Palgrave Macmillan Ser
Diploma

MW01040001

Series Editors
Kathy Fitzpatrick
University of South Florida
Tampa, FL, USA

Caitlin Byrne
Griffith Asia Institute
Griffith University
Brisbane, QLD, Australia

At no time in history has public diplomacy played a more significant role in world affairs and international relations. As a result, global interest in public diplomacy has escalated, creating a substantial academic and professional audience for new works in the field.

The *Global Public Diplomacy Series* examines theory and practice in public diplomacy from a global perspective, looking closely at public diplomacy concepts, policies, and practices in various regions of the world. The purpose is to enhance understanding of the importance of public diplomacy, to advance public diplomacy thinking, and to contribute to improved public diplomacy practices.

This series is indexed in Scopus.

Bruce Gregory

American Diplomacy's Public Dimension

Practitioners as Change Agents in Foreign Relations

Bruce Gregory
George Washington University
Washington, DC, USA

ISSN 2731-3883 ISSN 2731-3891 (electronic)
Palgrave Macmillan Series in Global Public Diplomacy
ISBN 978-3-031-38916-0 ISBN 978-3-031-38917-7 (eBook)
https://doi.org/10.1007/978-3-031-38917-7

This Palgrave Macmillan imprint is published by the registered company Springer Nature Switzerland AG.
The registered company address is: Gewerbestrasse 11, 6330 Cham, Switzerland

Paper in this product is recyclable.

For Paula

Keywords

Public diplomacy • Patterns of practice • Foreign service • Cultural diplomacy • International broadcasting • Soldiers • Democratization • Multidisciplinary scholarship • Practice theory • Societization • Digitalization

- Narrates the evolution of American public diplomacy from colonial times to the present
- Shows how practitioners transformed US diplomacy and shaped its public dimension
- Bridges diplomatic practice and multidisciplinary scholarship

Acknowledgments

In writing this book I have accumulated a mountain of intellectual debts to scholars, colleagues, former students, friends, and family. Two early mentors paved the way. As Professor Whittle Johnston's graduate teaching assistant at American University's School of International Service, I learned that history matters in theorizing diplomacy and international relations. From US Information Agency historian Murray Lawson, I developed an abiding interest in public diplomacy while researching archival records and drafting manuscripts on US international information, broadcasting, and cultural activities in the 1930s and 1940s.

Three outstanding practitioners shaped my thinking on the politics and practice of public diplomacy with gifts of their time and knowledge. Lou Olom, an executive director of the US Advisory Commission on Public Diplomacy, and Walter Roberts, a distinguished Foreign Service officer, teacher, and member of several advisory panels, were giants in twentieth-century public diplomacy. They gave me their personal papers and valuable insights during many hours of spirited conversations about issues on which we often disagreed but fundamentally shared common ground. Former Advisory Commission Chairman Tom Korologos, a master of Washington's folkways, genuinely cares about diplomacy's practitioners and taught many lessons that broadened my understanding of domestic politics and its implications for public diplomacy.

I owe an enduring debt to communities of scholars and staff at George Washington University's School of Media and Public Affairs (SMPA), Georgetown University's Master of Science in Foreign Service program (MSFS), the National War College (NWC), and the US Naval War College. I especially want to thank Sean Aday, Bob Entman, Kim Gross, Maria Jackson, Steve Livingston, Jerry Manheim, Yvonne Oh, Pat Phalen, Frank Sesno, Janet Steele, Silvio Waisborg, and Will Youmans at SMPA; Anthony Arend and Erin Guild at MSFS; Terry Deible, Lorry Fenner, Peter Galbraith, and Cynthia Watson at NWC; and Stephanie Helm and Carnes Lord at the Naval War College. I also benefited from the knowledge and leadership skills of Vince Vitto while serving on three Defense Science Board Task Force studies on strategic communication. At the University of Southern California's (USC) Center on Public Diplomacy, Geoff Cowan, Stacy Ingber, Adam Powell, and Jay Wang welcomed me as a non-resident faculty fellow and provided an online re-distribution hub for my bimonthly literature review.

A long list of practitioners and scholars, some no longer with us, have been sources of expertise and valuable advice. Many provided factual information and critical judgments on chapters in the book. I am indebted to Robert Albro, Sohaela Amiri, Matt Armstrong, Dick Arndt, David Arnett, Amelia Arsenault, Mark Asquino, Kadir Jun Ayhan, Len Baldyga, Judy Baroody, Martha Bayles, Jon Beard, Don Bishop, Paul Blackburn, John Brown, Katherine Brown, Robin Brown, Jim Bullock, Roxanne Cabral, Bob Callahan, Bea Campbell, Mike Canning, Brian Carlson, Steve Chaplin, Bob Chatten, Julie Gianelloni Connor, Bob Coonrod, Daryl Copeland, Nick Cull, Jeremy Curtin, Woody Demitz, Domenick DiPasquale, Chuck Dolan, Cynthia Efird, David Ensor, Alisher Faizullaev, Edwin J. Feulner, Jr., Ali Fisher, Mary Gawronski, Eytan Gilboa, Jack Hamilton, Craig Hayden, Bob Heath, Alan Heil, Jonathan Henick, Carl Herrin, Ellen Huijgh, Bud Jacobs, Mary Jeffers, Joe Johnson, Ross Johnson, Pat Kabra, Elaine Kamarck, Kenton Keith, Rob Kelley, Chris Kern, Wayne Knight, J. Michael Korff, Peter Kovach, David Kramer, Dan Kuehl, Graham Lampa, David A. Langbart, Teresa La Porte, John Lennon, Jodi Lewinsohn, Kristin Lord, Ilan Manor, Jessica Mathews, Mark Maybury, Michael McCarry, Jamie Metzl, Emily

Metzgar, Tom Miller, David Morey, Greta Morris, Ken Moskowitz, Sherry Mueller, Joseph Nye, Joe O'Connell, Robert Ogburn, James Pamment, Gene Parta, Chris Paul, Bill Pickering, Geoff Pigman, Mark Pomar, Evan Potter, Shawn Powers, Tony Quainton, Frank Ricciardone, Marie Ricciardone, Bill Rugh, Rick Ruth, Juliet Sablosky, Caitlin Schindler, Marianne Scott, Giles Scott-Smith, Phil Seib, Efe Sevin, Stan Silverman, Pamela Smith, Nancy Snow, Connie Stevens, Mark Taplin, Greg Tomlin, Art Tracy, Tom Tuch, Dick Virden, Vivian Walker, Matt Wallin, Betsy Whitaker, Dan Whitman, Doug Wilson, Rhonda Zaharna, and Barry Zorthian.

Online resources of the following organizations have been particularly helpful. The massive collection of Oral Histories assembled by the Association for Diplomatic Studies and Training (ADST) is extraordinary. Others include the *Foreign Relations of the United States* series maintained by the Department of State's Office of the Historian; annual reports of the US Advisory Commission on Public diplomacy (1948–present); the *Foreign Service Journal*; the journal *American Diplomacy*; the website of USC's Center on Public Diplomacy; and publications of the Public Diplomacy Council of America and Georgetown University's Institute for Diplomacy.

The following scholars deserve special mention. I am grateful to Jan Melissen for his thinking on the societization of diplomacy and public diplomacy's becoming woven into the mainstream of diplomatic practice. And to Paul Sharp for his foundational scholarship on relations of separateness in diplomacy theory and helpful comments on colonial era diplomacy. These founding co-editors of *The Hague Journal of Diplomacy* (*HJD*) have earned the appreciation of scholars and practitioners worldwide for the ample space they have given to public diplomacy in *HJD*. Geoff Wiseman's pathbreaking ideas on polylateral diplomacy and practice theory have been enormously helpful, as well as his encouragement at critical phases in writing the book and advice to stick with the term "diplomacy's public dimension." I learned from Brian Hocking's pioneering work on boundary spanning and national diplomatic systems. Alan Henrikson read every word of the book and provided many valuable comments. Kathy Fitzpatrick has been a rock of support for this project from the beginning. I deeply appreciate her subject matter expertise, knowledge of the publishing process, endless patience and readiness to respond to questions, and our many years of enjoyable "sparring" over issues.

Barry Fulton, Donna Oglesby, and Mike Schneider have been kindred spirits in our journey from public diplomacy careers to teaching and research. As diplomats they were outstanding innovators who honored tradition but resolutely worked to adapt patterns of practice to new environments. As respected teachers and scholars, they brought critical distance to analyzing practice and keen intelligence to concepts and ideas. I have benefited from our many conversations and the ways they have improved this project.

Anca Pusca and Isobel Cowper-Coles, accomplished professionals at Palgrave Macmillan, and their team have been a pleasure to work with in bringing this book to publication.

Finally, I am grateful to my family. For the love and support of my children, Scott, Donna, and Eric, my sister Ann, my brother Rob, my daughters-in-law Jasmine and Naina, and my niece, nephews, and grandchildren. My deepest appreciation is for the boundless patience and inspiration of my wife Paula Causey, whose distinguished career bridged public diplomacy and intelligence research. She patiently read every chapter many times over, offered countless editorial suggestions, shared practitioner stories, stood her ground as we energetically debated content, and supported me at every turn. More than anyone she has helped to make this book better and possible. The mistakes and errors of judgment are all mine.

About the Book

This is the first book to frame US public diplomacy in the broad sweep of American diplomatic practice from European settlers and Indigenous peoples to the present. It tells the story of how innovators and rival practitioner communities—foreign service officers, cultural diplomats, broadcasters, soldiers, citizen front groups, democratizers, and presidential aides—transformed traditional government-to-government diplomacy and moved diplomacy with publics into the mainstream. This deeply researched study blends practice and multidisciplinary scholarship. It documents historical turning points, analyzes evolving patterns of practice, and examines societal drivers of an American way of diplomacy: a preference for hard power over soft power, episodic commitment to public diplomacy correlated with war and ambition, an information-dominant communication style, and American exceptionalism. It is an account of American diplomacy's public dimension, the people who shaped it, current reform agendas, and the societization and digitalization that today extends diplomacy well beyond the confines of embassies and foreign ministries.

Praise for *American Diplomacy's Public Dimension*

"The book … represents a terrific compendium of accumulated observation and wisdom from one of the central figures in the field of public diplomacy studies."
—Professor Nicholas Cull, *University of Southern California, USA*

"Bruce Gregory presents a thorough and elegantly written history of American diplomacy's not always-successful efforts to influence the global public. This book will prove indispensable for public diplomacy scholars and practitioners."
—Philip Seib, *Professor Emeritus of Journalism and Public Diplomacy, University of Southern California, USA*

"In this original study, Bruce Gregory provides an account of how the public dimension to America's diplomacy was present before the creation of the Republic, evolved in response to historical turning points and changes in the technologies of communication, and remains of vital importance today. For anyone who wants to know what is exceptional about America's public diplomacy -for good and ill- and how the challenges it faces today might be addressed, Gregory provides much-needed answers."
—Paul Sharp, *Professor of Political Science, University of Minnesota Duluth*

"A captivating explanation of the unique origins of American style diplomacy with a focus on public diplomacy. This compelling — and easy-to-read — digest of the history of American diplomacy is a must-have for international affairs students, teachers, and especially practitioners. As a foreign policy practitioner, I wish I had read (and been able to reread) a book like this earlier in my career as it answers the question of why we do things a certain way and more importantly how we can use our past experiences, history, and culture to set us on the right course for the future."
—Roxanne Cabral, *US Department of State, USA*
View expressed herein is strictly her own and not necessarily those of the U.S. Government

"An authoritative, sweeping, yet highly readable work for the lay person and professional practitioner alike, certain to prove both a keystone reference and a standard text in diplomatic training institutes and schools of journalism and communication studies worldwide."

—Francis Ricciardone, *US Ambassador, ret. President, ret.*
The American University in Cairo

"Bruce Gregory has written a sweeping history of U.S. public diplomacy, packed with useful advice for practitioners and real-life examples of how individual leaders were able to shift U.S. government policies and practices. It should be essential reading for students, scholars, diplomats, and public diplomacy professionals."

—Kristin M. Lord, *President and CEO, IREX*

"[This book] is the first truly comprehensive history of the American way of engaging with other *peoples*, as distinct from other *states*. It is a dialectically open "conversation" about the past, present, and future of US public diplomacy. Deeply researched and factually informative, it is sure to become a landmark in the field."

—Alan K. Henrikson, *Founding Director of Diplomatic Studies,*
The Fletcher School of Law and Diplomacy, Tufts University

Contents

About the Author

Bruce Gregory is a visiting scholar at George Washington University's Institute for Public Diplomacy and Global Communication. He taught graduate and undergraduate courses for twenty years at George Washington University, Georgetown University, the US Naval War College, and the National War College. His government career included positions at the Department of State, the US Advisory Commission on Public Diplomacy, and the US Information Agency. Publications include peer-reviewed articles and book chapters, public policy reports, and a bimonthly literature review, *Diplomacy's Public Dimension*. He is a faculty fellow at the University of Southern California's Center on Public Diplomacy and a member of the International Studies Association (ISA), the Public Diplomacy Council of America, and the Washington Institute of Foreign Affairs. He received the Department of State's Superior Honor Award and was voted the ISA International Communication Section's Distinguished Scholar for 2024.

Abbreviations

ACDA	Arms Control and Disarmament Agency
ADST	Association for Diplomatic Studies and Training
AFGE	American Federation of Government Employees
AFRICOM	United States Africa Command
AFSA	American Foreign Service Association
BBG	Broadcasting Board of Governors
BIB	Board for International Broadcasting
CA	Civil Affairs
CAO	Cultural Affairs Officer
CCF	Congress for Cultural Freedom
CENTCOM	United States Central Command
CIA	Central Intelligence Agency
CIAA	Coordinator of Inter-American Affairs
CIC	Coalition Information Center
CIPE	Center for International Private Enterprise
COI	Coordinator of Information
CSIS	Center for Strategic and International Studies
CU	Bureau of Educational and Cultural Affairs (State Department)
DAS	Deputy Assistant Secretary
DCM	Deputy Chief of Mission
DRS	Distribution and Record System
DSB	Defense Science Board

ECA	Bureau of Educational and Cultural Affairs (USIA, State Department)
FIS	Foreign Information Service
FSI	Foreign Service Institute
FSIO	Foreign Service Information Officer
FSO	Foreign Service Officer
GAO	Government Accountability Office (formerly General Accounting Office)
GEC	Global Engagement Center
IBS	International Broadcasting Service
ICA	International Information and Cultural Affairs Agency (Stanton Panel proposal)
ICG	International Public Information Core Group
ICS	Information Center Service
IIA	International Information Administration
IIE	Institute of International Education
IIIS	Interim International Information Service
IIP	Bureau of International Information Programs
IMET	International Military Education and Training
IMV	Motion Picture and Television Service
INR	Bureau of Intelligence and Research
IO	Information Officer
IO	Information Operations
IPI	International Public Information
IPS	Press and Publications Service
IRI	International Republican Institute
IW	Information Warfare
IWG	Interagency Working Group
JCS	Joint Chiefs of Staff
JOT	Junior Officer Trainee
JUSPAO	Joint US Public Affairs Office
MBN	Middle East Broadcasting Networks
MISO	Military Information Support Operations
MIST	Military Information Support Team
NDI	National Democratic Institute for International Affairs
NED	National Endowment for Democracy
NPSB	National Psychological Strategy Board
NSA	National Student Association

NSC	National Security Council
NSDD	National Security Decision Directive
OCB	Operations Coordinating Board
OEX	Office of Educational Exchange
OFF	Office of Facts and Figures
OGC	Office of Global Communications
OIAA	Office of Inter-American Affairs
OIC	Office of International Information and Cultural Affairs
OII	Office of International Information
OMGUS	Office of the Military Government, United States
OPC	Office of Policy Coordination
OSI	Office of Strategic Influence
OSS	Office of Strategic Services
OWI	Office of War Information
PA	Public Affairs
PAO	Public Affairs Officer
PCC	Policy Coordinating Committees
PDD	Presidential Decision Directive
PME	Professional Military Education
PRT	Provincial Reconstruction Team
PSB	Psychological Strategy Board
PSYOP	Psychological Operations
RFA	Radio Free Asia
RFE	Radio Free Europe
RFE/RL	Radio Free Europe/Radio Liberty
RIAS	Radio in the American Sector
RL	Radio Liberty
SC	Strategic Communication
SPG	Special Planning Group
UNESCO	United Nations Educational, Scientific, and Cultural Organization
USACPD	US Advisory Commission on Public Diplomacy
USAGM	US Agency for Global Media
USAID	US Agency for International Development
USIA	US Information Agency
USICA	US International Communication Agency
USIS	US Information Service
VOA	Voice of America

1

Introduction

American diplomacy is rooted in the seventeenth-century politics, trade, and wars of European colonies and Native American tribes. Skilled diplomacy practitioners on both sides worked to bridge the considerable differences between colonists, for whom publics were peripheral to diplomacy, and Indigenous peoples, for whom publics and public ceremonies were essential. Their diplomatic practices foreshadowed what in the modern era has been called public diplomacy, strategic communication, information, and propaganda.

In diplomacy scholar Paul Sharp's classic formulation, people have always lived in groups. They use diplomacy to manage their "relations of separateness."[1] Diplomacy's core functions are communication and representation. Diplomats are agents who communicate on behalf of groups and act as representatives to other groups.[2] Diplomacy is an instrument of power. Uniquely, it has crosscutting relevance to other instruments: political, economic, and military. The historically contingent term "public diplomacy" is generally considered to have been adopted by retired US diplomat Edmund Gullion in 1965. The dean of the Fletcher School of Law and Diplomacy was searching for an alternative to propaganda and an umbrella phrase to take into account what in US practice was described as information, international broadcasting, and educational and cultural exchanges.

© The Author(s), under exclusive license to Springer Nature Switzerland AG 2024
B. Gregory, *American Diplomacy's Public Dimension*, Palgrave Macmillan Series in Global Public Diplomacy, https://doi.org/10.1007/978-3-031-38917-7_1

I prefer the term diplomacy's public dimension defined as an instrument used by states, associations of states, and some sub-state and non-state actors to understand cultures, attitudes, and behavior; build and manage relationships; and influence thoughts and mobilize actions to advance their interests and values.[3] This definition limits the concept, but it is broad enough to include diverse diplomatic actors, processes, spaces, and historical time frames. I use public diplomacy and diplomacy's public dimension interchangeably: public diplomacy in a nod to its continuing use by some scholars, practitioners, and organizations; diplomacy's public dimension in recognition of its centrality in modern diplomacy.

In defining diplomacy's public dimension, it helps to identify what diplomacy is not. It is not *foreign policy*. Foreign policies typically describe a political entity's public interests, values, and goals. Policies can be actions and statements, oral and written. Second, diplomacy is not *governance*, understood broadly as rules, norms, and institutions that guide and steer the shared activities of one or more groups.[4] It is an instrument of governance. Diplomacy is not *cross-cultural internationalism*. A huge array of individuals and organizations in civil society engage in cross-border relationships in pursuit of private interests. Some partner with governments. Some civil society actors in multi-actor networks, such as the International Committee of the Red Cross, can be viewed as independent diplomatic actors that advance public interests at scale based on their capabilities.

Four themes are at the heart of the book.

An American way of diplomacy. Societal drivers of an American way of diplomacy, manifest over the course of four centuries, have particular relevance to US diplomacy's public dimension.[5] (1) A preference for military and economic instruments of power over diplomacy. (2) Episodic interest in public diplomacy correlated with war and ambition. Time and again, from the Pequot War in the 1630s to the Afghanistan and Iraq wars after 9/11, Americans "discovered" public diplomacy when motivated by threats and fear. (3) A messaging and information-dominant communication style consistent with a culture that prioritizes individual freedom. (4) Belief in American exceptionalism characterized by the nation's outsized view of its virtue, democracy, and capacity to steer history.

Historical turning points. The diplomacy of the English colonist Roger Williams and Algonquian tribal chiefs before the Pequot War (1637–1638) is the book's starting point. Thereafter pivotal events signaled significant changes in diplomatic practice. The diplomacy of citizen diplomats (Benjamin Franklin, John Adams, Thomas Jefferson) in the royal courts, parliaments, salons, and coffee houses of Europe during the American Revolution. The state-sponsored diplomacy of "unofficial" private citizens in wartime beginning in the War with Mexico (1846–1848). The invention of the telegraph, which transformed diplomatic communication previously limited to the speed of sailing ships and foot travel. The Foreign Section of George Creel's Committee on Public Information in World War I, the first of many US government information organizations. The US decision to maintain public diplomacy organizations in peacetime after World War II. And a less precise turning point, the digitalization and societization that extend diplomacy well beyond the confines of embassies and foreign ministries in the twenty-first century.

Practitioner communities. Looking at American diplomacy's public dimension through the lens of practitioner communities with distinct identities and operational preferences strengthens traditional frameworks of analysis. Communities of practice span historical eras and transitory government organizations. They connect governments and civil society. This book focuses on the modus operandi of Foreign Service officers, cultural diplomats, international broadcasters, soldiers, citizen front groups, democratizers, and presidential aides. It examines their norms, tools, and methods, their differences and family resemblances. It argues change agents, rivalries, operational choices, and field-oriented behavior patterns fundamentally shaped diplomatic practice more than the mandates of presidents, lawmakers, and headquarters officials.

Multidisciplinary scholarship. Concepts drawn from international relations, diplomacy studies, communication theory, and a broad range of other academic disciplines illuminate historical and operational differences in diplomacy's public dimension: soft power, influence and relational communication models, strategic communication, public relations, cognitive framing, social psychology, network theory, nation branding, and polylateralism. Particularly useful is "practice theory," the approach of a growing number of scholars who assert study of diplomatic practices is a productive way to think systematically about diplomacy.[6] Analysis of diplomatic practice, past and present, helps scholars theorize about diplomacy and today's diplomats adapt to change.

Part I of the book exists because the literature on US public diplomacy overwhelmingly focuses on the Cold War and after. Studies that take a longer history into account typically point briefly to the public diplomacy of citizen diplomats during the American Revolution before moving quickly to the modern era. Missing is the cross-cultural blend of diplomatic practices that emerged in the century and a half before US statehood. The diplomacy of English colonies and Native Americans is foundational to the evolution of US diplomacy's public dimension and the American way of diplomacy. Chapters in Part I examine colonial era diplomacy, decisive turning points in the early public diplomacy of the United States, nineteenth-century cosmopolitans (abolitionists, women's rights advocates, humanitarians, missionaries), and dynamics that shaped behavior patterns of practitioner communities that emerged in the twentieth century.

Part II examines the practitioner communities that institutionalized government-to-people diplomacy, beginning with temporary practitioners—journalists, scholars, writers, filmmakers, and public relations experts—"borrowed" from civil society in wartime. Subsequent chapters discuss career Foreign Service officers and cultural diplomats, who built communities of practice based on what works best "in the field." A chapter on government media looks at the Voice of America and regional US government-funded grantees acting as domestic services in countries denied free media. Other chapters focus on the modus operandi of soldiers, citizen front groups, democracy builders, and presidential aides. These practitioners, intensely competitive and often given to unsparing internal discourse, built mature communities of practice and transformed traditional government-to-government diplomacy.

Part III contains chapters on issues in twenty-first-century diplomacy. They examine ways in which practitioners developed competing visions for a post–Cold War world, dealt with America's "rediscovery" of public diplomacy following the terrorist attacks of 9/11, and responded to global trends and "wicked problems" that are profoundly consequential for diplomacy's institutions and processes. The final chapter discusses damage done during the presidency of Donald Trump and problems in US diplomacy grounded in long-standing pre-existing conditions. It discusses recent reform proposals and ways of thinking about change in US diplomacy's public dimension. The book concludes with observations about questions scholars and practitioners are raising today on what constitutes diplomacy, where its boundaries should be drawn, and the challenges of "digitalized" and "societized" diplomacy.

Notes

1. Paul Sharp, *Diplomatic Theory of International Relations* (Cambridge University Press, 2009).
2. Christer Jönsson and Martin Hall, *Essence of Diplomacy* (Palgrave Macmillan, 2005), 67–116.
3. I introduced this definition in "Public Diplomacy: Sunrise of an Academic Field," *The Annals of the American Academy of Political and Social Science* 616, no. 1 (March 2008): 276.
4. Robert O. Keohane, *Power and Governance in a Partially Globalized World* (Routledge, 2002); Bruce Gregory, "Mapping Boundaries in Diplomacy's Public Dimension," *The Hague Journal of Diplomacy* 11, no. 1 (November 2016): 1–25.
5. Military scholars have written extensively about an American way of war. Literature on an American way of diplomacy is practically non-existent. Diplomacy scholar Geoffrey Wiseman's analysis of distinctive and interconnected characteristics of US diplomacy is a notable exception. My approach to an American way of diplomacy extends its time frame to the early colonial era. Two characteristics are similar to Wiseman's, a preference for hard power over soft power and low context messaging modes of communication. Two are different, episodic attention to public diplomacy and a self-image of American exceptionalism. See Geoffrey Wiseman, "Distinctive Characteristics of American Diplomacy," in *American Diplomacy*, eds. Paul Sharp and Geoffrey Wiseman (Martinus Nijhoff, 2012), 1–25.
6. Vincent Pouliot and Jeremy Cornblut, "Practice Theory and the Study of Diplomacy," *Cooperation and Conflict* 50, no. 3 (September 2015):

297–315; Costas M. Constantinou et al., "Thinking with Diplomacy: Within and Beyond Practice Theory," *International Political Sociology* 15, no. 4 (2021): 559–587; Geoffrey Wiseman, "Diplomatic Practices at the United Nations," *Cooperation and Conflict* 50, no. 3 (September 2015): 316–333.

Part I

Precursors and Concepts

2

Colonial-Era Foundations

The English Puritan Roger Williams left his home in Salem, Massachusetts, in January 1636 never to return. He entered the thick adjacent forest in a howling blizzard, alone and suffering from an extended illness, to escape imminent arrest under a warrant issued by the Governor's Council of the Massachusetts Bay Colony. He made his way in deep snow assisted by Native Americans with whom he had long enjoyed close personal relations. They saved his life during a 90-mile trek through the woods of southern New England. In the spring he gained their permission to establish a settlement for his family and co-religionists on Narragansett Bay.

Williams is well known for his views on religious freedom and pioneering role in the separation of church and state. Americans are familiar with a narrative that focuses on his emigration from England to Massachusetts in 1631, doctrinal disputes with Puritan authorities in Boston, conviction on charges of sedition and heresy that led to his banishment, and role as founder of the colony of Rhode Island. Williams remained a devout Puritan. Yet he was equally convinced it was "monstrous" to compel anyone to conform to his beliefs or the beliefs of others.[1]

Less known are his extraordinary skills and achievements as a diplomat. Williams is at the heart of the origins story of American diplomacy's public dimension. He undertook important diplomatic missions in two

B. Gregory, *American Diplomacy's Public Dimension*, Palgrave Macmillan Series in Global Public Diplomacy, https://doi.org/10.1007/978-3-031-38917-7_2

major wars: the Pequot War (1637–1638) and King Philip's War (1675–1676). His book, *A Key into the Language of America*, a dictionary of Native languages and guide to their ways of life published in London in 1643, gained widespread attention and facilitated communication between English settlers and Native Americans. For 40 years, Williams was at the center of the competing political and economic interests of the New England colonies, Dutch traders, and the region's Native tribes, the Wampanoag, Mohegan, Massachusett, Niantic, Nipmuck, Pequot, Showatuck, and Narragansett.[2]

As a young man in England Williams was a protégé of Sir Edward Coke, the great English jurist and politician. He graduated with honors from Cambridge University, but his "real education" in politics, writes historian John M. Barry, came from observing the business of the Privy Council and Coke's rivalry with the philosopher and statesman Sir Francis Bacon. Williams formed religious convictions and views on politics and law that shaped his life in the colonies. He became an accomplished orator who possessed a "combination of charm, confidence, and intensity which a later age would call charisma."[3]

In North America Williams developed lasting friendships with leading tribal chiefs, notably the Wampanoag sachem Massasoit and Narragansett sachem Canonicus. Through long stays in their villages, he learned their languages and developed a deep understanding of their customs and opinions. He brought them axes, knives, mirrors, spades, and clothes. In return they gave him furs and wampum, strings of shells that served as currency and confirmation of peace treaties and military alliances. He attended their feasts, games, dances, and harvest festivals. He advised them on inter-tribal conflicts and at times negotiated their treaties. Williams did not romanticize them. He could drive hard bargains, and he had no enthusiasm for living in what he called their "filthy smoak holes." He retained his English loyalty, habits, and manners throughout his life.

It was a political, intellectual, and cultural relationship grounded in his belief in a fundamental equality between Europeans and Indigenous peoples, his practice of buying rather than simply taking their land, and his keen understanding of the long-term economic and political advantages of collaborative relationships.[4] His home in Providence, Rhode Island, served as a cultural center. As Bruce Elliott Johansen writes:

Very quickly, Williams' house became a transcultural meeting place. He lodged as many as fifty Indians at a time—travelers, traders, sachems on their way to or from treaty conferences. If a Puritan needed to contact an Indian, or *vice versa*, he more than likely did so with Williams' aid. Among Indian nations at odds with each other, Williams became "a quencher of our fires." When citizens of Portsmouth needed an Indian agent, they approached Williams. The Dutch did the same after 1636. The Narragansetts' council sometimes used Williams' house for its meetings.[5]

Williams was not a tutor to Indigenous tribes, but a diplomat who represented English settlers to self-confident Native peoples.

The Pequot War was a bloody conflict born of fear and English, Dutch, and Native disputes over control of trade, wampum production, and Pequot land in the Mystic River Valley in southeastern Connecticut. In July 1636 the Massachusetts Bay, Plymouth, and Connecticut colonies began preparing for war. The Pequots were seeking alliances with the Narragansett, Mohegan, and other Algonquian tribes for an attack on the English. They threatened not only colonists in Connecticut but the Bay Colony itself.

Puritan leaders in Boston sought help from the recently banished Williams. Without hesitation he responded first by providing intelligence to Governor John Winthrop. Then, with no guarantees as to his personal safety, he undertook three days of authorized negotiations with the Narragansetts and Pequots who had gathered in a war council at the home of Canonicus. It was a high-risk mission. Although Williams expected to be welcomed by the Narragansetts, the Pequots were another matter. Given the violent hostilities between Pequots and the English in Connecticut, Williams wrote, he "could not but nightly looke for their bloody Knives at my owne throat allso."[6] Williams succeeded in persuading Canonicus and the Narragansetts to remain neutral and later to side with the colonies.[7]

The Pequot War was an opening chapter in a pattern of correlation between America's public diplomacy and perceptions of external danger. When facing existential threats, the Puritans set their theological differences with Williams aside and used his negotiating skills and long-term relationships with Native tribes to political and military advantage. When it was over, Winthrop proposed ending Williams's banishment in recognition of the extraordinary value of his diplomacy. This proved too difficult for the doctrinaire magistrates and clerics in Boston. His exile continued, and his name was not mentioned in official reports on the war. The Bay Colony's retreat from diplomacy continued until another threat to its vital interests loomed. At the outbreak of King Philip's War, it rediscovered diplomacy and turned again to Williams for help.

Beginning in June 1675 and for the next 14 months, Metacomet, a Wampanoag sachem who used the adopted name King Philip, attacked a number of English towns. After years of watching the colonies gain power and encroach on tribal lands, he put together an alliance of the Algonquian tribes, something the Pequots had failed to achieve. This time, the Narragansetts joined with the Wampanoag in Rhode Island, the Nipmuck and Pocumtuck in Massachusetts, and the Abenaki in Maine. Attacks from all sides raised the possibility the colonists would have to leave New England.

Williams provided intelligence to the colonies and tried through negotiations to keep the Narragansetts out of the war. He did not succeed. His home in Providence was attacked and burned, and he lived in poverty until his death in 1683. King Philip's War was the deadliest war in American history measured by casualties as a percentage of the population. The colonies prevailed and prospered. The New England tribes were ruined. The true measure of Williams's success is that his diplomacy had "helped to maintain a shaky peace along the frontiers of New England for nearly two generations after the Pequot war."[8]

Williams possessed the qualities and skills of an outstanding diplomat aware of the importance of diplomacy's public dimension. He demonstrated deep comprehension of the interests, beliefs, and opinions of others. He was intellectually curious and genuinely devoted to building and maintaining relationships among different cultures. He excelled in the "last three feet" of interpersonal communication not just with tribal leaders but also with their followers. He was a gifted linguist. He understood the importance of public ceremony in achieving political and economic interests. He was unhesitating in speaking truth to power and willing to take personal and professional risks. He was an accomplished orator and writer. He displayed personal charm. It's a skill set worthy of a top diplomat in any century.

"Relations of Separateness" in Colonial North America

Indigenous peoples in North America had managed long distance tribal relations for centuries through trade, diplomacy, and armed conflict before the Europeans arrived. Historian Alan Taylor writes that colonization by the Spanish, French, Dutch, and English brought together empires, Native tribes, and slavery in an "unprecedented mixing of radically diverse peoples—African, European, and Indian—under circumstances stressful for all." Within these racial and cultural groups was a complex variety of languages and sub-cultures. Groups that were previously separate, now unexpectedly connected, were forced to accommodate and adapt. Identities changed. Technologies changed. Environmental circumstances changed. "The colonial intermingling of peoples—and of microbes, plants, and animals from different continents—was unparalleled in speed and volume in global history."[9] Summarizing an abundance of recent scholarship, historian Ned Blackhawk argues the agency and survival of Native peoples—their diplomacy, trade, and warfare with Europeans—make Native-newcomer *interrelations* a compelling alternative to a traditional American story grounded in European discovery and expansion.[10]

European colonies differed considerably in their freedom of action and relations with Native Americans. Spain's missionaries came in search of converts. Its conquistadores came for gold and conquest as early as 1513. Their "smash and grab" approach stood in contrast to France's emphasis on forging alliances. Unlike the English, the Spanish did not come with families and settlers. Their power centers were in Mexico and Peru, and they viewed frontier settlements in Florida and New Mexico as military buffer zones against English and French empires to the north.[11]

France established trading posts in parts of Canada and small settlements in Quebec, Montreal, and Louisiana. The French were fur traders, merchants, and missionaries. They came "not as conquering invaders, but as a new tribe negotiating a place for itself in the diplomatic webs of Native North America."[12] They excelled in learning local languages and cross-cultural communication skills needed for trade and diplomacy. Their networks of influence with Huron, Iroquois, and Algonquian tribes offset their small numbers and slow population growth. French colonists used these skills and alliances to advantage until the 1760s.

Although they believed themselves more civilized in the business of empire than the Spanish, the English also used violence and harsh methods. Dependent at first on Native peoples for survival, the colonists' growing numbers soon led to major conflicts, first in Virginia in a reciprocal pattern of violence with the region's Algonquian tribes, then in New England's Pequot and King Philip's Wars. England's colonies benefited from superiority in weapons. They had considerable autonomy so long as they followed English law and remained loyal to the Crown.

English ambitions were fueled by an insatiable desire for land—valued for timber, raising crops, keeping domesticated animals, and the space it provided for waves of settlers seeking religious freedom and economic opportunity. In contrast to Native Americans, who viewed land as public commons to be shared, land for the English was private property. It was a means to economic flourishing. In the eighteenth century, waves of Scottish, Irish, Swiss, and German immigrants added to population pressures. Expansion of commercial shipping, favorable trade patterns, and escalation of the African slave trade, all supported by England's naval power, led to impressive economic growth. It was prosperity achieved by exploiting the labor of indentured servants and enslaved Africans and by taking land from Native Americans, for whom it was not a "New World."

England pursued supremacy in North America primarily in competition with the French in upstate New York, the Great Lakes region, and Canada. For a century and a half, alliances with Iroquois tribes in the Mohawk Valley and Algonquian tribes in New England and the mid-Atlantic were crucial to the commerce and conflicts of these European rivals. In the end, it was British colonies along the Atlantic coast from Maine to Georgia that dominated the continent and created powerful legacies for the United States.[13] Among them, an American way of diplomacy.

Diplomacy between imperial monarchs occurred primarily in foreign ministries and embassies with resident ambassadors in Europe's capitals. Theirs was the Westphalian diplomacy of sovereign states that emerged in the seventeenth century.[14] England's colonies were what today would be called sub-state actors. Their political relations with the Crown were those of domestic governance not diplomacy. When, for example, King Charles II sent a commission in 1664 to settle disputes between the colonies, his commissioners came not as diplomats but as government officials.[15] The colonies' interactions with Native peoples, however, evolved from initial encounters to continuous "relations of separateness," which included systematized processes of negotiation, collaboration, and public diplomacy.[16]

The colonists brought the methods and protocols of Europe's state-to-state diplomacy but not its institutions, which they did not establish until they united as an independent state. Natives used rituals and practices developed during centuries of diplomacy with other tribes and within their own confederacies.[17] They were determined protagonists whose methods of diplomacy often were highly effective. Colonies and tribes had no foreign ministries, no embassies, and no system of resident ambassadors. Nevertheless, both sides engaged in structured diplomacy, because it was indispensable to achieving their political, economic, and military goals. They learned to accommodate each other's diplomatic practices and understand the costs of not doing so. "European and Native American traditions and practices melded to produce a new, uniquely American form of cross-cultural diplomacy," Colin G. Calloway writes. "But it was never a perfect mix and was replete with opportunities for misunderstanding, deceit, and abuse."[18]

Colonial-era diplomatic practices turned on pragmatic interpretations of underlying legal issues. English kings viewed Indians as subjects, which in theory precluded diplomacy. Power realities, however, meant the Crown and colonial elites dealt with Native tribes as political entities with control over territory, trade, and armed force. Treaties with the Iroquois as early as 1642 recognized sachems as having authority to negotiate on behalf of their tribes.[19] The commissioners sent by King Charles II also were instructed "To ascertain the condition of the Indian Kings and Princes, what treaties have been made and how observed, that no violations may be permitted." Ambiguous English understandings on natives as subjects or peers can be seen in the commissioners' report: "The Nanhygansetts Sachems in 1664 surrendered themselves, people and country, to the late King's protection. ... The Sachems thankfully received two coats in his Majesty's name, and in acknowledgment of their subjection are to pay yearly on the 29th May two wolf skins; and did now send 'two caps of peag [wampum] and two clubbs inlaid with peag for a present to the King and a feather mantle and a porcupine bagg for a present to the Queene.'"[20]

Forest Diplomacy

Today it is almost impossible to imagine the ambient experience of "the woods" in colonial North America. For Europeans, vast and seemingly impenetrable forests were near, mysterious, and threatening. Strange fearful creatures lived in the woods. They could bewitch and kill. The woods were to be cleared and settled. For Native Americans, European settlements were likewise near, mysterious, and threatening. But the woods, which they also viewed as vast and scary, were to be cleared only as needed and otherwise preserved. Intense hostility grew out of these different experiences, but both sides viewed travel in "the woods" as a difficult necessity in war, trade, and diplomacy.

In the performative diplomacy of Native Americans, publics were essential participants in the ceremonies, rituals, speech making, and gift exchanges required to maintain alliances and trade agreements. Large numbers of observers, including women and warriors, legitimized diplomatic outcomes. Performances had to be done correctly. Mistakes could negate or undermine agreements.[21] Most Indians were not literate and therefore suspicious of written treaties. Rather, agreements were best achieved through a public "*process* of treaty making" leading to mutual obligations validated by a "perpetual process of negotiation and renewal." They conducted diplomacy by public oratory. They used stories, metaphors, body language, dancing, and pipe smoking rituals in large public settings to convey meaning. Not all negotiations were public. Both sides also valued private meetings, known to the Iroquois as discussions "in the bushes," where disagreements could be ironed out away from public ceremonies.[22]

English colonists typically treated negotiations as a "one and done" means to create written treaties that would be archived in London and colonial capitals as proof of a binding agreement. But they soon learned that success hinged on observing the customs of Native diplomacy. "Whosoever has any affairs to transact with Indians must know their forms and in some measure comply with them," declared Sir William Johnson, New York's superintendent of Indian affairs.[23] For their part, tribal sachems came to accept written agreements as inevitable and grew skeptical when negotiations did not lead to written records of the proceedings. "The point," diplomacy scholar Paul Sharp argues, "is not that these sorts of first principle differences had to be settled before relations could be conducted (often, they were never settled), but that relations had to be conducted by someone nevertheless, and in the midst of such differences."[24]

A communications frontier paralleled diplomacy on the physical frontier. Traders and missionaries carried news and information with their goods and bibles. Newspapers took hold in the early 1700s. Increased shipping added to the flow of transatlantic communication. Colonial newspapers, letters, pamphlets, taverns, and coffee shops created what Jurgen Habermas would call the "public sphere of civil society"—a domain of private autonomy separate from the public authority of governance entities.[25] Communication technology, which began with pen and paper, wampum strings and belts, walking trails, roads, horses, canoes, and sailing ships, was transformed by the arrival of the printing press (the first came to New England in 1638) and a postal service (initiated in the 1670s). Communication content, confined at first to talk, letters, rumors, legends, and hoaxes, became a more powerful influence on public opinion with widespread availability of pamphlets, books, and newspapers.[26]

"Go-Betweens" in Frontier Diplomacy

Europeans and Native Americans used "go-betweens" to carry messages, interpret languages and customs, investigate rumors, settle quarrels, and keep clear what Natives described as "the path between the peoples." They were not neutral in their loyalties. Almost all, historian James H. Merrell observes, "were firmly anchored on one side of the cultural divide or the other." "Indians and colonists called these people by many names: *agent, messenger, ambassador, Mr. Interpreter, Manager, Province Interpreter, mediator, ne horrichwisax, n'donasit, friend, a person to do Indian Business, thuwawoenachqata, Anhuktonheet, Guardian of all the Indians, a person to go between Us.*"[27] They constituted an unsystematic, but intentional, community of diplomatic practitioners with norms and patterns of practice.

Their diplomacy typically began with an "At the Woods' Edge Ceremony," where representatives of both sides met "between the thorny underbrush" and "the cleared land" to acknowledge and counter the power of the woods before negotiations could begin.[28] Natives and colonists believed a person emerged from dense forests traumatized by the ordeal. A ritual in which hosts comforted the traveler could minimize the trauma. The parties sat by a fire. Hosts engaged in ceremonial "wiping clean the throat, ears, and eyes [to] set things right."[29] These ceremonies derived from wariness of visiting strangers who could represent danger, and they demonstrated belief in the possibility of gradual rapprochement with outsiders.

Condolence ceremonies, another form of public diplomacy, were often precursors to negotiations. Iroquois condolence ceremonies were rituals with strict protocols in which the actors were Native leaders, colonial governors, and their go-betweens. For more than a century, they took place in Onondaga, the political center of the Iroquois Confederacy, and in Albany, Philadelphia, and other colonial towns. Their purpose was to comfort those who had recently lost a native chief or a colonial official. One side conducted the ceremony as the party unaffected by grief. The other side acted as mourners. Natives were accomplished performers of these ceremonies. Colonists were not, but rituals were flexible, and most

Natives appreciated their efforts to participate. If protocols were not observed, Natives would say "they had only heard from the English as a Noise in the Woods" or they heard nothing. Colonists likewise came to dismiss messages sent without appropriate rituals as "only a transient discourse."[30]

Colonial governors and militia commanders sought skilled go-betweens who knew the woods and had deep knowledge of Native American languages and cultures. Honesty and strong moral principles were a plus. George Washington, seeking tribal support when facing French forces on the Pennsylvania frontier in the 1750s, called for "a Person of Distinction acquainted with their language" or at least "a Man of Sense and Character" to be paid whatever it takes. Similarly, Native Americans chose individuals with strong rhetorical skills and knowledge of English language and customs. They almost always were men, and typically they were "'a person of Consequence' … 'a man of note' formally installed through ceremonies replete with talk of being 'sure our Business will go on well, & Justice be done on both sides.'"[31] Go-betweens were agents, not principals. They represented colonial governors and tribal chiefs.

Examples of go-betweens with exceptional ability included Pennsylvania's German-born Conrad Weiser (1696–1760). At age 16 he was sent by his father to live for a year with a Mohawk tribe in the Schoharie Valley, where he learned the language and Iroquois culture before returning to life as a farmer. In 1731 he represented Pennsylvania in negotiations with an Oneida go-between known as Shikellamy (?–1748), an overseer of the Shawnee and Lenape tribes in central Pennsylvania. They became fast friends—Weiser trusted by the Iroquois and Shikellamy by the English.[32]

Andrew Montour (c. 1720–1772) represented Virginia and Pennsylvania. He looked European, but many considered him a Native. He dressed in the garb of both and chose English or Native names when it suited. His father was an Oneida. His mother, her origins obscure, had English, French, and Iroquois family connections. "At home in a long-house and at a governor's table, able to perform the Iroquois Condolence Ceremony and explain Christian baptism to Indians, bearing a provincial captain's commission and a wampum belt with his credentials as an

Iroquois leader, wearing a hat on his head and paint on his face—Montour became a 'very useful Person' with 'a good Character' amongst White people and Indians."[33] Peter Chartier, the son of a French fur trader and Shawnee mother, represented Pennsylvania with the French and Shawnees. Like Montour, Chartier's embrace of English and Shawnees raised questions on both sides. "[He] can seem loyal to anyone when it suits him," Merrell writes, "But where does his heart truly lie?"[34] Twentieth-century US diplomats with deep cultural knowledge and long service in another country faced similar headquarters concerns about "going native."

These go-betweens never lost sight of fundamental differences. William Johnson spoke their languages, joined their dances, dressed in their clothing, and partnered with an Iroquois woman, but "nonetheless always remained an outsider and he knew it." As Shikellamy is reported to have said, "We are Indians and don't wish to be transformed into white men. The English are our Brethren, but we never promised to become what they are."[35]

Most go-betweens were not traders. Traders knew the woods, but their intentions were "sweet profits" not diplomacy. A trader "can with eagerness go thro the greatest hardships and Difficaltyes for the sake of Gaine."[36] With notable exceptions, most were unwilling to endure such difficulties for kings and colonial governors. In this they differ little from their twenty-first-century private sector successors. Traders then and corporations now might occasionally partner with governance actors in diplomacy when mutually beneficial, but their goals and roles are categorically different.

William Johnson and Chief Hendrick

William Johnson and a Mohawk leader known as Chief Hendrick to the British and Theyanoguin to the Iroquois were two of the most talented go-betweens in eighteenth-century America. They were prototypes of diplomacy practitioners that Americans would come to know well: the business leader who moves easily between private and public roles and the soldier/diplomat. Their public diplomacy skills were extraordinary.

Born in Ireland in 1715, Johnson came to New York in 1738. There he prospered in the fur trade and learned the Mohawk language and Iroquois customs. In 1746 Governor George Clinton appointed Johnson to be New York's agent to the Iroquois and a colonel to command Mohawks he recruited in raids against the French. A decade later Johnson was named Superintendent for Indian Affairs for the northern colonies. The Iroquois, however, regarded Johnson as their agent in New York. As one tribal leader explained to Clinton, "one half of Colonel Johnson belonged to his Excellency and the other to [the Mohawks]."[37] Johnson pursued business interests, diplomacy with Native Americans, and service as a Major General in the British Army until his death in 1774.[38]

The formidable Iroquois Confederacy used shrewd diplomacy, trade, warfare, and terrain advantage to project power in an arc that extended from Maine to the Carolinas. Reliable support from the Iroquois was vital to British interests. As Eliot A. Cohen observes, "The counterpoise to expanding French influence lay chiefly with one remarkable man, William Johnson, in his own right a force worth a small army."[39] His common-law relationship with Molly Brant, sister of renowned Mohawk chief Joseph Brant, and his eight children with Mohawk women added to his influence. He speaks to us "in our own way," one Onondaga Chief said, "which is more Intelligible to us, because more comfortable to the Customs and Manners of our Fore Fathers."[40] Johnson took delight in arriving at conferences dressed and painted as a Mohawk. On one occasion, thus attired, he led a party of Mohawk warriors into New York City. In the words of Cadwallader Colden, a fellow Irish émigré and go-between, Johnson "dressed himself after the *Indian* manner, made frequent Dances, according to their Custom when they excite to War, and used all the Means he could think of, at a considerable Expense, (which his Excellency has promised to repay him) in order to engage them heartily in the War against *Canada*."[41]

Johnson's public diplomacy was strengthened by his role as an agent for colonial war contracts and use of his personal estate, Johnson Hall, for large gatherings of tribal councils. He provided the Iroquois with abundant supplies of food, drink, clothing, weapons, and other material goods. This was not unique. Many colonial officials supplied Natives with goods and weapons. But, Timothy Shannon writes, they often

"saddled Indians with wagon loads of gifts" with "either a stubborn igno-
rance or callous disregard" for Native customs. Johnson had a "keen
appreciation for the culture of gift giving." His presents were selected for
intended recipients. Large one-time gifts were not sufficient. Effective
diplomacy, he declared, required "constant little Presents," which "from
the Nature of the Indians cannot be avoided and must be complied with."
He distributed gifts to warriors and to their women and children when
they were away. He kept meticulous records. Failure to observe these
norms jeopardized short-term bilateral negotiations and endangered geopolitical strategies. When Johnson's superiors in Albany neglected gift
protocols, the French took advantage.[42]

Johnson's Iroquois counterpart, Chief Hendrick (1692–1755), a
Mohican by birth, was adopted by the Mohawks and baptized as a
Protestant. In the 1740s he became a prominent Mohawk spokesman,
go-between, warrior, staunch ally of the British in their wars with the
French, and Johnson's trusted ally. Hendrick often dressed in the colonial
garb of laced hats, ruffled shirts, and scarlet coats, an attire that eased his
entrée in conferences with officials in New York, Pennsylvania,
Massachusetts, and Montreal. After his death, engravings of Hendrick in
colonial dress with a battle axe in one hand and a wampum belt in the
other sold in London.[43]

Hendrick was adept at promising to break ties with New York if Native
grievances over land fraud and trade agreement violations by colonial
governors were not satisfied. He was skilled at playing Massachusetts's
interests against New York's. The British came to respect Hendrick as a
gifted diplomat and reliable interlocutor. "He became," in the words of
Eric Hinderaker, "the most influential figure of his generation in Anglo-
Iroquois affairs."[44] Unlike go-betweens in other tribes who preferred to
act as mediators in Anglo-French disputes rather than as long-term allies
of either, Hendrick confined his diplomacy to representing the Iroquois
to British colonies.

To achieve peace and prosperity on the New York frontier, the colonists needed Hendrick and Johnson in Covenant Chain diplomacy—a
web of alliances, trade agreements, and treaties between the Iroquois and
the colonies and at times directly with England and France. The Chain
was a physical object (wampum belts, metal chains) that served as a

diplomatic symbol for reciprocal benefits and obligations: gifts of goods (clothing, food, weapons, tools, and liquor) from the British in exchange for furs, alliances, and peace from the Iroquois. Hendrick and Johnson used the Chain to mutual advantage in their diplomacy and wars with the French.[45]

Until the French and Indian War (1754–1763), the French had the upper hand in alliances with powerful Native tribes in the Ohio and Mississippi Valleys. Their strategy combined trade, military force, and the cross-cultural skills of Jesuit missionaries. The British colonies, divided politically and militarily, cared less about Native languages and cultures. New York governors lacked experience and sustained interest in Native affairs. When King George's War ended in 1748, Governor Clinton and the New York Assembly stopped payments for "expensive" gifts. In 1753 Hendrick declared the Chain broken due to widespread land fraud and failure of New York's leaders to observe diplomatic ceremonies and provide presents to maintain the alliance. Johnson had earlier resigned as Indian Agent, because the Assembly had ended his compensation. French expansion and lost trade followed. In London, the King's ministers noticed. The daunting prospect that the Iroquois would be neutral, or worse ally with the French, led the Board of Trade to order colonial governors to repair the damage.[46] New York turned again to diplomacy.

The process of mending the Chain began at a conference in Albany in 1754 where representatives of seven colonies, 150 Iroquois, and Benjamin Franklin participated. Diplomacy, ceremonies, and presents were renewed. The following year London sent two regiments of British troops commanded by General Edward Braddock to battle the French. Braddock made Johnson, his compensation by then restored, his agent to the Iroquois with a mandate to secure their assistance. On June 21, 1755, Johnson convened 1100 Iroquois men, women, and children at his estate, where he "relit the Council fire that the Mohawks had declared 'burnt out' in Albany." Then began nine days of public ceremonies, speeches, and feasts orchestrated by Johnson and Hendrick. Johnson's rhetoric and rituals were coordinated with those of Red Head, the chief Iroquois sachem.[47]

This time the British made good on their promises, "because to lose the Iroquois would be to completely expose the frontier regions of

New York and New England, which provincials and militias could not adequately protect."[48] Braddock's army was defeated in the Ohio Valley, but colonial and Mohawk forces led by Johnson and Hendrick prevailed in the Battle of Lake George in 1755 after taking heavy casualties that included Hendrick. Stories of Hendrick's death and his loyalty to the British war effort circulated widely in the colonies and London. Johnson received a baronetcy, gained additional fame from his capture of Fort Niagara in 1759, and became a legendary figure in British imperialism.

Like Roger Williams a century before, Johnson and Hendrick mastered the traits of the talented diplomat fully aware of diplomacy's public dimension. They had deep respect, authentic and pragmatic, for their counterparts in cross-cultural engagement. They bridged cultural differences—the individualistic culture and low-context communication modes of the British and the communitarian culture and high-context communication modes of the Iroquois. They understood the importance of the "last three feet" of personal communication. Americans had again turned to public diplomacy in wartime.

By the end of the French and Indian War, the British had defeated the French and in the Treaty of Paris in 1763 gained control of Canada. Because the Iroquois no longer had a strong French card to play, the colonists again cut expenses for diplomacy. British commander Jeffrey Amherst instructed army officers at frontier posts to stop giving presents and gunpowder to the tribes. Amherst's decree and expanding British settlements led the Ottawa's Chief Pontiac to attack Detroit and Fort Pitt in 1763. Again, the wheel turned with more diplomacy, presents, and ceremonies. In 1768 Johnson convened a conference of representatives from New York, Pennsylvania, Delaware, and Virginia and more than 3000 Natives from the Iroquois and other tribes to negotiate the Treaty of Fort Stanwix. Natives ceded huge tracts of land for which they received cash and presents.[49] Boundary lines were set and reset as English-speaking settlers moved west.

From the Covenant Chain to Dispossession

The American War of Independence intensified divides within the Iroquois Confederacy. Many tribes sided with British Tories, and some moved to Canada. Johnson and Hendrick were no longer there to mend the Chain. Natives who stayed neutral or cast their lot with Britain faced a Continental Army bent on retaliation and domination on the frontier. George Washington sent troops to invade Iroquois country in 1779. His orders to commanders were to achieve "the total destruction and devastation of their settlements ... that the country may not be merely overrun but destroyed."[50] The campaign to dispossess Iroquois who sided with Britain was not only a war measure, it was a way to seize control of their lands.[51]

At the end of the eighteenth century, the Iroquois, their powerful confederacy diminished, were confined to reservations along the US-Canada border. Newly elected President Washington and his Secretary of War Henry Knox at first treated all Indian tribes as "nations" with "limited sovereignty." The United States would negotiate treaties to regulate trade, purchase Native lands, and undertake "Rational experiments ... for imparting to them the blessings of civilization"—principles Congress incorporated in the 1793 "Act to Regulate Trade and Intercourse with the Indian Tribes."[52] But if Natives refused to give up their land and engaged in violent resistance, Knox ordered military commanders to impose peace through conquest and "extirpate" those committing "depredations." Treaties were made and broken; military campaigns in the Ohio country and Great Lakes region followed. As Thomas Jefferson subsequently put it to Michigan territorial governor William Hull, "if ever we are constrained to lift the hatchet against any tribe, we will never lay it down till that tribe is exterminated, or driven beyond the Mississippi."[53]

The US policy of negotiating with the tribes as "nations" was soon tested by the growing power of Spain and its allied Cherokees and Creek confederacy in Georgia and northern Florida who were resisting the encroachment of Georgia's frontier settlers. Lacking sufficient troops to put down their resistance, Washington and Knox negotiated a treaty with the formidable Creek leader Alexander McGillivray. Son of a Scottish father and a mother who was half French and half Creek, the diplomatically gifted McGillivray was well-read in British and European history; fluent in English, Spanish, and Creek; a skilled negotiator; and through his matrilineal heritage an authoritative voice of the Creeks and their neighboring tribes. The Creek case fascinates at several levels: the central role of public diplomacy, the War Department as diplomatic actor, and McGillivray's wily resistance to terms until tempted by a summit meeting and co-equal status with President Washington at the US capital in New York. As historian Joseph Ellis tells the story, Washington and Knox "had no way of knowing that they were dealing with the Talleyrand of the southern frontier."[54]

McGillivray made a ceremonial procession up the Atlantic coast in the summer of 1790 to negotiate a treaty that, in the words of one emissary, would "be as strong as the hills and lasting as the rivers."[55] He traveled in a carriage followed by 26 Creek chiefs on horseback in full ceremonial regalia. They were greeted by large cheering crowds and feted at dinners hosted by local dignitaries in Richmond, Fredericksburg, and Philadelphia. In New York they were "welcomed like European royalty" with ships firing salvos in the harbor and a parade past Federal Hall where all members of Congress came out to cheer. Washington greeted them at the presidential residence. As Ellis describes, "the extravaganza ended at City Tavern with a sumptuous dinner and more toasts, all punctuated by Creek songs and shouts that gave the occasion an exotic flavor by blending Indian and white versions of etiquette. It was what we might call a major multicultural event."[56] After nearly a month of negotiations during the day and celebrations in the evening, the Treaty of New York was signed establishing mutually agreed boundaries and "perpetual peace and friendship." It was the first treaty ratified under the US Constitution.

"Perpetual peace" proved to be temporary. White settlers rolled westward relentlessly, "making a mockery of all plans for an enduring Creek homeland."[57] McGillivray resumed ties with Spain, which continued to provide the Creeks with weapons. Diplomacy could not produce an agreement that would hold in the face of demographic pressures, settler ambitions, and the military costs of enforcing the treaty's obligations. Good public diplomacy was essential to reaching an agreement, but it had no bearing on whether the agreement could be sustained.

Concerned to keep the Iroquois out of ongoing wars with other tribes in the Ohio Valley, Washington, Knox, and their Indian agent Timothy Pickering returned for a time to Johnson-style diplomacy. Pickering patiently worked to mend the Covenant Chain and negotiate the Canandaigua Treaty of 1794. It restored some territory to the Onondaga, Oneida, Cayuga, and Seneca tribes and temporarily stabilized relations. For Washington and Knox, the Chain and Treaty signified a resolution of conflicts with the Iroquois. For the Iroquois, they symbolized their status as a sovereign nation and established a basis for claims litigation that continues today. Throughout their accommodation to political realities, they never conceded the legitimacy of their dispossession.[58]

The early US policy of managing affairs with Native Americans through negotiated treaties fell to forces that led to decades of westward expansion and Indian removal and survival. Native Americans were dispossessed of their lands though mass deportation, legal maneuvers, intimidation, and violence.[59] In the words of Jurgen Ostermammel, they were "no longer treated as negotiating partners but regarded as objects of military and administrative compulsion."[60] *Diplomacy* between the United States and tribal "nations" gave way to military and civilian *administration* of their decreasing numbers.

Foundations of the American Way of Diplomacy

Colonial and Native American diplomacy practitioners developed tools, methods, and patterns of behavior shaped by their governing authorities and broad societal currents that reveal characteristics of an American way of diplomacy: (1) a preference for military and economic instruments of power over diplomacy, (2) episodic attention to public diplomacy correlated with war and ambition, (3) a low-context communication style that emphasizes information and messaging, and (4) a self-image of American exceptionalism.

A preference for hard power. Europeans in the Americas used force, intimidation, terror, payments, and commerce in their quest for security, gold, goods, land, and a better life. As recent scholarly literature makes clear, duplicity and violence occurred continuously in frontier wars.[61] The Scots and Irish brought martial ways born of generations of clan warfare and conflicts with the English, which have done much to define the attitudes and values of the US military.[62] "Colonial North American history was not created in peace and interrupted by war," writes Ian K. Steele, "wars, rumors of war, and costs of war affected every generation of Amerindians and colonists."[63] For Malcolm Gaskill, England in the sixteenth century had "treated the Irish like an inferior species." In the seventeenth century, "what was good for Irish rebels was even better for Indians."[64] As Alan Taylor observes, the colonies came to view "resisting peoples as dirty, lazy, treacherous, murderous, and pagan savages, little if any better than wild animals."[65]

England's colonists pursued the destruction and displacement of their enemies with zealous intention and violence. They used fear to build domestic support for their military strategies and demonized enemies in ways that resonate today. Stories of the Natives' extreme brutality, historian Bernard Bailyn writes, became universalized in narratives that "cast them into popular literary idioms, and drove them, in ways one will never fully understand, deep into the American psyche."[66] There were differences in how colonists prioritized armed conflict. Elites in urban centers often preferred to achieve separation through negotiated dispossession. When Native tribes resisted, the remedy was force. Frontier settlers feared violence from tribes protected by treaties.[67] The priority the colonies gave to military and economic instruments of power became an enduring characteristic of American diplomacy.

The colonists had a unique early advantage in wars with Native peoples. Contemporaneous written accounts came almost entirely from one side. "As the colonists saw it," Jill Lepore writes, "violence itself was the Indians' only vocabulary." "If war is a contest of both injuries and interpretation, the English made sure that they won the latter, even when the former was not assured."[68] The absence of a written language did not mean that violence was the Native Americans' only tool. They were persistent adversaries who used the full spectrum of hard and soft power instruments.

Episodic attention to public diplomacy. The evidence is overwhelming. England's colonies turned to public diplomacy when threatened by war.[69] They did so because publics were essential as participants in the diplomacy of Native Americans and as witnesses who legitimized diplomatic process and outcomes. The performative diplomacy of the Iroquois was "a species of drama in which the Iroquois were the playwrights, the directors and teaching actors, and the joint producers with the colonial hosts."[70] It was not a dubious or marginal diplomatic activity, Paul Sharp argues, "it was taken for granted as both a fact and a good thing."[71] The colonies needed public diplomacy to recruit Native allies or convince tribes to remain neutral. But instead of playing a long game, when threats waned so did their public diplomacy. Colonists paid a price for this lack of consistency. As the Iroquois chief Scaraouyady put it to colonial leaders in Philadelphia in 1755, they "had been too negligent of Cultivating … Friendship with the Indians…" War on the frontier might have been avoided "if we had been more Conversant with each other."[72]

The correlation between threats and episodic attention to public diplomacy in the colonial era casts a long shadow. The United States turned to public diplomacy during the Revolutionary War, its war with Mexico, and the Civil War. Attention to public diplomacy re-emerged in the hot and cold wars of the twentieth century. After 9/11, the United States elevated public diplomacy again in its "war on terror."

Low- and high-context communication. Differences between low-context English, Scots, and Irish cultures and high-context Native American cultures point to a third element in the American way of diplomacy. Anthropologists and communication scholars maintain that differences in group cultures create variations in the methods and content of communication. Low-context cultures emphasize individuals and communication intended to achieve outcomes that serve goals of the communicator. English colonists prioritized written messages and short-term results. They had less regard for non-verbal cues and long-term relationships. High-context cultures embrace communitarian values, the context of communication, and relationships built over time. Native American cultures valued symbols and performative communication more than written and spoken messages.[73]

Speech and time were critical elements of difference. For the colonists speech was transient. Lies and faulty memories made speech unreliable. Words on paper were a more dependable record of what had been agreed to in the past. But for Natives paper was what Whites often used to rob them of their land. "[W]hen you have gott a writing ... from us," a Delaware Native complained, "you lock it up in ye Chest & no body Knows what you have bought or what you paid for it."[74] They came to realize the importance colonists gave to literacy, however, and tried to play by English rules, just as English go-betweens learned the value of wampum to the Natives. Both sides faced the problem of discerning signals in noise created by rumors, deceit, and human frailty.

Different perceptions of time influenced diplomacy. For high-context Natives the every day greetings of colonial emissaries were too perfunctory. Whites were too quick "to get down to business." Good diplomacy required constant attention. Colonists learned to engage in performative diplomacy when necessary, but their priority was information diplomacy—sending a message, influencing a target audience, quickly reaching agreement, and reducing it to a signed written document.[75] US diplomacy today has important relational and communitarian characteristics. However, low-context messaging and transactional pragmatism still dominate.

Colonial-era diplomacy also saw the beginnings of what in the twenty-first century is known as a "say-do gap" between words and actions. As the Onondaga sachem Red Head made clear to William Johnson in 1755, an Iroquois commitment would depend on the colonists' actions. By continuing to trade with the French even as war clouds gathered, they were putting their economic interests above the common good. "Your people are very faulty," Red Head said, "they are too thirsty for money." From long experience the Iroquois understood the British were good at the rhetoric of brotherhood, but greed and ambition often trumped their public diplomacy.[76] More than two centuries later, US armed forces recognized the "say-do gap" as "real or perceived differences between actions and words" that, if not mitigated, reduce credibility and negatively affect mission outcomes.[77] Gaps are easy to find in, for example, US rhetoric about war criminals and rule of law coupled with failure to ratify international treaties on the International Criminal Court and Law of the Sea.

Seeds of American exceptionalism. Many Americans have long believed the colonists came to a promised land where, through virtue and hard work, they created a uniquely exceptional nation defined by prosperity, freedom, and equality. For the Puritans, English civilization was intertwined with "Christ's blessings." As the resolves of the town of Milford, Connecticut, put it in 1640: "Voted that the earth is the Lord's and the fullness thereof; voted, that the earth is given to the Saints; voted, we are the Saints."[78] American identity was shaped by the colonists' belief in their moral superiority and fear that they might become like the savage Natives and lose their "Englishness."[79] The real story is more complex. Indigenous peoples, enslaved Africans, French and Spanish colonizers, disease, and relentless expansion also shaped the United States.[80] The treatment of African-Americans as enslaved peoples beginning in 1619 is central, but slavery is largely the domain of domestic governance and society, not diplomacy.

Tensions between ideals and self-interest came early. Colonists wrapped their territorial dispossession of Native peoples in the packaging of "civilization." There were exceptions. Roger Williams was no idealist, but he believed that "Nature knows no difference between Europe and Americans in blood, birth, bodies &c. God having of one blood made all mankind."[81] William Penn spoke of his desire "to sit downe Lovingly… freely confer & discourse" with Indian tribes.[82] Williams and Penn negotiated and paid for land. But most colonists held very different views. The colonial seal of New York shows two natives kneeling and offering furs to the king, who in return projects sovereign authority and Christianity.

American exceptionalism served then and serves now as a rationale for strategies that combine hard power—force, intimidation, bribery—and the soft power attraction of ideals, resources, and alliances. America's colonies, the theologian Reinhold Niebuhr would say three centuries later, had "pretensions of innocency." They saw themselves as God's chosen agents in a "new beginning for mankind." It was an "ironic incongruity" in which personal illusions masked the realities of self-interest.[83] It was an identity with profound consequences for the American way of diplomacy.

Diplomatic practices of colonists and Native Americans have enduring relevance. They help us understand the nation's occasional state-sponsored public diplomacy by private citizens in the nineteenth century. They shed light on twentieth-century tools and methods when Americans established government organizations and diverse communities of public diplomacy practice. They instruct today when whole of government diplomacy, new diplomatic actors, and digitalized and societized diplomacy are transforming diplomatic practices worldwide.

Notes

1. John M. Barry, *Roger Williams and the Creation of the American Soul: Church, State, and the Birth of Liberty* (Penguin Books, 2012), 390–396.
2. In the contested terrain of collective and individual names for Indigenous peoples, I have been guided by historians Colin Calloway, Ned Blackhawk, and Jill Lepore. Following Calloway and Blackhawk, I use *Native American* and *Indian* interchangeably. I adopted Calloway's interchangeable use of *tribe* and *nation*, convinced by his argument it does not mean Native American tribal nations "are either less than or the same as nation states." I follow Lepore's use of anglicized names familiar to most readers for Native tribes and individuals. She notes there are few clues to what Algonquians called King Philip's War. He was not a king, and his given name was not Philip. Ultimately, she asks, can the contest for meaning in names "ever be a fair fight when only one side has access to those perfect instruments of empire, pens, paper, and printing presses?" Colin G. Calloway, *Pen and Ink Witchcraft: Treaties and Treaty Making in American Indian History* (Oxford University Press, 2013), xii; Ned Blackhawk, *Violence Over the Land: Indians and Empire in the Early American West* (Harvard University Press, 2006); Jill Lepore, *The Name of War: King Philip's War and the Origins of American Identity* (Vintage Books, 1999), ix–xxiii.
3. Barry, *Roger Williams*, 1, 58–59.
4. Barry, *Roger Williams*, 155–166, 213–218; Bruce Elliott Johansen, *The Native Peoples of North America: A History* (Rutgers University Press, 2006), 1, 121–135.
5. Johansen, *Native Peoples*, 125.
6. Quoted in Alfred A. Cave, *The Pequot War* (University of Massachusetts Press, 1996), 124.

7. Cave, *Pequot War*, 122–128; Barry, *Roger Williams*, 233–242.
8. Johansen, *Native Peoples*, 130.
9. Alan Taylor, *American Colonies: The Settling of North America* (Penguin Books, 2001), xi.
10. Ned Blackhawk, *The Rediscovery of America: Native Peoples and the Unmaking of U.S. History* (Yale University Press, 2023).
11. Taylor, *American Colonies*, 67–90.
12. Alan Greer, *The People of New France* (University of Toronto Press, 1997), 5.
13. Taylor, *American Colonies*, xiv–xvii. Recent "Atlantic scholarship" gives needed attention to French and Dutch colonies, Spanish America, the British West Indies, and enslaved Africans. Diplomacy between English colonies and Native Americans, however, had the greatest impact on the American way of diplomacy.
14. Keith Hamilton and Richard Langhorne, *The Practice of Diplomacy: Its Evolution, Theory, and Administration*, 2nd ed. (Routledge, 2011), 37–90.
15. Murray N. Rothbard, *Conceived in Liberty* (Arlington House, 2011), 267–279; Noel W. Sainsbury, ed., *Calendar of State Papers, Colonial Series, America and West Indies, 1661–1668* (Longman, 1880), 200–204, 341–343.
16. On encounter, discovery, and re-encounter relations in diplomacy, see Sharp, *Diplomatic Theory*, 89–92.
17. Timothy Shannon, *Iroquois Diplomacy on the Early American Frontier* (Penguin Books, 2008).
18. Calloway, *Pen and Ink Witchcraft*, 12.
19. Frances Jennings, ed., *The History and Culture of Iroquois Diplomacy: An Interdisciplinary Guide to the Treaties of the Six Nations and Their League* (Syracuse University Press, 1985), xiv–xv.
20. Sainsbury, *State Papers*, 200, 342.
21. Sharp, *Diplomatic Theory*, 272; Sharp, email to author, November 18, 2021.
22. Shannon, *Iroquois Diplomacy*, 81–87, 96–100; Calloway, *Pen and Ink Witchcraft*, 14–15, 35–43.
23. Quoted in Calloway, *Pen and Ink Witchcraft*, 12.
24. Paul Sharp, "The Idea of Diplomatic Culture and Its Sources," in *Intercultural Communication and Diplomacy*, ed. Hannah Slavik (DiploFoundation, 2004), 372.

25. Jurgen Habermas, *The Structural Transformation of the Public Sphere: An Inquiry into a Category of Bourgeois Society*, trans. Thomas Burger (MIT Press, 1991), 23, 26.
26. Katherine Granjean, *American Passage: The Communication Frontier in Early New England* (Harvard University Press, 2015); Gregory Evans Dowd, *Groundless: Rumors, Legends, and Hoaxes on the Early American Frontier* (Johns Hopkins University Press, 2015).
27. James H. Merrell, *Into the American Woods: Negotiators on the Pennsylvania Frontier* (W. W. Norton, 1999), 27–34.
28. Merrell, *American Woods*, 19–41.
29. Merrell, *American Woods*, 153–154; Jennings, *History and Culture*, 105.
30. Merrell, *American Woods*, 186.
31. Merrell, *American Woods*, 62, 77–78.
32. Shannon, *Iroquois Diplomacy*, 11–13, 25–28, 83–96, 107–133; Merrell, *American Woods*, 54–55, 63–64, 167–172, 222–223.
33. Merrell, *American Woods*, 76–77
34. Merrell, *American Woods*, 75.
35. Merrell, *American Woods*, 102, 104.
36. Merrell, *American Woods*, 80.
37. Quoted in Timothy Shannon, *Indians and Colonists at the Crossroads of Empire: The Albany Congress of 1754* (Cornell University Press, 2000), 44.
38. James Thomas Flexner, *Mohawk Baronet: A Biography of Sir William Johnson* (Syracuse University Press, 2015); Fintan O'Toole, *White Savage: William Johnson and the Invention of America* (Farrar, Straus and Giroux, 2005).
39. Eliot A. Cohen, *Conquered into Liberty: Two Centuries of Battles Along the Great Warpath that Made the American Way of War* (Free Press, 2011), 47.
40. Quoted in Shannon, *Indians and Colonists*, 37.
41. Quoted in Eric Hinderaker, *The Two Hendricks: Unraveling a Mohawk Mystery* (Harvard University Press, 2010), 176.
42. Shannon, *Indians and Colonists*, 42–44.
43. Shannon, *Indians and Colonists*, 30–36; Shannon, *Iroquois Diplomacy*, 120–122, 133.
44. Hinderaker, *Two Hendricks*, 159.
45. Shannon, *Indians and Colonists*, 30–36, 149–173; Shannon, *Iroquois Diplomacy*, 103–106, 120–124.
46. Shannon, *Indians and Colonists*, 45–51; Merrell, *American Woods*, 221–224.

47. Shannon, *Iroquois Diplomacy*, 142–149; O'Toole, *White Savage*, 109–120.
48. Cohen, *Conquered into Liberty*, 48.
49. Peter Marshall, "Sir William Johnson and the Treaty of Fort Stanwix, 1768," *Journal of American Studies* 1, no. 2 (October 1967): 149–179.
50. Quoted in Alan Taylor, *American Revolutions: A Continental History, 1750–1804* (W. W. Norton, 2016), 256.
51. Colin G. Calloway, *The Indian World of George Washington* (Oxford University Press, 2018), 235–259.
52. Calloway, *Indian World*, 340–345.
53. Knox and Jefferson are quoted in Jeffrey Ostler, "'To Extirpate the Indians': An Indigenous Consciousness of Genocide in the Ohio Valley and Lower Great Lakes, 1750s–1810," *The William and Mary Quarterly* 72, no. 4 (October 2015): 607–617.
54. Joseph Ellis, *American Creation: Triumph and Tragedies at the Founding of the Republic* (Alfred A. Knopf, 2007), 142.
55. Calloway, *Indian World*, 364–365.
56. Ellis, *American Creation*, 152. On McGillivray's progress and public ceremonies in New York, see Ellis, *American Creation*, 127–164 and Calloway, *Indian World*, 346–377.
57. Ellis, *American Creation*, 160.
58. Shannon, *Iroquois Diplomacy*, 162–209; Calloway, *Indian World*, 440–444.
59. Guided by historians Claudio Saunt, Frederick E. Hoxie, and Ned Blackhawk, I use the terms *dispossession* and *survival* rather than *genocide*. For Saunt, genocide problematically elevates the term to the single question of whether extreme violence in the American past fits the definition of the crime described in the 1948 United Nations Convention on Genocide. Hoxie and Blackhawk write convincingly that genocide masks the agency of Indigenous peoples. "Native leaders from the seventeenth century forward," Hoxie observes, "were willing to negotiate treaties, learn new languages, travel to foreign capitals, publish broadsides, and adopt new religions as they struggled to force newcomers to recognize their humanity and sovereignty." In Blackhawk's account, "genocide complicates a fundamental premise of the American story.... Native peoples simultaneously determined colonial economies, settlements, and politics and were shaped by them." Claudio Saunt, *Unworthy Republic: The Dispossession of Native Americans and the Road to Indian Territory*

(W.W. Norton, 2020), xii–xiv; Frederick E. Hoxie, "Conquest and Agency," Letter to the Editor, *The New York Review* 67, no. 15 (October 8, 2020): 46; Blackhawk, *The Rediscovery of America*, 5.

60. Jurgen Ostermammel, *The Transformation of the World: A Global History of the Nineteenth Century*, trans. Patrick Cammiler (Princeton University Press, 2014), 60.

61. Greg Grandin, *The End of the Myth: From the Frontier to the Border Wall in the Mind of America* (Metropolitan Books, 2019), 16–23, 47–48; Bernard Bailyn, *The Barbarous Years: The Peopling of British North America—The Conflict of Civilizations, 1600–1675* (Alfred A. Knopf, 2012).

62. James Webb, *Born Fighting: How the Scots-Irish Shaped America* (Broadway Books, 2005).

63. Ian K. Steele, *Warpaths: Invasions of North America* (Oxford University Press, 1994), 1.

64. Malcolm Gaskill, *Between Two Worlds: How the English Became Americans* (Basic Books, 2014), xvi, xix.

65. Taylor, *American Colonies*, 123.

66. Bernard Bailyn, *The Peopling of British North America: An Introduction* (Vintage Books, 1988), 116.

67. Calloway, *Indian World*, 321–345.

68. Lepore, *Name of War*, 68.

69. Kathy R. Fitzpatrick, *The Future of US Public Diplomacy: An Uncertain Fate* (Martinus Nijhoff, 2010), 5–78; Bruce Gregory, "American Public Diplomacy: Enduring Characteristics, Elusive Transformation," *The Hague Journal of Diplomacy* 6, no. 3–4 (March 2011): 351–372.

70. William Fenton, "Structure, Continuity, and Change in the Process of Iroquois Treatymaking," in Jennings, *History and Culture*, 7.

71. Sharp, *Diplomatic Theory*, 272.

72. Quoted in Merrell, *American Woods*, 224.

73. Raymond Cohen, *Negotiating Across Cultures: International Communication in an Interdependent World* (United States Institute of Peace Press, 1991), 9–23; Glen H. Fisher, *Public Diplomacy and the Behavioral Sciences* (Indiana University Press, 1972), 127–160; R.S. Zaharna, *Battles to Bridges: U.S. Strategic Communication and Public Diplomacy After 9/11* (Palgrave Macmillan, 2010), 121–133; Edward T. Hall, *The Silent Language* (Doubleday, 1959).

74. Merrell, *American Woods*, 217.

75. Michael K. Foster, "Another Look at the Function of Wampum in Iroquois-White Councils," in Jennings, *History and Culture*, 103–110.
76. O'Toole, *White Savage*, 119.
77. Joint Chiefs of Staff, *Doctrine for the Armed Forces of the United States*, JP 1 (2013), I-12–I-13.
78. Steele, *Warpaths*, 94.
79. Lepore, *Name of War*, xii–xv, 5–8.
80. Alan Taylor, *Colonial America: A Very Short Introduction* (Oxford University Press, 2013), 6–7.
81. Quoted in Barry, *Roger Williams*, 158.
82. Quoted in Merrell, *American Woods*, 35.
83. Reinhold Niebuhr, *The Irony of American History* (1952; reis., University of Chicago Press, 2008), 24.

3

Turning Points in a New Nation, 1776–1917

Until shortly before the Declaration of Independence, few colonists imagined they would unite in a new nation. At the Albany Conference of 1754, where the colonies met to repair ties with the Iroquois, Benjamin Franklin proposed a Plan of Union. "Join, or Die" was the caption on his political cartoon depicting the colonies as a snake in pieces. His proposal was soundly defeated. When British troops emerged victorious after years of war with France in 1763, colonists lit fireworks, rang church bells, and celebrated their good fortune to be British subjects. James Otis, a leader of Boston's Patriot movement, spoke for many when he proclaimed the colonies' affection for a mother country "We love, esteem, and reverence" and a king we "adore."[1] Yet in April 1775, 12 years later, 13 colonies began their revolution and soon united in a sovereign state.

This chapter examines three turning points that signify fundamental changes in US diplomacy's public dimension before the twentieth century. We begin with diplomats, methods, and events that reveal the importance of public diplomacy when English colonies, no longer subgroups in Britain's empire politics, turned from a dominant focus on relations with Native Americans to diplomacy with sovereign states. A second turning point is the emergence of state-sponsored public diplomacy in the nineteenth century—occasional, unofficial, and mostly

© The Author(s), under exclusive license to Springer Nature Switzerland AG 2024
B. Gregory, *American Diplomacy's Public Dimension*, Palgrave Macmillan Series in Global Public Diplomacy, https://doi.org/10.1007/978-3-031-38917-7_3

during wartime—without government organizations fitted to the purpose. A third turning point occurred when human communication and transportation were transformed by the telegraph, railroads, and other industrial age technologies.

Citizen Founders of US Public Diplomacy

Americans who led a war for independence were gifted diplomats as well as revolutionaries. No longer only "go-betweens" on America's frontier, they practiced their diplomacy in the royal courts, parliaments, salons, and coffee houses of Europe's major cities. They were skilled in private negotiations and effective in wielding the tools of diplomacy's public dimension.

Benjamin Franklin. Ten years before the American Revolution, Franklin was a vigorous opponent of Britain's hated Stamp Act. The Act placed a tax on newspapers, books, legal documents, playing cards, and almost all paper circulating throughout the English colonies. Britain had won the war with France; now the colonies would help pay for it. Colonists begged to differ. Franklin took their case to the British people. His strategy: a systematic effort to influence British public opinion through reasoned argument, humor, and satire. His tools: a letter writing campaign, anonymous satirical essays, a political cartoon handed out on note cards in front of Parliament by a paid agent, conversations with British ministers and parliamentarians, access through his celebrity as a scientist, and four hours of testimony in the House of Commons in February 1766.[2] This was "domestic" politics. Franklin was still a loyal subject of the Crown. Later, he would use these tools as a US diplomat.

Within a decade the colonies were using public diplomacy as a government-sponsored instrument of foreign policy in the context of impending war. They began in Canada with a messaging strategy that relied on print media. Six months before shots were fired, the Continental Congress sent a long public letter to the French-speaking inhabitants of Quebec, which the British had conquered, to persuade them to form an alliance. The letter was translated into French and widely distributed as a pamphlet. It was a mixture of promises and threats: the benefits of freedom of religion, protection of property, and other civic rights if they associated with "the rest of North America" or war if they refused. "You have been conquered into liberty," the pamphlet concluded without apparent irony, "if you act as you ought." After the outbreak of revolution, a second public letter to the "oppressed inhabitants of Canada" appealed to their fears of British rule. The Continental Congress also sent Franklin to Montreal in April 1776 with instructions to explain representative democracy and offer the Canadians full membership in the united colonies. With little regard for consistency, Franklin was "instructed to establish a free press and … give directions for the frequent publication of such pieces as may be of service to the cause of the United Colonies."[3]

In November 1776 Franklin arrived in Paris as a diplomatic representative of the colonies seeking money and weapons. Through astute private and public diplomacy, he played a critical role in bringing France into an alliance that lasted nearly six years. He combined appeals to his hosts' interests with the skills of a master image builder and celebrity diplomat. He captivated the French aristocracy drawing crowds wherever he went. Franklin well understood the power of symbols. To great enthusiasm, he resumed his act as an American backwoods rustic and village sage dressed in plain linen and a fur cap. His image appeared everywhere in engravings and print. In the words of historian Gordon S. Wood, "Franklin's genius was to understand how the French saw him and to exploit that image on behalf of the American cause."[4]

Franklin was adept at what later would be called cultural diplomacy. He engaged easily in conversations with Voltaire, Condorcet, and other French *philosophes*. His writings on electricity and moral philosophy were translated into French and achieved great commercial success. He encouraged translation of America's colonial constitutions into French, gave copies to every ambassador in Paris, and circulated them throughout Europe. Franklin understood the value of personal contact and leveraged his many connections with France's political elites to diplomatic advantage.

At the same time, he was at home in the world of covert operations and disinformation. His pieces in the press often were anonymous or signed by others. One parodied the British practice of paying a bounty only for Hessian mercenaries who died, not for those who were wounded. Others used wit and satire to ridicule reports circulated by Britain's ambassador to France. His news releases often displayed scant knowledge of what was happening at home. Biographer Walter Isaacson describes his account of the British surrender at Saratoga as "filled with little details and large exaggerations."[5] In a skillful forgery intended to build support for treaty negotiations, Franklin circulated throughout Europe a "Supplement" to the Boston *Independent Chronicle* complete with phony advertisements. The hoax told of huge numbers of scalps taken by British troops from Continental Army soldiers, women, infants, and unborn children.[6]

The alliance with France in 1778 did not come easily. Louis XIV was reluctant to engage in war with Britain, and he resisted supporting a rebellion against another monarch. The Americans had little to offer the French, and the Continental Army's early defeats raised doubts about whether the revolution would succeed. Plus, there was resistance in the colonies. Most Americans had memories of recent wars with France and its Native American allies. Nevertheless, Wood concludes, Franklin's efforts were "the most potent weapon the United States possessed in its struggle with the greatest power on earth."[7]

John Adams. In February 1778 Adams sailed to Paris to join Franklin in negotiations with France. Operating largely behind the scenes, he clashed with Franklin and others in the American delegation. Adams was not "qualified by nature or education to shine in courts," his friend Jonathan Sewall observed. "His abilities are undoubtedly equal to the mechanical parts of his business as ambassador; but this is not enough. He cannot dance, drink, game, flatter, promise, dress, swear with the gentlemen, and small talk and flirt with the ladies; in short he has none of the essential arts or ornaments which constitute a courtier."[8] Adams's views on what moved nations were of a different order. "It is interest alone which does it," he informed Congress, "and it is interest alone which can be trusted."[9]

Adams traveled to Amsterdam in 1780 to negotiate a loan for the American war effort, and the following year he was an envoy to the Dutch government in The Hague. There he discovered his inner public diplomacy. According to biographer David McCullough, "He made a study of Dutch ways and temperament, read deeply in Dutch history ... struggled to learn the language, and in what seemed an equally daunting task, to fathom the complexities of the Dutch system of government." When the government resisted, he found support for the American cause among intellectuals, journalists, lawyers, mayors, and democracy activists. He took his case to the people and "cultivated an amazing range of friends among the press and in intellectual and financial circles." He encouraged them to petition their government to recognize the United States. He visited official residences in The Hague that housed delegations from 18 Dutch cities. He used skills and tools Franklin had developed in Paris: letters, newspaper reports, anonymous articles in French journals, and articles placed by agents in the British press. Adams, McCullough writes, was his "own office of information and propaganda."[10] His public diplomacy proved critical to securing Dutch loans and recognition of the United States in 1782.

Thomas Jefferson. Jefferson succeeded Franklin as US Minister to France in 1785. His assignments were to negotiate treaties of commerce with European nations, pay ransom to the Barbary pirates for release of American sailors, finalize a consular agreement with France, and convince host officials they could deal with an America still governed by the Articles of Confederation. He knew that to understand a country one needed to get away from its capital city. His travels for business and pleasure took him to Marseilles in the south, Nantes and Rennes in the east, Calais in the north, and beyond France to Brussels, Cologne, Rotterdam, Amsterdam, Genoa, and Milan.[11]

Jefferson maintained good relations with Count de Vergennes, the French Minister of Foreign Affairs, a diplomat who had supported the American Revolution. He also continued his friendship with the Marquis de Lafayette, whose influence in the French court "powerfully aided" his diplomatic efforts.[12] Jefferson reciprocated by collaborating unofficially with Lafayette and kindred French liberals in writing the Declaration of the Rights of Man and a constitution for a French Republic. In so doing, Jefferson encountered a perennial public diplomacy challenge. How should practitioners simultaneously carry out diplomatic relations with government officials in power and also engage with their citizens, some of whom may be actively seeking to gain power?

Public diplomacy practitioners routinely cite Jefferson's "decent respect to the opinions of mankind" that framed America's cause to the world in the Declaration of Independence. But there are many other ways he stands out as an exemplar of varieties of diplomatic practice—political influence campaigns, media relations, cultural diplomacy, nation branding, and disinformation. Biographer Jon Meacham catalogs his skills: listening as a political art, leveraging personal relationships, distilling complexity to reach emotions as well as minds, speaking and writing to audiences at home and abroad, and an understanding that politics in diplomacy and governance is not a "dispiriting distraction, but an undertaking that made everything else possible."[13]

Jefferson used his celebrity as author of the highly regarded *Notes on the State of Virginia* to advance US policies, respond to French curiosity about the United States, and satisfy his own endless curiosity about people, cultures, and the natural world. He spent much of his time in the company of intellectuals, artists, and writers. As he wrote to James Madison after arriving in Paris, "You see I am an enthusiast on the subject of the arts … as its object is to improve the taste of my countrymen, to increase their reputation, to reconcile them to the respect of the world, and procure them its praise."[14]

In an early example of nation branding, Jefferson went to the considerable trouble of having "the complete carcass and skeleton of an American moose, seven feet tall at the shoulders and with skin and antlers attached, shipped to him in Paris and reassembled and installed in the entrance hall of his residence, the elegant Hotel de Langeac in the center of town." Why? In the words of David G. Post, it was the "Wow" factor. He wanted people to see tangible evidence of the vast possibilities in a strange and largely unexplored "new world."[15] Jefferson's attention to the public dimension of diplomacy continued throughout his presidency and beyond. As he wrote to President James Monroe from retirement in Monticello three years after the War of 1812:

> I hope that to preserve this weather-gauge of public opinion, and to counteract the slanders and falsehoods disseminated by the British papers, the government will make it a standing instruction to their ministers at foreign courts, to keep Europe truly informed of occurrences here, by publishing in their papers the naked truth always, whether favorable or unfavorable. For they will believe the good, if we candidly tell them the bad also.[16]

Patterns of Public Diplomacy Practice. For Franklin, Adams, and Jefferson, public diplomacy was central to their roles as diplomats, and their skills, tools, and methods are models for contemporary practice. They understood the importance of languages and looking at history and culture through the eyes of others. They traveled beyond capital cities, and they communicated with the people in other countries as well as their governing elites.

Length of time in country expanded their knowledge and added to the depth and breadth of their contacts. Franklin was in London for 15 years and in France for eight. Adams served in France for two years, in the Netherlands for six, and as the first US Minister in Britain for three. Jefferson served in France for five years. They were multidisciplinary experts who played on political and cultural stages simultaneously. They chose contacts carefully among political, media, and military elites, and leading figures in science, literature, education, architecture, and the arts. This was easier before today's knowledge explosion. But they make a strong case for diplomats with broad lateral knowledge that fosters engagement with a range of experts and subject domains.

These practitioners understood the value of credibility, timing, enlisting interest, and building common ground. They also were keenly aware of diplomacy's relevance to domestic politics. Persuading Americans that French and Dutch support was attainable was as important as persuading France and the Netherlands that support for the American cause was in their interest. They would find legal restrictions on "domestic dissemination" of information impossible to imagine. In navigating contested political issues at home, they foreshadowed their twenty-first-century successors. They were idealists as well as national interest realists. They understood the power of ideas, and they framed the American project as "the cause of all mankind." They would be unsurprised by "indispensable nation" and "leader of the free world," phrases that come easily to the lips of Americans today. They also understood public diplomacy's limitations. Moving publics may not move governments when conflicts of interest are in play.

Thomas Paine—Emotions and Reason

Thomas Paine arrived in the United States in 1774, a debt-ridden former shopkeeper and recently fired London tax collector. He set up in Philadelphia as the editor of the *Pennsylvania Magazine*. His fiery prose soon attracted the attention of colonists bent on war with Britain. In January 1776, he published *Common Sense*, a pamphlet widely distributed (it sold 100,000 copies within weeks), excerpted in local newspapers, and read aloud in taverns throughout the colonies. Quoting the Bible and using emotionally charged words such as "tyranny," the "evil of monarchy," and "British barbarity," Paine demonized hereditary rule and King George III as a "Royale brute." He personalized the language of self-defense to legitimize the colonial cause. "We fight neither for revenge nor conquest," but because we have been attacked in our houses and lands by "enemies in the character of Highwaymen and Housebreakers." Praise for his prose came from all quarters, including Jefferson, who declared admiringly, "No writer has exceeded Paine in ease and familiarity of style; in perspicuity of expression; happiness of elucidation; and in simple unassuming language."[17]

Paine was a one-man information operation. George Washington immediately understood the pamphlet's "sound Doctrine and unanswerable reasoning" and ordered it read aloud to his demoralized Continental Army. His friends in Virginia agreed, writing that Paine's views were "working a powerful change there in the minds of men." Paine signed on as an aide to Army General Nathaniel Greene and became close friends with Washington. He followed with *The Crisis*, a collection of 13 essays honoring the 13 colonies, written by candlelight as the Army endured the miseries of its march across New Jersey in December 1776. This time, Washington himself read Paine's essays aloud to groups of soldiers.[18]

Paine's public diplomacy was on display with widespread circulation of *Common Sense* in Europe. It persuaded many to support the American cause and made him an international celebrity. In 1781 Congress appointed a young soldier, 26-year-old John Laurens, as a special envoy to France to support Benjamin Franklin in seeking a loan, war supplies, and naval support. Paine, who accompanied Laurens as his secretary, was given the task of energizing French support with his eyewitness accounts of the war. In a breach of protocol they handed a letter directly to King Louis XIV. The strategy worked. They returned with supplies and two-and-a-half million livres of silver. Paine went on to support the French Revolution, publish *The Rights of Man*, receive honorary French citizenship (along with Washington, Franklin, Alexander Hamilton, and James Madison), spend time in a French prison, publish *The Age of Reason*, return to the United States, and die in New York City.[19]

Paine played on fear and anger to strengthen the impact of his reasoned logic. His writings were skillful combinations of analysis and appeals to raw emotions in the context of external threats. His public diplomacy moved governments by using ordinary language to move their citizens. Years later John Adams would say he knew "not whether any Man in the World has had more influence on its inhabitants or affairs for the last thirty years than Tom Paine … Call it then the Age of Paine."[20]

Scholars today remind us of what Paine knew instinctively. Public emotions, Martha Nussbaum observes, have a Janus like quality. They can inspire groups to undertake great achievements on behalf of common purposes. They also can generate hatred of others and serve foolish or unjust causes. For Richard Ned Lebow, states and other governing bodies do not themselves have emotions. People project their psychological needs and passions on to the politics and diplomacy of their governing entities.[21]

Emotion in public diplomacy deserves greater attention—its role in the vilification of out-groups by fearful and angry publics, and its importance in political persuasion and interest-based narratives.[22] Seemingly dispassionate civil society cosmopolitans who pursue mutual understanding cannot escape the mix of feelings and reason that shapes discourse in inter-group cooperation and competition. Operationally, emotion can enable effective actions in situations where reasoned, time-consuming calculations are not possible. But it also can play havoc with critical reason and generate passions that lead to mistakes and bad outcomes. Separating emotion and reason creates a false dilemma, Michael Walzer explains, because they are "always entangled in practice."[23] They are necessary companions in political life, which is why they matter in public diplomacy.

Civil Society's Cosmopolitans

Americans in great numbers traveled the world in the nineteenth century pursuing niche agendas and private interests. Their global reach vastly exceeded the government's diplomatic connections just as it does now. Steamboats and railroads transformed ocean and land travel. The "horizons of modern society had opened out in every respect," wrote Frank Ninkovich, and a "narrowing of cultural distance was taking place on a global scale."[24] These civil society cosmopolitans shaped America's image and were a source of what Joseph Nye calls soft power.[25] There is a throughline from these cosmopolitans to twentieth-century democratizers, cultural diplomats, Peace Corps volunteers, citizen front groups, and other practitioners in diplomacy's public dimension.

Abolitionists. William Lloyd Garrison, Wendell Philips, Lucretia Mott, John Greenleaf Whittier, and other anti-slavery advocates traveling abroad found common ground with Europe's Chartists, Irish nationalists, John Stuart Mill, and other intellectuals. In 1846 Frederick Douglass met with parliamentarians and gave impassioned speeches in cities from London to Edinburgh to Dublin. Harriet Beecher Stowe's novel *Uncle Tom's Cabin* (1852), a grim portrayal of slavery in America, sold a million copies in Britain during its first year. She was lionized at meetings of anti-slavery societies and theatrical performances of her novel.[26] Although abolitionists achieved their central goal with the Thirteenth Amendment ending slavery in 1865, their civil rights activism continued. On a speaking tour before large audiences in Great Britain (1893–1894), African-American journalist, feminist, and anti-lynching advocate Ida B. Wells called for British sanctions in opposition to racist practices in Jim Crow America.

Women's Rights. During decades of meetings with women's rights advocates in Europe Elizabeth Cady Stanton, Susan B. Anthony, Rachel Foster Avery, and activists across Europe created a transatlantic network of women's rights organizations. Their efforts led to creation of the International Council of Women, an organization that now has consultative status with the United Nations.[27]

Peace activism. America's peace activists were convinced the power of public opinion, "which in the long run governs the world," would bring an end to armed conflict. They began to organize in the United States and Europe in the 1820s, where they distributed thousands of pamphlets and attended meetings to debate colonialism, disarmament, and international arbitration of disputes. Elihu Burritt, a journalist and advocate of what he called "people-diplomacy," worked with Quakers to build a grassroots pacifist movement in which workers would refuse to fight. The movement peaked with peace conferences in Brussels in 1848 and Paris in 1849.[28]

Free traders. For free trade advocates, the removal of tariff barriers was much more than a way to promote commerce. Its movement of merchants, manufacturers, workers, journalists, intellectuals, and political activists believed open markets would break down national barriers and realize "the unity of mankind" through enlightened public opinion. The nineteenth century would be an "admirable epoch," Victor Hugo declared, in which the "only fields of battle" would be "markets opening up to trade and minds opening up to ideas."[29]

Missionaries. America's most powerful grassroots force in the world were missionaries, Walter Russell Mead writes, "the chief bridge between Americans and the non-European countries in which the majority of the world's population lives." Saving souls, they discovered, meant learning languages, understanding cultures, feeding the hungry, educating students, promoting sanitation, and healing the sick. They were early proponents of the idea that Western countries had a duty to provide assistance and training in the Global South. They helped to spread democracy by promoting mass education, mass printing, voluntary associations, and colonial reforms. Missionaries built boarding schools, provided scholarships for study in the United States, and established Roberts College in Turkey, the American University of Beirut, and the American University in Cairo. Unlike the British, French, and Dutch, they were visitors in countries where America's founding documents influenced anti-colonial nationalists and intellectuals, many of whom were educated in missionary schools. Their international networks inspired humanitarian efforts by the YMCA and the American Red Cross, and decades later Rotary

International, the National Organization for Women, World Vision, Catholic Relief Services, and other NGOs.[30]

Jurists and humanitarians. In 1863 President Lincoln asked Columbia University professor Francis Lieber to make recommendations to the Union Army on the treatment of civilians and prisoners of war. He drafted what is known as the "Lieber Code" and initiated contacts with European jurists to discuss codifying laws of armed conflict. Their work led to the Hague Conventions on land warfare. Sixteen countries signed the first Geneva Convention in 1864 establishing legal rules guaranteeing neutrality and protection for wounded soldiers. Clara Barton, a nurse in the American Civil War, founded the American Red Cross. Her movement contributed to US adherence to the Geneva Convention. She later collaborated with the White House and State Department to provide humanitarian assistance in Cuba during America's War with Spain.[31]

Cosmopolitans in the second half of the nineteenth century, many motivated by the lethality of industrial age warfare, turned increasingly to public-private partnerships. Abolitionists, women's rights activists, jurists, and humanitarians on their own could not create sustainable solutions. Practical men and women came to realize they needed government support and binding legal commitments. Civil society can provide voice and expertise in relations between nations. But to achieve efficacy and durability, cross-cultural internationalism requires diplomats, negotiated agreements, and government organizations.

Public Diplomacy Without Government Organizations

The US Constitution, adopted in 1789, provided that "Ambassadors, other public Ministers, and consuls" be appointed by the president, with Senate approval. Congress created a Department of State, and President Washington appointed Jefferson, then US minister in France, as Secretary of State. He took office in March 1790 with a staff of eight that included two clerks, three assistant clerks, a part-time French translator, and two messengers.

US foreign policy in the nineteenth century was shaped by the nation's geographical advantages, a desire to engage in global commerce without involvement in Europe's politics and wars, and a belief that Americans had a "manifest destiny" to expand across the continent spreading their special virtues and institutions. Washington famously warned against "permanent alliances" with any nation, although he cautiously endorsed "temporary alliances for extraordinary emergencies." He went on to advise that "The great rule of conduct for us in regard to foreign nations is in extending our commercial relations, [and] to have with them as little political connection as possible."[32] The new nation regarded the diplomatic protocols of Europe's monarchies with suspicion. Jefferson established a small diplomatic service to handle political affairs and a separate consular service for maritime and commercial affairs and protection of US citizens. This was not a formula for robust diplomacy.

In 1800 the nation had six diplomatic missions and 52 consular posts. By 1900 the US presence abroad had risen to 33 missions and 252 consular posts. Chiefs of Mission all were men. Most were wealthy. Most were political allies of presidents. Consuls, who registered US vessels and rendered services to American citizens, far outnumbered diplomats. Some consuls were noted writers and artists such as Washington Irving, Nathaniel Hawthorne, James Fenimore Cooper, James Russell Lowell, William Dean Howells, and Bret Hart. Until 1893 Chiefs of Mission carried the rank of Minister, not Ambassador, which Americans viewed as too pretentious. Their missions were called legations, not embassies. With few exceptions diplomats were not paid until Congress authorized salaries in 1856. Instructions from Washington were often vague or nonexistent. Infrequent reports from the field sent by sea were often ignored. Not until the Rogers Act of 1924 did the United States establish professionally trained diplomatic and consular services.[33]

Nevertheless, as Walter Russell Mead argues, the United States was remarkably successful in achieving many of its goals. After independence, it settled with the Barbary pirates and pursued access to foreign markets. Following the Napoleonic Wars, the United States made the Louisiana Purchase, annexed Florida and Texas, moved its western boundary to the Pacific, negotiated the Canadian border, opened Japan to world commerce, seized the southwest from Mexico, persuaded Britain and France not to recognize Confederate independence, established hegemony in the Western Hemisphere, built a strong navy, and at century's end prevailed in the War with Spain.[34] Successes came through trade, military power—the Army in North America and the Navy's "gunboat diplomacy" abroad—and the global activities of the nation's civil society cosmopolitans.

External threats did not disappear in the nineteenth century. There was the war of 1812. Armed conflict with Britain and Canada was narrowly avoided during the Civil War. Violence was a constant presence on the domestic frontier. But overall, historian C. Vann Woodward observed, the United States enjoyed "free security" provided by "nature's gift of three vast bodies of water"—the Atlantic, Pacific, and Arctic oceans—"interposed between this country and any other power that might constitute a serious menace to its safety."[35] Americans supported a strong commercial fleet, a small, but growing, Navy, and an Army deployed largely in the American west. They saw little need for sustained government public diplomacy.

America's diplomats adhered to rules of the Westphalian state system in their government-to-government diplomacy. Government information and culture ministries did not yet exist in Europe, and in America they were unimaginable. However, in wartime the United States did engage in public diplomacy. In the War with Mexico, the Civil War, and the War with Spain, political leaders recruited private citizens to influence other governments and their publics in support of US interests.

War with Mexico. In 1846 President James Polk, intending to acquire territory, got Congress to declare war on Mexico. Americans were divided. Henry David Thoreau famously refused to pay taxes for a war of aggression. Congressman Abraham Lincoln introduced resolutions demanding to know who fired the first shots and where. But for many the war meant progress in the spread of democracy and civilization. It was "the best kind of conquest," wrote poet Walt Whitman, a voice of expansionist nationalism. "What has miserable, inefficient Mexico—with her superstition, her burlesque upon freedom, her actual tyranny by the few over the many—what has she to do with the great mission of peopling the new world with a noble race? Be it ours, to achieve that mission!"[36] Manifest Destiny, slavery, nativism, and anti-Catholicism, fueled by a three-decade increase in Catholic immigrants to the United States, inflamed debate over this reach for empire.

Protestant evangelicals led the war fervor that swept the country. For historian James C. Pinheiro, "Anti-Catholic rhetoric constituted an integral piece of nearly every major argument for or against the war and was so universally accepted among whites that recruiters, politicians, diplomats, journalists, soldiers, evangelical activists, abolitionists, and pacifists used it."[37] Historian Ted C. Hinckley holds that, although many Protestants militantly opposed Mexico's Catholicism, "there never materialized a national Protestant sentiment directed at transforming the struggle into a Protestant jihad south of the border." Nevertheless, evangelical rhetoric about sending American soldiers as "redeemers" to spread a "higher and purer Christian civilization" prompted widespread fear among Mexico's Catholics.[38]

Rumors that the United States intended to overthrow their religion and rob their churches created an operational problem for Polk and his generals. Polk had designs on Mexican territory, but not its religion, and the Army wanted no difficulties in recruiting Catholics to fight alongside Protestants. In a significant turning point for American public diplomacy, an alarmed Polk sought the assistance of New York City's Catholic Archbishop John Hughes. The Archbishop agreed to send Spanish-speaking priests to convince Mexico's clergy and laity that the United States would not interfere with their religion.[39] Polk also appointed Jesuit priests to serve as Army chaplains and show the Mexican people the United States was not seeking, as he noted in his diary, "to destroy their churches and make war upon their religion."[40] In an early instance of US military information operations, General Winfield Scott and other officers paid "conspicuous respect … to Mexican clergy, churches, and religious festivities."[41]

The Civil War. When the North and the South set out to influence foreign public opinion during the Civil War, they turned to private citizens for their public diplomacy.[42] The North wanted Europe's neutrality, respect for its blockade of Southern harbors, and denial of cotton imports. The South needed recognition, weapons, ships, and cotton exports. Both sides recognized the growing power of journalism enabled by the telegraph and increased literacy. Both sides sent journalists, clerics, and

political operatives to Europe to "give a right direction to public sentiment," openly and covertly. As US Minister to Belgium Henry Sanford,
who also coordinated the North's secret operations in Europe, wrote to
Secretary of State William Seward in 1861, "We ought to spend money
freely in the great centers in forming public opinion."[43]

Advocates for the North included General Winfield Scott, known
throughout Europe for his victories in Mexico; Episcopal Bishop Charles
McIlvaine sent to persuade British Anglicans; and Catholic Archbishop
John Hughes who came with messages for French Catholics and the
Papacy. Seward sent Thurlow Weed, a New York newspaper publisher
and skilled political operative, to influence opinion leaders and lawmakers in London. In the words of Amanda Foreman, Weed requested "a host
of unofficial representatives whose sole purpose was to shape public opinion," because, although US Minister to Britain Charles Francis Adams is
a "good man," he is "useless for anything other than strict diplomacy."[44]
Henry Adams, his father's private secretary, shared this view, complaining
to his brother Charles Francis Adams, Jr. that their father invariably
turned down invitations for public speaking. "Our agents abroad appar-
ently confine their efforts to cabinets and officials," he wrote, "and leave
public opinion and the press to take care of themselves."[45] Using his formidable public affairs skills, Weed primed 20 British MPs to speak for the
North in parliamentary debates on "the American question," focusing on
issues of neutrality, cotton economics, and perceptions of Union strength.

The Confederate State Department appointed Henry Hotze, an
Alabama journalist, to handle press relations in Britain. Described as
charming and fluent in French and German, he wrote speeches for pro-
South MPs in the British parliament and started a journal of opinion
named the *Index*, which he claimed was a British publication. Later, he
cultivated Auguste Havas, owner of the only telegraphic and foreign news
service in France. Hotze skillfully tailored the South's pamphlets, posters,
and draft editorials to the interests of diverse segments of British opinion.
Ultimately, however, he was more successful in shaping favorable perceptions of battle outcomes and raising questions about the North's ability to
pay its bonds than in persuading the British press to carry articles in
defense of slavery. Edwin De Leon, a diplomat-turned-writer and journalist, published articles in France and Ireland, where he sought to

discourage Irish immigrants from enlisting in the Union Army. He convinced Confederate President Jefferson Davis to support a well-funded campaign to "infiltrate the European press with our ideas and our version of the struggle."[46]

The *Trent* affair shows why public diplomacy mattered. On November 7, 1861, Confederate envoys James M. Mason and John Slidell boarded the British ship *Trent* in Charleston, South Carolina. Mason intended to establish a Confederate diplomatic mission in London; Slidell was en route to do the same in Paris. A Union naval vessel, acting without orders, intercepted the *Trent* outside of Havana. Mason and Slidell were captured and taken to Boston. The Northern press was exuberant. The *Trent*'s captain protested piracy and violation of British neutrality. An outraged British public clamored for war against the North. The Palmerston government, facing loud Tory protests, feared losing power. European observers viewed it to be a trap by the South to pull Britain into the war. The Union and Britain were at the brink of war.

John Bigelow, a New York newspaper publisher sent by Seward to Paris officially as US consul and unofficially "to put the public sentiment right," arranged a response in collaboration with Weed. It took the form of a letter drafted by Bigelow and signed by Winfield Scott. The letter expressed certainty that "the President and people of the United States" would be glad to release Mason and Slidell if in so doing they could "emancipate the commerce of the world."[47] The letter appeared in leading publications in London and Paris. Archbishop Hughes and Bishop McIlvaine championed the argument with their co-religionists. Weed wrote a letter to the London *Times* and arranged meetings with Palmerston's inner circle. Soon he was summoned by British Foreign Secretary Lord John Russell, who demanded the release of Mason and Slidell. Weed suggested the demand be framed "in a friendly spirit" and the United States would comply. Russell's message to Washington was considerably softened by Prince Albert. Lincoln released the Confederate envoys on Christmas Day, 1861.[48]

Events, interests, and leaders ultimately drove the outcome. Lincoln and Palmerston did not want war. Seward and Russell did not want war. Neither did Queen Victoria and Prince Albert. But inflamed passions came close to putting decisions beyond their control. As Don H. Doyle observes, the *Trent* crisis "taught timely lessons on the importance of the press and public opinion and on the urgency of having special agents, skilled in dealing with the press, on the ground and ready to put out fires." Weed, Bigelow, and the clerics Hughes and McIlvaine "pointed the way toward a promising new path in semiofficial public diplomacy."[49]

These and other citizens "of great knowledge and experience in public affairs," as Seward described them in Weed's letter of introduction to Minister Charles Adams, opened a fissure between traditional and public diplomats that persisted for more than a century. Adams took care to inform Seward of the "effective service" of these "loyal, high spirited and intellectual men of social position and character." They are "of material use" against Confederate emissaries who are "poisoning the sources of opinion" and "disseminating wholly erroneous notions" about the war. But Adams believed they served Union interests only in their "private position." He warned Seward of the dangers when they acted as "official representatives" and "necessarily occupy a false position in the face of the regularly accredited agent." They create a "perpetual danger of running into contradictions which neutralize the influence of both." Moreover, he argued, they create the impression that the official representative is not up to the task.[50] Adams was happy with positive outcomes in public opinion that might result from Weed's efforts, but he was decidedly unhappy with the means.

Lincoln continued to send private citizens abroad to engage in public diplomacy throughout the war. In 1862 Seward recruited Julian Sturtevant, a cleric, Charles W. Denison, a former Army chaplain, and Edward Everett, one of the greatest orators of his generation, to add to the work being done by Weed and others. Everett had quite the resume—a former Secretary of State, governor of Massachusetts, US representative and senator, minister to Britain a quarter century before Adams, and president of Harvard University. Lest his visit be "misconstrued," Lincoln wrote in a brief letter of introduction, Everett "bears no mission from this government." Yet, he declared, "no gentleman is better able to correct misunderstandings in the minds of foreigners, in regard to American affairs."[51] Whether foreign publics appreciate such distinctions is another matter. Likely to Adams's satisfaction, Everett declined to go after accepting the assignment.

Other efforts to use civil society activists were closer to what would later be known as cultural diplomacy. When naturalist Louis Agassiz, the philosopher William James, and a team of scientists began planning an expedition to Brazil, the US government, interested in countering Confederate influence in South America and opening the Amazon to trade, pledged its support. US officials entrusted Agassiz with messages for the emperor Dom Pedro II, a devotee of natural history who welcomed the team and arranged their meals, transportation, and other assistance. By 1865 the Civil War was no longer relevant to the government's support for their efforts, but the expedition gained some credit for the Amazon trade that followed.[52]

Secretary of State Seward operated his own international visitor program. He took foreign diplomats outside Washington to show them the Union Army's strength and later led them on a "grand tour" to New York's major cities and Niagara Falls. His aim was to demonstrate that the North was largely unaffected by the war.[53] Lincoln and Seward entertained and flattered the world-renowned William Howard Russell, an Irish war correspondent whose coverage of the war was influential in Europe. "The London *Times*," Lincoln told Russell, "is one of the greatest powers in the world—in fact I don't know anything which has more power—except perhaps the Mississippi. I am glad to know you as its minister."[54]

Lincoln's statements and actions were framed with public diplomacy in mind. He wrote public letters to British mill workers in Manchester thanking them for their resolutions of support and sacrifices endured due to cotton shortages. He expressed appreciation for their "sublime Christian heroism," which he declared was emblematic of "an energetic and reinspiring assurance of the inherent power of truth and of the ultimate and universal triumph of justice, humanity, and freedom."[55] Lincoln's personal secretary John Hay wrote anonymous newspaper reports that echoed Lincoln's views.

Lincoln added a line to the Emancipation Proclamation invoking "the considerate judgment of mankind." It was an opportunity, historian David Donald observed, "to use the White House as a pulpit, to speak out over the dissonant voices of foreign leaders to the common people, [that] daringly broadened the powers of the Presidency."[56] Historians debate the extent of the Proclamation's effect internationally. Henry

Adams, however, was in no doubt. It "has done more for us here than all our former victories and all our diplomacy," he wrote to his brother from London. "It is creating an almost convulsive reaction in our favor."[57]

In the end, events—the fortunes of armies and emancipation of the enslaved—were more decisive than articles in newspapers or speeches in parliaments. Seward was skeptical of public diplomacy except when passions were inflamed as in the *Trent* affair. "Foreign sympathy," he wrote to US consul Bigelow, "never did and never can create or maintain any state."[58] Nevertheless, the public diplomacy of Union and Confederate citizen volunteers was influential and a harbinger of what would come when the United States went to war in the twentieth century. Most nineteenth-century diplomats were not public diplomacy practitioners, but they cared about what public opinion meant for their diplomacy. Presidents cared even more. As Civil War historian Allan Nevins concluded, "No battle, not Gettysburg, not the Wilderness, was more important than the contest waged in the diplomatic arena and the forum of public opinion."[59]

Ascendant Hard and Soft Power

The decades after the Civil War saw the rise of America's global empire. The US military, more than diplomacy, was the face of America's ascendant power. Sea power strategist Alfred Thayer Mahan, the exploits of Admiral George Dewey, and US naval victories against Spain at Cuba's Santiago Bay and the Philippines' Manila Bay brought the Navy to worldwide prominence. Americans in government and civil society fashioned the elements of hard and soft power that would shape US diplomacy, commerce, and the nation's military and intelligence services in the twentieth century.

War with Spain. The War with Spain in 1898 lasted less than four months, not enough time to deploy citizens as unofficial public diplomacy practitioners. The Philippine-American War that followed lasted much longer. Most of the public diplomacy and information operations during the fighting and occupation of the Philippines were carried out by US military commanders. After the decisive battles that destroyed Spain's empire, the United States faced decisions on what to do with Cuba, Puerto Rico, Guam, and the Philippines. Spain recognized Cuba's independence and ceded Puerto Rico and Guam to the United States.

The Philippines took longer to settle due to a prolonged insurgency and American differences over independence or annexation. Dewey's naval blockade and supply of arms to the insurgents, together with independence leader Emilio Aguinaldo's belief in repeated US promises of independence, were a promising beginning. But when Spain surrendered, President William McKinley declared there would be "no joint occupation." The insurgents "must recognize the military occupation and authority of the United States." McKinley also proclaimed an American obligation to "uplift and civilize" the Filipinos.[60]

US armed forces used a combination of hard and soft power in the counterinsurgency campaign in the Philippines (1899–1913). The Army held Manila. Aguinaldo led a guerrilla campaign in the countryside. Where it was in control, the Army sought to win Filipino hearts and minds with sanitation projects, road building, hospitals, and education. In the countryside, American soldiers shot insurgents, cut off food supplies, raided and torched villages, tortured captives, and herded large numbers of rural Filipinos into fortified "reconcentration" camps. There they were "pacified." Rebel atrocities in response brought harsher counter measures in return.

Gaps between rhetoric and actions were on full display throughout the campaign. Instructions from Washington and military directives called for "kind and considerate treatment" of the Philippine people. But on the ground, "little brown brothers," "savages," "goo goos," and other racial slurs accompanied a pacification policy that was brutal and inhumane. Captain John Pershing (later World War I's General Pershing) exemplified these carrots and sticks perfectly. As US military governor in Mindanao, he made diplomatic visits to the indigenous Moros. He studied their language, ate their food, and counted many as "strong personal friends." He was elected a "datu," or sovereign prince, and became an honorary father to the wife of the sultan of Bayan. But as the insurgency continued, Pershing launched a surprise attack in which an estimated 200–500 Moros, including women and children, were killed.[61] Public outcry over these atrocities and Congressional hearings followed.

By 1899 the United States had acquired Hawaii, Guam, Pago Pago, Wake Island, and other islands in a chain that expanded its naval power in the Pacific. American political and economic power grew in China, and Secretary of State John Hay's Open-Door policy followed. His diplomatic notes urged equal commercial opportunities for all powers with spheres of influence in China. The United States had no defined sphere of influence, but it certainly had commercial interests. In 1900 McKinley sent 5000 troops to join a multi-national force established to protect diplomatic missions in China from the Boxers, a secret society intent on expelling foreigners. When it was over, China was forced to pay excessive indemnities to the intervening countries. Hay convinced Congress to use the funds to create two universities in China and support scholarships for Chinese students studying in the United States. The scholarships, administered by a China-US board, continued until China's Communist takeover in 1949. Hay's project set a precedent for the Fulbright scholarships and binational commissions later institutionalized in US cultural diplomacy.[62]

The United States followed similar militarized and economically driven policies in Latin America. Gun boats in harbors. Troop interventions. Support for authoritarian leaders hospitable to corporate enterprise. As Daniel Immerwahr summarizes, "U.S. troops entered Cuba (four times), Nicaragua (three times), Honduras (seven times), the Dominican Republic (four times), Guatemala, Panama (six times), Costa Rica, Mexico (three times), and Haiti (twice) between 1903 and 1934."[63] The only acquired territories were Puerto Rico, Guantanamo Bay, the Panama Canal Zone, the US Virgin Islands, and the Philippines until its independence in 1946. With these exceptions and its naval bases in the Pacific, US expansion did not call for planting the flag. Americans wanted open commercial relations, and, despite their militarized dispossession of indigenous peoples at home, they were outspoken in their opposition to Europe's imposed territorial colonization. Americans also wielded cultural soft power when missionaries and secular cosmopolitans brought ideas, democratic values, techniques, entertainment, and the English language to foreign countries, usually those of economic interest to the United States.

A professional military. The Army and Navy gave greater attention to professional military education as they strengthened their hard and soft power capabilities. The US Military Academy at West Point, established in 1802, had long educated a professional officer class that led the nation in war. The US Naval Academy in Annapolis, established in 1845, did the same for Navy commanders. These were undergraduate institutions. In 1884 the Navy, over the opposition of its old guard and many lawmakers, established the Naval War College in Newport, Rhode Island, to provide its officers with mid-career professional education in history and strategy. Lectures by Admiral Mahan, published as *The Influence of Sea Power upon History, 1660–1783,* became one of history's most important works on naval strategy. It gave purpose to the Navy's increasingly formidable fleet and provided an additional rationale for the nation's global ambitions. In 1901 the Army War College was established at Fort McNair in Washington, DC. Its purpose was to provide professional mid-career education to Army officers and respond to "military failings" in the War with Spain. It was also created to "advise the President, devise plans, acquire information, and direct the intellectual exercise of the Army" as an adjunct to the Army's General Staff. Nothing at all comparable was going on in American diplomacy, which, as retired diplomat Warren Zimmerman observed, "was mostly a patronage operation."[64]

Economic Soft Power. America's vibrant civil society and private sector also were drivers of the nation's growing power in the nineteenth century. Financiers, inventors, entrepreneurs, and huge monopolistic corporations combined to make the United States an economic great power well before its blue water Navy gave the United States a seat at the "high table" of world politics. By the mid-1880s America was a global leader in timber, steel, meatpacking, and mining. Its population was exploding. Americans held patents on most of the era's technological breakthroughs: turbines, alternating current, telephones, internal combustion engines, light bulbs, and radiotelegraphy. By 1893 the United States was the world's second largest trader behind Great Britain.[65]

Three industrialists and a financier personified America's economic growth. John D. Rockefeller, Sr. (1839–1937) founded the Standard Oil monopoly and pioneered the corporate "trust." Andrew Carnegie (1835–1919) bought out rival corporations and vertically integrated suppliers of raw materials with pig iron manufacture and steel production. In 1900 he sold his Carnegie Steel Company to financier J. Pierpont Morgan (1837–1913), after which it became the United States Steel Corporation. Henry Ford (1863–1947) experimented with self-propelled vehicles as Thomas Edison's chief engineer, founded the Detroit Automobile Company in 1899, introduced the Model T in 1908, opened Ford plants throughout Europe and Asia, transformed corporate public relations, and revolutionized mass production in manufacturing.[66] Standard Oil fought for overseas markets with ruthless price-cutting and privileged access to State Department reports on the Middle East and Southeast Asia. It functioned "as a shadow government with a foreign policy of its own."[67] Americans put a rhetorical gloss on what was happening. Their power rested on growing prosperity and the virtues of democratic principles, industrial capitalism, and a free and open society grounded in individual opportunity.

Huge fortunes amassed by Rockefeller, Carnegie, and Ford endowed the philanthropic foundations that bear their names. Their foundations funded vast knowledge networks, political projects, scientific research, and educational and cultural exchanges. In the twentieth century, primarily in the Global South, they supported political and economic development, established elite academic institutions, and funded cadres of experts in the natural and social sciences—activities that simultaneously advanced the goals of American corporations, diplomacy, and power projection. Global cosmopolitans in these foundations enhanced America's image and soft power, although most would not have associated what they were doing with governance and diplomacy.

Transformative Technologies, a Turning Point

Diplomats from ancient Mesopotamia to the nineteenth century traveled at the speed of horseback and sailing ships; their information was hand-carried. This time/space dimension put great distance between diplomats and those they represented. It gave them autonomy as representatives of political leaders and considerable freedom of action. In words difficult to imagine in an age of "real time" communication, President Jefferson is said to have told his Secretary of State James Madison, "We have not heard from our ambassador in Spain for two years. If we do not hear from him this year, let us write him a letter."[68]

Railroads and the telegraph. Railroads in the 1830s and the invention of the telegraph in the 1840s fundamentally transformed diplomatic practice. Railroads increased the speed of land travel over continental distances. Communication by telegraph meant messages could be sent without someone to carry them. Transmitted first by wire on landlines and later by underwater cables between continents, telegraphic messages were the primary means of long-distance communication during the second half of the nineteenth century. The telegraph changed how journalists gathered and reported news, how financial transactions were made, how military commanders positioned troops, and how diplomats received instructions, reported to their principals, and communicated with other governments. The importance of news and money meant journalists and financiers were first adopters. Military commanders were a close second. Diplomats were a distant third. Eventually the telegraph radically changed diplomatic practice in the field and the structures and functions of embassies and foreign ministries.[69]

In 1861 British diplomat Arthur Buchanan told parliament the telegraph "reduces, to a great degree, the responsibility of the minister. For he can now ask for instructions instead of doing a thing on his own responsibility."[70] Speculating in 1864 on the impact of a proposed transatlantic cable, US Minister Charles Francis Adams was ambivalent. He wished the enterprise success, but hoped it would occur after his London assignment ended. "I get so many dispatches per week [now] that I can with difficulty attend to them all satisfactorily," he observed. "[W]hat would be my fate if the cable succeeds, and I had to receive and answer them every day?"[71] And what, one wonders, would Adams have said about email and Twitter (renamed X in 2023)?

The telegraph strengthened foreign ministry hierarchies. In 1875 Secretary of State Hamilton Fish directed that "No messages are to be sent by the telegraph except those from the Secretary, or one of the Assistant Secretaries, or the Chief Clerk, or those authorized to be sent by one of the above."[72] His instruction foreshadowed State Department controls on diplomats using social media a century and a half later. When

John Hay became Secretary of State in 1898, State's Office of the Historian records, the Department was "an antiquated feeble organization enslaved by precedents and routine inherited from another century, remote from public gaze and indifferent to it. The typewriter was viewed as a necessary evil and the telephone was an instrument of last resort."[73]

The telegraph's impact on public opinion made management of international crises more difficult and foreign interventions more likely. As historian David Paull Nickles states, the speed of telegraphy, when combined with dramatic newspaper stories, created a sense of urgency in a crisis and raised public expectations that governments should "do something" about distant events more quickly. Nickles is careful not to exaggerate. Opinion surveys did not exist in the nineteenth century, and gauging the effects of public opinion was and is a tricky business. The telegraph did not determine policies or events. But it was an important factor in swings in the public mood and pace of diplomacy in the Crimean War, the Franco-Prussian War, and World War I. More than a century before debates on the so-called "CNN effect," the interplay of the media, public opinion, and political decisions was an important part of diplomacy's public dimension.[74]

Shortwave Radio. The telegraph and the telephone, patented by Alexander Graham Bell in 1876, are "one-to-one" technologies. The telegraph transmits content from point to point using the dots and dashes of Morse code. The telephone does the same with voice. They are not mass audience technologies. In 1894 Guglielmo Marconi began experimenting with wireless radio, and in 1902 he transmitted the first transatlantic radio signals from a station in Nova Scotia. Radio soon became a *one-to-many* broadcasting technology that enabled commercial and government broadcasters to communicate over long distances to government officials in other countries and directly to their citizens listening to receivers in their homes.

The shortwave band on the radio frequency spectrum was more advantageous than AM/FM frequencies in the early decades of international broadcasting. Shortwave signals sent to the ionosphere bounce back to earth where they can be retransmitted back to the ionosphere by relay stations. Through a series of such "hops," broadcasters could transmit voice and music beyond the curve of the earth for thousands of miles.

Shortwave's sound quality was vulnerable to weather conditions, sunspots, and jamming technologies. Radio signals on AM and FM frequencies provided clearer reception, but they traveled much shorter distances.

This chapter framed three turning points in the way America's leaders, diplomats, and citizens sought to communicate with and engage foreign publics: when America's revolutionaries made public diplomacy tools and practices integral to their diplomacy in Europe, when the US government deployed citizen practitioners in the War with Mexico, and when the telegraph transformed time and space in diplomatic practice. The following chapter introduces the US government's institutionalized public diplomacy in the twentieth century and the rival practitioner communities that emerged with separate but overlapping patterns of practice.

Notes

1. Quoted in Taylor, *American Revolutions*, 51.
2. Gordon S. Wood, *The Americanization of Benjamin Franklin* (Penguin Press, 2004), 105–120; Walter Isaacson, *Benjamin Franklin: An American Life* (Simon & Schuster, 2003), 226–232.
3. Quoted in Cohen, *Conquered into Liberty*, 134, 145–146, 159.
4. Wood, *Americanization*, 180.
5. Isaacson, *Benjamin Franklin*, 343; Caitlin E. Schindler, *The Origins of Public Diplomacy in US Statecraft* (Palgrave Macmillan, 2018), 41–74.
6. Dowd, *Groundless*, 187–201. Dowd notes that Franklin's hoax was circulated widely again in the run-up to the War of 1812. It continued to be taken as legitimate by some, and today it lives on the Internet.
7. Wood, *Americanization*, 171.
8. Quoted in David McCullough, *John Adams* (Simon & Schuster, 2001), 349.
9. Quoted in McCullough, *John Adams*, 233.
10. McCullough, *John Adams*, 234, 242–273.
11. On Jefferson's travels, see John B. Boles, *Jefferson: Architect of American Liberty* (Basic Books, 2017), 155–166.
12. Thomas Jefferson, *Autobiography*, The Avalon Project, Yale Law School website.

13. Jon Meacham, *Thomas Jefferson: The Art of Power* (Random House, 2013), xxiii, 35–36, 104–105.
14. Thomas Jefferson to James Madison, September 20, 1785, Founders Online, National Archives.
15. David G. Post, *In Search of Jefferson's Moose: Notes on the State of Cyberspace* (Oxford University Press, 2009), 13–18, 66–67, 209–211.
16. Thomas Jefferson to James Monroe, January 1, 1815, Founders Online, National Archives.
17. Quoted in Taylor, *American Revolutions*, 155–156.
18. Taylor, *American Revolutions*, 159; Ron Chernow, *Washington: A Life* (Penguin Books, 2010), 215, 271.
19. On Paine's diplomacy in France, see Craig Nelson, *Thomas Paine: Enlightenment, Revolution, and the Birth of the Modern Nation* (Penguin Books, 2006), 151–157 and Chernow, *Washington*, 391, 660–661, 689.
20. Quoted in Taylor, *American Revolutions*, 158.
21. Martha Nussbaum, *Political Emotions: Why Love Matters for Justice* (Belknap Press, 2013), 1–11, 204–225; Richard Ned Lebow, *A Cultural Theory of International Relations* (Cambridge University Press, 2008), 508–515.
22. Sarah Ellen Graham, "Emotion and Public Diplomacy: Dispositions in International Communications, Dialogue, and Persuasion," *International Studies Review* 16, no. 4 (December 2014), 522–539.
23. Michael Walzer, *Politics and Passion: Toward a More Egalitarian Liberalism* (Yale University Press, 2004), 126.
24. Frank Ninkovich, *Global Dawn: The Cultural Foundation of American Internationalism, 1865–1890* (Harvard University Press, 2009), 21.
25. Joseph S. Nye, Jr., *Soft power: The Means to Success in World Politics* (PublicAffairs, 2004).
26. W. Caleb McDaniel, *The Problem of Democracy in the Age of Slavery: Garrisonian Abolitionists & Transatlantic Reform* (Louisiana State University Press, 2013); David W. Blight, *Frederick Douglass: Prophet of Freedom* (Simon & Schuster, 2018), 166–177; Denise Kohn, Sarah Meer, and Emily Todd, eds., *Transatlantic Stowe: Harriet Beecher Stowe and European Culture* (University of Iowa Press, 2006).
27. Sandra Stanley Holton, "'To Educate Women into Rebellion': Elizabeth Cady Stanton and the Creation of a Transatlantic Network of Radical Suffragists," *The American Historical Review* 99, no. 4 (October 1994): 1112–1136.

28. Thomas Chalmers, "Thoughts on Universal Peace," in *The Works of Thomas Chalmers* (Towar, 1830), 295–303; Mark Mazower, *Governing the World: The History of an Idea* (Penguin Press, 2012), 33; Charles F. Howlett, "Elihu Burritt's Nineteenth Century Peace Education Efforts," Columbia University, n.d., https://www.tc.columbia.edu/epe/epe-entries/Howlett_Elihu_Burritt.pdf (accessed May 12, 2023).
29. Mazower, *Governing the World*, 38–48.
30. Walter Russell Mead, *Special Providence: American Foreign Policy and How It Changed the World* (Routledge, 2002), 132–162; Michael Mandelbaum, *The Ideas That Conquered the World: Peace, Democracy, and Free Markets in the Twenty-First Century* (PublicAffairs, 2002), 455, note 68; Robert D. Woodberry, "The Missionary Roots of Liberal Democracy," *American Political Science Review* 106, no. 2 (May 2012): 244–274.
31. On Francis Lieber, see Mazower, *Governing the World*, 67–68. On Clara Barton, see Schindler, *Origins of Public Diplomacy*, 114–120.
32. George Washington, "Farewell Address," September 19, 1796, Founders Online, National Archives.
33. On America's nineteenth-century diplomatic and consular services, see Harry W. Kopp, *The Voice of the Foreign Service: A History of the American Foreign Service Association* (Foreign Service Books, 2015), 1–10 and Peter D. Eicher, *Raising the Flag: America's First Envoys in Faraway Lands* (Potomac Books, 2018).
34. Mead, *Special Providence*, 6–8.
35. C. Vann Woodward, "The Age of Reinterpretation," *The American Historical Review* 66, no. 1 (October 1960): 2; John Lewis Gaddis, *Surprise, Security, and the American Experience* (Harvard University Press, 2004), 7.
36. Quoted in Kevin Peraino, *Lincoln in the World: The Making of a Statesman and the Dawn of American Power* (Crown Publishers, 2013), 21.
37. John C. Pinheiro, *Missionaries of Republicanism: A Religious History of the Mexican-American War* (Oxford University Press, 2014), 1–2.
38. Ted C. Hinckley, "American Anti-Catholicism During the Mexican War," *Pacific Historical Review* 31, no. 2 (May 1962): 121.
39. John Sigenthaler, *James K. Polk* (Times Books, 2004), 15–16.
40. Quoted in Hinckley, "Anti-Catholicism," 135–136.
41. Pinheiro, *Missionaries*, 136.
42. On the diplomacy of the North and South during the Civil War, see Amanda Foreman, *A World on Fire: Britain's Crucial Role in the American*

Civil War (Random House, 2010); Peraino, *Lincoln in the World*; Don H. Doyle, *The Cause of All Nations: An International History of the American Civil War* (Basic Books, 2015); Walter Stahr, *Seward: Lincoln's Indispensable Man* (Simon & Schuster, 2013); and Schindler, *Origins of Public Diplomacy*, 75–109.

43. Both quotes are in Doyle, *Cause of All Nations*, 3–4.
44. Foreman, *World on Fire*, 214–215.
45. Quoted in Foreman, *World on Fire*, 163.
46. Doyle, *Cause of All Nations*, 195; Foreman, *World on Fire*, 671–672.
47. Doyle, *Cause of All Nations*, 77.
48. For accounts of the *Trent* affair that discuss the public diplomacy of Weed, Bigelow, Scott, Hughes, Lincoln, Palmerston, their foreign ministers, and Prince Albert, see Foreman, *World on Fire*, 154–198 and Doyle, *Cause of All Nations*, 73–82.
49. Doyle, *Cause of All Nations*, 81–82.
50. Quoted in Schindler, *Origins of Public Diplomacy*, 90–91. I am grateful to Schindler for her discussion of the Union's public diplomacy and contrasting views of Lincoln, Seward, Adams, and Weed.
51. Quoted in Schindler, *Origins of Public Diplomacy*, 92. See also Foreman, *World on Fire*, 164–165.
52. Louis Menand, *The Metaphysical Club: A Story of Ideas in America* (Farrar, Straus and Giroux, 2001), 117–120.
53. Stahr, *Seward*, 367–368, 379.
54. Quoted in Foreman, *World on Fire*, 74.
55. Quoted in Peraino, *Lincoln in the World*, 218. Peraino notes that Lincoln's agents in Britain also provided funding for some of the meetings and drafted some of the resolutions.
56. David Herbert Donald, *Lincoln* (Simon & Schuster, 1995), 416.
57. Quoted in Peraino, *Lincoln in the World*, 219.
58. Quoted in Foreman, *World on Fire*, 164.
59. Quoted in Foreman, *World on Fire*, 806.
60. Robert W. Merry, *President McKinley: Architect of the American Century* (Simon & Schuster, 2017), 334–335.
61. Daniel Immerwahr, *How to Hide an Empire: A History of the Greater United States* (Picador, 2020), 88–107; Warren Zimmerman, *First Great Triumph: How Five Americans Made Their Country a World Power* (Farrar, Straus and Giroux, 2002), 404–417.
62. Richard T. Arndt, *The First Resort of Kings* (Potomac Books, 2005), 22, 50.

63. Immerwahr, *Hide an Empire*, 114.
64. Samuel J. Newland, "A Centennial History of the US Army War College," *Parameters* 31, no. 3 (Autumn 2001): 35; Zimmerman, *First Great Triumph*, 50, 88–101.
65. Zimmerman, *First Great Triumph*, 24–28.
66. Inderjeet Parmar, *Foundations of the American Century: The Ford, Carnegie, & Rockefeller Foundations in the Rise of American Power* (Columbia University Press, 2012), 41–58.
67. Parmar, *Foundations*, 42.
68. Quoted in Abba Eban, *Diplomacy for the Next Century* (Yale University Press, 1998), 92.
69. David Paull Nickles, *Under the Wire: How the Telegraph Changed Diplomacy* (Harvard University Press, 2003), 31–61.
70. Quoted in Johanna Neuman, *Lights, Camera, War: Is Media Technology Driving International Politics?* (St. Martin's Press, 1996), 107–108.
71. Quoted in Nickles, *Under the Wire*, 91.
72. Quoted in Nickles, *Under the Wire*, 35.
73. "The World in the Mid-19th Century," *A Short History of the Department of State*, Historical Documents, Department of State.
74. Nickles, *Under the Wire*, 79–102; Neuman, *Lights, Camera, War*, 25–40, 93.

4

Framing Practitioner Communities

Early in the twentieth century, the United States, and other countries in different ways, embarked on a journey that changed diplomacy. Centuries-old state-based institutions of *government-to-government* diplomacy gradually accepted *government-to-people* diplomacy. During World War I, another turning point, the United States established the first of many public diplomacy organizations. Thereafter, Americans resisted, misunderstood, and marginalized public diplomacy; turned to it enthusiastically in wartime; and eventually came to treat it as an essential and enduring instrument of foreign relations.

Until the 1950s the United States depended largely on journalists, writers, intellectuals, advertisers, and political activists willing to serve temporarily as public diplomacy practitioners. The threats and fears that drove Americans to create a National Security Council, Department of Defense, and Central Intelligence Agency in 1947, however, also led to continuation of organized foreign information and cultural activities. More practitioners stayed in government after World War II, and a new generation of public diplomats and broadcasters arrived to serve as career government employees.

The road to acceptance was bumpy. The emotional politics of anti-communism and McCarthyism undermined cooperation between

© The Author(s), under exclusive license to Springer Nature Switzerland AG 2024   **71**
B. Gregory, *American Diplomacy's Public Dimension*, Palgrave Macmillan Series in
Global Public Diplomacy, https://doi.org/10.1007/978-3-031-38917-7_4

Republicans and New Deal Democrats who had populated wartime information agencies. Commercial news media feared government competition. Career diplomats were concerned that information activities would change rules and norms of traditional diplomacy. Many Americans were wary of information and culture ministries and what they viewed to be government propaganda. Nevertheless, the United States made a commitment to "information," "cultural diplomacy," and "international broadcasting." Presidents Truman and Eisenhower, with bipartisan support from lawmakers, provided the necessary authorities and top-down leadership. But this did not mean agreement on how organizations should be structured, what they should do, or what they should be called. Policymakers and practitioners tangled over missions, methods, and norms. Reorganizations and advisory panels brimming with recommendations were a way of life.

US public diplomacy's government practitioners and their civil society partners constitute separate, but related, communities of practice— Foreign Service officers, cultural diplomats, international broadcasters, soldiers, covert operatives and front groups, democratizers, and presidential aides. Categorizing them as separate communities with distinct tribal cultures draws on Graham Allison's concept of organizational cultures. In Allison's account, practitioners in organizations generally agree on their basic mission, norms, and routines of behavior. Their identities are tied to how they perceive themselves, to "rules for matching actions to situations," and to distinctive beliefs they "have inherited and pass on to their successors."[1] Allison's logic contextualizes beliefs and practices of practitioner communities that are not confined to single organizations.

Each practitioner community developed its own modus operandi, meaning customs and continuities in its methods, discourse, and behavior. They constitute what practice theorists mean when they speak of "patterned ways of doing things."[2] Their repertoires of tools, methods, and ways of addressing problems became second nature. They created written and unwritten rules of conduct. Experiences and best practices became guides to professional excellence. As Iver B. Neumann explains, their guides to action distinguish practice from habit, and they have operational value because circumstances often require diplomats to improvise.[3] For scholars and practitioners, patterns of practice provide a basis for explanations of the past and, to a limited extent, expectations about the future.[4]

Public diplomacy's practitioners began as diplomacy's rebels. Forced to contend with lack of understanding in American society and the skepticism of most career diplomats, their communities devoted considerable energy to ensuring survival in addition to developing their modus operandi. Often led by change agents from within, they modified their tools and methods in response to unexpected events, environmental trends, and creative learning.[5] It helped considerably that their organizations were more agile and open to change than the Department of State. At the same time, like most professional communities, they often resisted change and reforms proposed by outsiders.

There are significant differences within and between these practitioner communities. Some practitioners are career professionals who devote full attention to public diplomacy. Others are political leaders and government officials with broad responsibilities who turn to public diplomacy intermittently. Some practitioners identify as public diplomacy actors. Others do not. Some are civil society organizations with contractual or informal connections to government organizations. Some connections are durable; others are temporary.

Public diplomacy's practitioner communities are rivals. They are turf conscious. They value independence. They compete for resources. Their practitioners rarely seek cross-community assignments. Broadcasters seldom invite Foreign Service officers to language service reviews, even though they concede the value of their expertise. Cultural diplomats acknowledge a role for policy advocacy, but often dismiss it as spin or propaganda. These tribal cultures are not hermetically sealed, however. The Secretary of State has a seat *ex officio* on US broadcasting's oversight board. Foreign Service officers carry out press and cultural activities in the field. Diplomats are assigned to military units; soldiers serve in embassies. Presidential staffs rely on career government employees on detail to the White House and the NSC.

Yet, there are family resemblances. All are "agents" of government. All seek to understand, engage, and influence the opinions and actions of citizens and their governments in other countries. Technologies shape their means and ends. Partnerships with non-governmental organizations amplify their knowledge and multiply their reach. Despite many operational differences, these practitioner communities are profoundly political and they serve public interests.

Big Ideas About Public Opinion

Early in the twentieth century the writings of two public intellectuals, Walter Lippmann (1889–1974) and John Dewey (1859–1952), revolutionized communication theory and media studies. In his book *Public Opinion* (1922), Lippmann distinguished between "the great blooming, buzzing confusion of the outer world" and "the pictures in our heads." Our "real environment is altogether too big, too complex, and too fleeting for direct acquaintance." An array of external factors (control of information at the source, socioeconomic norms, limited time, distorted words) and internal factors (fragile memories, finite minds, creative imagination, and stereotypes that simplify and impose conceptual order) mean we create cognitive maps, which he called "fictions." "We do not first see," Lippmann wrote, "We define first and then see." Because we can't know the truth about most issues of public significance firsthand, we choose between credible and untrustworthy authorities. "As congenital amateurs, our quest for truth consists in stirring up the experts."[6]

Like Lippmann, Dewey believed the telegraph, telephone, and radio had created a mediated world of events beyond immediate grasp. "We have inherited … local town-meeting practices and ideas. But we live and act and have our being in a continental national state."[7] Dewey praised Lippmann's contrast between a complex "world outside" and "pictures in our heads" as "a more successful statement of the genuine 'problem of knowledge' than professional epistemological philosophers have managed to give." It was also "perhaps the most effective indictment of democracy as currently conceived ever penned."[8]

But Lippmann and Dewey had profound differences that were foundational to the debates of generations of scholars, journalists, and public diplomacy practitioners. Because citizens could no longer render informed judgments on all or most issues in world affairs, Lippmann called for a top-down solution in which experts and political leaders would provide guidance and make democracy work. What society required, he argued, was practical truth provided by elites who could analyze the meaning of news and complex matters of public policy.[9]

Dewey's solution was a bottom-up model in which the problems of mediated complexity would be managed through dialogue. Lippmann's approach was too risky. Experts could be wrong. They might mislead or manipulate publics. What was needed, Dewey argued, was more democracy. In a confusing world, we come to know our minds by listening to others and explaining ourselves to them. Lippmann treated publics as "spectators." Dewey viewed publics as "participators." He had a deep belief in education and a conviction that what counts most is not information, but "face-to-face relationships by means of direct give and take." It is "dialogue," that "gives reality to public opinion."[10] Their century-old arguments continue to inform media, public opinion, and communication studies.

Lippmann's thinking fits with the modus operandi of public diplomacy practitioners who establish audience priorities, emphasize short-term advocacy programs targeted at elites, and prioritize communication with journalists and thought leaders who in turn communicate with readers and followers. Dewey's ideas contribute to the modus operandi of practitioners who emphasize dialogue and mutual understanding, manage exchange of persons programs, and engage in democracy promotion.

Public relations pioneer Edward Bernays channeled Lippmann's views in *Crystallizing Public Opinion* (1923), *Propaganda* (1928), and *Public Relations* (1945), books that framed public relations as a field of study and practice.[11] Their ideas caught on first with corporate executives and political campaign strategists. But soon the thinking of media, communication, and propaganda scholars began to influence the work of practitioners in government-to-people diplomacy. The term "propaganda" quickly became too burdensome. But "information" did nicely. As communications scholar Wilbur Schramm put it, "The abilities to command information, to gain access to the media, to sort out and interpret the available data, to command the cognitive skills necessary to work in such a specialized age are going to be sources of power comparable to the more traditional forms of economic, political, and military power."[12]

Actor-Centric Characteristics

Two dynamics—actor-centric and systemic—shape the modus operandi of practitioner communities in US diplomacy's public dimension. Actor-centric characteristics include: (1) instrumental communication, (2) perspectives on elite and mass publics, (3) short- and long-term time dimensions, (4) norms and methods imported from civil society, and (5) lagging adoption of technologies.

Instrumental communication. Jurgen Habermas's theory of "communicative action" distinguishes between instrumental communication intended to influence thoughts and actions and norms-based deliberative communication that is non-manipulative and seeks consensus.[13] Many postmodern scholars question the *possibility* of separating instrumental and deliberative communication.[14] Others question its *advisability*.[15] Although some practitioners give greater weight to persuasive communication and others to dialogue leading to mutual understanding, all public diplomacy at its core is instrumental in its intent to support a governing entity's interests, policies, and values.

Practitioner communities prioritize different communication tools and methods. Foreign Service officers emphasize face-to-face communication "in the field," media relations, and persuasive communication. As diplomat Christopher Ross explained, they "engage carefully targeted sectors of foreign publics in order to develop support for … the national interest articulated by their own government's strategic goals."[16] Government media entities gather and report news, and broadcast programs on thought, culture, and government policies. Cultural diplomats place a premium on dialogue, education, exchanges, reasoned argument, and projecting culture. They resist "engaging in 'propaganda' activities," diplomat Juliet Antunes Sablosky observed, and have "a general ambivalence about U.S. involvement in world affairs."[17]

Elite and mass publics. Differences between the public sphere and civil society are key to understanding the meaning of "publics" in public diplomacy. The public sphere exists as an ideational and communication domain between governance entities and society. As Manuel Castells observes, "The public sphere is an essential component of sociopolitical organization because it is the space where people come together as citizens and articulate their autonomous views to influence the political institutions of society." Quoting Habermas, "it is a network for communicating information and points of view." In contrast, "Civil society is the organized expression of these views." It includes the media, universities, cultural institutions, NGOs, and informal networks of citizens.[18] When public diplomacy practitioners speak of publics, however, they usually mean both the public sphere and people and groups in civil society.

Practitioners treat elite and mass publics differently. Policy advocates direct their attention to the media and leaders in civil society. They seek to influence journalists and opinion elites in the belief they in turn will inform and influence mass publics. Cultural diplomats give priority to elites, but with a difference. They engage scholars, students, artists, and professionals in a variety of fields, not to advance short-term policy agendas, but to break down barriers to cooperation and collaboration, and shape an environment that is receptive to policies and common goals. Broadcasters communicate to mass audiences segmented by language groups as well as to governing elites who monitor foreign broadcasts.

Time dimensions. Time priorities shape choices of tools and methods. Information practitioners typically respond to events and decisions of government officials. Short-term campaigns explain and advocate policies and actions and target selected publics over the course of months or a few years. Cultural diplomacy practitioners think in terms of years and decades. Results of exchanges and visitor programs are projected to occur over time as participants pursue their professions and maintain relationships. US diplomat Lois Roth observed, however, cultural diplomacy also includes programs in music, literature, and the arts that "transmit information about the cultural attainments of a nation" intended to influence perceptions in the moment.[19] For government media practitioners, time means daily news broadcasts, short-term news analysis and programs about American thought and institutions, and long-term relations with viewers and listeners over decades.[20]

Norms, methods, and firewalls. From the beginning US practitioners imported norms and methods from civil society. Similar to advertisers and political campaign strategists, they segment and target audiences—opinion leaders, decision-makers, and next-generation "comers." To persuade and build consent, publics must trust what they say and do. Credibility is undermined when words and actions do not match and when statements are inconsistent. Deception and undisclosed behavior are required methods in espionage and armed conflict, but not in public diplomacy. When the CIA's covert information and cultural programs were revealed in the 1960s, the United States put an institutional firewall between public diplomacy and covert information operations.

Cultural diplomats import educational and cultural norms, and create firewalls to protect the academic integrity, artistic merit, and "nonpolitical character" of exchanges and other programs. Distance from policy advocacy and "propaganda" shapes their identity, operating standards, and organizational preferences. They insist on peer review processes in decisions to award scholarships, professional exchanges, and grants to arts organizations. US lawmakers long ago ratified cultural diplomacy's operational norms. "The President shall insure that academic and cultural programs … shall maintain their scholarly integrity and shall meet the highest standards of academic achievement and artistic achievement."[21] International broadcasters imported norms and freedom of the press standards from American journalism. They created a firewall, enacted in legislation, to protect the credibility and journalistic integrity of their broadcasts.

Firewalls protect norms and methods in public diplomacy, not the ends. As distant as cultural diplomacy and international broadcasting may be from policy advocacy, they are instruments of power. "Cultural diplomacy," Cynthia Schneider maintains, "is a prime example of 'soft power,' or the ability to persuade through culture, values and ideas."[22] Cultural diplomats communicate values of freedom and democracy to influence next-generation leaders. Broadcasters influence as exemplars of press freedom and through discussions of US policies. Soft power is attractive power, not coercive. Nevertheless, it is still about power resources and tools intended to influence the thinking and behavior of others.

Oversight bodies, blue-ribbon advisory panels, and think tanks across the ideological spectrum have long offered advice on how to improve public diplomacy's operations and structures. Their reports number in the thousands.[23] Reorganization proposals figure prominently, and passionately contested structural changes often reflect divides in rival communities of practice. The enduring goal for broadcasters was independence from the United States Information Agency (USIA) and the State Department. Cultural diplomats pursued the holy grail of an organization comparable to the Smithsonian or the Endowments for the Arts and Humanities. Better days typically lay ahead in a reorganized promised land.

Lagging adoption of technologies. Although Americans invented many communication technologies, the United States often has been slow to use them in public diplomacy. Commercial and civil society organizations led in the adoption of the telegraph, shortwave radio broadcasting, film, satellite TV, digital technologies, and social media.[24] The first US government direct broadcast satellite service, the Alhurra Arabic-language television network, aired in 2004 more than two decades after CNN.[25] An exception was USIA's attractive public diplomacy website created in the 1990s soon after the invention of the World Wide Web.

Systemic Characteristics

Social and political forces in American society also shape the modus operandi of public diplomacy's practitioner communities. They include: (1) restrictions on domestic dissemination, (2) shallow institutional roots, (3) multidisciplinary scholarship, and (4) American exceptionalism.

Domestic dissemination. The United States has long maintained legal restrictions on dissemination of public diplomacy materials through amendments to the Smith-Mundt Act of 1948. Congress also routinely places riders in appropriations bills prohibiting the use of federal funds for publicity or propaganda purposes. These restrictions constitute a firewall meant to protect the American people from government propaganda. For more than a century, domestic dissemination issues have been a source of partisan debate, litigation, and operational challenges for practitioners.[26]

Concerns about domestic propaganda gave rise to conceptual and organizational boundaries between public diplomacy and public affairs. Former Under Secretary of State for Political Affairs Philip Habib put the issue in its classic form. "There is a distinct difference between public diplomacy and public affairs," he declared. "The word *diplomacy* means 'outside' and has nothing to do with what you are trying to do with the American people, which is altogether different."[27] The State Department's Public Affairs Bureau focused on the US press, and its spokespersons were rarely accused of propaganda. Public diplomacy describes the work of USIA and now a career track in the Foreign Service.

Advisory panels and practitioners have long sought to modify public diplomacy's geographically based restrictions. Satellite footprints and the internet's global reach blur the line between active dissemination and general availability. Moreover, presidential news conferences and media briefings by cabinet officials and military commanders simultaneously reach foreign and domestic audiences. Americans generally do not question these activities. Concerns about "domestic propaganda," practitioners argue, can be handled through media scrutiny and Congressional oversight. They also lament the impact on Americans' lack of understanding of the importance of public diplomacy.[28]

In 2012 Congress amended the Smith-Mundt Act to authorize making government broadcasting's content "available" to US audiences on request. It did not authorize US broadcasters to create program content for or broadcast to American audiences. In 2019 State merged its bureaus of public affairs and international information programs in a Bureau of Global Public Affairs.[29] Despite these moves, the deeply rooted issue of domestic propaganda is likely to endure.

Shallow roots. The presidency, the Army and Navy, the State Department, and overseas missions have been permanent US government entities shaped by laws and established routines since the nation was founded. Public diplomacy is different. Government organizations devoted to international exchanges, broadcasting, and embassy information and cultural programs were created in the twentieth century. Budgets and programs were in constant jeopardy. Frequent reorganizations were disruptive. Their lack of deep roots in American society made them vulnerable in ways that other foreign affairs institutions were not.

Leaders with vision and political access occasionally stood out. Nelson Rockefeller and Sumner Welles convinced Franklin Roosevelt and Congress to fund the first continuous exchange and information programs in Latin America. Acclaimed print and radio journalist Elmer Davis put his stamp on the Office of War Information. Poet Archibald MacLeish figured importantly in the origins of cultural diplomacy. The actor John Houseman looms large in VOA's history. Edward R. Murrow and Charles Z. Wick were influential USIA directors—the former remembered for his impact on the thinking of career practitioners and his relations with President Kennedy, the latter for a personal relationship with President Reagan that increased public diplomacy funding in the 1980s.[30]

Multidisciplinary scholarship. Early in the twentieth century, three categories of academic study began to have indirect and, in some cases, direct influence on US public diplomacy's tools and methods: public opinion research, communication studies, and the social sciences, primarily psychology and anthropology. In 1928 George Gallup graduated with a degree in the new field of Applied Psychology from the University of Iowa, "where everyone was talking about Walter Lippmann's 1922 book, *Public Opinion.*" Seven years later he established the American Institute of Public Opinion in Princeton. His method of analyzing population samples to measure opinions of mass publics soon drew the attention of journalists, politicians, and corporate executives.[31] Gallup and a cadre of opinion research experts, Hadley Cantril, Elmo Roper, Everett Carll Ladd, Arthur C. Nielson, Leo Crespi, and Daniel Yankelovich, who built careers in marketing and domestic politics, also helped to create and advise foreign opinion research staffs in the State Department and USIA. Crespi spent much of his career at the Agency, and Gallup and Nielson served on the US Advisory Commission on Information.[32]

Scholars who established communication studies as an academic field—propaganda studies, influence theories, and studies of mass media flows and effects—also contributed to public diplomacy practice. Influence theories held sway in the 1940s. "Who says what in which channel to whom and with what effect?" famously asked political scientist and propaganda expert Harold Lasswell. His one-way influence model was consistent with studies by Claude Shannon and Warren Weaver claiming that messages moved from a sender through a channel (airwaves, wires) to a passive receiver. Because channels created noise and distortions, frequent repetition of the same message to the same receiver was presumed to upgrade the chances for successful communication. Advertisers and political campaigns adopted the model. Critics soon challenged the influence model as too linear and asymmetric. Its "hypodermic needle" approach placed too much emphasis on the information sender. Receivers are not passive interpreters of messages, they argued; rather, they have a variety of meaning-making methods at their disposal. Theorists modified the influence model with feedback loops from receivers and pursued ways to make messages more effective.[33]

It is unlikely influence theorists had a direct hand in President Truman's "Campaign of Truth" speech in 1950. But he echoed their thinking when he sought to improve "the government's programs for telling the truth about the United States to the peoples of the world" [one-way messaging] and devise ways to break through Soviet jamming of VOA [channel interference] "to get our message across" to "millions of people who are uninformed or misinformed" [receivers].[34] Practitioners focused on delivering the right message. Information dissemination became a mantra in public diplomacy.

Beginning in the 1960s, a formidable group of scholars engaged in pioneering work on communication systems and their strengths and limitations as instruments of persuasion. They shaped communication studies and influenced diplomatic practice in the generation that preceded digital technologies. They divided into two overlapping camps: those who concentrated on technologies used to *transmit information* in the context of mediated political and economic power, and those who devoted their attention to *shared communication* in culture and society.

Many in the *transmit information* camp were advisors to government during the Cold War. Stanford University's Wilbur Schramm focused on channels, audiences, language, and the institutions of mass media. Columbia University sociology and journalism professor W. Phillips Davison wrote about audience analysis, prioritizing quality over quantity, and the political effects of mass media and international exchanges on US foreign policy. Sociologists Paul Lazarsfeld and Elihu Katz developed a theory of two step flows of information from mass media to opinion leaders and their followers. MIT's Ithiel de Sola Pool concentrated on communication technologies and their political and social effects. His Simulmatics Corporation pioneered in using computer algorithms to target voters and consumers. Robert M. Entman's cascading activation theory dealt with the effects of media power. W. Russell Neuman and Monroe E. Price bridged the analog and digital eras with influential studies of the communication effects of media technologies on mass audiences and state power.[35]

Scholars recognized the limitations of broadcasting and mass media technologies relative to personal dialogue. The media have power to focus attention, Schramm argued, but "The best evidence available indicates that face-to-face persuasion is more effective than persuasion on the audio-visual media." Davison observed, "In spite of the miracles of modern technology, the encounter where two or more individuals from different nations are present is still the most efficient way of arriving at a meaningful exchange of ideas."[36] Most public diplomats agree.

Scholars who turned to *shared communication* as a cohesive force in culture and community prominently included Canada's Harold Innis. A mentor to Marshall McLuhan, Innis influenced thinking on ways technologies benefited commerce and empire, as well as the expansion of human knowledge, discourse in the public sphere, and democratization.[37] Anthropologist Edward T. Hall explored cross-cultural patterns in communication without words, concepts of space and time in human relationships, and the impact of high- and low-context cultures.[38] Jurgen Habermas's path-breaking ideas on the public sphere and deliberative discourse and Antonio Gramsci's writings on the role of language in creating intersubjective reality in society also were influential.[39]

Scholars in other social science disciplines also influenced diplomacy practice. Social psychologists Herbert Kelman and Otto Klineberg studied conflict resolution and US-Soviet competition. Robert Jervis wrote on perceptions and misperceptions in sub-cultures in nation-states. Sociologist and cultural anthropologist Glen H. Fisher explored how social structures, perceptions, language, and patterns of thinking influence cross-cultural negotiations and diplomacy. Notably, Fisher and Hall taught training courses at the Department of State's Foreign Service Institute. Fisher, with credentials as a scholar and Foreign Service officer, wrote extensively about the value of theory to practice.[40]

For the most part these scholars influenced public diplomacy indirectly. A few Foreign Service officers had majored in communications in college and brought what they learned to their field operations. Civil Service practitioners engaged in opinion research were well read in relevant academic studies. But most public diplomacy practitioners did not ponder the thinking of Schramm, Davison, Katz, Hall, Fisher, and the others when developing programs and setting operational priorities.

Nevertheless, many of their ideas entered the bloodstream of public diplomacy. Practitioners, channeling Lippmann and Davison, understood that "Despite the popular image of the propagandist as a molder of opinion, communications by themselves are rather poor instruments for changing attitudes, especially in view of the powerful forces at work within each individual that protect the picture of the world he has already established."[41] Field officers assumed a two-step flow in the effect of mass media. Consistent with the views of Katz, Lazarsfeld, and other two-step flow theorists, however, practitioners knew that the views of people in communities influence opinion leaders more than media.[42] Public diplomacy practitioners became champions of interpersonal oral communication—a stance consistent with Ithiel de Sola Pool's argument that "The mass media alone, unlinked to word-of-mouth communication, fail in generating action but do not fail in creating information and desires … That is why a seemingly safe investment is made in the very slow-acting medium of education."[43]

In the 2000s scholars began to think of public diplomacy's potential as an emerging academic field. There was consensus that scholarship in a broad range of academic disciplines had much to contribute to research agendas. But then and now they faced questions on concepts, definitions, boundaries, research methods, and categories of practice.[44] From the outset, a key question turned on whether public diplomacy should be treated as an independent field of study. Two decades later this question remains. For some, the quest continues. There has been progress in developing the components of a field of public diplomacy study, they argue, although not in creating a central theory or analytical model.[45] Some scholars contend it may not be an independent field but rather "a subfield of international relations or public relations."[46] For others, public diplomacy has become mainstream in the practice of diplomacy.[47] This book argues it should not be treated as an independent academic field apart from diplomacy studies.

That diplomacy and public diplomacy now blend in diplomatic practice is widely acknowledged. Scholars who serve on advisory panels, provide contract services, and combine careers in government and academe can enhance knowledge, skills, and methods. Reform agendas emphasize professional education and developing a learning culture. Diplomats detailed to universities, corporations, and think tanks update previously acquired knowledge and enhance their ability to convene and connect experts who multiply their effectiveness in the field. Academic study increases knowledge about climate, disease, migration, cyber, and other complex issues in modern diplomacy. A survey published in 2021 shows that practitioners increasingly seek academic research and expertise, which they acknowledge can influence their views. However, they also perceive academic research as too abstract, untimely, and unclearly presented.[48] Scholars benefit too. What practitioners do is useful in theory building, teaching, and research.

American exceptionalism. The concept of "American exceptionalism" does not mean the United States is different from other countries or that Americans think of themselves as special. All countries are different, and their citizens take pride in their history and culture. The phrase itself is relatively recent.[49] But its meaning lies in the idea, going back to early colonial settlers, that Americans have a unique character and destiny. Its grip is strong. "Intellectually I know America is no better than any other country; emotionally I know she is better than every other country," novelist Sinclair Lewis declared in 1930, reflecting deeply held views of most Americans.[50]

American exceptionalism's narrative has two core elements. First, many Americans have an abiding faith that their nation is *uniquely* virtuous, a nation of great and incomparable character. The Puritans maintained they were chosen by God to fulfill a special role in the world. Jeffersonians believed Americans would triumph over old-world tyrannies and escape the forces of history. Generations later, Martin Luther King, Jr. wrote that freedom is "the sacred heritage of our nation and the eternal will of God." Republican Mitt Romney laid claim to "the absolute truth of American greatness." Its "beneficence and benevolence are unmatched by any nation on earth, and by any nation in history." Democrat Barack Obama stated, "What makes us exceptional—what makes us

America—is our allegiance to an idea articulated in a declaration made more than two centuries ago."[51]

A second element is a belief that America's ideals of democracy and freedom are *universally* relevant and the United States has an obligation to lead in world affairs. "If we have to use force," Secretary of State Madeleine Albright declared, "it is because we are America. We are the indispensable nation. We stand tall. We see further."[52] For President Joe Biden, "democracy is not just the foundation of American society, it is the well spring of our power." The United States must lead "not just with the example of our power, but also with the power of our example."[53] Scholars such as Michael Mandelbaum point to America's "responsibility for defending and sustaining … the global liberal order."[54] For Robert Kagan, American's strategy of global leadership is "a realism in the service of liberalism, of ideals and principles that they believed were universal and irrefutable."[55]

Critics of American exceptionalism fall into two camps. First, in the influential thinking of theologian and political activist Reinhold Niebuhr, America suffers from unjustifiable pride and illusions of innocence in a world where power creates great moral ambiguities. "[N]o society, not even a democratic one, is great enough or good enough to make itself the final end of human existence," he argued. Democracy is valuable as "a method of finding proximate solutions for insoluble problems," but Americans should not pretend to be "tutors to mankind." Niebuhr called for "a sense of modesty about the virtue, wisdom, and power available to us for the resolution of [history's] perplexities."[56]

A second critique is that a virtuous American exceptionalism is counter-factual. US expansion from 13 colonies across a continent and beyond was hegemonic and often cruel. As Stephen Walt argues, Americans eliminated and dispossessed much of the Native American population, fought numerous wars, and overall engaged in conduct that "has hardly been a model of restraint." The idea that the United States is uniquely virtuous is simply not true. Its self-regard as a democratic exemplar is undermined by its history of racism, its standing as the greatest debtor nation in human history, its disastrous wars in Vietnam and Iraq, its quagmire in and exit from Afghanistan, its support for unsavory dictatorships, its gridlocked politics, and growing perceptions of America's lack of regard for the interests of others.[57]

Although the United States falls short in important respects, the nation's ideals and soft power resources are a source of strength in its diplomacy. A challenge for practitioners engaging with foreign publics is to reckon with the complex narrative of American exceptionalism. As retired diplomat John Dickson argues persuasively, diplomats must understand their own and other country's histories, and be knowledgeable about how conflicting versions of history create differences and misunderstandings.[58]

Actor-centric and systemic dynamics provide context for the operational choices of US public diplomacy practitioner communities that emerged in the twentieth century. Chapters in Part II of the book examine how they developed their modus operandi in what can be called "traditional public diplomacy." What were their tools and methods? How did they think about and justify patterns of practice in the context of formal mandates? How did innovators respond to new circumstances through adaptation of tested methods rather than reflexive application of mission statements and communication theories? These chapters find fertile ground in a growing database of US practitioners' oral histories and greater online accessibility to historical records. They supplement top-down Washington-centric perspectives characteristic of much twentieth-century diplomacy literature. This blend of diplomatic and multidisciplinary theoretical perspectives benefits from and contributes to ideas in "practice theory."[59]

In the twenty-first century, many analysts embraced the ascendance of digital technologies, sub-state and non-state actors, whole of government diplomacy, relational methods, and societization of diplomacy with the term "new public diplomacy."[60] However, the term "public diplomacy" problematically conveys that it is bolted on to diplomacy rather than what is now central in diplomatic practice overall and better described as diplomacy's public dimension. Part III of the book will address these conceptual issues and changes in practice.

Notes

1. Graham Allison and Philip Zelikow, *Essence of Decision: Explaining the Cuban Missile Crisis*, 2nd ed. (Longman, 1999), 145–158.
2. Emanuel Adler and Vincent Pouliot, "Fulfilling the Promises of Practice Theory in IR," *International Studies Quarterly Online Symposium* (July 23, 2017): 2–4.
3. Iver B. Neumann, *At Home with the Diplomats: Inside a European Foreign Ministry* (Cornell University Press, 2012), 8–59, 62.
4. This approach draws on John Gaddis's ideas about historical explanations and what Alexander L. George and Andrew Bennett call "atheoretical process tracing." The process tracing of political scientists seeks to test theories, analyze causal explanations, and "forecast the future." Gaddis contends patterns are useful as explanations of past contingencies, but because historians generalize "only from the knowledge of particular outcomes, they make few if any claims about the future." Nevertheless, when patterns "show up frequently in the past, we can reasonably expect them to continue in the future. Trends that have held up over several hundred years are not likely to reverse themselves within the next several weeks." John Lewis Gaddis, *The Landscape of History: How Historians Map the Past* (Oxford University Press, 2002), 30–31, 62–66; Alexander L. George and Andrew Bennett, *Case Studies and Theory Development in the Social Sciences* (MIT Press, 2005), 210–216.
5. On issues relating to contingency, change, and tensions between routine regularities and transformation in practice, see Christian Bueger and Frank Gadinger, "The Play of International Practice," *International Studies Quarterly* 59, no. 3 (September 2015): 454–456. On social change and changes in diplomatic practice, see Neumann, *At Home*, 172–176.
6. Walter Lippmann, *Public Opinion* (Free Press Paperbacks, 1997), 3, 54–55; Ronald Steel, *Walter Lippmann and the American Century* (Transaction Publishers, 1999), 141–154, 171–185; Sue Curry Jansen, *Walter Lippmann: A Critical Introduction to Media and Communication Theory* (Peter Lang, 2012), 101–126.
7. John Dewey, *The Public and Its Problems* (Swallow Press, 1954), 113. Today, we can imagine he might say, "we have inherited nation-state practices and ideas, but we live and act in a globalizing world."

8. John Dewey, "Review of 'Public Opinion' by Walter Lippmann," *The New Republic* 30, no. 387 (May 3, 1922): 286–288.

9. Lippmann, *Public Opinion*, 201–230.

10. Dewey, *Public and Its Problems*, 217–219. On differences between Lippmann and Dewey, see James W. Carey, *Communication as Culture: Essays on Media and Society* (Routledge, 1992), 69–88 and Gregory, "Sunrise of an Academic Field," 274–290.

11. For an overview of how public relations concepts and practices have paralleled and interacted with public diplomacy, see Kathy Fitzpatrick, "Public Relations," in *A Research Agenda for Public Diplomacy*, ed. Eytan Gilboa (Edward Elgar, 2023), 139–154.

12. Wilbur Schramm, "The Effects of Mass Media in an Information Era," in *Propaganda and Communication in World History: A Pluralizing World in Formation*, eds. Harold D. Lasswell, Daniel Lerner, and Hans Speier (University Press of Hawaii, 1980), 3: 297–298. On Bernays' ideas and influence, see Stuart Ewen, "Introduction," in Edward Bernays, *Crystallizing Public Opinion* (Ig Publishing, 2011), 9–41.

13. Jurgen Habermas, *Between Facts and Norms: Contributions to a Discourse Theory of Law and Democracy*, trans. William Rehg (MIT Press, 1996); Danielle S. Allen, *Talking to Strangers* (University of Chicago Press, 2004), 53–68.

14. Edward Said questioned a "liberal consensus that 'true' knowledge is fundamentally non-political" in writings that focused on obscure relationships between culture and power in civil society and the "distribution of geopolitical awareness" in aesthetic and scholarly texts. Edward W. Said, *Orientalism* (Vintage Books, 1979), 9–11; Edward W. Said, "Orientalism and After," in *Power, Politics, and Culture: Interviews with Edward Said*, ed. Gauri Viswanathan (Vintage Books, 2001), 208–232. Michel Foucault argued power relations are embedded in all discourse and human interaction "in the whole network of the social." James D. Faubion, ed., *Power: Essential Works of Foucault, 1954–1984* (New Press, 2000), 3: 342–345.

15. Michael Walzer accepts the value of deliberation in political life, but contends politics has other values that are different and important, such as mobilization, organization, governance, and management of conflict. Michael Walzer, *Politics and Passion: Toward a More Egalitarian Liberalism* (Yale University Press, 2004), 90–109; Michael Walzer, "Deliberation

and What Else?" in *Thinking Politically: Essays in Political Theory*, ed. David Miller (Yale University Press, 2007), 134–146.

16. Christopher Ross, "Public Diplomacy Comes of Age," *The Washington Quarterly* 25, no. 2 (Spring 2002): 75.

17. Juliet Antunes Sablosky, "Reinvention, Reorganization, Retreat: American Cultural Diplomacy at Century's End, 1978–1998," *The Journal of Arts Management, Law, and Society* 29 (March 31, 2010): 30–31.

18. Manuel Castells, "The New Public Sphere: Global Civil Society, Communication Networks, and Global Governance," *The Annals of the American Academy of Political and Social Science* 616, no. 1 (March 2008): 78; Manuel Castells, *Communication Power* (Oxford University Press, 2009), 10–16; Jurgen Habermas, *The Structural Transformation of the Public Sphere*, trans. Thomas Burger (Polity, 1989).

19. Lois W. Roth, "Public Diplomacy: 1952–1977," *The Fletcher Forum* 8 (Summer 1984): 358.

20. Joseph S. Nye, Jr., *The Future of Power* (PublicAffairs, 2011), 105–107.

21. Bureau of Educational and Cultural Affairs, US Department of State, 22 U.S. Code §2460.

22. Cynthia Schneider, "Cultural Diplomacy: The Humanizing Factor," in *International Cultural Policies and Power*, ed. J. P. Singh (Palgrave Macmillan, 2010), 101–102.

23. For partial lists of these reports, see Christopher Paul, *Whither Strategic Communication? An Inventory of Current Proposals and Recommendations* (RAND, 2009) and *Public Diplomacy: A Review of Past Recommendations* (Congressional Research Service, 2005).

24. Amelia Arsenault, "Public Diplomacy 2.0," in *Toward a New Public Diplomacy: Redirecting US Foreign Policy*, ed. Philip Seib (Palgrave Macmillan, 2009), 135–153.

25. Shawn Powers and Ahmed El Gody, "The Lessons of Al Hurra Television," in Seib, *Toward a New Public Diplomacy*, 49–66.

26. Emily T. Metzger, *Seventy Years of the Smith-Mundt Act and U.S. International Broadcasting: Back to the Future?* (Figueroa Press, April 2018).

27. Philip Habib, "Concluding Remarks," in *Public Diplomacy: USA Versus USSR*, ed. Richard F. Starr (Hoover Institution Press, 1986), 283.

28. Matthew C. Weed, *U.S. Public Diplomacy: Legislative Proposals to Amend Prohibitions on Disseminating Materials to Domestic Audiences* (Congressional Research Service, 2021).

29. "Dissemination Abroad of Information About the United States," 22 USC Chapter 18, Subchapter V; "The Creation of the Bureau of Global Public Affairs," US Department of State website.
30. For an even-handed discussion of Murrow, a USIA director lionized by many public diplomacy professionals, see Nicholas J. Cull, "'The Man Who Invented Truth': The Tenure of Edward R. Murrow as Director of the United States Information Agency During the Kennedy Years," *Cold War History* 4, no. 1 (2003): 23–48.
31. Jill Lepore, *These Truths: A History of the United States* (W.W. Norton, 2018), 454–455.
32. On the role of opinion surveys in foreign affairs, see Ronald H. Hinckley, *People, Polls, and Policymakers: American Public Opinion and National Security* (Lexington Books, 1992), 3–7.
33. Wilbur Schramm, "Channels and Audiences," in *Handbook of Communication*, eds. Ithiel de Sola Pool, et al. (Rand McNally, 1973), 116–140; Steven R. Corman, Angela Trethewey, and H. L. Goodall, eds., *Weapons of Mass Persuasion: Strategic Communication to Combat Violent Extremism* (Peter Lang, 2008), 30–31, 152–159.
34. Harry S. Truman, "Address on Foreign Policy at a Luncheon of the American Society of Newspaper Editors" (April 20, 1950), Harry S. Truman Library.
35. Wilbur Schramm and Donald F. Roberts, eds., *The Process and Effects of Communication* (University of Illinois Press, 1954); Wilbur Lang Schramm, *Men, Messages, and Media: A Look at Human Communication* (Harper & Row, 1973); W. Phillips Davison, *International Political Communication* (Frederic A. Praeger, 1965); Elihu Katz and Paul Lazarsfeld, *Personal Influence: The Part Played by People in the Flow of Mass Communications* (Free Press, 1955); Ithiel de Sola Pool, *Technologies Without Borders: On Telecommunications in a Global Age* (Harvard University Press, 1990); W. Russell Neuman, *The Future of the Mass Audience* (Cambridge University Press, 1991); Robert M. Entman, *Projections of Power: Framing News, Public Opinion and U.S. Foreign Policy* (University of Chicago Press, 2004); Monroe E. Price, *Media and Sovereignty: The Global Information Revolution and Its Challenge to State Power* (MIT Press, 2002).
36. Schramm, "Channels and Audiences," 124; W. Phillips Davison, "International and World Public Opinion," in Pool et al., *Handbook of Communication*, 878.

37. Paul Heyer, *Harold Innis* (Rowman & Littlefield, 2002); Carey, *Communication as Culture*; Marshall McLuhan, *The Guttenberg Galaxy* (University of Toronto Press, 1962).

38. Hall, *Silent Language*; Edward T. Hall, *The Hidden Dimension* (Doubleday, 1966); Edward T. Hall, *The Dance of Life: The Other Dimension of Time* (Doubleday, 1983).

39. Habermas, *Structural Transformation*; David Forgacs, ed., *The Antonio Gramsci Reader* (New York University Press, 2002).

40. Herbert C. Kelman, *International Behavior: A Social-Psychological Analysis* (Holt, Rinehart, and Winston, 1965); Otto Klineberg, *The Human Dimension in International Relations* (Holt, Rinehart, and Winston, 1964); Robert Jervis, *Perception and Misperception in International Politics* (Princeton University Press, 1976); Glen H. Fisher, *Mindsets: The Role of Culture and Perception in International Relations*, 2nd ed. (Intercultural Press, 1997); Fisher, *Public Diplomacy*.

41. Davison, *International Political Communication*, 40–41.

42. Katz and Lazarsfeld, *Personal Influence*, 3–4.

43. Ithiel de Sola Pool, *Politics in Wired Nations* (Transaction Publishers, 1998), 210–211.

44. Kristin M. Lord, "What Academics (Should Have to) Say About Public Diplomacy" (paper presented at Political Communication Conference of the American Political Science Association, Washington, DC, August 31, 2005), author's copy; Jan Melissen, ed., *The New Public Diplomacy: Soft Power in International Relations* (Palgrave Macmillan, 2005); Eytan Gilboa, "Searching for a Theory of Public Diplomacy," *The Annals of the American Academy of Political and Social Science* 616, no. 1 (March 2008): 55–77; Gregory, "Sunrise of an Academic Field."

45. For recent scholarship on a multidisciplinary approach to public diplomacy as an independent field of study, see Gilboa, *Research Agenda*.

46. Gilboa, *Research Agenda*, 1.

47. James Pamment, "The Mediatization of Diplomacy," *The Hague Journal of Diplomacy* 9, no. 3 (2014): 253–280; Geoffrey Wiseman, "Public Diplomacy and Hostile Nations," *The Hague Journal of Diplomacy* 14, no. 1–2 (2019): 134–153; Gregory, "Mapping Boundaries."

48. Paul C. Avey, et al., "Does Social Science Inform Foreign Policy? Evidence from a Survey of US National Security, Trade, and Development Officials," *International Studies Quarterly* 66, no. 1 (2021): 1–19.

49. Some observers attribute its origins to Joseph Stalin, who deplored "the heresy of American exceptionalism" when he expelled the American

communist Jay Lovestone from the Communist International. James W. Cesar, "The Origins and Character of American Exceptionalism," in *American Exceptionalism*, ed., Charles W. Dunn (Rowman & Littlefield, 2013), 15; David A. Bell, "American Exceptionalism," in *Myth America: Historians Take on the Biggest Legends and Lies About Our Past*, eds. Kevin M. Kruse and Julian E. Zelizer (Basic Books, 2022), 13–24.

50. Quoted in Jon Meacham, *The Soul of America: The Battle for Our Better Angels* (Random House, 2018), 10.

51. Niebuhr, *Irony of American History*, 25; Anne-Marie Slaughter, *The Idea That Is America* (Basic Books, 2007), 232; Martin Luther King, Jr., "Letter from a Birmingham Jail" (April 16, 1963), University of Pennsylvania website; Mitt Romney, *No Apology: The Case for American Greatness* (St. Martin's Press, 2010), 47, 309; Barack Obama, "Inaugural Address by President Barack Obama,", January 21, 2013, White House website.

52. Quoted in Bob Herbert, "In America; War Games," *New York Times*, February 22, 1998.

53. Joseph R. Biden, Jr., "Why America Must Lead Again: Rescuing U.S. Foreign Policy After Trump," *Foreign Affairs* 99, no. 2 (March/April, 2020), 65.

54. Mandelbaum, *Ideas That Conquered the World*, 7.

55. Robert Kagan, *The Jungle Grows Back: America and Our Imperiled World* (Alfred A. Knopf, 2018), 31–37.

56. Reinhold Niebuhr, *The Children of Light and the Children of Darkness* (Charles Scribner's Sons, 1944), 118, 133; Niebuhr, *Irony of American History*, xiii, 71, 174.

57. Stephen M. Walt, "The Myth of American Exceptionalism," *Foreign Policy*, October 11, 2011; David Rieff, "Evangelists of Democracy," *The National Interest*, October 24, 2012.

58. John Dickson, *History Shock: When History Collides with Foreign Relations* (University Press of Kansas, 2021).

59. On practice theory, see Costas M. Constantinou, Pauline Kerr, and Paul Sharp, eds., *The Sage Handbook of Diplomacy* (Sage Publications, 2016), 1–10.

60. On "old" and "new" public diplomacy, see James Pamment, *New Public Diplomacy in the 21st Century: A Comparative Study of Policy and Practice* (Routledge, 2013); Melissen, *New Public Diplomacy*.

Part II

Twentieth-Century Practitioners

5

Borrowing from Civil Society, 1917–1947

Diplomacy's modern institutions made their early appearance with resident ambassadors and chanceries in the Italian city state system of the fifteenth century. In the seventeenth century, diplomacy took on characteristics of a profession with entry requirements and codes of conduct. Louis XIII and Cardinal Richelieu created the first foreign ministry in 1626 to maintain continuous relations with resident ambassadors. Books on diplomatic practice reflected these developments, notably *De la manière de négocier avec les souverains* published by François de Callières, a diplomat for Louis XIV. Other foreign ministries arrived in the eighteenth century, the British Foreign Office in 1782 and the US Department of State in 1789. In the nineteenth century, historians Keith Hamilton and Richard Langhorne write, diplomacy was institutionalized in centralized ministries, embassies, and "foreign services with regular career patterns and rules governing such matters as recruitment, education, promotion, retirement, pay and pensions."[1]

Chilean scholar/diplomat Jorge Heine calls this diplomacy's "club model." Diplomats restricted their contacts to club members who understood the rituals, vocabulary, and negotiating styles developed during several centuries of diplomatic practice in the Westphalian state system. They met "with government officials, among themselves, and with the

© The Author(s), under exclusive license to Springer Nature Switzerland AG 2024
B. Gregory, *American Diplomacy's Public Dimension*, Palgrave Macmillan Series in Global Public Diplomacy, https://doi.org/10.1007/978-3-031-38917-7_5

odd businessman or woman, and … [gave] an interview or speech here or there."[2] The 1928 Havana Convention on the duties of diplomatic officers codified long-standing rules of club diplomacy. Articles 12 and 13 ruled out public diplomacy. Diplomats were not to participate in the "domestic or foreign politics of states," and they were obliged to confine "their official communications" to ministers of foreign relations and other government authorities.[3] Communication with citizens was prohibited interference in a state's internal affairs.

Government-to-people diplomacy was resisted by club diplomats, and it was not understood or welcomed by most Americans. In the twentieth century, they reluctantly came to accommodate organized public diplomacy in wartime, but it was viewed largely as work for specialists not career diplomats. They remained wary of propaganda organizations in peacetime. Most Americans do not reject the need for consular services and diplomacy with other governments, and they want to project their values. But this can be done by example and the international activities of citizens and civil society organizations. In World Wars I and II, journalists, scholars, writers, filmmakers, advertisers, and public relations experts were "borrowed" from civil society. They had no rulebooks or traditions. They relied on their professional skills and experiences to solve problems and match means to ends. There was much they agreed on. But they had fundamental differences, and they came to value separation between "information," "culture," and "broadcasting."

After World War II perceptions of foreign threats and armed conflict drove the United States to accept public diplomacy as a legitimate category of diplomacy carried out by government organizations and separate communities of practice.[4] It was far from easy. Commercial media interests feared competition. Powerful lawmakers routinely cut budgets, leading historian Justin Hart to wonder why public diplomacy "repeatedly provoked a level of vituperation so disproportionate to the actual amount of time and money spent on the effort."[5] The emergence of institutionalized US public diplomacy is a story of ad hoc initiatives, organizational stovepipes, and rival practitioner communities competing over scarce resources and important questions.

Committee on Public Information, 1917–1919

George Creel, a muckraking Progressive-era journalist from Missouri and a close ally of President Woodrow Wilson; Arthur Bullard, a highly regarded foreign correspondent and author of *Mobilizing America* (1917); and noted suffragette Vira Whitehouse, together with many other talented civil society experts, were leading practitioners in the US government's first civilian public diplomacy organization. Wilson and Creel established the Committee on Public Information (CPI) on April 14, 1917.[6] Bullard and Whitehouse joined the CPI's Foreign Section. Captains Walter Lippmann and Heber Blankenhorn, both journalists, were pioneers in the Propaganda Subsection of the US Army's Military Intelligence Bureau (MIB).

The CPI's initial task was to mobilize public support for the war at home. Its mandate included censorship of sensitive information within a broader effort that Creel described passionately as "a great publicity bureau … to bring home the truths of this great war to every man, woman, and child in the United States, so they might understand that it was a just war, a holy war, and a war of self-defense."[7] Overseas, as he later put it, CPI was engaged in a fight "for the hearts and minds of people."[8] Philosopher John Dewey, however, called it the "conscription of thought."[9] Strongly supported by Wilson, Creel assumed full authority for the CPI. With little planning and much chaos, he mobilized the enthusiastic participation of patriotic Americans.[10]

CPI's Foreign Section. CPI's foreign operations began in October 1917 with the assignment to Russia of Edgar Sisson, managing editor of *Colliers* magazine; film campaigns in Italy and Spain led by Frank J. Marion, cofounder of the Kalem Company movie studio; and an overseas news service in New York directed by *Chicago Daily News* journalist Walter Rogers. Soon CPI was operating in each of the world's geographic regions. Its last field offices closed in June 1919.[11]

The Foreign Section was divided into three units. (1) A news service, known as the Wireless-Cable Service, circulated daily reports "beneficial to this country and the Allies" through US Navy and commercial channels. (2) A Foreign Press Bureau led by journalist, novelist, and playwright Ernest Poole distributed photographs, posters, leaflets, and other printed materials. Content ranged from government reports and speeches to feature articles about US war efforts and American society by William Allen White, Booth Tarkington, and other well-known writers. (3) A Foreign Film Division distributed movies obtained from commercial film distributors through export licensing controls. CPI placed its materials in allied, enemy, and neutral countries. Its goals: counter German propaganda and encourage separatist movements in Germany and Austria-Hungary; persuade neutral countries to support the allies or remain neutral; and build public support in allied countries for Wilson's war aims, postwar reconstruction policies, and vision for a League of Nations.

Bullard served as Creel's deputy before working with CPI's operations in Russia. Edward Bernays, a pioneer in the US public relations industry, managed operations in Latin America. University of Chicago political scientist Charles E. Merriam directed CPI's operations in Italy. Vira Whitehouse directed the CPI's office in Switzerland. Renowned graphic artist Charles Dana Gibson assembled a team to produce posters and other visual products. Movie executive Jules Brulatour directed CPI's film export activities. Many, such as Bullard and *McClure's* muckraking journalist Will Irwin, were highly skilled; others were hopelessly out of their depth. Wilson's crony James Kearny, editor of the *Trenton Times*, was sent to Paris with little ability and no French.[12]

CPI's field representatives included "commissioners," a few diplomatic and consular officers, and other Americans "acting as CPI agents." State Department diplomats expressed little enthusiasm for the activities of CPI's "commissioners" and often worked against them.[13] CPI's practitioners were convinced what they were doing could not be done by the Department. In August 1917 Walter Rogers wrote to Creel:

> Personally I do not believe this task can be handled by the State Department; the Department is not suitably manned or organized. A year ago last June 1 went to Mr. [Secretary Robert] Lansing and told him of the South American service inaugurated by the United Press—I knew all about it as, in a sense, it was my scheme—and suggested that the Department take advantage of this new service to explain systematically our attitude and

actions. The Secretary told me in so many words that it was not one of the functions of the Department to see that the American case was presented to the peoples of other countries.[14]

There were exceptions. Hugh Gibson, first secretary at the US Embassy in Paris and later US Minister in Poland and Ambassador to Belgium, was loaned to CPI to direct its operations in France. Ambassador John W. Garrett directed CPI's operations in the Netherlands; Ambassador E. V. Morgan did the same in Brazil. Paul Reinsch, the US Minister in China, translated CPI materials and assisted CPI Shanghai in screening and distributing films.

Despite his skepticism, Secretary Lansing made clear in his communications to US missions that Creel "has been personally charged by the President with direction of this undertaking."[15] Creel took care to tell Wilson, "I am not trying to be 'ambassadorial.'" He had advised Edgar Sisson in Russia "not to touch the political situation" and to "maintain the most friendly relations" with the Ambassador.[16] CPI's commissioners were instructed not to consider themselves embassy attachés. Merriam observed, "There is no disguising the fact that the diplomats of career look askance at the … [CPI] everywhere. I have done and will continue to do all in my power to cooperate with them cordially, but without surrendering the essential purposes for which I was sent."[17] He described a distance between public diplomacy practitioners and traditional diplomats that lasted for decades.

Tools and methods. Putting the word "information" in CPI's name was a deliberate choice. Creel and his colleagues occasionally described their work as propaganda, but they often denied it was what they did—reserving the term for Germany's "lies" and "obnoxious propaganda."[18] The Army's MIB used locutions such as a "campaign of foreign education (or US propaganda)" and routinely referred to CPI as "the Propaganda Section."[19] Europeans, who created an Inter-Allied Propaganda Board in Paris, used the term freely. US officials preferred "information," "publicity work," and "foreign educational campaigns." Information entered the vocabulary as a descriptor for US public diplomacy organizations and a framing term for activities relating to messaging, policy advocacy, and media relations.

Creel addressed the ideal qualifications and methods of CPI's representatives in allied and neutral countries. High on the list: expertise, language skills, and cultural awareness.

> The chairman of the central bureau in Paris should be a man of broad European experience, and the branch bureaus in London, Madrid and Rome and the Scandinavian countries should be directed by men who knew the country to which they were assigned sympathetically and spoke the language fluently, including an eminent scholar, a practical man of affairs, an economist, a journalist and others who would reach different institutions and classes of Society. Upon the choice of these men and the character of the chairman would depend the results of the work which would be carried on in a dignified, modest and thorough manner in keeping with the character of the New America as opposed to the America with which Europeans associate boasting, flamboyancy and commercialism.[20]

CPI's Foreign Section urged field representatives to "gather information for our use; about what the people are saying about us with a view toward ascertaining what our needs are in the way of propaganda." They were to report on public opinion in their countries and advise on ways to communicate to different audiences. A language qualified local contact, "someone who really understands the people," was essential, because "methods that go great with us, frequently fall down absolutely with them."[21] The CPI collaborated with the MIB on "Psychological Estimates" of public opinion, because, as the MIB's Colonel R. H. Van Deman put it to Creel, any "campaign … in order to be intelligently prosecuted relies of course, on accurate information." CPI will "want to keep up with the latest changes of popular feeling … as hidden behind what the newspapers give" and know "what methods of distribution work best" and "what methods have been tried and discarded."[22]

Most of CPI's resources went to messaging, policy advocacy, and dissemination of print and visual media materials. CPI existed to "help in the dissemination of news" and provide a "just presentation of the American point of view." It stressed it did not wish to compete with established news agencies and that it "exercises the greatest care in no way to misinterpret American policy."[23] Foreign publics should be allowed to draw their own conclusions. As Sisson put it, "facts should be built up so the reader gets his own opinion, not sign posted with the opinion desired to be conveyed." He emphasized information about actions. "The statement that one new ship was added to tonnage today will get wider publicity than the plan for a thousand in six months."[24]

Despite ample evidence of one-way messaging in CPI's methods, its field representatives understood the importance of personal contact, exchanges of people and ideas, validation by others, collaboration with non-state actors, and the value of deeds over words. "I am of the opinion that printed propaganda has worn itself out a little in all countries, and that word of mouth stuff is infinitely more valuable," Will Irwin observed. "I also know that the French are great on conferences and that public lecturers are excellent propagandists."[25] A report from Spain stated that "influence might be exerted among the intellectuals by professors of our universities, if they were sent to visit Spain," adding "such visitors would need to be of our finest, educated, urbane, masters of Spanish language and customs, and able to address critical audiences upon congenial topics."[26]

Anticipating the international visitor program decades later, Irwin encouraged CPI's representatives to send "star French journalists and literary men to come to America and write us up." He agreed to "have them taken in hand, given a good time and shown everything."[27] CPI's Robert Murray in Mexico sent foreign journalists to the United States to see America's war effort first hand. Visits by journalists from other countries in South America and Europe followed. Political leaders, civic organizations, and ethnic communities gave them warm welcomes and access to US factories and shipyards. Journalists were treated with "absolute frankness," Creel wrote after the war. They saw America "with their own eyes." They reported in ways that appealed to their readers, and "every column carried weight because it came from the pen of a writer in whom the readers had confidence." He described the visits as one of CPI's "most effective ideas."[28]

The CPI also initiated productive relations with non-state actors. The YMCA provided mailing lists and distributed its materials throughout Europe, Asia, and Latin America. The CPI worked closely with groups of Czechs, Italians, Austrians, Hungarians, Poles, and other "subject peoples." It sponsored their speakers, circulated their resolutions and speeches, and arranged visits with US political leaders, including in some cases President Wilson. It sponsored a European tour by American Federation of Labor President Samuel Gompers. Through cooperation with the American Chamber of Commerce, window displays were posted in the overseas offices of hundreds of US businesses. Inserts in multiple languages were given to American firms for placement in commercial catalogs shipped abroad. Collaboration with private citizens had occurred before in US public diplomacy, but the CPI was the first US government organization to engage in such practices. Its scope was global and the scale of its activities dramatically greater.

CPI was on common ground with America's allies when it communicated with people in enemy countries. Few opposed drops of leaflets in enemy territory and attempts to undermine the morale of German soldiers. But messages directed at allied countries raised concerns particularly when Washington's policies toward colonies and nationality groups did not align with the postwar policy goals of London and Paris. CPI's practitioners soon encountered one of public diplomacy's enduring challenges. Engagement with people out of power can be a source of conflict with their governments, but it can be beneficial if they eventually gain power. CPI also faced questions on how best to build support in neutral countries. Should it just provide news and factual information? Or should it seek tacit backing for the war effort? Should CPI's hand be seen or would it be more effective if hidden, when, for example, its field officers considered co-opting pro-German editors through bribes or offers of scarce newsprint?[29]

Vira Whitehouse stood out among the Foreign Section's representatives for her formidable skills. She was chair of the New York State Woman Suffrage Party, an effective fundraiser, and an early user of telephone polling. In 1918 Creel asked her to direct CPI's office in Switzerland, a move strongly resisted by the State Department, US diplomats in the Bern legation, and resident American journalists. Some objected to a role for women in diplomatic service, others to the appearance of propaganda. A State telegram, received in Paris when she was en route to Bern, stated, "It is not now and never has been the policy of the United States to conduct persuasive activities in any country."[30]

A promised diplomatic passport was not provided. Creel had attempted to calm the uproar by describing her purpose as studying "children's and women's issues." She was having none of it. She returned to Washington and soon went back to Bern with a diplomatic passport and two letters from President Wilson, one endorsing her work for CPI and the other making his "entire approval" clear to US Minister Pleasant Stovall.[31]

Whitehouse proved highly effective. Success, she believed, depended on being open and honest about American ideals and war aims. Lack of guidance from Washington was a plus; she wanted to be as "unhampered as possible." She persuaded the official Swiss news agency and other news organizations to carry CPI content translated into French and German. She traveled the country to meet with Swiss editors. She facilitated place-ment of CPI's motion pictures without violating Swiss neutrality. Even Allen Dulles, then a young US diplomat outspoken in opposition to her appointment, wrote to his uncle, Secretary Lansing, that "Mrs. Whitehouse—I am frank to admit—is doing good work … The influ-ence of America in Switzerland is tremendous now." Creel described her as "by far *the best* of our foreign representatives."[32] "I should like to cry from the housetops," Whitehouse wrote, "of the necessity and economy of a liberal policy of education publicity (which we must no longer call propaganda) in both allied and neutral countries."[33] After the war, she was eager to go home. "There was nothing difficult about the work of our office now. It could go on mechanically," she later recalled. "The demand for American news had become insistent. Commercial agencies could enter the field and supply it as a business proposition."[34]

When the war ended, some of CPI's leaders argued the Foreign Section should continue as a permanent part of America's diplomacy. Diplomats in US consulates throughout Russia, where a civil war was underway, reported that CPI's publications were enjoying "great popularity with [the] Russian public and press."[35] As Ernest Poole, who like many of his colleagues intended to return to a career in journalism, put it in a letter to Creel:

[I]t seems to me that a bureau along these lines should either be attached to the State Department or at least cooperate closely with it both here and in foreign countries … the need of such work being permanent appears to me plain and urgent. If we are entering an era of more and more open diplomacy, in order to make the policies of this government most effective abroad we must use the legitimate methods of publicity to reach widely the great masses of people in other countries with the significant facts about the life and purposes of this nation. To present such facts widely we need men especially trained in reaching the large public by presentation in popular form.[36]

His arguments persuaded few, including Creel, who was convinced the CPI "was a *war organization* only."[37] Congress terminated the CPI on June 30, 1919.

The Foreign Section's mixed legacy. The CPI's Foreign Section showed what institutionalized public diplomacy could do on a global scale. Its effectiveness hinged on presidential interest, the galvanizing effects of war, the creative energies of American citizens, and partnerships with the War Department, European allies, and civil society organizations. Many of its tools and methods were adopted in later US diplomatic practice.

Early criticism of Creel came from Lippmann who, in addition to his Army propaganda duties, had standing as a personal representative of Wilson's top advisor Colonel Edward House. The CPI showed little understanding of politics and journalism in Europe, he wrote to House, and it was no match for the Europeans, who in every country view propaganda "as an instrument of diplomacy and the men who direct it are high in the council of government." After the war, Lippmann described the CPI's general tone as "one of unmitigated brag accompanied by unmitigated gullibility."[38] Americans came to view Creel's campaigns as "too boisterous, too exuberant for a world that had hardly been made safe for democracy," wrote historian Alan Winkler. "Propaganda became a scapegoat in the postwar period of disillusion."[39]

Until the publication of John Maxwell Hamilton's monumental *Manipulating the Masses: Woodrow Wilson and the Birth of American Propaganda* in 2020, most scholars glanced only briefly at CPI's Foreign Section. The "surprisingly thin" literature on CPI, Justin Hart observed, reveals "residual hostility" toward its influence on subsequent propaganda.[40] For some critics, Creel's aggressive methods demonstrated America's preference for messaging and information campaigns in wartime and neglect of cultural diplomacy.[41] But a reductionism that equates CPI with George Creel and messaging misses the rich tapestry of people, methods, and ideas in CPI's field offices. They improvised and used a wide variety of tools despite often vague or no guidance from Washington. During a lifespan of less than three years, Hamilton writes, they "field-tested ideas that became staples of public diplomacy."[42]

The Inter-war Years—Rejection and Rediscovery

For 15 years after CPI's demise, the United States showed little interest in public diplomacy. The threat of war receded. Public discourse focused on the horrors of twentieth-century warfare, rejection of Wilson's global agenda, and investigations into CPI's domestic censorship and heavy-handed methods. Propaganda became synonymous with lying, a demonizing term for partisans looking to frame policy differences and critics seeking to oppose or trivialize public diplomacy.

Meanwhile, civil society's cosmopolitans continued to project American culture and shape attitudes overseas. Philanthropic organizations supported international exchanges. Hollywood dominated world markets with myths, materialism, and images of life in America. Major book publishers such as Random House, Alfred A. Knopf, Simon & Schuster, and Viking, established in the 1920s, quickly found international markets, as did entertainment and literary magazines. Americans did not forget dollar diplomacy. At the urging of bankers, corporations, and the State Department, Congress created a United States Foreign Service in the Rogers Act of 1924. For lawmakers and business leaders it was intended to strengthen diplomatic support for trade and corporate enterprise. For diplomats it meant increased professionalism, salaries, and benefits. Business interests also advocated successfully for a Foreign Commercial Service in 1927 and a Foreign Agricultural Service in 1930.[43]

Amid growing concerns about Axis penetration in Latin America and German broadcasts with a strong Nazi slant, the United States slowly returned to institutionalized public diplomacy in the mid-1930s. Chiefs of mission took small steps such as making official policy statements available to local journalists and news organizations. The State Department negotiated exchange agreements with countries in Latin America, created a Division of Cultural Affairs, and supported radio broadcasts of music and cultural programs "in the service of peace" by the Pan American Union.[44] European governments had begun broadcasting to foreign listeners via shortwave radio, which prompted debates on whether the United States should engage in public international broadcasting.

In 1933 US Ambassador to Italy Breckinridge Long wrote to his friend President Franklin Roosevelt to complain about a lack of news and information about the United States. US missions received an "Information Series" compiled by the State Department's Division of Current Information. It arrived by surface mail. Collections of American newspapers, official press releases, speeches, and news summaries took from ten days to two weeks to reach Europe and a month or more to reach Asia. Long spoke colorfully for many diplomats when he declared that information received two weeks late "in this fast moving world" was as useful to him as a "Roman ruin." His solution: use shortwave radio to send information via Morse code to US embassies equipped with receivers maintained by Navy operators who would decode and airmail copies to nearby US missions that lacked receivers.

Roosevelt agreed, and State sent a memorandum to the Navy Department. Nothing happened until two years later when a rising chorus of field complaints led State and the Navy to launch the first "Radio Bulletin" on March 30, 1935. It was sent by shortwave to US missions in Berlin, Geneva, Paris, and Rome; two naval installations in China; and the Panama Canal Zone. The "Radio Bulletin" became known as the "Wireless File," a name that survived as technologies evolved from radio-teletype to satellites and the Internet.[45]

Using electronic technologies to keep America's diplomats informed posed few political problems. Dissemination to foreign publics was another matter. Almost immediately, US missions and Michael J. McDermott, the Department's press spokesman, sought approval to distribute official statements by the President and Secretary of State to the local press, preferably in translation, to overcome "misinformation" and lack of "fair and impartial" information about the United States.

Wary of the appearance of propaganda and opposition from commercial news services, the Department denied these requests. Quietly, however, field officers were permitted to allow journalists and influential individuals to peruse the "Information Series" and "Radio Bulletin" on a non-attribution basis at US missions. At the mission's discretion, texts of official statements could be given to those who asked for them.

As war clouds gathered, pressures to disseminate the "Radio Bulletin" increased. In 1938 Assistant Secretary of State George S. Messersmith, alarmed by the rise of the Nazi party in Germany and Austria, ordered a draft circular instruction authorizing US missions to make the "Radio Bulletin" available to contacts in the American and foreign press. It would be used "to correct wrong stories, to give the proper slant, or to supply assistance in writing articles." The circular was not approved. German aggression continued, however, and field diplomats increasingly ignored the Department's risk-averse posture. In August 1941 the US embassy in Madrid circulated a weekly news summary in Spanish using abstracts from the "Radio Bulletin." In the Philippines, High Commissioner Francis B. Sayre was commended for giving texts of official speeches to the Associated Press and United Press "in these perilous and critical times." The Department never officially authorized use of the "Radio Bulletin" with foreign publics, even though the practice became widespread during the war.[46]

State was similarly cautious about appointing press attachés in US embassies. Messersmith in 1938 had approved US embassy London's request that "all press contact … be very largely centered in one man." McDermott drafted a worldwide message authorizing press relations as one of each mission's "finest opportunities" and "most essential functions." It was never sent. In 1941 a telegram from US Minister Edwin C. Wilson in Uruguay called for "our own system of propaganda to combat Nazi propaganda" and appointment of Spanish-speaking "press attachés" throughout the region. Under Secretary of State Sumner Welles agreed and called for a circular instruction on "press relations," assignment of officers to deal with the press, and a more active role for "the Department and the Foreign Service in the formation of public opinion." State cautiously permitted embassy officers to meet with journalists, but under no circumstances were they formally or informally to be called "press attachés" or "press officers." Such titles suggested they would be propaganda agents. Soon, however, three journalists were given one-year appointments as "Special Assistants" in Peru, Mexico, and Brazil using the President's Emergency Fund.[47]

Opposition to using journalists came quickly from lawmakers and US ambassadors. Instead, the Department should establish a training course for "a small group of Foreign Service officers … designated to handle these press relations duties." As one diplomat put it: "We feel that a first, second, or third secretary can speak with just as much authority in dealing with the press as can a 'press attaché' and perhaps to better advantage." The lawmakers' views were shaped in part through conversations during an oversight trip to the region.[48]

Events soon trumped caution. On August 29, 1941, the Department created a Foreign Service Auxiliary to undertake a variety of new responsibilities. One was the appointment of "Public Relations Assistants" whose duties included "maintenance of friendly relations with… the press, radio, and local institutions or organizations." Within a week after the Japanese attack on Pearl Harbor, 13 "Public Relations Assistants" were assigned to key missions in Europe, the Middle East, North Africa, and Asia. A Central Translation Office had been created in 1940, and soon after the United States entered the war State was translating official texts into Spanish, Portuguese, and French for rapid worldwide distribution.[49]

Wartime Practitioners, 1940–1945

As Americans rediscovered public diplomacy, few believed State was up to the task. Practitioners from journalism, advertising, academe, politics, and culture again led the way, and presidential decisions were crucial in determining structures and funding. This time the United States created multiple agencies with separate authorities: the Office of the Coordinator of Inter-American Affairs (CIAA), the Office of the Coordinator of Information (COI), the Office of Facts and Figures (OFF), the Office of War Information (OWI), the Voice of America (VOA), and US Information Service (USIS) offices in Europe, Africa, and East Asia.

Nelson Rockefeller's CIAA. In the late spring of 1940, a young energetic Nelson A. Rockefeller, philanthropist, political activist, heir to the Standard Oil fortune, and future Vice President, sent a memorandum to President Roosevelt. It conveyed deep concerns about Germany's growing influence in Latin America and its use of radio broadcasts, motion pictures, and subsidies to local newspapers to undermine US interests. The United States needed an independent agency to implement "emergency" counter measures—economic and technical assistance and a variety of media and cultural programs. On August 16 Roosevelt created the CIAA with a budget from the President's Emergency Fund. He named Rockefeller its director. A year later, an executive order defined the CIAA's responsibilities and its relations with State and other government departments. It would be a center for "coordination of the cultural and commercial relations … affecting Hemisphere defense," and implementation of programs, "in cooperation with the Department of State," involving the "use of governmental and private facilities in such fields as the arts and sciences, education and travel, the radio, the press, and the cinema."[50] As biographer Richard Norton Smith observed, "What became known in Washington shorthand as 'the Rockefeller Office' was a classic Rooseveltian expedient, born of frustration over the diplomatic establishment and its blinkered refusal to think, plan, or act unconventionally."[51] But Roosevelt's priorities were clear. As he told Rockefeller, "if it ever comes to a showdown between your office and State I will have no choice but to back the department."[52]

The Department tolerated CIAA as an emergency measure but sought to check its activities through a policy advisor and occasional interventions with the President.[53] Veteran diplomat Ellis O. Briggs spoke for many traditionalists when he recalled his astonishment that Rockefeller "had been given $5 million with which to make friends, with a job description that, to the extent it was intelligible, appeared to duplicate the functions of State."[54] Eventually, State welcomed transfers of CIAA funds for its cultural diplomacy and coordination committees that proved beneficial to both sides.

Among CIAA's practitioners were Rockefeller's business associates, accomplished journalists, and an array of prominent Americans. They included Yale law professor Carl Spaeth, *Washington Post* editorial writer

John Clark, architect Wallace Harrison, public relations guru Francis
A. Jamieson, motion picture producer Jock Whitney, and radio advertising executive Don Francisco. Rockefeller's influence led to partnerships
with Walt Disney, Orson Welles, radio executives David Sarnoff (NBC)
and William Paley (CBS), and New York's Museum of Modern Art.
CIAA sponsored shortwave broadcasts in collaboration with US commercial radio networks; published the magazine *En Guardia*; launched
American libraries and cultural centers; worked with publishers to disseminate books and other publications; managed exchanges of scholars,
journalists, and other professionals; sponsored orchestral performances
and traveling art exhibits; and maintained a mailing list of more than
378,000 individuals and groups. It was a tool kit in Latin America that
USIA would replicate worldwide.[55]

Archibald MacLeish's OFF. In October 1941 Roosevelt created the
Office of Facts and Figures "to facilitate a widespread and accurate understanding of the status and progress of the national defense effort" at home
and abroad.[56] He persuaded Archibald MacLeish, the acclaimed poet and
Librarian of Congress, to serve as director. MacLeish hoped a simple
"strategy of truth" without hyperbole and emotional rhetoric would suffice. But his strategy soon gave way to advocacy and selective framing of
events and policies. He recruited an all-star list of experts: anthropologists Ruth Benedict and Margaret Mead; psychologists Gordon Allport
and Erik Erikson; historian Arthur Schlesinger, Jr; political scientist
Harold Lasswell; pollsters George Gallup and Hadley Cantril; and well-
known journalists, such as Malcolm Cowley and E. B. White. Theologian
Reinhold Niebuhr and columnist Max Lerner were persuaded to write
pamphlets. The actor Robert Montgomery and poet Stephen Vincent
Benet provided talent for a series of radio plays. OFF's staff grew quickly
to 350 Americans.

OFF was controversial from the outset, a target of Roosevelt's partisan
critics and others with different policy and organizational agendas. Its
formal authority was weak, and it lacked capacity to coordinate and compete with other agencies. OFF lasted eight months. MacLeish remained
committed to a government role in providing persuasive information to
"badly informed" publics. He went on to work for the Office of War
Information and the Department of State.[57]

William J. "Wild Bill" Donovan's COI. On July 11, 1941, Roosevelt established the Office of the Coordinator of Information under the leadership of a Wall Street lawyer and decorated hero of the American Expeditionary Force in World War I. Although Donovan was primarily interested in intelligence gathering and covert information operations, he also created a small Foreign Information Service (FIS) led by Robert E. Sherwood, Roosevelt's speechwriter and a Pulitzer Prize–winning playwright, to engage in open information activities. Its writ was worldwide other than Latin America.

Donovan and Sherwood had fundamentally different objectives, and they quarreled constantly. Donovan preferred clandestine broadcasts, psychological warfare, and any means, covert or overt, that would effectively thwart enemy operations. Sherwood, like MacLeish, had faith that US information and cultural initiatives would persuade if they were open and truthful. "The truth coming from America, with unmistakable American sincerity, is by far the most effective propaganda," Sherwood stated.[58] They believed in the self-evident value of ideas and that America should be an example to the world, a "global beacon" of an exceptional democracy. FIS's methods included targeted messaging, opinion surveys, repetition, simplification, dramatic formats, and selective truths.[59]

Robert Sherwood's and Elmer Davis's OWI. Confusion over who would do what led quickly to the first of many reorganizations in US public diplomacy. By Presidential military order on June 13, 1942, Donovan's intelligence activities became the Office of Strategic Services (OSS), a precursor to the Central Intelligence Agency. On the same day, Roosevelt's Executive Order 9182 created the Office of War Information under the direction of Elmer Davis, an experienced *New York Times* reporter, editorial writer, and CBS news analyst. OWI consolidated Sherwood's FIS and MacLeish's OFF. Sherwood remained head of OWI's Overseas Branch based initially in New York, and MacLeish became assistant director for policy. Rockefeller kept his CIAA separate. State managed educational and cultural programs through its Division of Cultural Relations and continued to edge into press and information operations abroad. US military services expanded their psychological operations in war zones and pursued public affairs activities at home.

Although the State, War, and Navy Departments retained authority over their own activities, Roosevelt's Executive Order required that they conform to information policies formulated by OWI. Thus began the practice of creating inter-agency coordination responsibilities that looked good on paper but lacked sustained practical effect. Cabinet departments gradually developed an appreciation for the roles of information agencies in wartime. But they intervened when necessary to protect departmental equities. As Creel, who knew a thing or two about interagency rivalries, wrote in a letter to Davis, "I am more sorry than I can say that your control over Army, Navy, and State is not real in any sense of the word. I know admirals and generals, also [State's] Sumner Welles, and while you may think you have established an arrangement that will permit a free flow of news, just wait until an issue arises."[60] Numerous disputes led to a second Executive Order in 1943. It gave sweeping formal powers to OWI, but did little to reduce competition between turf conscious officials.[61]

OWI's practitioners included German-born and Harvard-educated James Warburg, who was a banker and composer of scores for musical comedies, as deputy for policy and The New York Herald Tribune's foreign editor Joseph Barnes as deputy for operations. Percy Winner, director for southern Europe, had impressive print and radio journalism credentials as did Edd Johnson, director of New York operations. China scholar Owen Lattimore directed Pacific operations. They and many others in OWI were talented communicators and committed internationalists, but most lacked experience in the folkways and rivalries of Washington.

Tapping civil society's skills and creative imagination was now a familiar pattern in US public diplomacy. This time, two things were different. First, OWI gave priority to government international broadcasting. Romanian-born actor John Houseman was the director of the newly established VOA. It hired large numbers of European refugees who combined language skills, knowledge of overseas audiences, and a commitment to broadcasting as a way to shape the US war effort and the postwar world. Second, many OWI recruits remained to build public diplomacy organizations and serve in the career Foreign Service after the war.

OWI managed a worldwide press service that transmitted news, photos, and feature articles. It distributed magazines, leaflets, pamphlets, posters, and technical publications. It arranged for translation and publication of books by American and foreign publishers. It organized speaker programs and facilitated educational and cultural exchanges. It produced, acquired, and distributed newsreels, documentaries, and entertainment films. In 1944 OWI published *Amerika*, later called *America Illustrated*, a Russian language photo magazine about the United States that patterned the content, high-quality paper, and bright colors of *Life* magazine. USIA published the final issue 50 years later in 1994.

In the field, OWI established "outposts" known as US Information Service posts, a name that continued under USIA. Beginning with an American library in London in 1943, OWI established libraries in liberated Europe and eventually in each USIS post worldwide. OWI also engaged in psychological operations with Allied military forces against enemy countries ("strategic propaganda") and in the battlefield ("combat propaganda"). Priority tools were leaflets, mobile radios, and field printing units.[62] OWI's approaches to challenges within and outside the organization became enduring characteristics of public diplomacy's practitioner communities.

Emerging Tribal Cultures. Staffing a new organization with European émigrés, many with homeland political agendas, and recruits from diverse professions in the United States was not a formula for cohesion and policy discipline. Tensions between OWI's Washington office and its VOA broadcasters in New York existed from the beginning. Journalists who brought press freedom norms to a government enterprise were now obliged to consider policy relevance in selecting and framing news and information. The priorities of OWI's foreign language broadcasters at times did not align with US policies. OWI's practitioners and diplomats in the State Department's Division of Cultural Relations held different views on methods and organizational structures. These tribal cultures became rival communities of practice, each passionately committed to its own beliefs about what mattered most: field operations, broadcasting, press relations, cultural diplomacy, democracy building. They valued separateness and freedom of action.

Field/Washington Dynamics. OWI's field practitioners, like their CPI predecessors and USIA successors, had competing loyalties: to ambassadors and military commanders overseas and to headquarters offices in Washington. First-hand knowledge, they believed, meant they knew best how to engage and influence in local circumstances. Wary of large bureaucracies in Washington, they regarded what they did in the field as "the real work" of public diplomacy. Tensions between the field and head-quarters are a generic characteristic of government-to-government diplomacy. But they play out in public diplomacy with a significant complicating difference. Foreign *publics* are stakeholders.

At home, OWI's leaders juggled a variety of daunting tasks. These included standing up a new government organization, putting policies and procedures on the skeletons of broad and ambiguous executive orders, staffing new field posts, contracting with media and civil society partners, and making a public case for resources and why OWI mattered. Additional challenges were the daily requirements of managing relations with Congress, the American press, and large, well-established government organizations.

Truth, Secrecy, and Credibility. OWI made clear from the beginning it would "stick to the truth abroad as well as at home." Truth "is a very powerful weapon," Elmer Davis told Congress, "because it is important to create confidence in the story we are telling." His reasoning was pragmatic. "We do not tell the truth just for fun, we use the truth in such a way as to win and shorten the war." He elaborated, "We tell a true story to every area, but to each one we tell the kind of true story that will best serve our interests." OWI withheld information that would endanger military security or adversely affect a diplomatic negotiation, but, Davis argued, "We do not consciously add anything to the truth."[63] His criteria—selectivity, credibility, relevance, timing, and attention to the requirements of other instruments of statecraft—endure in public diplomacy.

Controversies were a hallmark of OWI's relations with lawmakers and government officials who expected its output would simply mirror and advance foreign policy and military objectives. OWI created three planning categories. Long-term plans (broad goals and themes) had value in Washington, particularly in Congressional testimony. Medium-range weekly plans and short-term daily guidance were more useful to USIS posts where practitioners had diverse views on how best to credibly inform and persuade local populations.[64]

A "strategy of truth" was fine in principle, but it masked operational difficulties. American sympathy with anti-colonial movements continued to complicate diplomatic relations with European allies. Varnished versions of America's history with racial minorities failed to convince foreign critics who charged hypocrisy and African-Americans who found them patronizing. Southern lawmakers slashed funding for a government agency that strongly supported racial equality. Entertainment programs, especially motion pictures, could build audiences, but many lawmakers viewed them as frivolous or partisan. US officials often viewed them as beside the point. In 1943 Congress voted to defund entirely the Bureau of Motion Pictures.[65] But OWI had one advantage its successors did not have. There were fewer sources of reliable news and information in the 1940s than decades later when information overload, not scarcity, became a central challenge for public diplomacy practitioners.

Policy Formulation and Interagency "Coordination." US policymakers in varying degrees supported OWI's role in *communicating* war information policies. At no time did they invite OWI to participate in the *formulation* of policies. OWI's practitioners, however, believed their role was also to advise on how policies would be understood by foreign publics. Turning to public diplomacy for messaging after policies had been decided became another enduring characteristic. "What do we tell the press about this?" was the usual afterthought as policymaking meetings came to a close. The point is not that foreign opinions should determine policies, practitioners and advisory panels repeatedly argued, but they should be taken into account in making and communicating policies.

OWI's Director chaired a committee to *formulate and advise* on "war information policies" made up of representatives of the Secretaries of State, War, the Navy, the Joint Psychological Warfare Committee, the CIAA Coordinator, and others the President might designate. The committee was expected to *coordinate* information policies to ensure they were "accurate and consistent." This led to a host of questions. What is "war information"? What exactly is "coordination"? Is it just sharing information? What happens when civilian and military agencies, each with independent information activities and access to the president, disagree or refuse to cooperate? OWI owed its existence to Roosevelt, but he intervened only occasionally leaving resolution of differences to the competition of bureaucratic rivals.

For the State Department, OWI was a low priority. State was slow to provide OWI's representatives with passports and facilitate their travel. VOA director Houseman resigned and returned to Hollywood in 1943 after State denied him clearance to inspect OWI's operations in Europe and North Africa.[66] State occasionally held up transmission of OWI's messages. Cooperation between OWI and US missions was uneven. OWI valued speed; State's policy guidance was often slow—a pattern that changed little in following decades. Personalities mattered, and relations improved when Archibald MacLeish became State's Assistant Secretary for Public and Cultural Affairs in 1944.

The War and Navy Departments focused on safeguarding operational information and conducting psychological operations in war zones. They provided liaison officers and intelligence to OWI, but they viewed its contribution to the war effort as secondary. Although Davis, Sherwood, and MacLeish had personal access to Roosevelt, they soon came to understand OWI's limitations and act accordingly. The cabinet departments also adjusted their views. As OWI's Charles Thomson later summarized, "The propagandists reduced their estimates of what they could do in the whole war effort, and the military and political leaders lost their earlier unfamiliarity, distrust, or contempt for the function."[67]

Congressional support for OWI as an emergency wartime measure diminished with success on the battlefield. Some lawmakers viewed OWI as a tool of New Deal Democrats and objected to its publications on domestic economic and social issues. Some were suspicious of its employment of aliens and possibly communists. Ultimately, OWI's fate was caught up in debates over the future of America's role in the world and distrust of government propaganda.[68] It had champions in Congress and American society, but overall it encountered skepticism and widespread lack of understanding of its role. Public diplomacy's future would remain closely tied to perceptions of external threats.

Peacetime Turning Point, 1945–1947

With the war coming to a close, the United States again faced a decision about what to do with information organizations in peacetime. There were three options. First, close OWI and CIAA, then called OIAA. This would leave America's overseas information and cultural activities largely to non-governmental organizations, to the modest press and cultural programs the State Department had reluctantly initiated, and to the military's information programs in occupied Germany, Austria, and Japan. Second, consolidate OWI and OIAA into an independent organization. Third, fold the agencies into the State Department, which would continue some activities and abolish others.

Elmer Davis advocated option three, a view shared by MacLeish and advertising executive William Benton, his successor as Assistant Secretary of State for Public Affairs. In the summer of 1945 OWI's leaders sent a memorandum to President Truman that "emphatically" urged him to expand the government's "information service to the rest of the world." Their reasoning: "Never again should America as a nation let the telling of its official story be left to chance ... Never again should the nation ... be satisfied with an unbalanced picture of America which must result if private telling in many media is left wholly unsupplemented."[69]

On August 31, 1945, President Truman's Executive Order 9608 abolished OWI and OIAA. It consolidated all activities "concerned with informing the people of other nations about any matter in which the United States has an interest" in an Interim International Information Service (IIIS) within the Department of State.[70] Truman directed Secretary of State James Byrnes to recommend a permanent arrangement that would not compete with "American private organizations and individuals in such fields as news, motion pictures, and communications." Rather, it would assist and supplement their activities and "see to it that other peoples receive a full and fair picture of American life and of the aims and policies of the United States Government." For a cautious State Department, taking on large and often controversial media and program activities was risky, but it had no choice. "The nature of present day foreign relations," Truman asserted, "makes it essential for the United States to maintain informational activities abroad as an integral part of the conduct of our foreign affairs."[71]

In January 1946 IIIS was renamed the State Department's Office of International Information and Cultural Affairs (OIC). Its staff of 3000 was much smaller than the combined 11,000 in OWI and CIAA. Under Benton's leadership, the OIC established five area offices to match the Department's five regional bureaus. It also created five divisions: International Broadcasting (the Voice of America); International Press and Publications, Libraries and Institutes; International Exchange of Persons; and International Motion Pictures. Benton cut programs from wartime levels substantially. The Newsfile's 100,000 words per day leveled off at 20,000 words per day. All magazines were eliminated except for *Amerika*. The OIC ended production of pamphlets and translations of books. It abolished OWI's worldwide radiophoto network and transferred some of its production activities to the War Department. It shut down radio broadcasting activities in San Francisco, and cut funding for VOA's broadcasting services in New York, educational and cultural exchanges, and American libraries.[72]

OIC developed ambitious plans for assigning USIS public affairs officers overseas. There would be one or more full-time American employees in 66 US missions worldwide; in 22 smaller missions there would be a part-time officer. Many OWI and CIAA practitioners returned to their private sector careers; others, however, remained permanently in government service. Most who served in media programs and radio broadcasting activities in New York and Washington became Civil Service employees. Those assigned overseas became Foreign Service Reserve Officers, a personnel category that emerged as the State Department came to recognize it would need a variety of skills to deal with occupied countries, economically devastated allies, and new trade, economic, and development issues in a postwar world.

Truman's decision marked a fundamental turning point. Priorities, functions, budgets, and organizations changed, but there were no more gaps in the US government's public diplomacy. The future belonged to government practitioners and their civil society partners.

Notes

1. Hamilton and Langhorne, *Practice of Diplomacy*, 76–80, 93–94; Raymond Cohen, "Diplomacy Through the Ages," in *Diplomacy in a Globalizing World*, 2nd ed., eds. Pauline Kerr and Geoffrey Wiseman (Oxford University Press, 2018), 21–36.
2. Jorge Heine, "From Club to Network Diplomacy," in *The Oxford Handbook of Modern Diplomacy*, eds. Andrew F. Cooper, Jorge Heine, and Ramesh Thakur (Oxford University Press, 2013), 60.

3. "Havana Convention on Diplomatic Officers, 1928," G. R. Berridge, Havana Conventions, http://grberridge.diplomacy.edu/havana-conventions/ (accessed May 13, 2023).

4. Walter R. Roberts, "The Evolution of Diplomacy," *Mediterranean Quarterly* 17, no. 3 (Summer 2006): 55–64; Hamilton and Langhorne, *Practice of Diplomacy*, 141–184.

5. Justin Hart, *Empire of Ideas: The Origins of Public Diplomacy and the Transformation of U.S. Foreign Policy* (Oxford University Press, 2013), 13.

6. "1. Editorial Note," *Foreign Relations of the United States, 1917–1972, Public Diplomacy, World War I*, Historical Documents, Department of State.

7. Quoted in John Maxwell Hamilton, *Manipulating the Masses: Woodrow Wilson and the Birth of American Propaganda* (Louisiana State University Press, 2020), 107.

8. George Creel, *How We Advertised America* (Harper & Brothers, 1920), 3.

9. Quoted in Lepore, *These Truths*, 395.

10. Hamilton, *Manipulating the Masses*, 111, 268–269; Hamilton, email to author, December 20, 2020.

11. On CPI's overseas activities, Hamilton's *Manipulating the Masses*, 261–321, is indispensable. See also James Mock and Cedric Larson, *Words That Won the War: The Story of the Committee on Public Information, 1917–1919* (Princeton University Press, 1939); Sarah Ellen Graham, *Culture and Propaganda: The Progressive Origins of American Public Diplomacy* (Ashgate Publishing Company, 2015), 21–28; David Greenberg, *Republic of Spin: An Inside History of the American Presidency* (W. W. Norton, 2016), 106–117; Jansen, *Walter Lippmann*, 75–83; and Vira B. Whitehouse, *A Year as a Government Agent* (Harper & Brothers, 1920).

12. Hamilton, *Manipulating the Masses*, 268–269; Hamilton, email to author, December 20, 2020.

13. Hamilton, *Manipulating the Masses*, 264–270; Hamilton, email to author, December 4, 2020.

14. "2. Letter from Walter S. Rogers to the Chairman of the Committee on Public Information (Creel)," *Public Diplomacy, World War I*.

15. "3. Editorial Note," *Public Diplomacy, World War I*.

16. "6. Letter From the Chairman of the Committee on Public Information (Creel) to President Wilson," *Public Diplomacy, World War I*.

17. Quoted in Mock, *Words That Won*, 319.

18. Hamilton notes that CPI's use of the word "propaganda" "is emblematic of the chaotic way Creel and CPI operated. Its use of 'propaganda' was as confusing as it[s] organizational chart, which changed all of the time." Hamilton, email to author, December 4, 2020.

19. "13. Memorandum From the Chief of the Military Intelligence Section, Department of War General Staff (Van Deman) to the Chairman of the Committee on Public Information (Creel)," *Public Diplomacy, World War I.*

20. "11. Memorandum by the Chairman of the Committee on Public Information (Creel)," *Public Diplomacy, World War I.*

21. "18. Letter from the Director of the Foreign Section, Committee on Public Information (Irwin) to the Committee on Public Information Commissioner in France (Kerney)," *Public Diplomacy, World War I.*

22. "13. Memorandum." *Public Diplomacy, World War I.*

23. "12. Report Prepared in the Division of Foreign Press, Committee on Public Information," *Public Diplomacy, World War I.*

24. "21. Telegram from the Embassy in the United Kingdom to the Department of State," *Public Diplomacy, World War I.*

25. "18. Letter," *Public Diplomacy, World War I.*

26. "5. Report from the Embassy in Spain," *Public Diplomacy, World War I.*

27. "18. Letter," *Public Diplomacy, World War I.*

28. Creel, *Advertised America*, 229, 269, 273.

29. Mock, *Words That Won*, 263–284; Lauren Claire West, "The Uneasy Beginning of Public Diplomacy: Vira Whitehouse, the Committee on Public Information and the First World War," MA thesis, (Louisiana State University, 2018).

30. Quoted in Hamilton, *Manipulating the Masses*, 274.

31. Hamilton, *Manipulating the Masses*, 272–278.

32. Quoted in Hamilton, *Manipulating the Masses*, 281–282.

33. Quoted in Hamilton, *Manipulating the Masses*, 278.

34. Whitehouse, *Government Agent*, 6, 267–268.

35. "42. Telegram From the Consulate in Irkutsk to the Department of State," *Public Diplomacy, World War I.*

36. "40. Letter From the Director of the Foreign Press Bureau, Committee on Public Information (Poole) to the Chairman of the Committee on Public Information (Creel)," *Public Diplomacy, World War I.*

37. Creel, *Advertised America*, 455.

38. Quoted in Steel, *Walter Lippmann*, 146–147.

39. Alan Winkler, *The Politics of Propaganda: The Office of War Information 1942–1945* (Yale University Press, 1978), 3.
40. Hart, *Empire of Ideas*, note 3, 218.
41. R. S. Zaharna, *Battles to Bridges*, 73–75; Arndt, *First Resort of Kings*, 27–36.
42. Hamilton, *Manipulating the Masses*, 294.
43. Frank Ninkovich, *The Global Republic: America's Inadvertent Rise to World Power* (University of Chicago Press, 2014), 119–143; Emily S. Rosenberg, *Financial Missionaries to the World: The Politics and Culture of Dollar Diplomacy, 1900–1930* (Harvard University Press, 1999); Kopp, *Foreign Service*, 12–14, 18–19.
44. Hart, *Empire of Ideas*, 17–21.
45. Murray Lawson and Bruce Gregory, *The United States Information Agency: A History, Origins, 1933–1945* (1970), 1-2-42–1-2-52, 1-3-5–1-3-13, RG 306, Entry A1-1089: HISTORIES OF THE USIA, 1969–1999, Records of the United States Information Agency, National Archives and Records Administration, College Park, MD; Bruce Gregory, *The Broadcasting Service: An Administrative History* (1970), RG 306, National Archives; Howard Oiseth, *The Way It Was: USIA's Press and Publications Service, 1935–1977* (1977), unpublished manuscript, author's copy.
46. Lawson and Gregory, *Information Agency*, 1-2-53–1-2-57, 1-3-5–1-3-13.
47. Lawson and Gregory, *Information Agency*, 1-3-13–1-3-24.
48. Lawson and Gregory, *Information Agency*, 1-3-22.
49. Lawson and Gregory, *Information Agency*, 1-3-24–1-3-37.
50. Franklin D. Roosevelt, "Executive Order 8840 Establishing the Office of Coordinator of Inter-American Affairs," July 30, 1941, American Presidency Project.
51. Richard Norton Smith, *On His Own Terms: A Life of Nelson Rockefeller* (Random House, 2014), 143.
52. Quoted in Cary Reich, *The Life of Nelson A. Rockefeller: Worlds to Conquer, 1908–1953* (Doubleday, 1996), 207.
53. On the origins of CIAA and Rockefeller's role as Coordinator, see Reich, *Rockefeller*, 174–244; Smith, *On His Own Terms*, 123–164; and Arndt, *First Resort of Kings*, 75–97.
54. Quoted in Arndt, *First Resort of Kings*, 79.
55. Charles A. H. Thomson, *Overseas Information Service of the United States Government* (Brookings, 1948), 117–157.

56. Winkler, *Politics of Propaganda*, 23.
57. Greenberg, *Republic of Spin*, 238–249; Hart, *Empire of Ideas*, 73–77.
58. Quoted in Winkler, *Politics of Propaganda*, 76.
59. Graham, *Culture and Propaganda*, 86–92.
60. Quoted in Winkler, *Politics of Propaganda*, 35.
61. Franklin D. Roosevelt, "Executive Order 9182 Establishing the Office of War Information," June 13, 1942, American Presidency Project; Franklin D. Roosevelt, "Executive Order 9312, On the Office of War Information, March 9, 1943, American Presidency Project; Thomson, *Overseas Information Service*, 17–21; Winkler, *Politics of Propaganda*, 8–37.
62. Thomson, *Overseas Information Service*, 53–75; Cull, *United States Information Agency*, 13–21; John B. Hench, *Books as Weapons: Propaganda, Publishing, and the Battle for Global Markets in the Era of World War II* (Cornell University Press, 2010); Winkler, *Politics of Propaganda*, 73–148.
63. Quoted in Thomson, *Overseas Information Service*, 41.
64. Thomson, *Overseas Information Service*, 48–49.
65. Hart, *Empire of Ideas*, 88–103; Mark Harris, *Five Came Back: A Story of Hollywood and the Second World War* (Penguin Press, 2014), 226.
66. Graham, *Culture and Propaganda*, 103.
67. Thomson, *Overseas Information Service*, 22.
68. Thomson, *Overseas Information Service*, 27–29; Hart, *Empire of Ideas*, 102–103.
69. Quoted in Hart, *Empire of Ideas*, 105–106.
70. Harry S, Truman, "Executive Order 9608—Providing for the Termination of the Office of War Information, and for the Disposition of Its Functions and of Certain Functions of the Office of Inter-American Affairs," August 31, 1945, American Presidency Project.
71. Harry S. Truman, "Statement by the President Upon Signing Order Concerning Government Information Programs," August 31, 1945, American Presidency Project.
72. Thomson, *Overseas Information Service*, 185–197; Cull, *United States Information Agency*, 22–29, 36–41.

6

Foreign Service—Building a Foundation, 1948–1970

"Every major foreign office in the world is doing things today which it would have considered startling, if not improper, ten years ago." In a speech at Duke University in 1949, State Department Foreign Service officer George V. Allen gave voice to a fundamental change in US diplomacy.[1] Communication with foreign publics, no longer the preserve of civil society experts on loan, would be carried out by career diplomats and other foreign affairs professionals. Allen, an exemplar of the accomplished traditional envoy, was US Ambassador to Iran, India, Nepal, Yugoslavia, and Greece. He also had been a journalist. Remarkably for a Foreign Service officer in the 1940s, he understood diplomacy could no longer be confined to relations "through a little group of selected officials called diplomats." The United States needed "to penetrate into the living-room of every individual" in other countries.[2]

Allen's views and skills led to his appointment as Assistant Secretary of State for Public Affairs following passage of the United States Information and Educational Exchange Act of 1948 (the Smith-Mundt Act), a law that remains, together with the Fulbright-Hays Act of 1961, the foundational legal authority for US public diplomacy. He oversaw the State Department's Office of International Information and Educational Exchange, formerly OIC, until his assignment overseas in 1949. In 1957

President Eisenhower recalled him to Washington to be the director of the US Information Agency (USIA), an independent agency created in 1953.[3] Allen was an important bridge figure in America's institutionalization of public diplomacy. He had standing with his Foreign Service peers and senior officials in the Department. He worked effectively with Congress and the White House. He was a committed, albeit cautious, advocate for using information, broadcasting, and exchanges as tools of diplomacy.

Allen's pioneering approach was "soft sell." USIA's objectives were more to explain and inform, than to advocate and persuade. His nuanced rhetoric was not about truth as a weapon or wars of ideas. As he put it in a letter to the US Ambassador in Liberia:

> I do not like bringing "propaganda" to the forefront of our government. It gives the impression that we are as much concerned with what we say as with what we do. It looks as if we are copying the Agitprop ideas of the Nazis and Commies. I do not like to give "propaganda" such importance—and no matter how we slice it, USIA's work is propaganda. I like to think it is enlightened propaganda, but even so, we should at least give the appearance of modesty.[4]

Allen was a pragmatist. Because all nations engaged in propaganda, "We Americans must become informed and adept at its use, defensively and offensively, or we may find ourselves as archaic as the belted knight who refused to take gunpowder seriously 500 years ago."[5]

Allen strongly supported long-term cultural programs and English teaching. Together with Voice of America director Henry Loomis he sought to make VOA "an instrument for relaxing international tensions rather than for making Cold War points." He commissioned surveys by opinion research organizations despite opposition from Secretary of State John Foster Dulles. Importantly, Allen worked hard to give USIA's field officers status equal to their Foreign Service counterparts in State. When Congress failed to provide the needed legal authority, he gave them limited Foreign Service "Reserve" appointments and created State-USIA examining boards to manage recruitment and promotions in what would become a career service.[6]

Many of these first-generation USIA officers were talented linguists and communicators. Some were émigrés recruited for language skills and knowledge of their countries of origin. Many brought media, journalism, and exchange management skills from their service in wartime information agencies. The politically ambitious hitched their wagons to ambassadors and USIA directors, but few became ambassadors. Allen and John Reinhardt in the Carter administration were the only career diplomats to serve as Agency directors. Most believed they were pioneers in a "hard hitting, fast moving information program" in which the field was preeminent. Most also believed their work could best be carried out free from "the confines of a cautious tradition-bound foreign office."[7]

Smith-Mundt Act

Practitioners have passionately debated goals, methods, and organizational structures for decades, but the first US public diplomacy mission statement was surprisingly durable. The Smith-Mundt Act framed two goals: "to promote a better understanding of the United States in other countries, and to increase mutual understanding between the people of the United States and the people of other countries." It authorized the State Department to create an information service "to disseminate abroad information about the United States, its people, and policies" and an educational exchange service to cooperate with other nations in "the interchange of persons, knowledge, and skills."[8] What could be more straightforward? Some practitioners would communicate information to achieve *better understanding*. Others would manage exchanges to achieve *mutual understanding*. Except it wasn't that simple.

The Smith-Mundt Act did not address whether the goal is just to disseminate information or also to influence attitudes, motivate behavior, and undermine the ideological campaigns of adversaries. And what precisely is the purpose of "mutual understanding?" Are exchanges a public good in themselves, or are they intended to support short-term policies as well as long-term interests?

In developing their tools, methods, and structures, practitioners faced a host of operational questions. What are the cost/benefit tradeoffs between fast media (radio broadcasting, radio teletype) and slow media (books, magazines, films)? Should the government's hand in disseminating information be apparent? Or is some "truthful" information more credible and persuasive if not attributed to the US government? Should information be disseminated to elites or mass audiences or both? Should information and exchange services be organized in or outside the Department of State? How should they be guided by foreign policies? Intense debates occurred within and between rival practitioner communities dedicated to "information," "culture," and "broadcasting"—a discourse that for generations produced a stunning number of advisory panel reports and Congressional hearings.[9]

Some Americans thought the Act was unnecessary. Congressman John Bennett (R-MI) spoke for many when he observed that America communicates best by example. "For more than 200 years—even in the remotest corner of the earth—people have known that the United States meant freedom," he argued. "Things which are self-evident require no proof."[10] Walter Lippmann now opposed government information organizations. He still believed in the political importance of "managing public opinion," but he viewed it as "inseparable from leadership." A competent leader did not need "a public relations expert between himself and the people."[11]

Others feared a US government information organization would manipulate public opinion in ways contrary to the public interest. Its tools were the weapons of dictators, not democratic leaders. It would be partisan. It would employ immigrants with alien ideas. It would compete with commercial media. Information was another term for propaganda, and an information service was a slippery slope to the abuse of political power. Renowned poet Archibald MacLeish spoke of his unease:

> I hated information work. I was asked to do it, and I always detested it. I suppose that in times of peace, so-called, you could probably devote yourself to information … But in war you were always on the verge of propaganda and … although some of the propaganda you could give your whole heart to, some you couldn't … As soon as I felt that I could honorably get out of it, I did.[12]

Europeans might be comfortable with government information and culture ministries. Most Americans were not.

Consultants and Advisory Panels

War in Korea and the Soviet Union's nuclear tests, however, drove fears of threats from abroad and complaints that the United States was losing the war of ideas to a spreading communist ideology. Republicans, out of power for two decades, made neglect of the information instrument a central part of campaign politics in the 1952 election. Campaigning in San Francisco, Dwight Eisenhower, a retired general who understood the psychological dimensions of power, forcefully made his case in a speech written by C. D. Jackson, a *Time* magazine executive who had served with the OSS and later in the Psychological Warfare Division of Allied forces in Europe. "Psychological warfare is the struggle for the minds and wills of men," Eisenhower declared. "Don't be afraid of that term just because it's a five-dollar, five-syllable word."[13] He promised stronger international information policies, activities, and structures, arguing they are central to US national security.

Advisory panels, brimming with ideas and enthusiasm, flourished. After the election, Eisenhower appointed Nelson Rockefeller to head an Advisory Committee on Government Organization in the executive office of the President. Its writ was government wide. In foreign affairs, Rockefeller proposed transferring the State Department's foreign information and assistance functions to independent agencies, a plan that appealed to Secretary Dulles who wanted to devote full time to formulating foreign policy. An agency for international information and broadcasting activities and a foreign aid agency, "subject to policy guidance from State," would be global versions of Rockefeller's wartime CIAA.[14]

Eisenhower appointed William H. Jackson, a New York investment banker who had served with the OSS and as deputy director of the CIA, to head a second advisory panel, the President's Committee on International Information Activities. Most committee members had military and intelligence experience. They included C. D. Jackson, its most active member; Robert Cutler, soon to be Eisenhower's first NSC advisor;

Gordon Gray, Truman's Secretary of the Army; Abbott Washburn, a former OSS officer who would become a deputy director of USIA; and Henry Loomis, a physicist and board member of the MIT affiliated Mitre Corporation. Eisenhower directed the "Jackson Committee" to make recommendations that would enable him to lead "a unified and dynamic effort" in international information policies and activities.

The Committee's report to the President on June 30, 1953, had a profound impact on the international information and broadcasting activities of USIA and the CIA. Information activities are essential to national security, it argued, and they should no longer be subordinate to the diplomatic, economic, and military instruments of power. The United States should speak with one voice as directed by the president and the NSC. Government information programs are justified if they persuade others "it lies in their own interest to take actions which are also consistent with the national objectives of the United States."[15]

The Committee recommended a range of methods and tools. Two methods were essential: (1) a deep understanding of foreign audiences and (2) "purposeful activities suited to the requirements of local audiences." Staffs in Washington should provide policy direction and concentrate "on conception, planning and coordination of global propaganda campaigns." Field officers should follow policy guidance, maximize use of qualified local employees, accentuate freedom and democracy, and forcefully refute Soviet lies and disinformation. They should have adequate funding and freedom to choose tools they thought appropriate. These included print media, people-to-people exchanges, radio broadcasting, motion pictures, libraries and information centers, book publishing, and television, "a new propaganda program of potential effectiveness." Practitioners should strengthen partnerships with private American organizations and coordinate information programs with foreign governments and international organizations.[16] Critics faulted the Committee's emphasis on one-way messaging and covert methods. But its views on understanding foreign audiences, tools and methods, and empowering field officers with broad discretion became bedrocks of practitioners' modus operandi.[17]

A third group, the bipartisan, presidentially appointed US Advisory Commission on Information, established in 1948, provided full-throated support for institutionalizing US public diplomacy in an independent agency. Now called the US Advisory Commission on Public Diplomacy, its politically well-connected and often nationally recognized members have long been ardent supporters and informed critics.[18] Their reports typically call for more resources, improvements in tools and methods, and greater understanding of public diplomacy by the American people.

The Jackson Committee, which wanted "the closest possible integration of foreign information activities with the development of foreign policy," made no organizational recommendation. Bowing to the preferences of Eisenhower and Dulles, however, it accepted "strong arguments in favor of taking the information program out of the State Department."[19] Senator J. William Fulbright, who feared putting "his" scholarship programs launched in 1946 in a propaganda agency, succeeded in keeping educational and cultural exchanges anchored in the State Department. Eisenhower made the decision: the US government's first peacetime information agency would be independent; its directors would report to the President and take policy guidance from the State Department.

Eisenhower's USIA Mission Statement

USIA was the organizational home for public diplomacy's community of Foreign Service practitioners during the second half of the twentieth century. Its overseas operations continued to be called the United States Information Service (USIS). Guided by two mission statements, Eisenhower's in 1953 and Kennedy's in 1963, these practitioners used common sense, a growing knowledge of what worked, and evolving communications technologies to create customs, norms, and methods that became patterned practices they passed on to their successors.

Eisenhower directed USIA "to submit evidence to the peoples of other nations by means of communication techniques that the objectives and policies of the United States are in harmony with and will advance their legitimate aspirations for freedom, progress, and peace." His statement called on the Agency to give foreign publics a better understanding of the United States and its policies by "explaining and interpreting" them clearly, by "depicting imaginatively" their correlation with the aspirations of others, by "unmasking and countering hostile attempts to distort or to frustrate" those objectives and policies, and by "delineating … important aspects of the life and culture of the people of the United States." The statement contained a classified paragraph that authorized the Agency, except in the case of VOA, "to communicate with other peoples without attribution to the United States government."[20] The stated mission was to convey information; the unstated mission was to persuade.

Eisenhower's mission statement did not reflect the contested issues and often heated rhetoric of politicians, officials, and advisory groups in the early Cold War. The Soviet Union in 1950 was spending an estimated $1.5 billion, 60 times the US information budget, on an aggressive "Hate America" campaign.[21] Senator Joseph McCarthy's accusations of communist subversion in the State Department included charges that broadcasters in VOA were disloyal and books by communist authors were on the shelves of American libraries in Europe. The NSC at first refused to provide USIA with National Intelligence Estimates on foreign countries. When newly appointed VOA Director Henry Loomis learned of this, he immediately called NSC Advisor Robert Cutler, who he knew as "Bobby" from their days at MIT and service on the Jackson Committee. As Loomis recalled:

> So I called Bobby and said, "What the hell goes here? How can you possibly expect the Information Agency to know what your policy is if it can't get the papers?" He said, "Oh, they're a bunch of commies, you can't trust them." I said, "The hell they are, and if they are, go ahead and fire them but at least put somebody in there that will do it. And besides, they're not commies." So we then had an arrangement where the papers were sent to me personally, not to the Agency … That lasted for three or four months, before I got it turned over to Policy, where it belonged.[22]

USIA's early practitioners admired Loomis, an innovator who combined operational skills and political influence.

A New Breed of Career Diplomat

USIA's first group of 50 entry-level officers was sworn in on September 27, 1954. They were joining the Agency to build careers in a new diplomacy with new tools and methods. Some were recruited from universities. Others applied after leaving military service. Some transferred from the State Department. Field officers rotated from post to post, carrying their rank "in-person." Civil Service employees were hired for their specialized competence. They held their rank "in-position." Some Civil Service officers transferred to USIA's Foreign Service Reserve. Agency directors and the Advisory Commission on Information called repeatedly for integration into the career Foreign Service. It took 15 years.

In 1960 USIA's Deputy Director Abbott Washburn asked Arthur Goodfriend, a field officer returning from assignment in India, to survey Agency practitioners about their experiences. His 132-page report, "Inside USIA: A Self-Appraisal," was based on interviews with 140 field officers, Civil Service employees in Washington, junior officer trainees, locally employed foreign nationals, and several ambassadors. It portrays an emerging cadre of career practitioners deeply committed to their mission, intensely competitive, and convinced improvement lay not in a recitation of past achievements but in examination of operational lessons learned.[23] His interviews reveal a professional culture given to relentless internal debate that typically closed ranks in response to outside critics.

These practitioners knew they accounted for only a small part of America's impact on the world. They told Goodfriend that commercial media, films, tourists, business executives, soldiers, and missionaries—as well as US and foreign government policies and actions—"have decisive effect on public opinion." Their job was to be influential in areas where they could make a difference. This meant fewer meetings in embassies and less paperwork. "Coordination is becoming a golden cow—our excuse for spending more time with ourselves than the Koreans," one officer lamented. "I can't give a speech at the university in the afternoon because I'll miss a must meeting in the office." Embassy walls were "a major barrier to communication." New methods also meant activities tailored to circumstances, not scattershot, one-size-fits-all approaches.

"We have been going bang-bang-bang and then looking to see if we hit anything," one officer observed. "That's a sure way to ruin a good bird dog." Importantly, they emphasized understanding audiences, building long-term relationships, and choices about which audience segments mattered most.[24]

What Works Best "Out in the Field?"

Tradecraft loyalties, competition for resources, and "the field knows best" mindsets drove spirited professional differences in a young agency. "The main impediment to better operations is over-emphasis on programming by Washington," one Public Affairs Officer (PAO) stated. "The field should do the programming, but it is crippled by lack of funds. The big Washington operation eats up the money." Washington's regional area directors, policy guidance officers, and managers of media units, particularly in VOA, saw things differently. As a media chief in Washington, whose first loyalty was to creativity and quality products, put it: "Others take the PAO's idea as the word of God. I don't. I'll listen to whatever the PAO has to say, but I reserve judgment as to the action."[25]

USIA's practitioners debated four fundamental issues: short-term vs. long-term goals, elites vs. mass audiences, communicating with people in and out of power, and non-attribution. In different contexts, shaped by digital technologies, these issues continue today.

Short- and long-term goals. Practitioners had different time priorities. Information officers and broadcasters focused on short-term objectives, but they understood that long-term exchanges and cultural activities can shape environments that make policy advocacy, press relations, and news broadcasts more successful. Cultural officers prioritized long-term goals. However, they understood their activities could influence behavior that served US interests in the short-term. PAOs and ambassadors were responsible for managing both.

Target audiences. Most USIA practitioners, other than in VOA, favored targeting elites because they were literate, urban, and influential. "Target audiences," also known as "gate-keepers," "opinion-makers," and "multipliers," were civil society leaders and government officials. The reasons were pragmatic. In a country such as India with a population then of 400 million, the only feasible approach was to engage urban elites who could influence larger audiences. This meant, Goodfriend summarized, "the first task of a PAO is to identify the influentials in the host country. By cultivating the few people at the top of the social, political, economic and cultural structure, many USIS officers believe they are making the most effective use of their time and money."[26] Understanding the influence environment and local culture was crucial. Their approach was congruent with theories of "two-step flow communication" advanced by Wilbur Schramm, Paul Lazarsfeld, and Elihu Katz.[27]

Some USIA practitioners, however, believed mass audiences mattered in "the real world" and should have priority. The revolt of the Cuban people put Fidel Castro in power. Communists appealed to mass audiences believing they would pressure their leaders. Rioting Japanese citizens caused President Eisenhower to cancel his visit to Tokyo in June 1960. Support for NATO depended on Europe's people, not just their governments. "Every time I go out to the Far East I come away with the feeling that half the world's population … [is] searching for something— food, better homes, health and education," one regional director observed. "We must forget all the talk about our limited resources, and start talking to these people. We have to get away from the idea that only the elites are important."[28] Goodfriend believed in the importance of mass audiences. His report gave ample emphasis to the consensus on the priority of elites, but he also included his own views:

> The rationalization of the mass audience concept is that content and direction are important in communication. That the message—couched in an idiom, verbal and visual, that masses can comprehend, and carried as close as possible to the people—has a better chance of reaching its destination than one inspired by, and aimed at elites … [They] cannot be counted on to decode a message that does not have within it, originally, before decoding, meaning to the masses.[29]

Messaging was central for proponents of both approaches. Their differences turned on whether to prioritize communication with elites (top down) as a way to reach mass audiences or to communicate with mass audiences directly (bottom up).

For Goodfriend, USIA's early doctrine was "largely empirical"—an informal mix of ideas from practitioner experiences, "studies of other nation's propaganda techniques," and "principles and techniques of intercultural communication."[30] The priority most field officers gave to audience segmentation and messaging choices derived from their knowledge of what worked best given constraints of time and scarce resources, not a close reading of communication theories. They had little time for the abstractions of theorists. Junior officer training occurred almost entirely during a year of interning with mentors in the field rather than in Washington studying text books. In retirement, Goodfriend worked as a consultant at the State Department and the East-West Center in Honolulu. He went on to teach at the University of Hawaii drawing on his experiences. His writings combine analytical distance and continuation of spirited arguments on methods and structures that, in the nature of a family quarrel, were part of USIA's culture.[31]

People in and out of power. Communicating with people and groups whose views were harmonious with those of their governments was relatively easy. Communicating with publics whose views differed from those in power or were seeking to replace them was more challenging, particularly when human rights, democratization, and free media issues were in play. A study of 61 USIA country plans in the late 1950s showed diverse audience categories: government officials, political leaders, journalists, media executives, labor unions, educational and cultural leaders, intellectuals, students, business executives, soldiers, religious groups, farmers, immigrants, and refugees. Field officers tailored messages and engaged in talent spotting. Engagement with promising future leaders often paid off when they became influential—a strategy that became the basis for international visitor programs, young political leader grants, media training, and educational and professional exchanges.

USIA's practitioners navigated a course that balanced communication with European allies, many of them colonial powers seeking to stem the tide of anti-colonialism, and aggrieved publics in colonies pursuing independence.[32] They maintained connections with leaders in autocratic anti-communist regimes—often supported by powerful lawmakers and factions in the United States—while building relations with civil society groups seeking to change the status quo. In Latin America, one State Department official observed, "A handful of politicians, socialites, [and] admirals run the show today. None of us would dream of having anything to do with anybody else … but the main job of USIS ought to be to connect with ordinary folk who, sooner or later, are going to make their presence felt. We need to get into trade unionism, land reform, education, and other activities that affect the poor people."[33] In Spain, PAO Burnett Anderson informed the Franco regime he would "operate in the normal fashion" with all segments of society including opposition parties organizing for a change in government. Any reprisals, he promised, would lead him to hold a press conference to complain. As he later explained, "you've got to stay in with the outs or someday you're going to be out with the ins."[34]

It was a delicate dance. When practitioners influenced the opinions and actions of publics, they were involved in the politics of other countries. Often this led to host government charges of interference in their domestic affairs. The skills needed to communicate simultaneously and effectively with people in and out of power became central to public diplomacy tradecraft then and in the decades that followed, notably during the anti-apartheid era in South Africa, the collapse of communism in Central and Eastern Europe, and the rise of the Muslim Brotherhood in Egypt. It called for a willingness to take political risks beyond embassy comfort zones, and street smarts to avoid offending their hosts and diplomatic colleagues.

Non-attribution. The question of attribution was often framed in the color codes of propaganda discourse. "White propaganda" is true, overt, and attributed to the source. "Gray propaganda" is true, but not attributed to the source, although it may be "attributable." That is, the sponsor makes no attempt to hide an association with the information. "Black propaganda" is covert. Every attempt is made to conceal the source.[35] Most in USIA understood overt, gray, and covert to be legitimate instruments of statecraft. Each had its place, and theirs was overt.

Nevertheless, the CIA's covert operations complicated public diplomacy through actions that ranged from planting press items to interfering with elections to toppling regimes—actions that could undermine

USIA's programs and credibility. As USIS officer Harry H. Kendall recalled, "[In Chile] Our colleagues from the 'other agency' (a euphemism for CIA) were also very active with the news media. For USIS it was difficult trying to conduct an out-front type of operation where you knew that press outsiders in fact planted commentaries that appeared to be locally originated." When the United States through economic sanctions and covert operations sought to overturn Chile's Allende government, "USIS continued to operate but had difficulty gaining access to anything but opposition media."[36] Many USIS officers understood the value of the CIA's local contacts, however, and some used them discretely to channel materials to journalists and political activists.

Non-attribution was the choice of the Eisenhower administration's Jackson Committee. "As a general rule, information and propaganda should only be attributed to the United States when such attribution is an asset. A much greater percentage of the information program should be unattributed."[37] The Committee was convinced foreign audiences are likely to reject information provided by other governments. Self-praise and emphasis on America's economic prosperity also could create envy and antagonism. USIA would be more successful if it channeled unattributed information through experienced local employees and private American organizations active abroad.

In 1959 Eisenhower appointed Mansfield Sprague, a lawyer and political advisor, to head another blue-ribbon commission, "The President's Committee on Information Activities Abroad." The "Sprague Committee" took a more cautious approach to non-attribution. "Unattributed activities should be used [only] when they can contribute to our objectives more effectively than overt activities and involve acceptable risks." USIA "is openly in the information business." The Agency could use open, factual information without attribution, but it would take ownership of "attributable" information if asked.[38]

For many early practitioners, shifting guidance created uncertainty. As one USIS officer put it, "the Agency veers, yaws, and drifts. Now we're in a Pollyanna phase. The next Director may want us to be Machiavellis. All manner of men have tried to shape our mission—advertising men, shortwave specialists, missionaries, school teachers, politicians. All their concepts are still at war within the agency." That USIA should no longer "impinge on gray propaganda" meant, in Japan for example, field officers could no longer feed "pro-American materials" to an "editor with close contacts with leftist writers. This was rejected as an activity more appropriate to an Agency other than ours … The shift leaves many USIS people overseas in a state of confusion."[39]

In 1963 President Kennedy ended the non-attribution policy in a memorandum to USIA Director Edward R. Murrow. "The influencing of attitudes is to be carried out by *overt* use of the various techniques of communication—personal contact, radio broadcasting, libraries, book publication and distribution, press, motion pictures, television, exhibits, English-language instruction and others" [emphasis added].[40] Non-attribution disappeared from the Agency's repertoire. Tom Sorenson, a seasoned USIA field officer and brother to Kennedy's speechwriter and special counsel Ted Sorenson, explained the evolving policy on attribution:

> It is important to distinguish between *attributed* activities and what is unlabeled but a*ttributable.* Not all Agency materials carry the USIA label … and it is not desirable that they should. Such a label is bound to be a notice to the reader to "watch out, this is something the Americans want me to believe." Sometimes such notice is desirable; for example, in the dissemination of official U.S. policy statements. But more often it is not. In nearly all circumstances … USIS is always prepared to acknowledge its authorship if necessary … Unattributable material, on the other hand, is that which is prepared or disseminated in such a way as to obscure or mislead the audience as to its origins. USIA does not engage in this kind of propaganda, leaving it to the Central Intelligence Agency, which specializes in covert operations.[41]

Field practitioners in the Eisenhower administration were putting meat on the bones of a mission statement. Goodfriend's report summarizes their agreements, differences, and the evolution of distinct information, cultural, and broadcasting practitioner communities:

> Information specialists feel the Agency's role is primarily to project news and official texts. Cultural officers with educational backgrounds place heavier stress on English language instruction, libraries, American studies, exchange of persons programs, Binational Centers, books, book translations,

seminars and college contact programs. The Director's [George Allen] stress is said to be on the long-range, cultural concept. "But the machinery to bring it about doesn't exist," according to an Agency view. "It conflicts with other objectives, and with activities performed by various media, many of which give priority to fast news operations."[42]

Kennedy, Murrow, and Johnson

With the election of John F. Kennedy in 1960, the country signed on to a Democratic administration and a new generation of leaders. USIA played a role in this pivot. Republican candidate Richard Nixon's campaign claimed that US prestige abroad had never been higher thanks to eight years of the Eisenhower administration's foreign policy. Kennedy used USIA's foreign opinion polls, leaked to *The New York Times*, to claim otherwise. As president, Kennedy's interest in public opinion led him to strengthen the Agency's research capacity and use its surveys to shape his rhetoric and build support for his policies.[43]

Anti-communism remained a driving force during the Kennedy and Lyndon Johnson administrations, but hostilities became more manageable when the United States and the Soviet Union walked back from the nuclear brink in the Cuban missile crisis of 1962. An ascendant non-aligned movement, constituted largely of countries with colonial pasts, sought to influence superpower conflicts to advantage in wars of national liberation. Kennedy launched the Peace Corps and the Alliance for Progress. Public diplomacy practitioners encountered an array of new challenges: perceptions of a missile gap with the Soviet Union, the failed Bay of Pigs invasion in Cuba, a buildup of American troops and counter-insurgency warfare in Vietnam, and apartheid in South Africa. Civil rights struggles, urban riots, a manned space program, an anti-establishment counterculture, women's rights, and demonstrations against the war in Vietnam shaped their domestic environment.

Legendary CBS journalist Edward R. Murrow was USIA's director during the Kennedy years. In the Johnson administration, the Agency was led first by Carl Rowan, a former journalist, Deputy Assistant Secretary of State for Public Affairs, and US Ambassador to Finland, and then by communications lawyer Leonard Marks.[44] As usual, outsiders had plenty of advice, much of it focused on headquarters operations and organizational structures. The Sprague Committee had submitted nearly 100 pages of detailed recommendations at the end of the Eisenhower administration. But Kennedy and his team had their own ideas and created new study groups during the transition.

A task force led by Lloyd Free, a former USIA employee who became head of the Institute for Social Research, and the RAND Corporation's W. Phillip Davison urged transferring State's Bureau of Educational and Cultural Affairs (CU) to USIA. Other recommendations addressed tools, methods, and training, and greater sensitivity by State's diplomats to their "blind spot" on "the psychological aspects of foreign policy."[45]

Donald M. Wilson, who led Kennedy's USIA transition team and was later its deputy director, urged increased attention to "the revolution of rising expectations" in Africa, Asia, and Latin America; more funding for opinion research, English teaching, books, and magazines; and career legislation for USIA's Foreign Service employees. He advised the President to preserve USIA's independence but leave exchanges in State as Senator Fulbright's strong views and "the political facts of life dictate." Murrow, Wilson declared, would "kindle an enthusiasm" among practitioners based on his "ability to attract talent to the Agency and to make the most of the talent already in USIA."[46]

Tom Sorenson also provided detailed recommendations to the President-elect. USIA's purpose, he argued, should be to persuade as well as to inform, and create climates of opinion conducive to achieving policy goals. The Agency should remain independent, take policy guidance from State, and advise policymakers on the public opinion implications of proposed policies and foreign public reactions to them.[47]

The US Advisory Commission on Information reaffirmed judgments made during a decade of USIA oversight: more funding for opinion research, more education and training, recognition of the important role of ambassadors in disseminating information about the United States and its policies, and better interagency coordination to ensure the US government speaks with one voice in foreign affairs. The Commission reasserted its view that USIA should be elevated to cabinet status, and its director should have direct access to the President to advise on foreign public opinion.[48] There were few takers on cabinet status. As Wilson put it, cabinet rank would inevitably lead to conflicts with the State Department. State's job is to make policy; USIA's role is to explain and promote policy. He voiced strong support, however, for USIA's advisory role. USIA "should always be able to offer its views on the international psychological effects of policies before they are put into effect."[49]

All agreed USIA's director should be an individual of ability and stature. This was achieved with the appointment of Murrow. Most also believed USIA's goals should be more clearly defined. This took longer. Building on their experiences in the field and the views of Murrow, Wilson, and Sorenson, USIA's practitioners drafted a new statement of mission, which Kennedy issued as a presidential directive in 1963. It endorsed Eisenhower's emphasis on disseminating information about American life and evidence that US policies were in harmony with the interests of others. But it moved beyond these objectives in two important ways. First, USIA should support US policies through "overt use of various techniques of communication." Gone was Eisenhower's classified language on non-attributed information. Explicit was an assertion that effective communication should seek to persuade as well as inform. As Murrow famously declared, "To be persuasive we must be believable; to be believable we must be credible; to be credible we must be truthful. It is as simple as that."[50]

Second, Kennedy's mission statement made clear that USIA should advise the President and diplomats abroad "on the implications of foreign public opinion for present and contemplated" US policies. This meant that even though Kennedy abolished Eisenhower's interagency coordinating structure that included USIA, the Agency nevertheless should "aggressively and expertly advise the Executive Branch" in the policy formulation process, not just communicate those policies after they were decided.[51] As Murrow also observed, USIA should be "in on the takeoffs, and not just the crash landings."[52] This was fine in theory, but hard to achieve in practice.

At his swearing in of Leonard Marks in 1965, President Johnson reflected on changes in the global environment. Information was more abundant. Communication technologies and jet travel were increasing mobility and global connectivity. Yet there was no corresponding gain in attention and understanding. Effective communication in such complexity, he stated, puts an emphasis on truth and disavows "propaganda." The United States "has no propaganda to peddle" since "we are neither advocates or defenders of any dogma so fragile or doctrine so frightened as to require it."[53] Marks considered issuing a new mission statement, but agreed with a USIA staff study that concluded no change was needed. The Kennedy statement remained in effect until 1978.

USIA's practitioners in the Kennedy and Johnson years faced challenges that did not fit perfectly within the four corners of mission statements and advisory panel reports. There was no letup in spirited debates on tools and methods. In a small agency, professionals often knew each other. Personal connections influenced decisions on assignments and program priorities. This was beneficial when they were based on merit; there were downsides when rivalries and score settling inevitably came into play.

Overseas, American and locally employed staffs were led by PAOs who reported both to their ambassadors and to USIA's director through geographic area directors. With occasional exceptions, they were valued partners in "country teams." PAOs prepared annual "country plans" to guide resource decisions and program priorities. In most embassies, they supervised press attaches and information officers (IOs) and cultural attaches and cultural affairs officers (CAOs). The latter were USIA officers who managed exchanges and cultural programs in the field that were funded and directed primarily by State. This PAO/IO/CAO model generally worked well despite overlapping reporting responsibilities and professional differences between IOs and CAOs.

In Washington USIA's director and deputy director, both presidential appointees, provided overall direction. A Deputy Director for Policy and Research formulated policies and communication themes based on State Department guidance and, beginning in 1966, directed an office of foreign opinion and media research. Geographic area offices led by assistant directors were responsible for managing field operations. Other offices included an inspector general and offices for administration and budget, personnel and training, congressional liaison, public affairs, and security.

USIA's largest Washington organizations, also led by assistant directors, were four media services: Broadcasting (IBS), Press and Publications

(IPS), Motion Picture and Television (IMV), and the Information Center Service (ICS). These were staffed mostly by Civil Service employees, specialists skilled in creating and disseminating media products who were not obliged to serve worldwide. USIA's Foreign Service officers were worldwide available. This Washington structure—Agency direction and management services, geographic area offices, and media services—lasted four decades.

Training, Unpaid Spouses, and Career Legislation

Public diplomacy training. USIA's officers at the outset did not take Foreign Service entrance exams; they took written and oral exams administered by the Agency. They were trained in foreign languages and regional studies at the State Department's Foreign Service Institute (FSI). But FSI offered no tradecraft courses in public diplomacy. The Agency was on its own, and it took the challenge seriously. It developed a junior officer trainee (JOT) program that combined courses in Washington with a yearlong apprenticeship abroad. Arriving officers began with a two-week introduction to USIA, followed by six weeks in FSI's basic officer course, two weeks of specialized study and briefings, sixteen to twenty-four weeks of language study, and a week of pre-departure orientation for their first assignment. Overseas, JOTs participated in nine months of mentoring and rotational work assignments at a USIA post and three months of training assignments in an embassy or consulate. They learned by doing.[54]

These early JOTs encountered skeptics and resistance. Many senior officers brought into USIA when it was created "were old OWI and OSS and State Department people as well as a collection of old news people, many of whom weren't really sure about the JOT program." As a junior officer, Bob Chatten recalled, "I encountered … a lot of resistance to the notion that a bunch of youngsters who had not gone through the school of hard knocks, as they had, were going to inherit the Agency." Time took care of this generational divide. But State Department skeptics proved more durable. "I encountered at our first post, Manila, something that became standard later on: State Department people saying, 'You seem like a bright, young man. Why don't you get out of this Mickey Mouse peripheral thing you're doing and get into the real Foreign Service.'"[55] Public diplomacy's career practitioners took pride in their JOT program. Its demise was high on their list of grievances when USIA merged with the State Department decades later.

Three major changes occurred in USIA's training programs during the Johnson administration. First, the Agency initiated a mid-career program, known as Phase II or "Career Take-off," to provide a broad range of professional training to be completed in three years. Included were management skills, theory and practice in political communication, rotational training assignments in USIA's Washington offices and State's Bureau of Educational and Cultural Affairs, and a year of intensive area and language study. Second, the Agency launched a five-week Phase III training program for senior officers. It focused on management and budget training, key issues in American society, and the operation of information and cultural programs. Third, USIA increased its overall language and area training requirements and placed greater emphasis on a year of professional education at US universities and military service colleges. Notable was the link between language study and promotion: "until language competence was achieved, middle and senior grade officers would be limited to one promotion."

USIA also expanded its training for foreign locally employed staff. This entailed longer training assignments at the Agency's Washington headquarters, home stays and travel across the United States, and observation of operations at other overseas posts. Another initiative included recruitment of labor information officers, most of whom had prior experience with unions affiliated with the AFL-CIO. Training for US-based employees received less emphasis, but USIA did increase training for support staff and a management training program for Civil Service executives.[56]

USIA's training requirements and professional education opportunities stood in marked contrast to those in the Department of State. Although its entrance requirements were rigorous and its officers for the most part remarkably talented, State gave relatively little attention to training beyond foreign language instruction, consular training, and regional studies. Nor did it value professional education. State assumed

Foreign Service officers could meet diplomacy's challenges with a good early education, the ability to pass tough entrance exams, and language skills. USIA's attention to training and professional development paid dividends. Its field officers on the whole were more proficient in foreign languages than their State counterparts. Although State's resistance meant most could not aspire to ambassadorial rank, they were routinely asked to step in as chargé d'affaires in the absence of a chief of mission.

Spouses—unpaid diplomats. Until the 1970s, the spouses of US career diplomats, almost all female, were expected to host luncheons and dinners, network with contacts in host country societies, assist with tourist activities of Congressional and other US visitors, and otherwise participate in the "representation" responsibilities of US missions. Although their roles were not defined in regulations, how they performed this uncompensated work was documented in the performance evaluations of their Foreign Service spouses. These tacit requirements and psychological pressures fell particularly hard on the spouses of public diplomacy officers in the field, whose work focused principally on foreign publics. In 1972 the State Department issued a directive, "Declaration on Spouses," that ended the practice of including spouses in officer evaluation reports.[57] This eased some of the pressures, but spouses of officers in entry-level training were expected to attend the "Wives Seminar." There they were instructed in the importance of "getting out and networking." As Stephanie Kinney explained, "We were to bring people to the table, into American homes and thereby facilitate relationships."[58]

Attitudes of spouses varied from those who justifiably resented their exploitation as free labor to those who thrived in their "in-house" role or who pursued professional goals independently. Older women who had paid their dues enjoyed the power and perks of being the spouse of a senior diplomat. Many came to resent their loss of status when State in effect moved "on to a new game without them" after the 1972 directive was issued.[59] Younger, career-oriented spouses who had bridled at uncompensated expectations welcomed the new policy. Some, in the manner of volunteers in many American institutions, flourished as the spouses of PAOs and other USIS officers—juggling USIS outreach responsibilities, raising children, and in the case of Tessa McBride (wife of accomplished cultural officer and PAO Edward McBride) pursuing a PhD.[60] Still others, including famously Julia Child (*Mastering the Art of French Cooking, The French Chef*), pursued independent careers. Child, who had worked for the OSS, became a culinary celebrity as the wife of USIA Foreign Service officer Paul Child. She took great pride in her professional accomplishments and role as an unofficial "cultural diplomat."[61]

Career legislation. A consequential development occurred in 1968 when Congress, recognizing that "USIA is here to stay," created a statutory personnel system for the Agency's field officers who served under the non-career reserve authority of the Foreign Service Act of 1946. As the Senate Foreign Relations Committee summarized, "It is not proper for the Agency to be required to carry out vital responsibilities in the conduct of our foreign policy while its professional, operational officers are by law only temporary employees."[62] Public Law 90-494 (the Pell-Hays Act) established the career Foreign Service Information Officer (FSIO) corps with the same rights, entrance exams, salary scale, and retirement benefits as State Department Foreign Service Officers (FSOs).[63] The Senate confirmed the first group of 592 FSIOs on October 4, 1968. They were statutorily equal, but the "I" in FSIO signified a difference in a pecking order that mattered to traditional FSOs. Invidious distinctions were common in the corridor culture of the Department of State. Nevertheless, it was a major milestone. Public diplomacy's overseas practitioners were now career diplomats.

By the end of the Johnson administration Americans had institutionalized a community of practice—Foreign Service professionals recruited and trained to understand, influence, and build relationships with foreign publics. As advisors and managers in Washington they provided needed perspectives, but it was their work "in the field" that gave them standing. It was where they preferred to be. There they had greater freedom to experiment, seize opportunities, and pursue imaginative agendas. Field activities were central to their self-identity, and they defended them with energy and determination. USIA's Foreign Service practitioners were central drivers of change as the norms and rules of government-to-government diplomacy throughout the world evolved to include public diplomacy.

Reflecting on his career, Tom Sorenson wrote vividly about USIA's work overseas:

Modern diplomacy is no longer conducted exclusively in hushed, high-ceilinged chanceries. It also takes place in the press, in the marketplace, and in the street, in a daily, unremitting war of words. This makes the overseas propagandist as much a diplomat, and sometimes as important a diplomat, as the embassy's Political or Economic Officer.

The first-rate American propagandist usually speaks the language of those he is seeking to persuade, and has a reasonable grasp of their history, aspirations, prejudices, motivations, and thought processes. He also is knowledgeable about the United States and its people, history, culture and policies. He understands the media of communication which are the tools of his trade, and can skillfully engage in one or more of the following: writing a news story, laying out a pamphlet, administering an exchange-of-persons program, making a speech, preparing a radio or film script, operating a public library, or designing an exhibit. He is willing to put up with monsoons, insects, and inadequate schooling for his children. He is willing to live on a government salary and away from the familiarity and security of his own country, amidst a different people of a different culture—and sometimes amidst hostility.

The successful PAO is equally effective as an administrator, counselor, and communicator. He must plan a program, persuade his ambassador and Washington of its validity, and then direct his staff in carrying it out. He must counsel the senior embassy staff on the propaganda implications of what they were doing. He must be able to entertain gracefully and purposefully, for persuasion is as often effected over a drink as over a desk.[64]

Sorenson wrote with the flair of the journalist he once had been. His prose reflected the gender habits of his day. He was comfortable with the rhetoric of "propaganda" calling it "an integral part of modern diplomacy." After all, he asked, what good is government-to-government diplomacy if it is not supported by public opinion? Champions of cultural diplomacy challenged his advocacy and information dissemination priorities. Traditional diplomats often sniffed at USIA's practitioners as "upstarts." Nevertheless, Sorenson described professional diplomats whose identity and views were driven more by experiences with foreign publics than views of Washington officials, reports of advisory panels, and scholarly studies.

Notes

1. Quoted in John W. Henderson, *The United States Information Agency* (Praeger, 1969), 4.
2. Quoted in Hart, *Empire of Ideas*, 133.
3. The place to begin in the literature on USIA is Nicholas J. Cull's masterful *The Cold War and the United States Information Agency*. Other studies, many by former practitioners, include Wilson P. Dizard, Jr., *Inventing Public Diplomacy: The Story of the U.S. Information Agency* (Lynne Rienner, 2004); Hans N. Tuch, *Communicating With the World: U.S. Public Diplomacy Overseas* (St. Martin's Press, 1990); Edward T. Barrett, *Truth is Our Weapon* (Funk & Wagnalls, 1953); Alan L. Heil, Jr., *Voice of America: A History* (Columbia University Press, 2003); Thomson, *Overseas Information Service*; Arndt, *First Resort of Kings*; and Graham, *Culture and Propaganda*.
4. George V. Allen to Ambassador Elbert G. Mathews, May 13, 1960, author's copy.
5. Quoted in John Brown, "The Purposes and Cross Purposes of American Public Diplomacy," *American Diplomacy*, August 2002.
6. Thomas C. Sorenson, *The Word War: The Story of American Propaganda* (Harper & Row, 1968), 104–107.
7. Howard Oiseth, *The Way It Was: USIA's Press and Publications Service, 1935–1977* (1977), 11, unpublished manuscript, author's copy.
8. "United States Information and Educational Exchange Act of 1948 (Smith-Mundt Act)," Historical Documents, Department of State. The legislation was co-sponsored by Senators H. Alexander Smith (R-NJ) and Karl Mundt (R-SD).
9. For an assessment of these questions, see Roth, "Public Diplomacy: 1952–1977."
10. Quoted in Frank Ninkovich, *The Diplomacy of Ideas: U.S. Foreign Policy and Cultural Relations, 1938–1950* (Cambridge University Press, 1981), 124–125.
11. Steel, *Walter Lippmann*, 423. In Steel's account, Lippmann used this argument in turning down an invitation from Secretary of State James Byrnes to direct Office of War Information activities transferred to the Department of State at the end of World War II. Lippmann also urged closing the Voice of America and opposed creation of the US Information Agency in 1953. See Jansen, *Walter Lippmann*, 22.

12. Bernard A. Drabeck and Helen E. Ellis, eds., *Archibald MacLeish: Reflections* (University of Massachusetts Press, 1986), 155.
13. Quoted in Greenberg, *Republic of Spin*, 275.
14. On the Rockefeller Committee and its plan to create an independent information agency, see Kenneth Osgood, *Total Cold War: Eisenhower's Secret Propaganda Battle at Home and Abroad* (University Press of Kansas, 2006), 76–78, 88–90.
15. "[370] Report to the President by the President's Committee on International Information Activities, June 30, 1953," *Foreign Relations of the United States, 1952–1954, National Security Affairs, Volume II, Part 2*, Historical Documents, Department of State. This version of the Jackson Committee's report does not include sections relating to the CIA's covert broadcasting and political action programs, which were not made public until 2011.
16. "[370] Report to the President," *National Security Affairs*.
17. For assessments of the Jackson Committee's recommendations see Osgood, *Total Cold War*, 78–81; Cull, *United States Information Agency*, 94–96; Shawn J. Parry-Giles, "The Eisenhower Administration's Conceptualization of the USIA: The Development of Overt and Covert Propaganda Strategies," *Presidential Studies Quarterly* 24, no. 2 (Spring 1994): 263–276; and Roth, "Public Diplomacy: 1952–1977," 361–363.
18. The Commission's first Chairman was Mark Ethridge, a respected journalist who helped build the *Louisville Courier-Journal* into a nationally known newspaper. Other members were Erwin "Spike" Canham, editor of the *Christian Science Monitor*; Philip Reed, Chairman of General Electric; Mark May, Yale psychology professor and consultant to the War Department; and Justin Miller, Chairman of the National Association of Radio and Television Broadcasters. Later members included pollster George Gallup, *Reader's Digest* editor Hobart Lewis, CBS President Frank Stanton, historian John Hope Franklin, founding Heritage Foundation president Edwin J. Feulner, Jr., and Washington lobbyist Tom C. Korologos.
19. "[370] Report to the President," National Security Affairs.
20. "Report to the National Security Council by the Executive Secretary (Lay)," October 24, 1953, *National Security Affairs*, https://history.state.gov/historicaldocuments/frus1952-54v02p2/d357. The "Mission of the United States Information Agency" is enclosed in Lay's report.
21. Cull, *United States Information Agency*, 52.

22. Henry Loomis Oral History, interviewed by "Cliff" Groce, Foreign Affairs Oral History Collection, ADST, Arlington, VA.
23. Arthur Goodfriend, "Inside USIA: A Self-Appraisal," unpublished manuscript, December 1960, author's copy.
24. Goodfriend, "Inside USIA," 4–8, 46.
25. Goodfriend, "Inside USIA," 9–10.
26. Goodfriend, "Inside USIA," 23–24.
27. Wilbur Schramm, "How Communication Works," in *The Process and Effects of Communication*, eds. Wilbur Schramm and Donald F. Roberts (University of Illinois Press, 1954), 3–26; Elihu Katz and Paul Lazarsfeld, *Personal Influence: The Part Played by People in the Flow of Mass Communications* (Free Press, 1955).
28. Goodfriend, "Inside USIA," 26.
29. Goodfriend, "Inside USIA," 1–15.
30. Goodfriend, "Inside USIA," 79.
31. Arthur Goodfriend, "The Dilemma of Cultural Propaganda: 'Let It Be,'" *The Annals of the American Academy of Political and Social Science* 398, no. 1 (November 1971): 112; Arthur Goodfriend, *The Twisted Image* (St. Martin's Press, 1963).
32. Jason C. Parker, *Hearts, Minds, Voices: US Cold War Public Diplomacy and the Formation of the Third World* (Oxford University Press, 2016), 92–115.
33. Goodfriend, "Inside USIA," 28.
34. Burnett Anderson Oral History, interviewed by Jack O'Brien, Foreign Affairs Oral History Collection, ADST, Arlington, VA.
35. Nicholas J. Cull, *Public Diplomacy: Lessons from the Past* (Figueroa Press, 2009), 22; Osgood, *Total Cold War*, 93.
36. Harry H. Kendall, *A Farm Boy in the Foreign Service: Telling America's Story to the World* (1st Books, 2003), 167, 175.
37. "[370] Report to the President," *National Security Affairs*, 61.
38. "The President's Committee on Information Activities Abroad [Sprague Committee Report]," 1960, 76–77, Box 1, Walter R. Roberts Papers, George Washington University Library.
39. Goodfriend, "Inside USIA," 11.
40. "144. Memorandum From President Kennedy to the Director of the U.S. Information Agency (Murrow)," *Foreign Relations of the United States, 1961–1963, Volume XXV, Organization of Foreign Policy;*

Information Policy; United Nations; Scientific Matters, Historical
Documents, Department of State.

41. Sorenson, *Word War*, 64–65. On the distinction between attributed and
attributable information, I am indebted to conversation with Michael
Schneider, February 17, 2017.

42. Goodfriend, "Inside USIA," 14–15.

43. Mark Haefele, "John F. Kennedy, USIA, and World Public Opinion,"
Diplomatic History 25, no. 1 (Winter 2001): 63–84.

44. For accounts of USIA's activities during the 1960s, see Gregory
M. Tomlin, *Murrow's Cold War: Public Diplomacy for the Kennedy
Administration* (Potomac Books, 2016); Cull, *United States Information
Agency*, 189–292; Dizard, *Inventing Public Diplomacy*, 83–99; and
Sorenson, *Word War*, 139–213.

45. "5. Report Prepared by the Task Force on the United States Information
Agency," *Foreign Relations of the United States, 1917–1972, Volume VI,
Public Diplomacy, 1961–1963*, Historical Documents, Department
of State.

46. "3. Report prepared by Deputy Director-designate Donald M. Wilson,"
Public Diplomacy, 1961–1963; "8. Memorandum From the Acting
Director of the United States Information Agency (Wilson) to President
Kennedy," *Public Diplomacy, 1961–1963*.

47. "2. Memorandum Prepared by Thomas C. Sorenson of the United States
Information Agency," *Public Diplomacy, 1961–1963*. On reports by the
Sprague Committee, Lloyd Free and W. Philips Davison, Donald
M. Wilson, and Tom Sorenson, see Sorenson, *Word War*, 117–122 and
Roth, "Public Diplomacy, 1952–1977," 367–370.

48. *The Sixteenth Report of the United States Advisory Commission on
Information* (1961), US Advisory Commission on Public Diplomacy
Reports. USIA's directors reported to the President through the National
Security Council. In practice, their access was limited. USIA's advisory
role was usually contingent on the personal relationships between the
Agency's directors and Presidents and White House officials. The State
Department seldom supported the Agency's advisory role.

49. "3. Report Prepared by Deputy Director-Designate Donald M. Wilson,"
Public Diplomacy, 1961–1963.

50. Quoted in Sorenson, *Word War*, 4.

51. On Kennedy's statement of mission, see Sorenson, *Word War*, 142–146.

52. Quoted in Alexander Kendrick, *Prime Time: The Life of Edward R. Murrow* (Little, Brown, 1969), 456. Although widely attributed to Murrow, the phrase was used in comments on bipartisanship by Republican Senator Arthur H. Vandenberg, who attributed it to Republican presidential candidate Harold Stassen. See Suzy Platt, ed., *Respectfully Quoted: A Dictionary of Quotations Requested from the Congressional Research Service* (US Government Printing Office, 1989), 260–261. On Murrow's views on USIA's advisory role and years at USIA, see Tomlin, *Murrow's Cold War.*

53. Quoted in Murray G. Lawson, Bruce N. Gregory, Hugh W. Olds, Jr., and Irving R. Wechsler, *The United States Information Agency During the Johnson Administration, 1963–1968* (1970), 1-11–1-12, RG 306, Entry A1-1089: HISTORIES OF THE USIA, 1969–1999, Records of the United States Information Agency, National Archives and Records Administration, College Park, MD.

54. On the early JOT program, see Beatrice Camp, "Learning the Ropes Through Rotations," *Foreign Service Journal* 100, no. 2 (March 2023): 31–33 and Henderson, *Information Agency*, 125.

55. Robert L. Chatten Oral History, interviewed by Fred A. Coffey, Jr., Foreign Affairs Oral History Collection, ADST, Arlington, VA.

56. For accounts of USIA's training initiatives in the 1960s, see Lawson, et al., *Johnson Administration, 1963–1968*, 3-22–3-28 and Henderson, *Information Agency*, 124–126.

57. "Wives and Women in the Foreign Service: The Creation of the Family Liaison Office," March 6, 2015, ADST, Arlington, VA, website.

58. Stephanie Smith Kinney Oral History, interviewed by Charles Stuart Kennedy, Foreign Affairs Oral History Collection, ADST, Arlington, VA. Kinney began her career as a Foreign Service spouse in 1971. In 1976 she passed the Foreign Service exam. She and her husband then became what is known as a "tandem couple." Her activism on women's issues contributed to changing attitudes in the Department, new policies on "working spouses," and creation of its Family Liaison Office and counterpart offices in embassies known as Community Liaison Offices.

59. Kinney Oral History, interviewed by Charles Stuart Kennedy, 56.

60. Tessa McBride Oral History, interviewed by Jewell Fenzi, Foreign Affairs Oral History Collection, ADST, Arlington, VA.

61. Julia Child Oral History, interviewed by Jewell Fenzi, Foreign Affairs Oral History Collection, ADST, Arlington, VA; Henry Breed, "Julia

Child as a Cultural Diplomat, *Alex Prud'homme* (blog), November 8, 2012,https://alexprudhomme.com/2012/11/13/julia-child-as-a-cultural-diplomat/.

62. Quoted in Henderson, *Information Agency*, 122.
63. On USIA's career Foreign Service legislation, see Lawson, et al., *Johnson Administration, 1963–1968*, 3-28–3-34 and Henderson, *Information Agency*, 121–124.
64. Sorenson, *Word War*, 56–58.

7

Foreign Service—Transforming Diplomacy, 1970–1990

The 1970s brought a new generation of change-oriented diplomacy practitioners. In the State Department, reformers known as "Young Turks" lamented the Department's diminished authority in a galaxy of independent foreign affairs agencies. Their 1968 manifesto, *Toward a Modern Diplomacy*, challenged Foreign Service leadership by a "hidebound old guard" and called for restoration of the prestige and special character of a career Foreign Service protected from political patronage.[1] USIA's practitioners looked to strengthen an instrument of diplomacy coming of age and show that traditional diplomacy could not succeed without public diplomacy.

A changing environment shaped their agendas. The Cold War continued, but in the spirit of détente. Nixon's trips to China and the Soviet Union ended rigid bipolarity and tamed America's strident anticommunism. Americans were seeking an exit from Vietnam. A loose coalition of Global South nations came together under UN auspices in the G-77 to promote a New World Economic Order and build support in UNESCO for a New World Information and Communication Order. At home, civil rights unrest, inflation, energy uncertainties, and Nixon's Watergate scandal dominated politics. A counterculture movement valued society more than government and people more than established

© The Author(s), under exclusive license to Springer Nature Switzerland AG 2024
B. Gregory, *American Diplomacy's Public Dimension*, Palgrave Macmillan Series in Global Public Diplomacy, https://doi.org/10.1007/978-3-031-38917-7_7

institutions. Public diplomacy's practitioners wanted USIA's programs to reflect these new realities.[2]

Barbara White and Walter Roberts, Foreign Service officers who had risen to the top career position in USIA, set the table for the next two decades of public diplomacy practice. They were improbable change agents. They were not junior officers looking to overturn an old order; both began their careers in 1942. White, a graduate of Mount Holyoke College and Harvard University, had managed overseas information and cultural programs for the OWI in Cairo and Rome. Roberts, Austrian born and educated at Cambridge University, began as a German language broadcaster for VOA. They joined the Department of State, transferred to USIA in 1953, and became accomplished field practitioners who skillfully navigated the minefields of Washington. Although their views differed in important ways, they framed debates that were central to building a mature community of practice and the transformation of US diplomacy.

Barbara White's Overseas "Communication"

In 1973 White wrote a report on "U.S. Government Overseas Communication Programs: Needs and Opportunities in the Seventies." It was based on extensive interviews with USIA's practitioners and, like Arthur Goodfriend in 1960, she also examined post inspection reports, advisory panel reports, and academic studies. She presented it as "'gut wisdom' accepted, if not unanimously, at least by a majority of field officers" to USIA director James Keogh and Assistant Secretary of State for Educational and Cultural Affairs John Richardson. Although the term "public diplomacy" was gaining traction in the Agency, White used "overseas communication programs" to frame "direct communication with peoples of other countries, whether through media or through exchanges and personal contact."[3]

White's logic was field driven. Communication with people in other countries was now an "integral arm of foreign policy" for all nations. The US government needed ways to present its "policies, and the reasons for them, clearly and persuasively to foreign audiences." To do this well,

career professionals must advise policymakers on the implications of foreign opinion for the *formulation* and *conduct* of foreign policy. The task
was to strengthen understanding between peoples in the United States
and other countries and foster shared approaches to common problems.

Her report addressed USIA's strengths and limitations. Its strengths
included the growing experience of its practitioners, extensive communication networks, and the "impressive results" of long-term investments in
people and institutions. Its limitations: a reluctance to take full advantage
of opinion research, operational rigidities and slowness to change, a
Washington bureaucracy insufficiently responsive to field needs, and preoccupation with lectures, handouts, one-way "frontal assault," and short-
term activities. Effective communication, she argued, required an
approach that prioritized dialogue, mutuality, common interests, and
working where possible through local institutions. Her examples of common interests—"population, environment, law of the sea, urbaniza-
tion"—resonate a half-century later. The United States should offer its
views and experiences when sought by others in the "spirit of mutuality,
not of determining a solution for others."[4]

White projected the thinking of pragmatic practitioners who were less
ideological than their predecessors. Confrontational anti-communism
and one-way messaging were ineffective in a world of information overload and growing skepticism about government output. Public diplomats
should communicate in depth on fewer issues—focusing on what "priority audiences want" and is "in the U.S. interest to provide." Quality and
selectivity meant fewer events in cultural centers, fewer speakers, fewer
print and video products. Why? Because one top expert recruited on a
subject of high mutual interest would have greater impact than multiple
speakers of lesser quality. One excellent television production placed in a
media-saturated country met the same test. This approach called for less
original USIA content and more acquisition from the best American
sources. There were also things USIA would not do. Psychological warfare would be solely the responsibility of the US military. The Agency
would not provide surrogate information services in countries lacking
free media. Nor would it engage in trade and tourism promotion.

Communication concepts informed the thinking of White and other
USIA change agents. They understood attitudes are resistant to change

and that media can draw attention to issues, but seldom alter deeply held beliefs. Channeling Walter Lippmann, they believed people perceive their "reality worlds" through mental images. They knew from experience that policies and actions are more powerful than words and messages. Audiences were well aware of the anti–Vietnam War and civil rights movements.[5] White's report emphasized listening and face-to-face communication. "*By listening more,*" she explained, "*the U.S. would gain greater understanding of the mind-set, motivations and attitudes of its audiences. Few if any steps … would do more to increase the effectiveness of the [USIA] programs in both operating and advisory roles*" [emphasis in the original].[6]

New ideas emerged amid spirited debates, personality conflicts, and bureaucratic infighting. A group of junior Foreign Service and Civil Service officers in USIA formed a Young Officers Policy Panel to encourage innovative thinking. Senior officers, many with strong egos and sharp elbows, advocated and opposed changes in tools and methods. Some were critical of the Agency's nation-building role in Southeast Asia. Others sought ways to build support for America's involvement in Vietnam. It was a time of ferment and critical self-reflection.

Alan Carter's Radical Innovations

One approach with far-reaching consequences was transformation of USIA's operations in Japan. PAO Alan Carter and talented young officers such as Barry Fulton and Paul Blackburn, who would later rise to top leadership positions in the Agency, led the effort. They began by updating contact lists still dominated by the postwar occupation. They prioritized a younger generation of Japanese poised to shape Japan's future. Fulton created an Audience Record System, which was later computerized and adopted Agency-wide as a Distribution and Record System (DRS). It identified key audiences, documented post outreach activities, and maintained updated records of audience participation in USIA's programs. American libraries in Japan, re-named "Infomats," were outfitted with state-of-the-art technologies, modular furniture, and modern design features. Drastically reduced collections of print and video materials focused on five thematic areas: security and US-Japan relations, economics, American society, the arts, and "toward the year 2000." Their changes were radical and controversial. As Blackburn recalled, each of the Infomats "had exactly the same 3,000 titles, 2,000 of them for circulation and 1,000 to meet the reference needs of our audiences … The standard 2,000 circulating titles were divided equally among the five major themes—or post objectives—that also guided our speaker programming." No more than 100 books or other items could be more than five years old. Each year 60 new books would replace 60 books in the collection. Programs centered on expert speakers in a thematic field accompanied by relevant print and video media products. It was a rigid approach, endorsed by Carter and his team, but rejected as too mechanistic by others.[7]

How did the Agency respond? It sent a senior officer, Jim Moceri, to Japan to determine whether Carter's "revolution" should be terminated, kept but only in Japan, or mandated in other USIS posts. Moceri concluded it might have limited validity in Japan, but it was too rigid and had significant flaws. Blackburn's description of what happened next provides insights into USIA's culture and capacity for innovation.

Alan was summoned back to Washington for what some called a "star chamber Hearing" to respond to Moceri's criticisms. According to those who attended, it was among the most dramatic confrontations in the Agency's history. People stood along the walls of the packed conference room for the four or five hours that Alan and Jim went head to head over nearly every aspect of the program. The upshot was that Alan prevailed, at least as far as Japan was concerned—which was all that he had been arguing for in the first place. The Agency's leaders congratulated him on putting together such a fine and carefully considered program, but reserved judgment about its applicability elsewhere.

As it happened, many of Alan's innovations did spread to other countries in the following years—for example, using modern design to draw trendy young audiences to the USIS centers, placing emphasis on getting the most up-to-date reference materials into the hands of key contacts, and instituting more rigorous distribution systems. In addition, USIS Japan's targeted speaker program, and the heavy demands it put on disparate Washington elements, prompted a full revamping of USIA's field program support apparatus....

[Years later] the Infomat had become an Information Resource Center. We had gone back to having an Information Officer, instead of a Media Relations Officer, and the Cultural Attaché portfolio belonged to the Cultural Affairs Officer. The Audience Record System, now the DRS, was more sophisticated ... More important was what was kept—the attention to carefully selected audiences, the dedication to constant upgrading of communications and A/V support technology, and a willingness to pass up activities that were "nice to do" in favor of a disciplined focus on our primary objectives. This approach continues to this day.[8]

Carter remained a thought leader with devoted followers and critics. As he summarized his views, "*the process of communication* differs substantially from *communication activities*" [emphasis added]. When diplomats string together many "different programs on different subjects for different audiences, on a sporadic and hyperactive basis, you have nothing more than a helluva' lot of activity." But when "an issue of consequence is discussed with an audience of consequence on a continuing basis (continuing does not mean daily; but it does mean occasionally), you have described process. Activity requires a lot of energy but not much thought. Process requires a lot of thought."[9]

USIA's change agents also were busy in Washington. Under the leadership of experienced field practitioners Hal Schneidman, Bill Haratunian, and Ed Schulick, the Agency's Information Center Service created rapid response Thematic Programming Units linked to requests and annual plans of USIS posts. It strengthened the Agency's ties with America's cultural and arts communities, built a studio to create inexpensive video products for field use, and modernized its book, exhibits, and American studies programs.[10]

White and her colleagues wanted to improve field operations through communication with targeted elites in and out of power. "Audiences ... must necessarily be limited to influentials, present and potential rather than the masses ... the [Agency's] programs must seek out not only today's opinion leaders but also tomorrow's."[11] With one exception, she was content to list contending reorganization proposals without voicing an opinion. "It is an anomaly," she wrote, "to have the programs of USIA and the Bureau of Educational and Cultural Affairs (CU) administered together in the field [and] separately in Washington." But she recommended no change for "the seventies." The arrangement overseas is efficient, cost-effective, and "permits concentration of effort on priority subjects."[12]

After finishing her report, White left USIA and took a position with ambassadorial rank in the US delegation to the United Nations. A year later she sent a five-page paper to Walter Roberts that addressed organizational weaknesses and recommended radical change. First, USIA's advisory role was "very poorly performed," she wrote, although some PAOs occasionally did the job well. Second, "longer range functions do not get due attention in the present USIA structure." Third, even though "mutuality" was built into some field operations, it was "largely window dressing, except for the CU programs, which have a different legislative base." Her solution was to put public diplomacy's advisory role and support for foreign policy in the State Department. "Indirect support" should be provided by a separate "agency of educational, cultural, and scientific exchange." VOA should be a separate government-funded agency with a public-private board of directors.[13] White's heart was in higher education and strengthening exchange programs. In 1976 she left government to become President of Mills College in California.

Walter Roberts and the Stanton Panel

Walter Roberts succeeded White in USIA's top career post. He played a pivotal role in the organizational disputes that preoccupied Washington in the 1970s. Should USIA remain an independent agency that managed the State Department's educational and cultural activities overseas? Or should these activities be fully integrated into USIA? Should international broadcasting be independent? Should some of USIA's "information" activities return to State? Powerful actors in Congress, the executive branch, and civil society energized these debates. On the surface they were about structure. Fundamentally they were about unresolved conceptual and professional practice differences in information, exchanges, and broadcasting.

These issues came to a boil in 1973. A year earlier, Congress had authorized a Commission on the Organization of the Government for the Conduct of Foreign Policy with Ambassador Robert D. Murphy as chair. The "Murphy Commission's" task was to recommend ways to improve the formulation and implementation of US foreign policy. It created a committee headed by Rep. Clement Zablocki (D-WI) to look at organizational issues in public diplomacy. The Commission issued a massive seven-volume report in 1975.

The Advisory Commissions on Information and on Educational and Cultural Affairs, which had long wanted organizational changes, formed a separate Panel on International Information, Education, and Cultural Relations to conduct an independent study. The Center for Strategic and International Studies (CSIS), then located at Georgetown University under the leadership of its co-founder David Abshire, agreed to host the study with funding from US foundations. The respected former CBS President Frank Stanton, who for nine years had chaired the Advisory Commission on Information, chaired the group. It soon became known as the "Stanton Panel." Peter Krogh, Dean of Georgetown's School of Foreign Service, was vice chair. Walter Roberts resigned as Associate Director of USIA and left government to become the Panel's project director and guiding influence.

The Stanton Panel's members embraced the term "public diplomacy." Their goal was to convince the American people of its value and fundamentally change how the nation's international information, broadcasting, and exchange activities were organized. Their 85-page report in 1975 was radical in its assumptions, original in its recommendations, and consequential in its influence—both for what it did to lift up public diplomacy and for the strong opposition its ideas generated. It sparked profound disagreements in practitioner communities, lengthy Congressional hearings, and decisions by the incoming Jimmy Carter administration in 1977 to change USIA's name, mission, and structure.

The Panel began by distinguishing between *policy information* and *general information*. Policy information involves "the official articulation and explanation of U.S. foreign policy overseas." Its practitioners are policy advocates and advisors on foreign public opinion. General information meant "information about American society and American perceptions of world affairs." It includes "subjects traditionally named 'cultural' (such as music, literature, and film making) but also subjects of international and public politics (e.g., energy, inflation, economics, ecology, American history)." Its purpose is to create a favorable image of the United States and shape the context in which policies can be understood, "but no intimate connection to daily policy operations is necessary or desirable."[14] As Stanton argued:

> We insist upon the separation of this "policy information" from all "general information" about American culture for the simple reason that in this country, unlike authoritarian states, the government does not control culture. The genius of this country—political, economic, social, and especially artistic—lies in its intensely private and individualistic nature. For us to represent that society and culture overseas in a fashion which mixes it all up in the partisan advocacy and defense of our government's foreign policy is a betrayal of the very ideals we stand for. How can we expect foreign peoples to believe what we say about our free, open and private society when they hear it from someone whose primary job is to persuade them to support the latest US policy moves vis-a-vis Moscow or at the UN?[15]

It followed that the two categories of information should be located in different organizations. The Panel was influenced by Roberts' regard for how European countries "organized their public diplomacy efforts" in separate institutions. Roberts was particularly impressed with the British model: information in the British foreign office, culture in the British Council, and broadcasting in the BBC World Service. He understood, however, that funding for all three flowed from parliament to the foreign office, which channeled funds to the Council and World Service.[16]

For general information and exchange of persons, the Panel recommended an Information and Cultural Affairs Agency (ICA). The ICA should be autonomous with its own budget "for reasons of credibility, long-range vision, and work with the private sector." At the same time, it should have a "delicate but wholly feasible relationship with the Department of State" to ensure its activities would be harmonious with "long range objectives of U.S. foreign policy" and acceptable to Congress and the American people. It would be "personally defined and defended by the Secretary of State," which would appeal to partners in educational and cultural exchanges who "find State Department auspices familiar and prestigious." The Panel also called for merger of the two Advisory Commissions, continued use of the term "USIS" overseas for brand continuity reasons, and management of ICA's field programs by "Information-Cultural Counselors/Attaches."[17]

The Panel recommended an Office of Policy Information within the State Department headed by a Deputy Under Secretary for Policy Information and two Assistant Secretaries: one for International Press Relations and one for domestic Public Affairs. Overseas, "Press Counselors/Attaches" would carry out the work at large- and medium-sized posts; political officers would take on this role in small posts. The position of PAO would be eliminated.

VOA would become independent under a five-member Board of Overseers. Two Overseers would be the Deputy Under Secretary of State for Policy Information and the Director of ICA. State would provide policy guidance and be given "direct and unqualified access to broadcast time." Foreign Service officers would continue to be assigned to VOA for regular tours of duty. The Panel strongly opposed any connection between VOA and Radio Free Europe/Radio Liberty given their "completely different missions."[18]

The Panel's proposals drew widespread opposition, largely because if adopted USIA would cease to exist. Two Panel members objected. Leonard Marks abstained and Edmund Gullion wrote a strong letter in opposition, which the report printed with a rebuttal by Stanton. USIA Director Keogh and former directors were outspoken in their opposition. The US Advisory Commission on Information issued a report that opposed the Panel's recommendations and urged placing State's Educational and Cultural Affairs Bureau in USIA. The General Accounting Office (GAO) put out a report critical of the Panel, and US Comptroller General Elmer Staats personally voiced strong opposition in Congressional testimony.[19] Another strong opponent was George Meany, president of the AFL-CIO. The labor federation received grants from USIA and worked closely with the Agency's labor information officers.

These critics found a champion in Rep. Dante Fascell (D-FL), whose House International Relations subcommittee held nine days of hearings in 1977. Most witnesses opposed the Panel's findings.

Supporters of the Stanton Panel included CSIS's David Abshire, members of the Murphy Commission and its Zablocki committee, CU's John Richardson, America's exchange organizations, international broadcasters, and the American Foreign Service Association (AFSA). They were handicapped by a lack of strong backing from Henry Kissinger's State Department. State for decades had not cared enough about public diplomacy to work out whether it wanted it in or outside the Department. Adding to the Panel's difficulties was its unofficial standing as a privately funded group in a think tank housed at Georgetown University.

In the end, Stanton and Roberts did not prevail. USIA and its allies viewed the Panel's proposals as an existential threat and worked harder in opposition than the Panel's supporters. Although many in the cultural diplomacy community had long preferred an independent organization, they were content to keep headquarters activities for educational and cultural affairs in State. Broadcasters welcomed the Panel's call for an independent VOA but offered little beyond rhetorical support in Congressional testimony.

USIA's career practitioners went beyond defending organizational preferences. Roberts, a respected former colleague, and Stanton had advanced conceptual and operational issues that deserved scrutiny. Most objected that a conceptual divide between policy information and general information—and an operational distinction between policy advocacy and building mutual understanding—failed analytically and in practice. "The fields of 'information,' 'culture' and 'education' are not separable and mutually exclusive," Gullion, a former practitioner, wrote in his dissent. "All are part of public diplomacy and need to draw upon one another to be most effective and appealing."[20] A group of USIA's Foreign Service and Civil Service mid-career professionals signed a petition in 1976 calling for a "reasonable and workable public diplomacy" that would facilitate "understanding of American policy as well as the society and values from which it flows." They also rejected a reorganization that would "compound the fragmentation that already exists in Washington" and "create fragmentation overseas where none exists."[21]

A year later some 500 USIA practitioners signed a paper on "USIA and the Future of Public Diplomacy." FSIOs Robert Nevitt, Juliet Antunes Sablosky, Hal Morton, and Sandy Rosenblum testified on its findings in the Fascell hearings. Most practitioners, they declared, agreed on three principles. First, "it is impossible and artificial to separate policy information from general information. They are strictly interrelated and in talking with any informed public overseas, eventually you must get into the broader social, economic, and cultural context out of which policies emerge." To present policies persuasively, we must present American "society and its values with candor" and "responsible non-government opinion," which might "at times be critical of those policies."[22]

Second, they stressed the importance of "listening" and "dialogue." On this they were not at odds with Roberts and Stanton; they were challenging the Panel's "arbitrary and awkward" separation of information and cultural programs that deprived the United States of their mutually reinforcing value. "Both relate to policy; both relate to the society we represent." It was an interest-based mix of realism and idealism—a public diplomacy that was "politically sophisticated, culturally sensitive, [and] experienced in international communications."

Third, the FSIOs combined a holistic approach to public diplomacy with a professional culture "fundamentally different from that of the Department of State." The relationship between elite and mass audiences "is clearly complementary." Short-term and long-term goals are compatible; relations with "essential interpreters" in other societies achieve both. Public diplomacy is less risk averse than government-to-government diplomacy, they declared. "If caution is the preserve of the State Department, boldness must be that of USIA."[23] As USIA Counselor Donna Oglesby later observed, "our ties are a little wider, our earrings a bit bigger and bolder, and our rhetorical flourishes just a wee bit more in keeping with the spirit of St. Patrick's Day." This was more than a matter of diplomatic style. "We wanted to be present and engaged well beyond capital and major cities," she explained. This advanced foreign policy objectives and was useful to embassy colleagues. "We were better able to be weathermen knowing which way the societal wind was blowing."[24]

Employee unions weighed in. The American Federation of Government Employees (AFGE), which had long paid close attention to professional issues in its newsletters and Congressional hearings, vigorously opposed the Panel's recommendations.[25] AFSA, led largely by State Department diplomats, supported "full integration of the function of public diplomacy" into the Department.[26] AFGE's views were shared by most USIA Foreign Service officers and were key in its defeat of AFSA in a representation election in 1976. For the next 16 years, an AFL-CIO union represented USIA's Foreign Service.[27]

US International Communication Agency

Fascell's hearings settled most issues raised by the Stanton Panel, and a year later the new Carter Administration rejected its recommendations. NSC advisor Zbigniew Brzezinski informed the President that abolishing USIA, eliminating PAOs, and spreading their functions around "would make US information programs harder to manage and less amenable to White House influence." He added that "Opposition to Stanton's ideas has been widespread" and the report was produced at "the Georgetown Center [headed by David Abshire] where Kissinger is now located … with the aid of Walter Roberts, who has played a very partisan role."[28]

The administration submitted a different reorganization plan that Congress quickly approved. It transferred State's Bureau of Educational and Cultural Affairs to USIA, merged the two Advisory Commissions, and gave the Agency a new name that lasted four years: the US International Communication Agency.[29] Carter appointed two career Foreign Service officers, USIA's John Reinhardt and State's Charles Bray, as Director and Deputy Director.

Carter's mission statement, drafted by senior practitioners, made clear there would be no divide between policy information and general information. The Agency would (1) "encourage, aid, and sponsor the broadest possible exchange of people and ideas"; (2) "give foreign peoples the best possible understanding of our policies and our intentions, and sufficient information about American society and culture to comprehend why we had chosen certain policies over others"; (3) "ensure that our government adequately understands foreign public opinion and culture for policy-making purposes"; (4) "assist in the development and execution of a comprehensive national policy on international communications"; and (5) "conduct negotiations on cultural exchanges with other governments." It would undertake no "covert, manipulative, or propagandistic" activities. It would "put its faith in the powers of ideas" and assume "that a great and free society is its own best witness."[30]

Information, exchanges, and broadcasting were located in a single government agency for the next two decades. "Public diplomacy" gradually became the umbrella term of choice. The merged commissions were renamed the US Advisory Commission on Public Diplomacy, a move intended by Fascell and the Commission to give traction to the term. In a 1980 speech on "The Future of Public Diplomacy," Reinhardt displayed his field practitioner's perspective in a firm rejection of "'either-or' divisions":

> If we are going to strengthen—truly strengthen—mutual understanding between peoples, and if we are truly going to strengthen rationality in international dialogue, we must use wisely all the means of communication at our disposal. Those of us who work in educational and cultural exchanges should see the VOA news and commentary as in a sense extensions of our own activities, with all the critical interest and concern that that implies. And the press officer in a post abroad who enunciates official U.S. policy, should understand that the Fulbright and international visitor programs provide increasing numbers of his audiences with background and experience of our culture which brings that policy into perspective.

"We are obligated to listen," he declared, "and we are bound, in our two-way communication, to reflect the plurality of American culture. But as the official component of this country's public diplomacy, supported by tax dollars, we cannot cut ourselves loose from policy."[31]

The Reagan administration restored the name USIA in 1982 and kept the Carter administration's organizational structure. As veteran field officer David Hitchcock stated in a report written for CSIS at the end of Reagan's second term, "No recent or incumbent secretary of state, NSC advisor, or USIA director favors fragmenting USIA's responsibilities among several other agencies." The CSIS's ever-agile David Abshire introduced Hitchcock's paper saying it "dramatizes the need for coherence" and "is in exact harmony with CSIS's findings and recommendations."[32] Abshire, who had enthusiastically championed the Stanton Panel, now saw the whole issue as a politically inconvenient minefield.

Stan Burnett, an experienced FSIO knowledgeable on the politics of the US decision to deploy intermediate range nuclear (INF) missiles in Europe, provided a clear example of the connection between long-term cultural diplomacy and short-term policy advocacy. Survey research showed that most European "opinions on the INF issue were not the product of calculations about the issue itself; they came from deep within … experiences that had been untouched by information officers but in which cultural attaches may have been heavily involved." European attitudes were a product of the languages they spoke, where they had traveled, and "how they felt about the United States, the Soviet Union, and the new Europe's role in the world." Advocacy came along "at the last minute to make a small difference in the context of these predispositions." Anyone who thinks educational and cultural programs are not connected with fundamental national interests, Burnett argued, would be dissuaded quickly by "debating United States policy with the tough editor of a European daily newspaper."[33]

For practitioners in the field, Washington's organizational debates were largely irrelevant. Foreign publics did not care about them. Diplomats and broadcasters were regarded as voices of the US government and the American people. It mattered little which government organization paid their salaries.[34] What counted most for practitioners was how public diplomacy worked on the ground. Just give them tools, resources, and freedom to operate among the people and spare them Washington's turf wars.

Strengthening Professional Practice

USIA's FSIOs in the last decades of the twentieth century were in the vanguard of a revolution in diplomatic practice with implications still being worked through. Diplomacy with publics was becoming essential not just something nice to have. They self-identified as specialists doing work that called for particular skills and methods—and a separate Foreign

Service career track. They needed to be fluent linguists, adept at cultural interpretation, effective oral and non-verbal communicators, skilled at media relations and networking, informed on a broad range of foreign policy issues, and knowledgeable about American history, politics, economics, society, and culture. They also had to be competent program and personnel managers. FSIOs supervised large locally employed staffs in USIS posts, cultural centers, libraries, binational centers, and English teaching and educational counseling centers.[35] Locally hired foreign nationals provided indispensable knowledge about the host country and professional and administrative support. The best provided program continuity and links to the country's key political and cultural elites. They served as policy interpreters, covered for inept FSIOs, and often were the face of the USIS post.

Customs and regularities in what these practitioners were doing in the field became an accepted modus operandi. The "last three feet" of face-to-face conversation was their holy grail.[36] Although some cultural officers objected to colocation of cultural programs with media and information activities, most agreed with veteran PAO Hans "Tom" Tuch who stated, "The programs are not only interrelated but also interactive, depending on each other for reinforcement and support."[37] Ample evidence can be found in their stories, street smarts, and willingness to take political risks:

South Africa (1972)

I regularly traveled to Eastern Cape Province because there were several significant educational institutions in the region and also because of the political ferment in the region … [I was] told on my first visit that I would not be allowed to meet with students … I began to hear about Stephen Biko and to meet with some of his student associates and hear about SASO, the South African Student Organization, which was established by black students as an exclusively black student organization. Stephen and his SASO colleagues broke away from NUSAS, the National Union of South African Students … I tried to convince Donald [Woods, a former NUSAS vice president and editor of the *East London Daily Dispatch*] certainly the most courageous newspaper editor in South Africa, that he needed to meet with Stephen and his close associates and hear them out … Donald and I became fast friends from our first meeting … Donald met Stephen and they became very close. (Branch PAO Robert Gosende)[38]

Paraguay (1979–1982)

[I recall] programming the Orpheus Chamber Orchestra in [military dictator Alfredo] Stroessner's Paraguay. Orpheus performs without a conductor; a fact that challenged the authoritarian constructs of the regime's supporters to such an extent that the politics of our decision to bring Orpheus to Paraguay were subject to great editorial debate in the newspapers of the time. Orpheus was magnificent; democracy came to Paraguay. Not quite a neat cause and effect; but, I know deeply that Orpheus and the jazz groups USIS made a point of bringing to Paraguay during those years spoke volumes about our values and our support for those working for political liberalization in that nation. (PAO Donna Oglesby)[39]

Poland (1976)

Warsaw Press and Cultural Counselor James Bradshaw reported January 26 (Warsaw 0617–C) on the highly successful and effective showing of the feature film ONE FLEW OVER THE CUCKOO'S NEST (United Artists) January 25 in Warsaw … The Polish and diplomatic audience heaped "superlatives" on the film, not only for its artistic merit ("This film should get all the Oscars in the world"), but (in the Embassy's judgment) for "… its deeper philosophical implications," which were readily grasped by the audience and characterized by an important Polish film director who said, "This is a film about us. You have to be from this part of the world (referring to film director Milos Forman) to make such a film—in America." Aside from the impressive effect of CUCKOO'S NEST on the audience as a cinematic tour de force, the Embassy foresees a "multiplier effect" in pressure on the Polish authorities to obtain the film for public showing. The anticipated refusal of Polish authorities to import it for public release would "demonstrate another dimension to the Polish (government's) claims about importing so many Western films: that such acquisition is selective and politically regulated and not determined by any artistic merit." (Press and Cultural Counselor James Bradshaw)[40]

Indonesia (1973)

Indonesia … is an autarchic country, extremely tightly controlled … part of the tightrope walk was that part of our natural constituency were the intellectuals, the educators and the artists, all of whom were in the opposition. We developed a very close relationship with them … We had to do it without offending the government. We always had something on geography or something else innocuous. I traveled around Indonesia, went to the universities, and there was a great exchange. The thing was, at least in Indonesia, that we were not considered political officers or intelligence officers, and we were safe to be seen with. That was a big thing. And they would talk like a blue streak, and we were very well informed. (PAO Alexander Klieforth)[41]

At home, Civil Service employees included writers, film producers, radio broadcasters, exhibits creators, magazine editors, survey researchers, and administrators. Some achieved national reputations. Before he was a Pulitzer Prize–winning historian, David McCullough launched and edited USIA's Arab language magazine *Al-Majal*. Abe Brumberg, founding editor of the Agency's highly regarded academic journal, *Problems of Communism*, was a frequent contributor to *The Economist*, *Dissent*, and *The New York Review*. Filmmaker George Stevens, Jr. oversaw films such as *John F. Kennedy: Years of Lightening*, *Day of Drums*, and the Academy Award–winning *Nine from Little Rock*. Singer, folk song writer, and union organizer Joe Glazer, known at home and abroad as "labor's troubadour," was a labor information officer.

USIA's designer Jack Masey won worldwide acclaim for his exhibits on culture, technology, and American life. His model American kitchen exhibit provided the backdrop for Richard Nixon's "kitchen debate" with Nikita Khrushchev on the merits of capitalism and communism. He later engaged Buckminster Fuller to design the geodesic dome that was the main attraction at Expo '67 in Montreal. USIA's exhibits in the Soviet Union and their young Russian-speaking American guides were among the Agency's most successful Cold War programs.[42] In a forerunner to today's State Department Global Engagement Center, USIA's counter-disinformation unit, headed by Herbert Romerstein, responded to the Soviet Union's bogus claims that the United States invented HIV/AIDS in a lab at Fort Dietrich, Maryland, used biological weapons in Cuba, and supported a trade in baby parts for transplant surgery. USIA's survey researchers were a talent pool for America's leading opinion research organizations. Comptroller Stan Silverman, a master at explaining public diplomacy's complex budgets, was indispensable to Agency directors and lawmakers for decades. Some found government too confining for their creative instincts; most were intensely loyal to what was now a mature dimension of diplomatic practice.

In 1988 US ambassadors overwhelmingly affirmed the importance of public diplomacy in response to a worldwide survey conducted by the US Advisory Commission on Public Diplomacy. Many lamented being outspent by other countries; all claimed more opportunities than resources. Some addressed shortcomings—a systemic imbalance between operations and language training, a gap between media skills training and the growing demand for ambassadors and PAOs to explain US policies on television, and the adverse impact of State's policy of worldwide rotational assignments on the language proficiency and deep cultural expertise that could be achieved through multiple assignments to the same country or region. The Commission and GAO documented areas for improvement in their reports.[43]

Country Plans, Research, and Evaluation

Country plans. Beginning in 1952, annual country plans were used to connect field operations and budgets with foreign policy guidance from the White House and State Department and headquarters guidance on themes and methods. Plans were written by PAOs and approved by chiefs of mission. A typical plan began with a short essay on mission priorities, political and social indicators in the host country, and the bilateral communication relationship. An audience analysis section arranged institutions and audiences in two categories: media "gatekeepers" (journalists, editors, opinion writers) and cross-cultural interpreters (scholars, writers, artists, and government officials concerned with education and culture).[44]

Field officers often chafed at the process and questioned Washington's mandates to state specific objectives and measure performance outcomes. Bob Gosende liked the improvisational spirit that bloomed when officers had freedom to do what they thought best. "We got away with murder," he stated in an interview.[45] But, as the GAO cautioned, this approach allowed field officers to improvise and rationalize almost any activity.[46]

Planning mattered, but chance also played a role. As Brooks Spector put it, reflecting on South Africa's Soweto uprising, "virtually everyone who was in a noticeable leadership position was somebody we had identified as a potential grantee or a person with whom you would want to deal with on projects. When you do this job right, it is not that you predict the future, but … If you are good at it and you are a little bit lucky, you pick the right people to deal with."[47] Decades later, Canadian diplomat Daryl Copeland observed that in diplomacy's new ecology, "Doing things by the book … awaiting instructions, and referring to operating manuals rarely suffice." Diplomats must be "inventive and prepared to improvise" imaginatively outside embassy comfort zones.[48]

Most FSIOs came to appreciate country plans, especially the audience analysis section. The country plan might sound "dry and bureaucratic," Paul Blackburn recalled, but it "was widely praised as an excellent planning document" that was "never improved on over a period of two decades."[49] When audience analysis was marginalized after USIA's merger with State in 1999, it was much lamented by veteran practitioners.

Research and Evaluation. Diplomats acknowledged the value of audience research, and most knew that what others hear is more important than what diplomats say. As Al Hansen put it, quoting Trinidadian calypso: "Talk my talk, man And jump my way. Else I ain't listen, To nothing you say."[50] But few used opinion research consistently in operational planning. Many preferred to rely on intuitive judgments. Any field practitioner "worth his salt should know off the top of his head who the post is reaching and who it is not."[51] Opinion surveys and focus groups were administrative burdens and an easy target when budget cuts were required.

A similar gap between principle and practice existed in the evaluation of field programs. Few questioned holding field activities to a high standard. But, as with opinion research, lawmakers routinely failed to provide the funds needed to do evaluation well, and practitioners preferred to put scarce resources into operations. Many used quantitative measures to report successful *outputs*. Column inches of press placement. Numbers of visitors to information centers and exhibits. However, they generally resisted evaluating public diplomacy's *outcomes*, understood as impact on attitudes and behavior in host countries. Such impacts rarely could be linked to discrete USIS programs. Field officers knew outcomes often occurred over many years, not within annual planning cycles.[52] There was also the problem of justifying tax dollars spent on art, music, and cultural exchanges. "It all looks pretty fuzzy to a bean counter," Donna Oglesby recalled.[53] Practitioners also were skeptical, Nicholas J. Cull stated, "about the 'discovery' of evaluation by successive generations of administrators," who "were unaware of previous work in the field and unprepared to provide the resources necessary to evaluate the work effectively."[54]

By the end of the twentieth century, public diplomacy's Foreign Service practitioners were confident about their tools and methods and realistic about what could be achieved at home and abroad. There were disputes on best practices and priorities, occasionally bitter and personal. Debates on resource allocation pitted practitioners in Africa, the Middle East, and Latin America against those in Europe and Asia, whose budgets were larger due to Cold War geopolitics and higher operating costs. And they had not achieved full acceptance in the Foreign Service. The State Department had promised Congress in the 1960s that USIA's officers would receive equal treatment with State colleagues. But two decades later they still carried the FSIO label with its implication of second-class status, and few were assigned as ambassadors and deputy chiefs of mission (DCMs).

The Foreign Service Act of 1980, however, had signaled change. It eliminated the FSIO designation. USIA's field officers—who faced the same working conditions and hardships and who were tested, promoted, and retired under the same rules as State Department officers—were now Foreign Service Officers (FSOs). The Act also instructed State to ensure USIA's officers could "compete for chief of mission positions and have opportunities outside their area of specialization on the same basis as other Foreign Service officers."[55]

A Foreign Service culture dominated by State's political officers increasingly recognized public diplomacy's value, but as a specialized sub-set of diplomatic practice. It was still easy to sideline specialists in the competition for ambassadorial assignments. The ratio in 1983 was typical. USIA's officers constituted 19 percent of the Foreign Service. Of 86 career diplomats serving as ambassadors, 84 were State Department officers; two were from USIA. State's officers filled 128 DCM assignments; USIA's filled three. USIA's officers faced a dilemma. How could they reconcile their belief they were specialists only until it came time to compete for chief of mission assignments? Following USIA's merger with State in 1999, assignments across career tracks and appointments as chiefs of mission gradually increased.

Twentieth-century public diplomacy practitioners were reformers and builders. In the twenty-first century a successor generation of reformers learned to navigate the world of digitalized diplomacy and became increasingly wise to the folkways of the Department of State.

Notes

1. On the reform efforts of the "Young Turks," see Kopp, *Foreign Service*, 60–73. Although they were activists by temperament, Kopp contends their manifesto "was more conservative than radical." It praised the Foreign Service Act of 1946 as "an almost ideal instrument" that had become "a fiction."
2. Thomas W. Zeiler, "Historical Setting: The Age of Fear, Uncertainty, and Doubt," in *Reasserting America in the 1970s: U.S. Public Diplomacy and the Rebuilding of America's Image Abroad*, eds. Hallvard Notaker, Giles Scott-Smith, and David J. Snyder (Manchester University Press, 2016), 9–24.
3. Barbara White, "U.S. Government Overseas Communication Programs: Needs and Opportunities in the Seventies," July 1973, 1–5, 37, Box 1, Walter R. Roberts Papers, George Washington University Library.
4. White, "Overseas Communication Programs," 15–18.
5. I am grateful to Donna Oglesby for pointing out how foreign public awareness of the US government's duplicity on Vietnam affected the work of public diplomacy's practitioners in the 1970s. Email to author, August 26, 2018.
6. White, "Overseas Communication Programs," 55.
7. For a discussion of USIA's Japan innovations in the 1970s, see Paul Blackburn Oral History, interviewed by Charles R. Beecham, Foreign Affairs Oral History Collection, ADST, Arlington, VA.

8. Blackburn Oral History, interviewed by Charles R. Beecham, 29–30.
9. Alan Carter, "Viewpoint: Reflections and Episodes," *USICA World* (March 1979); Carter, explanatory note to author, April 11, 1979, author's copies.
10. Michael Schneider, conversation with author, June 2019.
11. White, "Overseas Communication Programs," Attachment, Paper #11.
12. White, "Overseas Communication Programs," 60–61.
13. Barbara White to Walter Roberts, working paper, August 23, 1974, Box 3, Walter R. Roberts Papers, George Washington University Library. On White's evolving views see Roth, "Public Diplomacy, 1952–1977," 374–375.
14. "103. Report of the Panel on International Information, Education, and Cultural Relations," *Foreign Relations of the United States, 1969–1976, Volume XXXVIII, Part 2, Organization and Management of Foreign Policy, Public Diplomacy, 1973–1976*, 6–7 (hereafter cited as Stanton Panel Report).
15. *Public Diplomacy and the Future: Hearings Before the Subcomm. on International Operations*, 95th Cong. (1977) (Frank Stanton to Elmer Staats, Comptroller General of the United States), 11–17.
16. Stanton Panel Report, 5.
17. Stanton Panel Report, 15–23.
18. Stanton Panel Report, 33. For analysis of the origins and report of the Stanton Panel, see Gifford D. Malone, *Political Advocacy and Cultural Communication: Organizing the Nation's Public Diplomacy* (University Press of America, 1988), 33–48; Roth, "Public Diplomacy, 1952–1977," 375–379; Arndt, *First Resort of Kings*, 480–498; and Cull, *United States Information Agency*, 340–345.
19. *1977 Twenty-Eighth Annual Report.* United States Advisory Commission on Public Diplomacy Reports; *Public Diplomacy in the Years Ahead—An Assessment of Proposals for Reorganization* (US General Accounting Office, 1977).
20. Edmund Gullion to Frank Stanton, March 7, 1975, printed in Stanton Panel Report, 80–83.
21. "1. Petition Prepared by Employees of the United States Information Agency," *Foreign Relations of the United States, 1977–1980, Volume XXX, Public Diplomacy*, Historical Documents, Department of State.

22. *Public Diplomacy and the Future*, 95th Cong. (1977) (statements of USIA FSIOs Robert Nevitt, Juliet Antunes, Hal Morton, and Sandy Rosenblum), 139–144.

23. *Public Diplomacy and the Future*, 95th Cong. (1977), 111.

24. Donna Marie Oglesby, "USIA and the Foundations of Public Diplomacy," remarks, conference on "U.S. Public Diplomacy: A Look to the Past, A Look to the Future," US Department of State, November 12, 2013, author's copy. Oglesby's "rhetorical flourishes" quote was first used in a speech to the American Foreign Service Association, March 17, 1994, email to author, January 27, 2018.

25. *Public Diplomacy and the Future*, 95th Cong. (1977) (statement of Bruce N. Gregory, President, American Federation of Government Employees, Local 1812), 120–126.

26. *Public Diplomacy and the Future*, 95th Cong. (1977) (statement of Patricia A. Woodring, President, American Foreign Service Association), 130–135.

27. Bruce Gregory, "Union Representation in the Foreign Service," paper presented at the International Studies Association, St. Louis, MO, March 1977, author's copy.

28. "22. Memorandum from the President's Assistant for National Security Affairs (Brzezinski) to President Carter," March 18, 1977, *Volume XXX, Public Diplomacy.* There is no evidence that Roberts and Stanton were motivated by partisan concerns. Throughout his career Roberts displayed a talent for working with both Democrats and Republicans with the test being how they might advance his views on public diplomacy and possibly his career. He became the only career Foreign Service officer appointed to the bipartisan US Advisory Commission on Public Diplomacy. Senator Claiborne Pell (D-RI) facilitated his nomination as an "independent." Roberts ended his career as a teacher, writer, and mentor to younger professionals. Most who remembered his work on the Stanton Panel still objected to his recommendations, but they respected his distinguished career and pioneering role in public diplomacy.

29. Reorganization Plan No. 2 of 1977, International Communication Agency, 91 Stat. 1636 (1977).

30. Quoted in Roth, "Public Diplomacy: 1952–1977," 389–391.

31. "203. Address by the Director of the International Communication Agency (Reinhardt)," *Volume XXX, Public Diplomacy.*

32. David I. Hitchcock, *U.S. Public Diplomacy* (Center for Strategic and International Studies, 1988), v–vi, 4.
33. Stanton H. Burnett, "U.S. Informational and Cultural Programs," in *Public Diplomacy: USA Versus USSR*, ed., Richard F. Staar (Hoover Institution Press, 1986), 77–79.
34. Foreign publics generally did not care whether US diplomats worked for the State Department, USIA, USAID, or some other civilian department and agency. They did care, as did public diplomacy practitioners, about a bright line distinction between diplomacy and the CIA's covert operations.
35. William A. Rugh, *Front Line Diplomacy: How U.S. Embassies Communicate with Foreign Publics* (Palgrave Macmillan, 2014), 25–35.
36. Rugh, *Front Line Diplomacy*, 65; William P. Kiehl, ed., *The Last Three Feet: Case Studies in Public Diplomacy* (Public Diplomacy Council, 2012).
37. Tuch, *Communicating with the World*, 43.
38. Robert Gosende, "Our Man in Pretoria: Three Tours in South Africa," in *Outsmarting Apartheid: An Oral History of South Africa's Cultural and Educational Exchange with the United States, 1960–1999*, ed. Daniel Whitman (State University of New York Press), 235–236, 239–240.
39. Donna Marie Oglesby, "Reflections: Mission and Meaning," remarks, Women's Action Organization Luncheon, Washington, DC, June 20, 199, author's copy.
40. "6. Information Memorandum From the Assistant Director, Motion Pictures and Television Service, United States Information Agency (Scott) to the Acting Director (Kopp)," *Volume XXX, Public Diplomacy*.
41. Alexander A. L. Klieforth Oral History, interviewed by Cliff Groce, Foreign Affairs Oral History Collection, ADST, Arlington, VA.
42. Shawn Dorman, "Up Close with American Exhibit Guides to the Soviet Union, 1959–1991," *Foreign Service Journal* 100, no. 4 (May 2023): 24–47.
43. Nicholas J. Cull, *The Decline and Fall of the United States Information Agency: American Public Diplomacy, 1989–2001* (Palgrave Macmillan, 2012), 1–13; *1989 Annual Report*, US Advisory Commission on Public Diplomacy Reports; *U.S. International Communication Agency's Overseas Programs: Some More Useful Than Others* (US General Accounting Office, 1982), 14–15.
44. Henderson, *Information Agency*, 209–217.
45. Quoted in Cull, *Decline and Fall*, 10.

46. *Communication Agency's Overseas Programs*, US General Accounting Office, 8–9.
47. Brooks Spector, "'Do You Sell Stamps or Don't You?' (Breaking the Cultural Boycott)," in Whitman, *Outsmarting Apartheid*, 48.
48. Daryl Copeland, *Guerrilla Diplomacy: Rethinking International Relations* (Lynne Rienner, 2009), 208.
49. Blackburn Oral History, interviewed by Charles R. Beecham.
50. Allen C. Hansen, *USIA: Public Diplomacy in the Computer Age*, 2nd ed. (Praeger, 1989), Epigraph.
51. *Communication Agency's Overseas Programs*, US General Accounting Office, 34.
52. Michael Schneider, email to author, May 30, 2019.
53. Oglesby, "Reflections: Mission and Meaning."
54. Nicholas J. Cull, "Preface: Evaluation and the History of U.S. Public Diplomacy," in *Data-Driven Public Diplomacy: Progress Toward Measuring the Impact of Public Diplomacy and International Broadcasting Activities* (2014), US Advisory Commission on Public Diplomacy Reports, 12.
55. *1983 Annual Report*, US Advisory Commission on Public Diplomacy Reports, 35.

8

Cultural Diplomats

The Department of State established a Division of Cultural Relations on June 28, 1938. It marked the beginning of institutionalized cultural diplomacy in the United States. Foreign Service officers, locally employed foreign nationals, Civil Service employees, and civil society partner organizations at home and abroad developed a community of practice with distinct norms, methods, and structures—never fully integrated into public diplomacy, never completely independent.

Cultural diplomacy's roots lie in the educational, artistic, and cosmopolitan impulses of American society. The Division's first director was the highly regarded University of Denver educator Ben Cherrington. We are not "a diplomatic arm or a propaganda agency," he explained. Our activities are "definitely educational in character" and will focus on "genuine cultural relations." Just as the United States has no "official culture," it will have no "culture ministry." Cultural exchange, Cherrington believed, was the responsibility of people acting through universities, foundations, publishers, museums, NGOs, and citizen volunteers. Government, at the "beck and call" of private interests, would broker useful foreign connections, provide information and resources, and occasionally administer programs.[1]

The State Department and its civil society partners shared a common goal: to facilitate cross-cultural connections between peoples that would

B. Gregory, *American Diplomacy's Public Dimension*, Palgrave Macmillan Series in Global Public Diplomacy, https://doi.org/10.1007/978-3-031-38917-7_8

foster dialogue and "mutual understanding." It was a goal envisioned in President Roosevelt's Good Neighbor policy. "The essential qualities of a true Pan Americanism," he declared in 1933, "must be the same as those which constitute a good neighbor, namely, mutual understanding, and through such understanding, a sympathetic appreciation of the other's point of view. It is only in this manner that we can hope to build up a system of which confidence, friendship and good-will are the corner-stones."[2] Department officials developed the principle in public statements and international conferences throughout the 1930s. USIA's historians summarized their logic:

> According to this view, cultural intercourse between nations leads to "greater mutual knowledge" of each other's people, institutions and policies; mutual knowledge leads to better "mutual understanding" of each other's aspirations, fears and motivations; mutual understanding leads to more "sympathetic understanding" of each other's point of view, orientation and conduct; sympathetic understanding leads to more "friendly relations" with each other across the political, economic and social spectrum; friendly relations lead to "friendly cooperation" in international affairs of mutual concern; and friendly cooperation leads to "a civilized world order under law"—and to world peace.[3]

From Private Initiatives to Government Organizations

As with public diplomacy overall, enthusiasm for cultural diplomacy correlated with wars and external threats. It had the advantage, however, of a deep base of support in civil society. In creating the Carnegie Endowment for International Peace in 1910, Andrew Carnegie's goal was no less than to "abolish war." Through peaceful settlement of disputes, war would come to be regarded "as disgraceful to civilized men" and discarded in the same way as dueling, slavery, and other social evils.[4]

The Endowment's founding president, Elihu Root, a corporate lawyer who had served as Secretary of War and Secretary of State, and his successor Nicholas Murray Butler, President of Columbia University, were pillars of America's East Coast establishment. Their combined 35 years of leadership shaped a philanthropic organization committed to resolving conflicts through international law and bridging cultural differences through people-to-people contacts. In 1919 the Endowment established the Institute for International Education (IIE) and created what historian Frank Ninkovich calls the "standard repertory" adopted by government cultural diplomacy—"exchanges of professors and students, exchanges of publications, stimulation of translations and the book trade, the teaching of English, [and] exchanges of leaders from every walk of life."[5]

Other organizations, notably the Rockefeller, Guggenheim, and Ford Foundations, and a host of universities and learned societies partnered with IIE to create a community of educators and philanthropists with shared beliefs. The power of education and free movement of ideas. Faith in American volunteerism. Distrust of government interference in intellectual and cultural affairs. A seamless connection between culture and trade. Belief in the power of functional internationalism apart from the state. Faith that educational and cultural exchanges would overcome differences and frictions leading to war.

Why then create government cultural diplomacy? Answers lie in the private institutions and threats from abroad. Each of the organizations had its own objectives, areas of geographic interest, and bureaucracy. Because they also engaged in domestic programs, internal struggles occurred over funding priorities. They were better at planning foreign programs than carrying them out. The foundations were affluent, but their resources were limited, and partnerships with government promised funding streams, coordination, and local support abroad. The early idealism of Roosevelt's Good Neighbor policy gave way to concerns about the growing influence of German and Italian immigrants with fascist sympathies in Latin America. US cultural diplomacy was driven by fears of Nazi Germany's political and economic penetration and propaganda activities in the region.[6]

State's Division of Cultural Relations

The Convention for the Promotion of Inter-American Cultural Relations, adopted by 21 countries in 1936, provided for the reciprocal exchange of scholars, graduate students, and teachers. The United States also signed two other agreements: the Chilean Convention on Artistic Exhibitions, providing facilities for government-sponsored artistic exhibitions, and the Peruvian Convention on Interchange of Publications, authorizing the exchange of official and library publications. Congress quickly ratified the first two treaties, which came into effect on September 16, 1937. Library of Congress objections to funding mandates and the scope of the agreement on publications delayed its ratification for two years.[7]

During the negotiations Assistant Secretary of State Sumner Welles had stated casually that the US Office of Education would "of course" manage implementation. But in the spring of 1938, Welles, by then Under Secretary of State, and Latin America division chief Laurence Duggan, the son of IIE's founding executive Stephen Duggan, thought otherwise. Given "the increasing importance of the promotion of cultural relations" and "the necessity for final policy decisions on all matters directly affecting the conduct of international relations to rest with the Secretary of State," Duggan argued, the Department needed a Division of Cultural Relations. It would mean "more effective control" over cultural activities arising from the treaties and "at some future time … the improvement of cultural relations with all countries of the world." Within three months the Division was approved by State, discussed informally with American stakeholders, funded by a special Congressional appropriation, and operating under the direction of Cherrington, who reported directly to Welles. The Department also created an advisory committee to provide "the experienced counsel" of distinguished Americans in the nation's "cultural and intellectual life."[8]

It was a remarkable decision for a foreign ministry not given to experimentation. Cautious officials repeatedly declared they would not trespass on the dominant role of private activities in cultural relations. Government would do no more than 5 percent of the work; private initiatives would comprise 95 percent.[9] Government's responsibility was to provide grants of public funds and use its good offices to assist, coordinate, and avoid duplication. Nevertheless, a half-century after France's Alliance Française led Europe in using culture for diplomatic purposes, the US government had made a commitment to cultural diplomacy. Its role grew as external threats continued and exchange organizations came to depend on public funding.

Partnership with America's educational and cultural organizations gave cultural diplomacy a deeply rooted base of support. Government funding expanded to a growing number of partner organizations that influenced the modus operandi of government practitioners. As a result, the litera-ture on US cultural diplomacy tends to focus less on field operations and more on politics, policies, organizations, reorganizations, and relations between government and civil society in the United States. Some scholars consider exchange of persons and managed export of culture to be sepa-rate core components of public diplomacy.[10] This book treats them as blended components within a cultural diplomacy community of practice that manages flows of people and knowledge in a variety of academic, professional, and arts domains.

Support at US missions came first from a handful of interested Foreign Service officers. Some observers had proposed appointing cultural atta-chés, but the Department firmly rejected the idea. One reason, Assistant Secretary of State for Administration George Messersmith explained, is "because we like to consider that every one of our foreign service officers in the field is chosen with adequate care so that he is considered in a degree a cultural attaché." But another reason was fear it would encour-age Germany and Italy to do likewise. Their cultural attachés in Europe were viewed as propagandists and "poorly concealed political agents" engaged in subversive activities. Britain and France had refused to accept them, and the term had "acquired a certain amount of odium."[11]

Soon after his appointment, Cherrington proposed that "two Foreign Service Officers with extensive experience in Latin America affairs be del-egated to serve as counselors in the field" to assist with "uncertainty as to what should be attempted locally and how to proceed." Welles and State's regional division rejected the idea of "roving cultural envoys." The need to "coach" US missions on their cultural relations responsibilities could be met with lengthy field visits by Washington officials. The Department also promised to encourage interest in cultural matters by Foreign Service officers who, as Cherrington now accommodatingly noted, had a duty to "represent the best of the cultural tradition of our country."[12]

War in Europe soon led State to adopt a more enterprising approach. By 1941 it was clear Foreign Service generalists could not handle the Department's greatly expanded field activities. In July State obtained Roosevelt's approval to establish "a non-career temporary Foreign Service Auxiliary" to (1) take "adequate countermeasures" against "the constantly shifting propaganda techniques of Axis countries" and (2) support "the very considerable expansion of the [Department's] cultural relations program in Latin America."[13]

By December State had appointed 11 cultural relations officers. Most were university professors, many with country or regional expertise. They were "American intellectuals by any definition," renowned cultural diplomat Richard Arndt observed. They were expected to have broad knowledge of social, educational, and cultural trends in the United States, but few thought they needed further preparation. Success in academe was assumed to mean competence in diplomacy. By the end of 1942 "high caliber cultural officers were in place all around the globe," and the designation "Cultural Relations Attaché" was approved in 1943.[14]

Their deceptively brief mandate was to strengthen cultural relations between the United States and other countries. But to this, Cherrington listed an astonishing array of duties in his "Outline of a Tentative Program for the Division of Cultural Relations," which the Department endorsed and circulated widely. The Division would implement international exchanges agreements; facilitate exchanges of professors and students; provide travel subsidies; engage in "personalized relationships"; cooperate with local universities and education ministries; make US visits of professional, educational, and cultural leaders "as purposeful as possible"; distribute books and documents; encourage translations; facilitate distribution of educational films; support English language teaching; advise on educational opportunities in the United States; advise and support cultural institutions; participate in international conferences; manage US participation in expositions; study and investigate propaganda and cultural methods; and encourage closer relations between unofficial organizations engaged in cultural and intellectual activities.[15] There were no training programs for these new diplomatic functions, no existing body of practice, and no consensus on what these practitioners meant by culture.

Cultural Diplomacy and Cross-cultural Internationalism

Culture is difficult to describe and measure. It is often modified by adjectives—high culture, popular culture, Asian culture, Western culture. By the end of the twentieth century, most cultural anthropologists had abandoned culture as a master concept for a way of life in a country or region. As constructivism took hold in the humanities and social sciences, they came to view cultures as domains for struggles over meaning in the knowledge, beliefs, behavior, and expressions of groups.

Despite its centrality to their profession, cultural diplomats pay little attention to what they mean by culture. For Welles and Duggan in the 1930s, "culture" was a sphere distinguished from, but "inextricably linked together" with, the "political" and the "economic." Cultures were intellectual domains of ideas and values—non-material patterns of thought, knowledge, and symbolic structures that varied among countries and regions. National cultures could be understood and expressed through exchanges of people and ideas. Cherrington basically agreed, but differed on culture's provincialism. "Culture in its essence is cosmic," he argued. To nationalize or regionalize culture would diminish its inherent universalism.

Philosopher Charles Frankel included material elements of culture. "'Culture,'" he wrote before his appointment as Assistant Secretary of State for Educational and Cultural Affairs in 1965, "stands for ... all the modes of behavior, preferences, ideas, and conscious or unconscious reactions to experience that are 'second nature' to a man or people." Looking at decades of twentieth-century US practice, Arndt concluded that most diplomats use "culture as the anthropologists do to denote the complex factors of mind and values which define a country or group, especially those factors transmitted by the processes of intellect, i.e., by ideas."[16]

In a survey of 51 active and retired practitioners in 2011, anthropologist Robert Albro found "tremendous variability" in their definitions of culture. Responses included 21 synonyms (world view, ideology, structure of meaning), 22 basic units of culture (values, beliefs, symbols), and 31 expressions of culture (music, art, film). Some voiced frustration with the question, arguing its meaning is obvious or that "culture" has multiple meanings ("It means what it means"). There was no common thread, he decided.[17]

Most practitioners accept a distinction between *cross-cultural internationalism* and *cultural diplomacy*—categories developed by Akira Iriye, a scholar born in Tokyo in 1934 who taught for many years at Harvard University. Cross-cultural internationalism, he argues, transcends national entities and consists of cognitive and material connections in all aspects of human endeavor: cultural, economic, political, and other "cross-national activities by individuals and groups." They pursue *private* interests in global networks of ideas, movements, and institutions. Their networks can generate stability, solve problems, create behavioral norms, and help counter pathologies of hard power. The domain also includes networks of criminals, corrupt businesses, and violent political actors. Cultural diplomacy for Iriye is an analytically distinct instrument of sovereign states that serves governance and *public* interests by supporting people-to-people exchanges predominantly through partnerships with civil society actors. His classic distinction is central to our understanding of cultural diplomacy.[18]

European scholars Jessica C. E. Gienow-Hecht and Mark C. Donfried find common ground among practitioners on four propositions. First, successful cultural diplomacy rests in part on the extent to which it is separate from political and economic agendas. Second, reciprocity and interactive structures increase cultural diplomacy's sustainability. Third, cultural diplomacy creates opportunities to avoid or minimize clashes between cultures. Finally, it fulfills short-term and long-term goals tied to state interests. The state "fills an important role by ensuring that the private agendas of civil society groups work in tandem with the national priorities and challenges."[19]

US cultural diplomats know their diplomacy is a government instrument related to foreign policy. Rose Hayden, a director of the American

Council on Education and a senior exchange official in the Carter administration, framed the idea nicely. "While scholars and other cultural representatives must be generally responsive to overall foreign policy goals, they can never be subordinated to them, nor mouthpieces for them. It is one thing to be in sight of the flagpole, another to be tied to it, to the long-term detriment of all."[20]

"What Do You Do, Mr. Brown?"

Most early practitioners were temporary hires from civil society who signed on for two years during World War II. Some remained through the war before returning to academe; a few became career diplomats. They brought enthusiasm and the norms and skills of higher education. They contended with the pecking order of US diplomats (political officers ruled) and variations in receptivity (missions in Latin America, China, and the Near East welcomed the newcomers; in Europe not so much). They encountered tensions between those who favored educational cooperation, others committed to spreading American values and democracy, and still others seeking to connect artists, scientists, and technical professionals. They navigated multiple lines of authority and endless bureaucratic struggles between "information" and "culture." It was a new kind of diplomacy—complex, challenging, and by turns frustrating and rewarding.[21]

These cultural diplomats spent their days improvising. Those who paused to reflect tended to focus on multiple encounters rather than strategies. John L. Brown had earned his doctorate from France's École Nationale des Chartres, written a critical anthology of American literature, served as a cultural officer with OWI, and continued as a highly regarded career CAO with USIA until the 1970s. He described his world with entertaining insight. "The Cultural Attaché is … a rather curious and complicated figure whose qualifications have never been satisfactorily defined, whose job description is the despair of orderly personnel people, and whose real accomplishments can rarely be measured."

Brown handled his formal requirements well—managing exchanges (a process "as complicated as a Dr. Seuss machine"), writing countless letters politely saying "no" to bizarre requests, and dealing with a host of problems "sent over to culture" because they didn't fit neatly in the embassy's political, economic, military, information, or administrative pigeonholes. But this was the price of freedom. What I do much of the time is "nonsense," he explained, in describing "the hallowed rituals of telephoning, conferring, meeting, lunching, exchanging memoranda, writing efficiency reports and giving evidence of effectiveness." The CAO soon learns "that if he wants to avoid the most stultifying aspects of his métier, he should make sure to get out of his office as much as possible." He travels thousands of miles outside capital cities. He accepts as many invitations as possible to "speak, to inaugurate, to 'manifest.'" He is under no "illusion the people he *really* should know will make an appointment to see him in his office. Professional 'friends of America' may—but few others." Pausing to wonder whether his self-selecting endeavors might be acts of self-indulgence, he rejected the idea. "No amount of theoretical knowledge can replace such contact with reality." When asked "What do you do, Mr. Brown?" he replied, "A cultural officer should not Mean but Be."[22]

Others took more openly instrumental approaches. Some were proponents of American exceptionalism. Sociologist Donald E. Webster, appointed to Turkey in 1943 as the first cultural attaché outside Latin America, saw his role as "secular missionary." "We want to have this small but strategically located country not only friendly to us but also able to think things through in patterns similar to our own in politics, economics, social welfare, and the many other phases of our culture." More cautiously, State Department Middle East expert Gordon Merriam wrote that "The Turks are not Americans and never will become Americans, but it will be a fine thing if we can help them to be good Turks." Cornelius van Engert, US minister in Kabul, wrote that American teachers would help "to make American idealism and justice and vision a positive and constructive force in the whole of Central Asia." This would work, he argued, so long as the Afghans believed in the "disinterestedness of our motives."[23]

Wilma Fairbank expressed the views of many CAOs. She had joined the Division in 1943 before becoming Cultural Attaché in China in 1945. Cultural diplomacy is in the "national interest," she wrote in an official history of exchange programs in China. But its methods should not entail the imposition of one culture on another. Cultural programs must serve the interests of both countries and be carried out "in the main" by indigenous cultural institutions outside government. Fairbank also advocated the crucial importance of personal relationships. Objectives can be learned in Washington, but what is "accomplished is more subtle and less easily assessed," she stated. "It involves determining what happened at the Point of Contact. How, for example, did Americans react to the Chinese scene or Chinese to the American? Were the ideas flowing in both directions absorbed or rejected by recipients at either end? Effectiveness at the various Points of Contact is the only effectiveness, in my view."[24]

State's cultural diplomacy during the war and its founding principles took hold with enduring effect. Programs were modified to meet wartime demands. Greater emphasis was placed on exchanges of journalists. CAOs distributed films and other materials developed by OWI. Cultural assistance turned to democracy promotion. Cultural diplomacy took on a fundamental duality that continues today. Its origins and core principles are rooted in an idealistic belief in the value of mutual understanding and reciprocity. Its budgets and programs thrive when framed in the context of external threats, national security, and the export of American democracy. As Frankel explained, what we do rests on a "tangle of purposes."[25]

Cold War Cultural Diplomacy

Things changed when Germany and Japan were defeated. Funding took a nosedive. Professors returned to their universities. The new global context, however, brought new demands for cultural diplomacy. It had a role in nation building (in occupied Germany and Japan), in bringing democracy to China (until 1949), in shaping goals and activities of the United Nations Educational, Scientific, and Cultural Organization (UNESCO), in assisting newly independent former colonies in Asia and Africa, and in ideological struggles with the Soviet Union.[26] Scholars were no longer recruited for temporary duty, apart from a few appointed to short-term assignments as "super CAOs." Partnerships continued with exchange program agencies, universities, learned societies, volunteer international visitor committees, and museums.

The Fulbright Act of 1946, the Smith-Mundt Act of 1948, and the Fulbright-Hays Act of 1961 provided permanent authorities and new organizational structures. Arguments for a minimal government role and a bright line between foreign policy and culture continued among cultural diplomacy enthusiasts, but the trends were obvious to all. Government provided most of the funding. IIE at this point in its history was almost wholly financed through government grants. The Cold War also meant cultural relations roles for the CIA and the US military. The idealism of State's Division of Cultural Relations continued, but cultural diplomacy was now an instrument in the worldwide struggle between democracy and communism. Historian Louis Menand was blunt about what was going on: "[C]ultural diplomacy just *is* propaganda. It puts a national brand on art and ideas."[27]

Senator J. William Fulbright's (D-AK) amendment to the Surplus Property Act of 1944 was crucial in institutionalizing cultural diplomacy. By making foreign currency proceeds from the sale of US property available for educational purposes within the country of sale, the Act provided operating funds without political opposition at a time when Congress was slashing appropriations for information and cultural programs. Diplomats began to negotiate binational agreements (the first with China in 1947), leading to a worldwide network in which foreign governments collaborated with US embassies and educational organizations in managing educational exchanges.

Fulbright had discovered the value of academic exchanges as a Rhodes scholar. Exchanges of scholars and students, he believed, would bring about "a fairer understanding" of other countries—and through the multiplier effect of international education "achieve changes in our manner of thinking about the world" and "how to avoid war in the future."[28] To this, however, he added a healthy dose of realism. My amendment "inherently has an element of promoting mutual security," he told the Senate Appropriations Committee. "I was looking for intellectual leaders who could be political leaders," he later recalled.[29] His rhetoric conflated mutuality with American values and educational exchanges as an "instrument of foreign policy, designed to mobilize human resources." The world will be influenced "by how well we communicate the values of our society."[30] Fulbright's means were those of an educator, not a propagandist. But his goals were pragmatic and interest-based. His mix of idealism and realism is at the core of the US government's flagship academic exchange program. Practitioners became deeply committed to "The Fulbright Difference" and its impact on the lives of hundreds of thousands of alumni in the United States and abroad.[31]

Although the views of some academics were too toxic for government, people-to-people exchanges overall were less vulnerable to partisan attacks than paintings and books. In 1946 the State Department sent exhibits of critically acclaimed abstract American paintings to Europe to counter views among intellectuals that America was a materialist culture devoted to comic books and cowboys. US officials viewed abstract art as expressive of American individualism and freedom, a fit response to Soviet realism. Congressional conservatives and Hearst newspapers soon attacked the paintings as obscene, radical, and un-American. President Truman joined in. "If this is art, I'm a Hottentot," he declared. The Department cancelled the exhibits, and Congress cut funding the following year.[32] For virtually every government-sponsored art exhibition after 1946, wrote Menand, "there were domestic complaints about the style of the art and the politics of the artists."[33]

During Congressional hearings in 1947, lawmakers found too many objectionable books and too few anti-communist books in American libraries. A State Department directive in 1949 bravely declared that "works of art, literature, science, or scholarship" should be judged on their "merit alone without regard to the political affiliation or leaning of its producers." Books by American communists or sympathizers should not be excluded arbitrarily, but included in a "balanced presentation" of the total culture. In an about-face three years later, however, the Department required US publishers to certify that books purchased for overseas libraries were not written by communists or fellow-travelers.[34]

Cultural diplomats mixed heroism and political compromise in dealing with inspections of US libraries in Europe by Senator Joseph McCarthy's (R-WI) staffers Roy Cohn and David Schine in 1953 and visits elsewhere by Republican lawmakers. CAO Alan Dodds resigned from the Foreign Service after defending USIA's libraries in West

Germany. He was later rehired. Frankfurt's America House director Hans "Tom" Tuch reported showing Cohn the location of Dashiell Hammett's mysteries on the shelves, evidence for Cohn that a communist author was in the collection. CAO David Nalle in Afghanistan concealed his Dashiell Hammett mystery in a desk drawer prior to a visit by Republican Senator William Knowland. Yale Professor Robin Winks, a Fulbright scholar in Malaysia, declined to give his lecture notes, based in part on assigned readings by Karl Marx, to the CAO for review. Fulbright effectively defended the Board of Foreign Scholarships in an hour-long exchange with McCarthy, who thereafter chose not to challenge him again.[35]

Historian David Caute cites estimates that State removed some 300 titles by 40 authors; cautious USIA librarians in the field removed many more on their own. The Agency's overseas library director Franklin L. Burdette removed Thoreau's *Walden* as the world celebrated the centenary of its publication, because it had influenced communists. Ambassador to Germany James Conant told McCarthy he favored taking any books by communist authors off the shelves of USIA's 40 libraries in Germany, observing, however, it would be best if done so without publicity.[36] These attacks led US officials to consider alternatives. Among the reasons for the CIA's covert funding of scholars, writers, and artists in the 1950s was awareness that it enabled government support for a spectrum of cultural expression with less political risk.

The Fulbright-Hays Act

Practitioners argued over funding tradeoffs between exchanges and other cultural activities. Protecting bureaucratic turf was one reason. But their differences also reflected the skepticism of many Americans about government's role in cultural relations. The Smith-Mundt Act had used the term "educational exchange" rather than "cultural affairs." It focused on "the interchange of persons, knowledge, and skills" primarily through "the two-way travel of students, professors, and other specialized personnel." The Act did call for "interchange of developments in … education, the arts, and sciences," but the arts and sciences were secondary.[37]

The Fulbright-Hays Act of 1961 consolidated scattered legal authorities and authorized new activities listed separately as "education" and "culture." Activities included tours by individuals and groups representing the arts, sports, "or any other form of cultural attainment"; US representation in cultural events and exhibitions; a "reverse flow" of foreign fine and performing arts to the US; centers for cultural and technical exchange; research on problems of educational and cultural exchange; US-sponsored scholarly meetings; exchanges in environmental science and promoting respect for religious freedom; and support for American studies, foreign language training, and area studies. A US Advisory Commission on Educational and Cultural Affairs replaced the US Advisory Commission on Educational Exchange.

The law cemented the headquarters location of cultural diplomacy in State's Bureau of Educational and Cultural Affairs (CU). But it kept cultural diplomacy's field operations in the hands of USIA's CAOs. One CAO lamented, "Eighty-five percent of my program comes from CU, but I am hired or fired, praised or damned, promoted or demoted, supervised or tyrannized—and above all transferred—by USIA."[38] Dual lines of authority generated calls to separate CAOs from USIA. Frankel argued, either transfer the CAOs to an upgraded CU led by an undersecretary or take cultural diplomacy out of State and USIA and place it under a quasi-public foundation for educational and cultural affairs. The Smithsonian Institution, British Council, and National Endowments for the Arts and Humanities were acceptable models.[39]

Goals, Means, and Organizations

Mutual understanding remains the cardinal precept of cultural diplomacy practitioners. The mission of the State Department's Bureau of Educational and Cultural Affairs, its website proclaims, "is to increase mutual understanding between the people of the United States and the people of other countries by means of educational and cultural exchanges that assist in the development of peaceful relations." The often-quoted definition of political scientist Milton C. Cummings elaborates that cultural diplomacy is "the exchange of ideas, information, art, and other aspects of culture among nations and their people in order to foster mutual understanding."[40]

But educational and cultural activities are also conducted, Frankel observed in 1965, "to impart or acquire skills and information; to affect or enter sympathetically into the beliefs, attitudes, and concerns of others; to share with people elsewhere objects of enjoyment or admiration in one's own society or in theirs."[41] His desire to "affect" others foreshadowed a willingness by cultural diplomacy practitioners to make a pragmatic case for resources by relating their goals to national security policies, repairing damage to America's image, and the benefits of exchanges to the domestic economy.

Means include cultural centers, Fulbright scholarships, young leader visits, youth exchanges, city-to-city connections, American studies, English teaching, student advising, and exchanges of athletes, journalists, scientists, artists, musicians, writers, and others in a broad range of fields. "The best cultural diplomats do what other diplomats do," Arndt summarized, but they "operate with different tools, with different audiences, in different time frames, and at a different pace."[42] This modus operandi raises two central questions. Is cultural expression self-evident to others?[43] What is cultural diplomacy's political intent and what are its political effects?[44] "The desire to break down cultural barriers is hardly innocuous or innocent," Frank Ninkovich declared. "Whatever … [cultural diplomacy's] actual impact, it is difficult to imagine a foreign policy activity that is more serious, even subversive in intent."[45]

Organizational preferences are a critical element in cultural diplomacy. Echoing Cherrington, Fulbright insisted that State manage exchanges not USIA with its taint of propaganda.[46] Close association with America's educational, philanthropic, scientific, and arts communities led cultural diplomats to favor private institutions in their work and a minimal role for government—apart from their constant desire for more public funding.

A presidentially appointed Board of Foreign Scholarships has determined broad policies and approved candidates for Fulbright grants since 1947. Its principal responsibilities are to act as a "firewall" to ensure merit-based competition and insulation from partisan politics and short-term foreign policy goals. In 1978 Congress required the US Advisory

Commission on Public Diplomacy to report annually on the academic integrity and non-political character of US-funded exchanges. Cultural diplomats, watchful professionals in IIE and other partner organizations, and respected educators and intellectuals appointed to manage exchanges—Ben Cherrington, Archibald MacLeish, Charles Frankel, Philip H. Coombs, and Alice Ilchman—worked to maintain protections for educational and discourse norms.

Cultural diplomacy rests on three pillars: commitment to long-term goals; exchanges of people, knowledge, and ideas; and structures that protect norms and methods. Summarized thusly, the road to an institutionalized community of practice seems coherent and harmonious. It was not. Its odyssey was marked by political vulnerabilities and the indifference or hostility of many Americans to a government role in cultural relations. Partisan controversies over ideas and forms of cultural expression were common. Norms of reciprocity did not fit easily with perceptions of American exceptionalism and the nation's global power projection. Reorganizations and competition for resources added to the turbulence.

Making the Hard Case for the Soft Stuff

A controversial budget decision in the early Reagan administration was a turning point for cultural diplomacy. Foreign policy conservatives came to Washington in 1981 determined to cut government funding and respond forcefully to the Soviet Union's propaganda and active measures. USIA director Charles Z. Wick initiated a campaign labeled "Project Truth." It featured rapid response "Soviet Propaganda Alerts" distributed by Herbert Romerstein, the Agency's counter-disinformation officer, aggressive advocacy programs, a documentary film "Let Poland Be Poland," and a wireless magazine, *Dateline America*. To pay for these initiatives, while absorbing a White House–mandated budget reduction of $67 million, Wick put the burden on exchanges. Grants would be cut by 40 percent. Exchanges in 120 countries would be trimmed to 59 countries. Annual International Visitor numbers would drop from 1500 to 750. Humphrey Fellowships and support services for foreign students in the United States would be terminated. Fulbright scholarships, managed by non-profit partner organizations, would be absorbed by the Agency. Cuts in VOA, however, would be a modest $1.8 million. The rationale: large reductions would permanently damage "staff intensive" VOA, whereas grants for exchanges could be restored later.

Outrage from the exchange community was widespread and effective. Harvard University President Derek Bok proclaimed there is no better government investment "dollar for dollar" than exchanges of scholars. University of Minnesota President Peter Magrath protested the demise of the Humphrey program. American University President Richard E. Berendzen, Chairman of the American Council on Education's National Commission on Foreign Student Policy, argued the cuts would come "very close to ending the Fulbright program," adding, "I can't tell you how strongly those of us in higher education feel about this."

Republican Senator Lowell Weicker led a bipartisan coalition urging a 9 percent increase for exchanges. Democratic Senator Claiborne Pell added an amendment to double the exchange budget in five years and protect it from use for unintended purposes. The US Advisory Commission on Public Diplomacy, led by Edwin J. Feulner, Jr., proclaimed US public diplomacy was "woefully underfunded" and lagged behind the spending of other countries. Wick got the message. He made larger budgets for public diplomacy a hallmark of his tenure and declared his increases in exchange funding exceeded those of the Carter administration.[47] The 1980s and early 1990s saw the highest sustained levels of constant dollar spending in the history of US public diplomacy.[48]

The United States had often prioritized information programs over exchanges. Universities and non-profit organizations had protested before. It was a familiar routine. This time two things were different. First, cultural diplomacy's supporters were done with ad hoc responses. They needed a powerful and permanent organization to represent their interests in Washington. Second, although they preferred to talk about mutual understanding, they knew arguments linking exchanges to economic and national security concerns are more convincing to lawmakers. Librarian of Congress James Billington, a former Fulbright scholar, later observed, we needed "to make the hard case for the soft stuff."[49]

Non-profit groups committed to educational exchanges and foreign language study had formed an International Exchange Liaison Group in

1980. Among the leaders were Alan H. Kassof (International Research and Exchanges Board), Cassandra "Cassie" Pyle (Council for International Exchange of Scholars), Wallace Edgerton (Institute of International Education), John Richardson (Youth for Understanding), Arthur Dudden (Fulbright Alumni Association), Rose Hayden (National Council for Foreign Language and International Studies), Jack W. Peltason (American Council on Education), and Charles F. McCormack (Experiment in International Living).

A second group, the International Exchange Association, represented Sister Cities International, Partners for the Americas, Rotary International, and other organizations committed to citizen exchanges. The two coalitions coordinated their efforts during the 1980s and eventually merged in 1993 to form the Alliance for International Educational and Cultural Exchange (later renamed the Alliance for International Exchange). The Alliance became the public policy voice of the US educational and cultural exchange community.[50]

Its unity of effort and grassroots constituencies became a powerful combination. A small Washington office staff afforded direct access to lawmakers and executive branch agencies. Under the leadership of its long-time executive director Michael McCarry, a former USIA Foreign Service officer, the Alliance learned that mobilizing supporters in meetings with lawmakers in Congressional districts made a difference when they returned to vote on Capitol Hill. Building on the Fulbright and Humphrey Fellowship models it encouraged new exchange programs named for leading lawmakers in both political parties.[51] It sponsored political advocacy training and hosted forums where members collaborated and shared ideas. Working with Congressional staffs and government officials, the Alliance used its expertise to influence legislation and policies on funding, visas, grant management, staffing, program quality, participant selection safeguards, and other issues of broad interest to the exchange community.

Practitioners turned readily to making "the hard case" for soft power. The founding statement of the International Exchange Liaison Group declared that "exchange programs are of critical importance to the security and competence of the United States in world affairs." If Americans are to have the knowledge needed to compete in global commerce, counter authoritarian ideologies, and reverse declines in the nation's influence abroad, they must dramatically increase their investment in exchanges. They amplified the argument with global comparisons: the United States was significantly outspent by foreign adversaries (Soviet "expenditures are … at least four times U.S. investments") and allies (citing GAO reports showing France, Germany, Britain, and Japan spent more on exchanges). They pointed to huge increases in the US military budget. "If the erosion of U.S. influence and power internationally is serious enough to necessitate a $33 billion increase in defense spending," they asked, "is not an equally substantial increased investment called for to provide an American 'arsenal of ideas'?"[52]

Cultural diplomacy's pragmatists tailored their arguments to the moment. Retired CAO Yale Richmond attributed the Cold War's outcome in great measure to Soviet exchanges with the West. Joseph Nye drew a link between Russian intellectual Alexander Yakovlev's year studying democratic pluralism at Columbia University and his influence on Soviet leader Mikhail Gorbachev's glasnost (openness) and perestroika (restructuring). Exchanges could help temper hostilities in Bosnia and Kosovo and support democracy in Eastern Europe and the former Soviet Union. After 9/11 cultural diplomacy was a way to influence societies that support terrorism and offset anti-Americanism. As the Alliance's board chair Kenton Keith put it, "To win the war on terrorism … we must also engage the Muslim world in the realm of ideas, values, and beliefs … [through] exchange components of our public diplomacy."[53]

Practitioners also fine-tuned their pragmatism in the context of diplomacy. Exchanges create "a foundation of trust" diplomats "can build on to reach political, economic, and military agreements." They enlarge circles of cultural interpreters, build relations that endure beyond changes in governments, and create a "neutral platform" for contacts with individuals not reachable through embassy functions. Shared values encourage others to give the US "the benefit of the doubt on specific policy issues or requests for collaboration."[54]

For some practitioners, cultural diplomacy masks political intent. "One of the best arguments for cultural and educational programs," career diplomat William Rugh observed, is they "can at least appear to be non-political and be carried out despite political hostility." Scott-Smith writes, "The more a program functions as if it is nonpolitical in intent, the more it can achieve a political effect." Others seemed to rule out politics altogether. President Clinton's White House Conference on Culture and Diplomacy managed simultaneously to hold the views that "'Culture' is a central element of all relations among peoples because it relates to human creativity beyond the scope of politics" and that "cultural programs are central … to the success of American foreign policy."[55]

Within the Alliance, members have competing priorities. More money for academic exchanges can reduce funding for the arts and professional exchanges. Priority for Western Europe and Asia can mean less funding for Africa and Latin America. Tensions can occur within exchange categories such as in the Fulbright program: faculty vs. students, humanities vs. science, researchers vs. lecturers.[56] The Alliance focuses primarily on educational and visitor exchanges, including visitors on J-1 Visas in the Exchange Visitor Program: camp counselors, au pairs, and students in temporary summer work jobs.[57] It gives priority attention to exchanges managed by the State Department and USAID rather than other departments and agencies.

Cultural diplomacy's practitioners have learned to operate politically at home in ways that strengthen their capacity to act with political intent abroad. Americans typically do not lobby Congress demanding more support for State Department and embassy information programs. They frequently do lobby Congress to support Fulbright scholarships, international visitor programs, and a host of other educational and cultural exchanges.

Cultural Diplomacy's Limitations

Although cultural diplomacy's outcomes are inherently hard to evaluate, practitioners provide countless examples of those who say a "Fulbright grant changed my life." They point to cultural diplomacy's endurance in human history as testimony to its self-evident value. Wedded enthusiastically to this narrative, they devote less attention to arms-length evaluation and cost/benefit implications. Anecdotes and ubiquitous lists of internationally known scholars, artists, and political leaders who participated in exchange and visitor programs may impress casual observers, but they are not systematic evidence of effectiveness.[58]

Consider first that inter-personal contact can reinforce negative perceptions and stereotypes. Often it is precisely because people are closely connected that hostility and competing values become more evident. Next-door neighbors at odds. Faculty departments warring like Capulets and Montagues. Divorce courts filled with people who know each other well. Sayyid Qutb, the Egyptian Brotherhood activist whose ideas inspired Al Qaeda's leaders and a generation of Islamist radicals, attended colleges in Colorado and Washington, DC. He encountered a culture that amplified his alienation and hostility toward the West. US diplomat Moorehead Kennedy, writing of his experience as a hostage in Tehran, described the ambivalence of Iran's English-speaking guards. Many had studied in the United States. One was "returning to Georgetown." They mixed resentment of an imperial America and its "great crimes" with admiration for its people and educational opportunities.[59]

Like all forms of power, cultural diplomacy is context dependent. It is more likely to succeed when others share a country's cultural values and are attracted to its institutions and practices—its forms of governance, languages, business opportunities, higher education, technological innovation, and entertainment products. Success is less likely when groups are divided by hostilities or when in-groups seek to strengthen their identity and self-esteem through out-group bias—French laws that prohibit Islamic headscarves in schools, Iran's fatwa condemning the author Salman Rushdie.

Situational factors range from macrocultural characteristics to the project goals and experiences of participants. In a study of US foreign leader visitor programs, Giles Scott-Smith concluded that, because exchanges "are primarily a potent weapon for sustaining the status quo rather than changing it," they have been more successful in Europe and Latin America than in countries where status, hierarchy, and tradition generate resistance to cultural penetration. In a longitudinal study of military exchanges, Carol Atkinson found successful exchanges (defined as outcomes that benefit the values and policies of the sponsor) tend to occur when participants' social interactions are extensive during the exchange experience, when a sense of community exists between participants and their hosts, and when participants return to influential positions in their home country.[60]

In training courses at the State Department's Foreign Service Institute, diplomat Glen Fisher, who had a teaching background in the social sciences, examined reasons why systematic understanding of the mindsets of *all* parties in an exchange situation enhances the quality of the experience. Many diplomats, he argued, are problematically inattentive to their own mindsets and culture. Retired US diplomat John Dickson has written powerfully about the "history shock" that occurs when diplomats confront differently constructed understandings of shared history. Among many examples: US and Mexican memories of the 1846–1848 "War of North American Intervention"; Nigerian views of US civil rights history through the prism of Malcolm X and Black consciousness; Haitian memories of long-withheld US recognition of its independence in 1804 due to slavery issues.[61] When pressed, most cultural diplomats acknowledge the validity of these mindset considerations, but they tend not to become part of their DNA.

Evaluations of exchanges and cultural programs have existed since the mid-twentieth century. US agencies contracted for evaluation studies immediately after World War II and occasionally thereafter. Small evaluation units (long a fixture in USAID) were not a continuing presence in USIA and the Department of State until the 1990s. Cultural diplomacy practitioners typically turn to evaluation when pressured by lawmakers, White House budget examiners, and advisory panels.

What accounts for this persistent lack of enthusiasm for evaluation? Field concerns about privacy and invasive data collection in surveying exchange alumni is one explanation. Methodology weaknesses in many studies are another. Studies by International Research Associates for the State Department for five years in the 1950s examined whether exchanges introduce, reinforce, or broaden "skills, information or attitudes" and whether they lead participants to "disseminate newly acquired information and ideas in their native lands." Researchers found evidence of success in "scholastic achievements, professional competence, and work proficiency." But numerous factors beyond the reach of their research designs were not studied. "The influence of personality factors, the expectations and motivations of selectees, different approaches in pre-trip and post-trip orientation, variations in programming and length of stay," and other variables, made it impossible to reach even modest conclusions as to whether experiences were pivotal in changing views and behavior.[62]

In her research on 24 studies of the US international visitor program conducted between 1951 and 1973, Sherry Mueller found they were uncoordinated, methodologically deficient, and lacked relevance to practitioners. They were not based on representative samples or data collected over time. They ignored the effects of exchanges on Americans, despite their goal of fostering mutual understanding and two-way communication.[63] Mueller's finding that these studies did not reflect the academic and industry research standards of the day foreshadowed an enduring pattern. Scholars and advisory groups nearly 50 years later agree that research and evaluation are still limited by broad structural constraints and not on a par with best practices in civil society. Many practitioners do not require evaluation as a pre-condition for program grants or designate funds for evaluation within grants at levels consistent with private sector standards.[64]

Cultural diplomacy is now a whole of government effort with wide variations in sponsoring agencies, program categories, and numbers of participants. State Department exchanges are a minority share of the total US investment in international exchange and training programs carried out by USAID, Defense, Health and Human Services, Energy, and other departments. Systematic cross-program planning is rare. In budget requests, ambassadors, senior officials, and program managers seek "more" for program silos. White House budget examiners and lawmakers respond by raising or lowering program budgets based on existing and anticipated resource levels rather than crosscutting assessments of which programs in which agencies are best suited to achieve results in a particular country or region. Practitioners find it difficult to transfer funds to meet unexpected contingencies, and easy to multiply lots of "drop in the bucket" activities. Seldom are priorities grounded in "more of this, less of that" choices between cultural diplomacy and other instruments in diplomacy's public dimension.

Cultural diplomats have constructed a community of practice with a distinct modus operandi in US diplomacy's public dimension—an accepted and respected instrument that connects government and society, values and power. They prefer the rhetoric of mutual understanding, but they justify what they do with a pragmatic vocabulary. Frank Ninkovich illuminates with great insight the evolution of America's "diplomacy of ideas." He goes too far, however, when he asserts US cultural diplomacy's justification has "never been geopolitical in any traditional sense," but rather it is "based at bottom on an act of faith."[65] Cultural diplomacy is not just an act of faith; it can be evaluated and judged empirically. It is not the cross-cultural internationalism of cosmopolitans pursuing private interests; it is an instrument of governance and diplomatic practice that supports public interests.

Notes

1. Quoted in Ninkovich, *Diplomacy of Ideas*, 31–32.
2. Franklin D. Roosevelt, "Address on the Occasion of the Celebration of Pan American Day, Washington," April 12, 1933, *American Presidency Project*.
3. Lawson and Gregory, *Information Agency*, 1-2-6–1-2-7.
4. "Mr. Carnegie's Letter to the Trustees," December 14, 1910, Carnegie Endowment for International Peace, website.
5. Ninkovich, *Diplomacy of Ideas*, 12. On the cultural internationalism of America's philanthropic foundations, see Richard Pells, *Not Like Us: How Europeans Have Loved, Hated, and Transformed American Culture Since World War II* (Basic Books, 1997), 22–31.
6. Graham, *Culture and Propaganda*, 51–55.
7. Lawson and Gregory, *Information Agency*, 1-2-8–1-2-12.
8. Lawson and Gregory, *Information Agency*, 1-2-12–1-2-16. Congress gave the Division an initial budget of $27,920 for a staff of five professionals, two clerk-stenographers, and one messenger.
9. On the creation and early work of the State Department's Division of Cultural Relations, see Charles A. H. Thomson and Walter H. C. Laves, *Cultural Relations and U.S. Foreign Policy: A New Dimension in Foreign Relations, Education, Science, Art, and Technical Skills* (University of Indiana Press, 1963), 36–46; Philip H. Coombs, *The Fourth Dimension of Foreign Policy: Educational and Cultural Affairs*, with foreword by J. W. Fulbright (Harper & Row, 1964); Charles Frankel, *The Neglected*

Aspect of Foreign Affairs: American Educational and Cultural Policy Abroad (Brookings, 1965); Ruth McMurry and Muna Lee, *The Cultural Approach: Another Way in International Relations* (University of North Carolina Press, 1947), 208–229; J. Manuel Espinosa, *Inter-American Beginnings of U.S. Cultural Diplomacy, 1938–1948* (Department of State Publication 8854, 1976), 49–60; and Lawson and Gregory, *Information Agency*, 1-2-13–1-2-21, 1-3-38–1-3-80.

10. Nicholas J. Cull, "Public Diplomacy: Taxonomies and Histories," *The Annals of the American Academy of Political and Social Science* 616, no. 1 (March 2008): 31–54.

11. Quoted in Lawson and Gregory, *Information Agency*, 1-3-59–1-3-69; Espinosa, *Inter-American Beginnings*, 98.

12. Espinosa, *Inter-American Beginnings*, 128–129, 142; Lawson and Gregory, *Information Agency*, 1-3-64–1-3-65.

13. Lawson and Gregory, *Information Agency*, 1-3-67–1-3-69.

14. Arndt, *First Resort of Kings*, 123.

15. Espinosa, *Inter-American Beginnings*, 124–129; Lawson and Gregory, *Information Agency*, 1-2-16–1-2-19.

16. For the definitions of Welles, Duggan, and Cherrington, see Ninkovich, *Diplomacy of Ideas*, 24, 30; Frankel, *Neglected Aspect*, 67; and Arndt, *First Resort of Kings*, xviii.

17. Robert Albro, "Models as Mirrors or Cultural Diplomacy?" *CPD* (blog), February 15, 2012, http://uscpublicdiplomacy.org/blog/models-mirrors-or-cultural-diplomacy.

18. Akira Iriye, *Cultural Internationalism and World Order* (Johns Hopkins University Press, 1997), 1–12. See also Giles Scott-Smith, "Cultural Diplomacy," in *Global Diplomacy: Theories, Types and Models*, eds. Alison R. Holmes and J. Simon Rofe (Westview Press, 2016), 176–190.

19. Jessica C. E. Gienow-Hecht and Mark C. Donfried, "The Model of Cultural Diplomacy," in *Searching for a Cultural Diplomacy*, eds. Jessica C. E. Gienow-Hecht and Mark C. Donfried (Berghahn Books, 2010), 13–29.

20. *Public Diplomacy and the Future*, 95th Cong. (1977) (statement of Rose L. Hayden, Director, American Council on Education), 429.

21. On the qualifications and work of the US government's first cultural officers, see Arndt, *First Resort of Kings*, 123–141 and Frankel, *Neglected Aspect*, 9–23.

22. John L. Brown, "But What Do You Do?" *Foreign Service Journal* 41, no. 6 (June 1964): 23–25; Arndt, *First Resort of Kings*, 126, 357–359. For a highly skilled practitioner such as Brown, laissez-faire cultural diplomacy worked well. Lesser mortals could succumb to doing what might be easiest or most enjoyable.

23. Webster, Merriam, and Van Engert are quoted in Ninkovich, *Diplomacy of Ideas*, 53–54.

24. Wilma Fairbank, *America's Cultural Experiment in China, 1942–1949* (Department of State Publication 8839, 1976), vii–ix, 5.

25. Frankel, *Neglected Aspect*, 80–98.

26. On cultural diplomacy and UNESCO, see James Marshall, "International Affairs: Citizen Diplomacy," *American Political Science Review* 43, no. 1 (February 1949): 83–90.

27. Louis Menand, *The Free World: Art and Thought in the Cold War* (Farrar, Straus and Giroux, 2021), 221.

28. J. W. Fulbright, foreword in Coombs, *Fourth Dimension*, ix–xiii.

29. Quoted in Leonard R. Sussman, *The Culture of Freedom: The Small World of Fulbright Scholars* (Rowman and Littlefield, 1992), 18.

30. J. W. Fulbright, foreword in Coombs, *Fourth Dimension*, ix, xi.

31. On the origins of the Fulbright program, see Ninkovich, *Diplomacy of Ideas*, 140–144 and Thomson and Laves, *Cultural Relations*, 59–63. For essays by scholars and diplomats on the life-changing effects of Fulbright exchanges, see Richard T. Arndt and David Lee Rubin, eds., *The Fulbright Difference, 1948–1992* (Transaction Publishers, 1993) and David Nalle, "Changing the World," *Foreign Service Journal* 71, no. 3 (March 1994): 45–47.

32. Greg Barnhisel, *Cold War Modernists: Art, Literature, and American Cultural Diplomacy* (Columbia University Press, 2015), 55–58; Graham, *Culture and Propaganda*, 147–149.

33. Menand, *Free World*, 220.

34. *Overseas Information Programs of the United States, Hearing before a Subcomm. of the Committee on Foreign Relations*, 83rd Cong. (1954) (Department of State Directive, August 18, 1949 Canceled, October 7, 1952), 1600–1601, https://babel.hathitrust.org/cgi/pt?id=uc1.aa0008077075&view=1up&seq=3 (accessed May 16, 2023).

35. On Dodds, Nalle, and Winks, see Arndt, *First Resort of Kings*, 155, 461–462. On Tuch, see Tuch, *Communicating With the World*, 19. On Fulbright, see Thompson and Laves, *Cultural Relations*, 105.

36. David Caute, *The Dancer Defects: The Struggle for Cultural Supremacy During the Cold War* (Oxford University Press, 2003), 26–27. On McCarthyism and cultural diplomacy, see Pells, *Not Like Us*, 76–82; Arndt, *First Resort of Kings*, 462–463; Thompson and Laves, *Cultural Relations*, 99–105; and Tuch, *Communicating with the World*, 18–22.

37. Thomson and Laves, *Cultural Relations*, 67–68.

38. Quoted in Richard T. Arndt, "Public Diplomacy, Cultural Diplomacy, The Stanton Commission Revisited," in *Rhetoric and Public Diplomacy: The Stanton Report Revisited*, ed. Kenneth W. Thompson (University Press of America, 1978), 88–89.

39. Frankel, *Neglected Aspect*, 138–146.

40. Bureau of Educational and Cultural Affairs, US Department of State, https://eca.state.gov/about-bureau; Milton C. Cummings, Jr., *Cultural Diplomacy and the United States Government: A Survey* (Americans for the Arts, 2003), https://www.americansforthearts.org/sites/default/files/MCCpaper.pdf (accessed May 16, 2023).

41. Frankel, *Neglected Aspect*, 71.

42. Arndt, *First Resort of Kings*, 546–547.

43. Robert Albro, "Cultural Diplomacy's Representational Conceit," *Public Diplomacy Anthropologist* (blog), March 2012, https://robertalbro.com/2012/03/cultural-diplomacys-representational-conceit/ (accessed May 16, 2023).

44. Giles Scott-Smith, "Mapping the Undefinable: Some Thoughts on the Relevance of Exchange Programs Within International Relations Theory," *The Annals of the American Academy of Political and Social Science* 616, no. 1 (March 2008): 173–195.

45. Frank Ninkovich, *U.S. Information Policy and Cultural Diplomacy* (Foreign Policy Association, 1996), 44.

46. Hart, *Empire of Ideas*, 24.

47. Rushworth M. Kidder, "The Selling of America – on a Tight Budget," *Christian Science Monitor*, November 17, 1981; Barbara Crossette, "Budget Cuts Threaten Cultural Exchange Projects," *New York Times*, October 24, 1981; Murray Marder, "U.S. Sharpening Information Policy Overseas," *Washington Post*, November 10, 1981; "Minutes of Meeting December 16, 1981," US Advisory Commission on Public Diplomacy, author's copy; Cull, *United States Information Agency*, 406.

48. *2017 Comprehensive Annual Report on Public Diplomacy & International Broadcasting*, US Advisory Commission on Public Diplomacy Reports, 14–15.
49. James H. Billington, "The Intellectual and Cultural Dimensions of International Relations," remarks, President's Committee on the Arts and the Humanities, Washington DC, February 28, 1991.
50. Alliance for International Exchange website, http://www.alliance-exchange.org.
51. These include the Benjamin A. Gilman International Scholarship Program, the Mike Mansfield Fellowship Program, Kennedy-Lugar Youth Exchange and Study (YES) program, the Paul Simon Study Abroad Program, and several bilateral parliamentary exchanges such as the Congress-Bundestag program.
52. "Enhancing American Influence Abroad: International Exchanges in the National Interest," statement of the International Educational Exchange Liaison Group, May 1981, National Library of Medicine Digital Collections, https://collections.nlm.nih.gov/catalog/nlm:nlmuid-101584906X15108-doc.
53. Yale Richmond, *Cultural Exchange and the Cold War: Raising the Iron Curtain* (Pennsylvania State University Press, 2003); Joseph S. Nye, Jr., "You Can't Get Here from There," *New York Times*, November 29, 2004; *Hearing on Public Diplomacy Before the Senate Committee on Foreign Relations*, 108th Cong. (2003) (statement of Kenton W. Keith).
54. *Cultural Diplomacy: The Linchpin of Public Diplomacy* (Advisory Committee on Cultural Diplomacy, September 2005), US Advisory Commission on Public Diplomacy Reports.
55. Rugh, *Front Line Diplomacy*, 129–159; Scott-Smith, "Mapping the Undefinable," 179, 190; *White House Conference on Culture and Diplomacy* (White House, November 28, 2000), http://www.culturaldiplomacy.org/pdf/white_house.pdf (accessed May 16, 2023).
56. On tensions in the Fulbright program and related exchange activities, see Sussman, *Culture of Freedom*, 91–105.
57. "Does the Summer Work Travel International Exchange Program Work?" EurekaFacts, August, 28, 2017, https://www.eurekafacts.com/2017/08/28/summer-work-travel-program-works/. The Alliance argues the purpose of these unfunded exchanges is mutual understanding and that participants overwhelmingly list the cultural exchange

experience as their prime motive more than the work. Michael McCarry, conversation with author, July 14, 2018.

58. On positive and negative consequences of dialogue and global transparency, see Kristin M. Lord, *The Perils and Promise of Global Transparency: Why the Information Revolution May Not Lead to Security, Democracy, or Peace* (State University of New York Press, 2007), 45–56; and Geoffrey Cowan and Amelia Arsenault, "Moving from Monologue to Dialogue to Collaboration," *The Annals of the American Academy of Political and Social Science* 616, no. 1 (March 2008): 10–30.

59. David Von Drehle, "A Lesson in Hate," *Smithsonian Magazine* (February 2006); Cull, "Taxonomies and Histories," 45–46; Moorehead Kennedy, "Lessons From Captivity," *Princeton Alumni Weekly* (January 30, 1985): 9–12.

60. Giles Scott-Smith, *Networks of Empire: The US State Department's Foreign Leader Program in the Netherlands, France and Britain, 1950–1970* (Peter Lang, 2008); Scott-Smith, "Mapping the Undefinable," 180; Carol Atkinson, "Does Soft Power Matter? A Comparative Analysis of Student Exchange Programs, 1980–2006," *Foreign Policy Analysis* 6, no. 1 (January 2010).

61. Fisher, *Mindsets*; Dickson, *History Shock*.

62. Elmo C. Wilson and Frank Bonilla, "Evaluating Exchange of Persons Programs," *Public Opinion Quarterly* 19 (March 1955): 20–30; Scott-Smith, "Mapping the Undefinable," 178–180.

63. Sharon Lee Mueller Norton, "The United States Department of State International Visitor Program: A Conceptual Framework for Evaluation," PhD diss., (Fletcher School of Law and Diplomacy, 1977).

64. *Data-Driven Public Diplomacy*, US Advisory Commission on Public Diplomacy Reports. For an excellent overview of challenges and multi-disciplinary scholarship in evaluating exchanges, see Giles Scott-Smith, "International Exchanges," in Gilboa, *Research Agenda*, 249–264.

65. Ninkovich, *U.S. Information Policy*, 58–59.

9

Government Media

US international broadcasters are a community of practice divided into separate but closely connected parts: an official broadcaster with global reach, the Voice of America, and regional broadcasters acting as "surrogates" in countries denied free media. By law and professional commitment, they operate with journalism norms and structures that protect their independence. Yet they are government funded, and their broadcasts must be consistent with the broad foreign policy objectives of the United States. External forces and internal tensions shaped their modus operandi and how they navigated the choppy waters between journalism and foreign policy.

Broadcasters and public diplomats have much in common. They support American interests. They seek to understand, engage, and influence citizens and government officials in other countries. They value trust and credibility. But there are important differences. Broadcasters rely on electronic media to overcome distances measured in thousands of miles; diplomats emphasize personal contact. Broadcasters prioritize reporting news, press freedom, and distance from government. Public diplomats privilege policy advocacy, exchanges, and a central role in the activities of US missions.

211
B. Gregory, *American Diplomacy's Public Dimension*, Palgrave Macmillan Series in Global Public Diplomacy, https://doi.org/10.1007/978-3-031-38917-7_9

A Late Beginning

European nations were the first to beam radio broadcasts to the people of other countries. Radio Moscow's World Service aired in 1929 with daily news, music, and politically oriented programs in Russian, French, German, and English. Others launched colonial services: the Netherlands in 1927, France in 1931, Britain's BBC Empire Service in 1932, Belgium and Portugal in 1934. Pope Pius XII launched Vatican Radio in 1931. In 1933 Germany, followed by Italy in 1934 and Japan in 1935, began broadcasting to support expansionist policies in Europe, Asia, and the Western Hemisphere. The United States was a latecomer. VOA went on the air in February 1942, two months after the attack on Pearl Harbor.[1]

Early advocates of US international broadcasting were a handful of Naval officers, State Department officials, and lawmakers concerned about controlling a dominant share of the high frequency radio spectrum for military purposes and satisfying a legal requirement that the frequencies were being used. This fit with their desire to counter Axis inroads in the Western Hemisphere. Many Americans, however, objected to the idea that democracies should broadcast to citizens of other countries in peacetime. Commercial broadcasters, fearing government competition, voiced relentless opposition. President Franklin Roosevelt vacillated, telling both sides what they wanted to hear.

German broadcasts of Nazi propaganda to Latin America prompted the State Department to consider "the use of radio broadcasting in the service of peace" and a government-owned shortwave radio station as early as 1936.[2] Rep. Emanuel Celler (D-NY) and Senator Dennis Chavez (D-NM) introduced bills to create a government station. None were enacted. Roosevelt privately encouraged their efforts; publicly he withheld his support.

In 1937 an independent station supported by charitable foundations with the call letters WRUL (World Radio University for the Listener) began transmitting speeches by Secretary of State Cordell Hull to Latin America. Commercial broadcasters, CBS, NBC, and General Electric, did the same. Although strongly opposed to a government station, they were happy to air speeches and occasional government programs as "ambassadors of international goodwill." Welcoming this opportunity, State's Division of Cultural Relations in 1938 offered guidance on radio programs created by the Departments of Education and Agriculture. In 1940 Nelson Rockefeller's CIAA developed programs in English, Spanish, and Portuguese, which were transmitted to Latin America by WRUL and commercial broadcasters. In June 1941 the Foreign Information Service in William Donovan's Coordinator of Information Office placed programs on commercial broadcasts to audiences in Europe and Asia.[3]

In VOA's first broadcast, William Harlan Hale announced, "Today, and daily from now on, we shall speak to you about America and the war. The news may be good for us. The news may be bad. But we shall tell you the truth."[4] His oft-quoted statement framed US broadcasters' highest priorities, news and truth. They developed a modus operandi that embraced gathering, reporting, and analyzing news; information and music programs; foreign language skills; audience research; and evolving communications technologies.

US Broadcasting's Braided Narrative

VOA was established as a government station that would reach global audiences. Early in the Cold War, Americans added new surrogate stations with a regional focus and a very different approach to government broadcasting. The first was Radio in the American Sector (RIAS), a station created by US occupation authorities in Berlin in 1946, followed by Radio Free Europe (RFE) and Radio Liberty (RL). Later, the US added other surrogate networks: Radio/TV Marti in Spanish to Cuba, Radio Free Asia (RFA) to China and Southeast Asia, and the Middle East Broadcasting Network (MBN).

VOA and the surrogate networks have overlapping goals. Both support freedom and democracy. Both seek to achieve "good will," counter propaganda, undermine hostile regimes, and advance US political, economic, and military interests. They also face the same basic questions. Why do audiences listen to foreign government broadcasts? Which technologies, languages, audiences, and mix of programs deserve priority?

What are appropriate norms and standards? How should they evaluate outcomes and impact?

Although they occasionally self-identify as two sides of the same coin, these broadcasters have divergent objectives and methods. They work in dissimilar organizations. They have separate and, in many cases, duplicate language services. They are intensely competitive in their quest for resources, market share, and organizational separation. VOA faces fewer questions about its rationale, but more questions about its relationship with policymakers. Surrogate broadcasters face questions when media environments become freer. Do they go out of business or reinvent themselves?

VOA's Charter

"Government journalism" creates constant tensions between broadcasters, whose credibility and market share rest on objective news and information, and policymakers who regard them as the government's voice. The first of many tests came quickly. After Mussolini's fall in 1943, Italy's King Victor Emanuel III, who had supported Mussolini for decades, stayed on the throne. His new prime minister announced Italy would remain Germany's wartime ally. A VOA commentary referred to Victor Emanuel as a "moronic little King." *New York Times* columnist Arthur Krock wrote that VOA had undermined international negotiations with the King and threatened the lives of US soldiers. Following President Roosevelt's public rebuke of the broadcast and a showdown at the White House, senior VOA broadcasters in New York lost their jobs.[5]

Attacks on VOA's news coverage continued after the war. Especially harmful were Senator Joseph McCarthy's charges in the 1950s that VOA broadcasters were soft on communism. The attacks damaged morale and created tensions between pro- and anti-McCarthy elements within VOA. The Hungarian revolution in 1956, riots in Poland, the Suez Canal crisis, Eisenhower's deployment of federal troops in Arkansas, the Soviet launch of Sputnik I, and Fidel Castro's revolution in Cuba afforded many opportunities for critics to question VOA's reporting.

Broadcasters wanted a statement of principles that would clarify their mission and protect their journalism. As VOA's program manager Barry Zorthian explained, there was "a lot of discussion about the need for the news to be balanced, objective, [and] non-policy-oriented … [N]o one had ever said the news should lie. Everyone gave it lip service, but the amount of guidance, the amount of selectivity—policy by selection, hesitation on balanced reporting … was a continuing issue." We believed in "straight news," but every time there was turnover at the top, "we'd have to go over the God-damn thing again. So gradually the realization grew that we needed to institutionalize this principle, and get it in writing."[6]

Henry Loomis, VOA's incoming director in 1958, agreed. But what should a mission statement say? "Should we be hard-hitting, propagandistic, furthering the interests of the United States? Or were we an overseas CBS, washing all our dirty linen in public?" Broadcasters wrote multiple drafts. In the end, Loomis gave them to Jack O'Brien, his Foreign Service deputy, who boiled them down to three principles. USIA Director George Allen issued the VOA Charter as a directive, which Eisenhower endorsed shortly before leaving office. Now iconic, it was posted on the walls of VOA's newsroom and studios.[7]

Voice of America Charter: The long-range interests of the United States are served by communicating directly with the peoples of the world by radio. To be effective, the Voice of America must win the attention and respect of listeners. These principles will therefore govern Voice of America (VOA) broadcasts:

(1) VOA will serve as a consistently reliable and authoritative source of news. VOA news will be accurate, objective, and comprehensive.

(2) VOA will represent America, not any single segment of American society, and will therefore present a balanced and comprehensive projection of significant American thought and institutions.

(3) VOA will present the policies of the United States clearly and effectively and will also present responsible discussions and opinions on these policies.[8]

Tensions heightened again during the war in Southeast Asia. Ambassador John Gunther Dean demanded that VOA not report on student demonstrations against a weakening Cambodian government as the Khmer Rouge gained ground in the countryside. In April 1975 US Ambassador to Vietnam Graham Martin insisted VOA broadcast only official statements about US evacuation of civilians as the South was falling rapidly to North Vietnamese/Vietcong forces. The NSC issued a directive that VOA broadcast only White House statements and information on government actions. When parts of a report by VOA's White House correspondent Philomena Jurey were deleted, broadcasters were outraged. *The Washington Post* and other media outlets carried stories about "censorship."

Policymakers pushed back. This is about responsibility not censorship, White House press spokesman Ron Nessen explained. VOA "is the official voice of the United States government overseas … it must operate I think with some constraints on occasion." USIA's deputy Gene Kopp called the directive "unique" in a volatile situation where speculation about evacuation could endanger American lives.[9] But VOA saw it as a violation of the Charter. VOA's broadcasters "don't believe in selective reporting," protested newsroom director Bernie Kamenske. "They know, and I know, that we are an important source of truth in the world, and we destroy the sum total of knowledge if we … moderate, adjust if you will, a Charter principle."[10] Besides, he added, the wire services, most commercial networks, and the BBC were carrying reports of the evacuation.

VOA's practitioners worked to put their Charter into law. In 1975 Kamenske and his deputy Alan Heil began quiet conversations with Scott Cohen, a senior aide to Senator Charles Percy (R-IL). Letters followed from Percy, Senator Lloyd Bentson (D-TX), and Rep. William Cohen (R-ME) to Secretary of State Kissinger and USIA Director James Keogh objecting to clearance of broadcast copy with US ambassadors. "We do not need to stoop to the level of the propagandists of other nations," Cohen wrote. In budget hearings, Percy grilled Keogh for over an hour on "censorship" of VOA's broadcasts.[11] In 1976 Percy and the House Foreign Affairs Committee's Bella Abzug (D-NY) included the Charter in the Foreign Relations Authorization Act, which President Gerald Ford signed on July 12.

The Charter's principles are clear, but broadcasters had to work out their operational meaning. Is objectivity an absolute standard or a method of verification grounded in transparency, sourcing rules, and reliability that emerges over time? "Truth" cannot mean absolute truth. Broadcasts are necessarily subjective and partial versions of events within the strictures of time and information abundance. Should they report just "facts" or also their best judgment about what they mean? Does "balance" require coverage for widely held views believed on evidence to be false?[12] And how should content take into account "the interests of the United States" and win "the respect and attention of listeners?"

The Charter's most contested provision deals with the presentation of US policies. During the Carter administration, VOA broadcast policy "commentaries" labeled and aired separately from other programs. USIA's clearance was required.[13] Reagan administration officials mandated daily "editorials." VOA "in the best tradition of American journalism" would broadcast hard-hitting editorials reflecting the views of its government "publisher."[14] Broadcasters argued government-labeled editorials undermined their credibility. The Charter's policy standard could best be achieved by reporting on White House and State Department press briefings and airing responsible discussions of US policies by informed analysts.

Two years after the Charter became law, VOA issued guidelines for its foreign correspondents recommended by an advisory panel of journalists chaired by Chalmers Roberts, senior diplomatic correspondent for *The Washington Post*. Henceforth they would no longer have offices within US embassies or travel with official or diplomatic passports. They would carry journalist visas. They would have no access to classified information. They would not look to embassies for residential and administrative support or use their postal and commissary facilities.[15]

The Charter and the guidelines did not satisfy some American journalists. On March 17, 1980, the Committee of Correspondents for Congressional Press Galleries voted unanimously to continue rules that denied accreditation to VOA's reporters. VOA might "operate in the tradition of privately owned news media," the Committee argued, but this did not "alter the basic fact that VOA is a branch of the federal government."[16] President Reagan's appointees to the US Advisory Commission on Public Diplomacy, Edwin J. Feulner, Jr. and Tom Korologos, led a public campaign to challenge the decision. In Congressional hearings they pointed to the Charter and the Committee's inconsistent practice of accrediting Tass, Radio Moscow, Xinhua, the BBC, NPR, and other government-funded correspondents. The Committee capitulated and admitted VOA's reporters as non-voting members but otherwise to be treated "in a manner identical to all other Congressional correspondents."[17]

Broadcasting's "Firewall"

To give the Charter operational meaning, broadcasters believed VOA should be independent from USIA. Nearly two decades after the Charter was enacted, they achieved their goal. In 1994 Congress consolidated VOA and RFE/RL as separate entities under an independent, bipartisan, presidentially appointed Broadcasting Board of Governors (BBG).[18] The BBG "is essential to providing what I call an 'asbestos firewall,'" Senator Joseph Biden (D-DE) declared, "an arms-length distance between the broadcasters and the foreign policy bureaucracy."[19] But critics responded that foreign policy interests require limits on unfettered journalism in broadcasts funded by taxpayers. Conservative lawmakers Jesse Helms (R-NC) and Dana Rohrabacher (R-CA) argued VOA should not broadcast ideas contrary to America's interests and values. It is not censorship to insist that VOA tell America's story of freedom and justice in no uncertain terms.

In 1997 US Ambassador to China James Sasser and other Clinton administration officials tried unsuccessfully to stop VOA from broadcasting an interview with Chinese dissident Wei Jingsheng, arguing it would undercut efforts to gain release of other dissidents. A year later US Ambassador to Turkey Mark Parris insisted that State halt a broadcast interview with "notorious international terrorist leader, Abdullah Ocalan of the Kurdistan Worker's Party, or PKK."[20] After 9/11 State's spokesperson Richard Boucher objected to VOA's interview with Afghanistan's Taliban leader Mullah Omar. It "would be confusing to the millions of listeners to what is essentially a US Government broadcast, paid for by the US Government."[21] William Safire's column "Equal Time for Hitler" in *The New York Times* protested that "U.S. taxpayer-supported broadcasting is supposed to be on our side."[22]

In each instance broadcasters invoked the firewall and defended their interviews as newsworthy and shining examples of a free press. "I happen to believe that any legitimate news organization in the world would do that [Mullah Omar] interview," BBG Chairman Norman J. Pattiz explained. "And if the United States is going to be a proponent of a free press, it has to walk the walk." He then marshaled structural arguments. The firewall legitimized the BBG's independence, budget autonomy, and distance from the NSC's interagency coordinating directives. It also gave the State Department deniability when foreign governments complained about broadcasts.[23] Surrogate broadcasters had their own firewall. They were government grantees, "not an institution of the United States Government," and "did not carry VOA's burden" of pressures from policymakers.[24]

Many broadcasting decisions are not about news integrity: funding levels for VOA and surrogate broadcasting, audience research, and media technologies; decisions on which foreign languages and how many; ratios of broadcasts in minority and majority languages (e.g., VOA's Serbian and Albanian programs in Kosovo); and trade-offs between broadcasting and other instruments of public diplomacy. In the words of one advisory panel report, "Broadcasting represents nearly half the spending on public diplomacy, and it must be part of the public diplomacy process, not marching to its own drummer with its own goals and strategy, sources of funding, and [management] board." The BBG instantly shot back that this "would tear the firewall that separates broadcasters from partisan politics."[25] This was another Washington turf battle of little interest to foreign audiences who wanted reliable news and information.

VOA's Operational Issues

VOA's broadcasters by the 1970s had institutionalized a durable community of practice. They faced three far-reaching challenges: new communication technologies, deficiencies in audience research and evaluation, and decisions on languages and programs best suited to attract audiences in dense media environments.

Modernization. VOA's dominant technology for half a century was shortwave radio. Signals were sent from studios in Washington to foreign relay stations where they were retransmitted to listeners as far as 6000 miles away. Shortwave signals can be jammed, which the Soviet Union, China, and Cuba did in patterns that mirrored levels of political tension. Until the 1990s, most VOA broadcasts aired on World War II vintage transmitters from studios with vacuum tube equipment maintained by talented engineers who kept the aging system going.[26]

A Reagan administration NSC directive in 1982 called for VOA and RFE/RL to undertake a long-term program of modernization. Policymakers and broadcasters assumed shortwave would "remain for the foreseeable future the primary medium of US international broadcasting," although AM and FM were "preferable wherever technically and politically feasible."[27] VOA launched a $1.3 billion plan to build 16 new shortwave stations and renovate headquarters facilities. Ten years later, due to contracting delays, lack of funds, and difficult site negotiations, GAO reported VOA had fallen well short of its goal with only two stations completed and two under construction.[28]

The world, however, was moving to television, direct broadcast satellites (DBS), fiber-optic cable, audio-diskettes, microelectronics, and computers—with the Internet and smart phones on deck. VOA used alternatives (AM broadcasts, placement of programs on local stations), but it continued to rely on shortwave for most broadcasts. DBS would take years to develop, they argued, and receivers for satellite signals would not replace shortwave receivers in Africa, Asia, and the Middle East anytime soon.[29] Practitioner rivalries also were a factor. In 1985 USIA Director Charles Z. Wick initiated Worldnet television—a point-to-point closed-circuit audio–video satellite network enabling government officials in Washington and opinion leaders at USIS posts to discuss policies and issues. As VOA veteran John Lennon recalls, "VOA radio broadcasters worked stubbornly alone in their fenced-off area of interest, and Worldnet television producers and editors did the same." Neither side wanted "the loss of resources and effectiveness and impact and reputation that, they feared, would surely result from consolidation—or, even from a working partnership."[30]

VOA's studios and control center proved easier to modernize. In 1986 a team led by Chris Kern, a talented young VOA writer with an aptitude for computers, created the System for News and Programming (SNAP), a multilingual word processing and database management network connecting writers, editors, translators, producers, engineers, and managers. Kern moved out of the newsroom to head a VOA Computer Division, which, in association with Xerox Corporation, developed software to move texts in more than 40 languages, including Chinese ideographs. In 1987 a VOA Master Control Center went online with automated switching of programs.[31] That same year VOA developed a capability for point-to-point satellite placement of radio programs on local stations and networks, beginning in Latin America.[32] By 1991 VOA was gathering information through a gateway between SNAP and the Internet. Two years later it was taking steps to use the Internet for program dissemination.

Broadcasters who had been doubling down on shortwave, were now giving priority to satellites, television, computers, and multimedia networks.[33] As the world moved to narrowcasting and streaming, broadcasters adopted the term US global media.[34]

Audience Research. Until the 1980s VOA's audience estimates relied on casual attention to listener mail. But letters received are no measure of audience size. Voices within and outside VOA argued better audience research was needed to inform decisions on new transmitter locations, better frequencies, and program content.[35]

VOA created a small audience mail analysis staff in 1982, and three years later USIA created a Media Research Branch led by Foreign Service officer Sherwood "Woody" Demitz, an advocate of moving beyond national surveys. Audiences are increasingly local and urban, he explained, and markets are more competitive. His unit began using targeted audience surveys, market analysis, focus groups, BBC data, and other tools. VOA was placing more programs on local AM/FM stations, and it needed market research to shape content for station gatekeepers interested in attracting advertising. Broadcasters also turned to outreach methods used by diplomats. Studies showed regular "personal contact with station managers plays a strong role in determining how much VOA programming they use."[36] But progress was slow. In 1992 GAO found VOA's spending on audience research was "roughly one-tenth that of ... BBC, RFE or RL."[37] In 2016 VOA and other networks refined an "Impact Model" to evaluate how their programs affected the lives and needs of their audiences. Analysts welcomed the move, but called for increased spending and strategies regarding the implications for their broadcasts.[38]

Languages and programs. There are trade-offs in what media scholar Monroe Price calls competition in "markets for loyalties."[39] Which languages should be added or dropped? What combination of news, current affairs, and entertainment works best for which audiences? Decisions are shaped by audience research, turf conflicts, and pressure from outside groups.

Language service creation is seldom straightforward. In 1979 the State Department successfully objected to adding three local languages in southern Africa, because they would be seen as favoring some political groups. In 1990 a Senate bill authorized a VOA Kurdish service. Turkey's government and Turkish groups in the US were outraged. State advised that "Kurdish broadcasts will do serious, perhaps irreparable damage" to US relations with a strategically located NATO ally. This time, domestic politics favored advocates; VOA Kurdish went on the air in 1992 and continues to broadcast.[40]

Dropping languages is often harder. Opposition from nationality groups, foreign governments, Congress, and State overturned repeated VOA decisions to end broadcasts in Thai, Uzbek, Greek, Turkish, and other services based on low audience numbers. Thailand's Prime Minister protested it would signal reduced US commitment to an Asian ally. Conservatives argued VOA "serves as a beacon of democracy" in the gas-and-oil-rich Uzbekistan dictatorship. Plans to cut Greek and Turkish produced the first ever collaboration by the Congressional Turkish and Hellenic Caucuses. "[I]t is critical that the VOA sustain its radio and television programs to Turkey, Greece and Cyprus, a geographical area with a combined population of more than 80 million people," their joint statement declared.[41]

US media practitioners make daily decisions on program content, tempo, and production techniques in keeping with professional standards. What is the best mix of news, Americana, and entertainment for direct broadcasts, local placement, and Internet streaming? VOA is now a multimedia platform with digital-age networks. Its competition for "market loyalties" takes place in a more complex broadcasting environment. It seeks to combat disinformation, promote freedom of expression, support free media, advance trade and investment, combat extremism, quell ethnic strife, fight disease, mitigate climate change, and engage underserved audiences, including women, youth, and marginalized populations—as well as serve as a source of objective news and authoritative information.

Surrogate Broadcasting: Origins

The US is the only world power to create and maintain government-funded surrogate broadcasting networks. Early stakeholders were national security officials, civil society activists, and émigrés from the Soviet Union and occupied countries in Eastern Europe with plans, memories, resentments, and hopes of return to their home countries. George Kennan, director of the State Department's Policy Planning Staff, worked with these exiles to create a National Committee for a Free Europe. A planning paper called them "the most effective agents to destroy the communist myth of the Soviet paradise."[42] The Committee channeled their enthusiasms, gave them work, and in 1950 put their voices on RFE broadcasts to Czechoslovakia, Romania, Hungary, Poland, and Bulgaria "in their own languages, in familiar tones." In 1953 RL began broadcasting in Russian and 15 other languages to the Soviet Union.[43] Both stations were nonprofit corporations secretly funded by the CIA.

RFE/RL's "home service" broadcasts covered local politics, sports, religion, culture, and entertainment. They highlighted contradictions and deficiencies in target countries and the attractiveness of life in the West. They called for freedom of expression and religion, and challenged state control of the arts and sciences. "We must play the role of an inner opposition radio," RFE's policy advisor William Griffith declared; our role is "promoting liberalization … under conditions of continued Communist rule." Lacking foreign correspondents, RFE/RL depended on information from travelers, escapees, scholars, journalists, business executives, *samizdat* literature, US intelligence, and other sources.[44]

US officials saw the Radios as a political tool to contain and weaken Soviet power. Émigrés viewed them as ways to pursue national political agendas and liberate "enslaved peoples." Tensions and political rivalries were inevitable. They broadcast in foreign languages with considerable autonomy and light guidance from the CIA. This gave them freedom and audience relevance, but it enabled polemics, rumors, and personal attacks that usually were discovered, if at all, only in post-broadcast audits. Émigré politics also played out in VOA, lessened somewhat because language-qualified Foreign Service officers usually managed broadcast services.

Poland and Hungary, 1956. RFE/RL's early broadcasts were strident and bellicose. Consider this broadcast from the 1950s:

> This is Radio Free Europe, the voice of freedom calling the captive countries behind the Iron Curtain—speaking to them in their own languages in more ways than the obvious. American propaganda of hope sizzling through the air with messages musical and spoken that the Communists don't want their slaves to hear—messages that should be a warning to the Reds that all their carefully canned dogma can't quite blot out the simple human urge to think and say what you please.[45]

RFE's Policy Handbook in 1951 stated that, as "a non-governmental station," RFE is free "to express independent views" regarding other countries. Yet it also cautioned against broadcasts "contrary to United States Government policy or to the beliefs of the American people" and warned against promises of Western intervention. The goal was to support "legitimate" opposition, raise morale, and bring "hope to our friends and confusion to our enemies."[46]

In practice RFE/RL country directors pursued a variety of objectives. For the CIA's Frank G. Wisner, they included "Developing an atmosphere favorable to the growth of resistance movements, for ultimate exploitation in war, or, at a propitious moment, in peace time." This could mean "character assassination," promises of "retribution" against quislings, or "gray or even black propaganda should the situation warrant it."[47] Cord Meyer, who directed CIA's oversight of the Radios, conveniently recalled stricter guidelines decades later: the Radios "were not to provoke premature and suicidal internal revolt by any implied promise of external assistance." Nor were they to engage in disinformation campaigns against East European leaders.[48] The CIA wanted maximum pressure in the struggle for freedom but not assurances of US military support for violent opposition inconsistent with the policy of containment.

Many RFE broadcasts were professional and imaginative. Others fell well short of Handbook standards. When Soviet premier Nikita Khrushchev's "peaceful co-existence" campaign prompted riots and labor unrest in Poland in 1956, RFE's Polish service director Jan Nowak, a popular journalist and former resistance fighter against the Nazis, covered the events as news. His commentaries encouraged citizens to be firm in their demands. But they should be prudent and calm: "Russia with its enormous military might is near, and the United States is too far away to effectively protect Poland from Soviet attack." Poland's reformers gained better working conditions, ended collectivization of farms, and avoided a Soviet military crackdown. Analysts view RFE's Polish service at the time as a model of successful surrogate broadcasting.[49]

RFE's Hungarian broadcasts had different consequences. When news of uprisings in Poland reached Hungary, mass protests led to a few days of democratic government under Imre Nagy. Bloody suppression by Soviet troops and tanks followed. Thousands of Hungarians fled. Others were executed or imprisoned. For some analysts the "voice of Free Hungary" was responsible for fomenting revolution and carelessly endangering lives. Meyer described its broadcasts as perhaps "more exuberant and optimistic than the situation warranted." He called out one script that implied the US Congress might approve armed intervention if the Hungarians kept fighting. It "violated basic policy guidelines and should never have been broadcast."[50] US Ambassador to the Soviet Union Charles E. Bohlen affixed a brighter sheen: "There was nothing in any of the broadcasts which could have been interpreted as an offer to help." One broadcast "may have been a little injudicious, but it spoke only in general terms of the sympathy and support of the outside world for the efforts of the Hungarian people to free themselves."[51]

Later assessments by RFE/RL director Ross Johnson and other practitioners rejected claims that the Hungarian service had incited violent revolution. But they faulted RFE on several grounds. Emotional broadcasts voicing Western solidarity with the insurgents failed to make clear this did not mean the US would intervene. Derogatory condemnations of Nagy as a Soviet Trojan horse violated RFE guidelines against taking positions on individual personalities. Some broadcasts offered tactical military advice. In broadcasting the rebels' formal demands, amplifying their early victories, and rebroadcasting the content of local stations back into Hungary, RFE was complicit in the revolution. Oversight from its Munich headquarters was lacking, and for a time the Hungarian service was "out of control."[52]

For the next decade, RFE/RL continued to broadcast to large audiences in Eastern Europe and the Soviet Union with CIA funding. The lessons of Poland and Hungary were pivotal. "Liberalization" supplanted "liberation" in RFE's Handbook. RL director Howland Sargeant confined RL's broadcasts to news reporting with no original commentary or opinion pieces from global media. In the CIA, many believed the Radios had outlived their usefulness, although it funded Radio Swan, a "black" station intended to undermine the Castro government in Cuba in 1961.

In 1967 a story in *Ramparts* magazine was pivotal for surrogate broadcasting. Its explosive disclosure that the CIA was funding National Student Association activities was followed by media accounts of CIA's support for RFE/RL and a variety of foundations and front groups. President Johnson appointed a committee consisting of Under Secretary of State Nicholas Katzenbach, Health, Education, and Welfare Secretary John Gardner, and CIA Director Richard Helms that in two weeks recommended ending the CIA's support for all civil society organizations. RFE/RL was a different matter. State and CIA were not ready to shut them down. Johnson disagreed. "I'm going to close down those Radios," he privately told Helms. When Helms objected, Johnson agreed he could seek Congressional funding without White House support. Helms obtained temporary funding, and US officials dithered for four years over what to do with RFE/RL.[53]

The decision to continue surrogate broadcasting occurred for several reasons. Officials, democratizers, and anti-communist hardliners in both parties considered RFE/RL's $32 million annual budget a worthwhile

investment in mobilizing opposition to Communist regimes short of violence.[54] Shuttering the Radios would convey acquiescence in a permanent division of Europe. Lawmakers and political candidates looked at
the Radios and saw voting blocs. Ambassadors walked a line between
outreach to RFE/RL's audiences and relations with foreign ministries
hostile to the Radios. Their dispatches contained observations on the
value of RFE/RL's reporting on the Soviet invasion of Czechoslovakia,
the improved quality of the broadcasts, and West Germany's fears that
controversies over RFE might trigger international boycotts of the 1972
Munich Olympic Games. Broadcasters, fighting to survive, pointed to
the knowledge and skills of their language-qualified staffs, their unique
research archives on targeted countries, and studios and transmitters that
would be difficult or impossible to recreate if disbanded.[55]

Multiple government studies chewed on three options: continue CIA
funding, channel public funding through State or USIA, or create a public–private board. The CIA recognized secret funding risked "press and
public relations problems." State wanted RFE/RL to continue but not
the organizational responsibility. VOA had no interest in a merger fearing
loss of credibility. The Radios wanted no part of VOA's policy guidelines
and worried Congress would cut their budgets and expose them to public
scrutiny. Target countries would view association with "an official propaganda arm of the U.S. government" skeptically, and émigré broadcasters
might leave. Open sponsorship by government, whether direct or under
a public–private board, "would be a contradiction in terms for a gray
radio."[56]

Powerful voices in the media and the Senate joined the fray. In a widely
read *Washington Post* opinion column in 1968, Rowland Evans and
Robert Novak questioned whether the incoming Nixon administration
would continue to fund RFE/RL through the CIA or "as a regular congressional appropriation subject to normal congressional procedures."
Senator Clifford Case (R-NJ) accused the CIA of denying Congress "its
constitutional role of approving the expenditures" and RFE/RL of deceiv-
ing its listeners and American taxpayers. His solution, supported by
Senators Frank Church (D-ID) and Stuart Symington (D-MO), was to
fund the Radios openly through State Department grants. Foreign
Relations Committee Chairman J. William Fulbright questioned "our
meddling in the internal political affairs of other countries" and declared

it was time for the Radios "to take their rightful place in the graveyard of cold war relics."[57] As usual when choices were hard, it was time to create a blue-ribbon commission.

Board for International Broadcasting. In 1972 Nixon asked former Johns Hopkins University President Milton S. Eisenhower to chair a Presidential Study Commission on International Radio Broadcasting. It recommended creation of a Board for International Broadcasting (BIB) to receive Congressional appropriations, make grants to RFE and RL, which would be constituted as private, nonprofit corporations, and oversee the stations. The BIB would safeguard their "professional independence … with the *sole limitation* that the stations not operate in a manner inconsistent with broad United States foreign policy objectives." It would have seven members, five (including the chair) appointed by the President and confirmed by the Senate, and the chief executives of RFE and RL as *ex officio*, non-voting members.[58]

The "Eisenhower Commission" drew a bright line between RFE/RL and VOA. RFE/RL's mission is "to function as a surrogate free press" and "fill the information gaps created by communist government restrictions on the free flow of information." VOA, as the official radio of the US government, "gives preponderant emphasis to American developments." It saw no conflict between the missions, but it argued a merger of VOA and RFE/RL would "defeat the purposes of both." The Commission thought it unlikely free media in the Soviet sphere would occur any time soon, but when it is a reality "it will be time to consider termination of the stations."[59] Congress implemented the recommendations in the Board for International Broadcasting Act of 1973. The law provided organizational stability for the next two decades. Nevertheless, questions about the purposes, budgets, and operations of entities in US broadcasting's braided narrative persisted.[60]

Surrogate Broadcasting Today

Until the 1980s there was no serious effort to change the two-track VOA and RFE/RL broadcasting model. But when the Cold War ended, did the US still need surrogate broadcasting? As usual, decisions came on the heels of multiple reports, Congressional debates, and jockeying among broadcasters. Nationality groups favored expanding surrogate broadcasting to Cuba, Asia, and the Middle East—and new opportunities for RFE/RL. Politicians reflected interest group pressures. The White House and State Department followed the prevailing winds. When the dust settled, surrogate broadcasting services not only survived, they propagated like mushrooms.

Radio and TV Marti. The first signal that the US would expand surrogate broadcasting came in 1980 when Cuban exiles in Florida and conservatives in Congress attempted to label VOA's Spanish broadcasts to Cuba as "Radio Free Cuba." Reagan administration officials, VOA, and the US Advisory Commission on Public Diplomacy objected, arguing VOA's mission might be compromised.

President Reagan signed the Radio Broadcasting to Cuba Act, creating Radio Marti (in honor of Cuban independence leader Jose Marti) in 1983. It would "promote freedom in Cuba, while maintaining the high standards of the Voice of America for accuracy and reliability." Liberal lawmakers placed it in VOA to ensure it would operate in a manner consistent with the Charter. Broadcasts aired in 1985. An Advisory Board for Cuba Broadcasting, chaired for many years by Jorge Mas Canosa, the powerful head of the Cuban American National Foundation, heavily influenced its policies and programs. In 1990 Congress authorized TV Marti. Daily telecasts were transmitted from a tethered Air Force balloon in Marathon Key, Florida. The stations broadcast news, entertainment, and commentary about life in Cuba from studios in Miami.[61]

Critics protested the stations were pawns in the exile politics of Mas Canosa's Foundation. Cuba alarmed US commercial broadcasters when it demonstrated retaliatory jamming could knock AM stations off the air in Iowa and Utah. It also blocked TV Marti's signal. Multiple oversight reports concluded the stations had small audiences. Programs lacked objectivity. Poor management, low employee morale, inadequate training, allegations of fraud, and political controversies were endemic. Broadcasts continued with the support of the Cuban-American community and presidential candidates aware of Florida's influence in the Electoral College.[62]

Radio Free Asia. In 1989 images of pro-democracy protests in Beijing's Tiananmen Square caught the world's attention just as Vaclav Havel, Lech Walesa, and other European reformers were voicing heartfelt thanks for RFE/RL's Cold War broadcasts. Pressured by democratization activists and powerful Asian-American lobbies, lawmakers began drafting bills to create Radio Free Asia (RFA), a new "Home Service" station to bring news about events in China to the Chinese people and promote freedom and human rights in the region. A White House Task Force on US Government International Broadcasting recommended "a new U.S. surrogate broadcasting entity" for Asia. The Center for Strategic and International Studies convened experts to discuss the pros and cons of a "Radio Free China." Senators Joe Biden and Jesse Helms teamed up to create a "Commission on Broadcasting to the People's Republic of China."[63]

Armed with the bipartisan support of Biden and Helms, RFA's advocates argued the relevance of RFE/RL's "Freedom Radios" to China's denial of free media and abysmal record on human rights.[64] But critics responded the Cold War model was outdated. A flood of information now reached China via radio, television, VCRs, fax, computers, and large visitor flows. Surveys showed television was the primary source of news for most Chinese adults. Radio was important, but VOA, which had been broadcasting in Mandarin since 1942, and other international broadcasters were providing news about the outside world *and* internal developments in China. RFA's costs outweighed its potential benefits. USIA's field practitioners called for more Fulbright scholarships, visitor programs, and book translations in China. The State Department argued RFA would be detrimental to US relations with China on trade and other policy issues.[65]

Passionate arguments on *ends* triumphed over reasoned arguments on *means*. After four years of spirited debate, the International Broadcasting Act of 1994 authorized RFA's surrogate services to China, Burma, Cambodia, Laos, Tibet, Vietnam, and North Korea.

RFE/RL's Future. Early in 1990 House Foreign Affairs Committee Chairman Dante B. Fascell (D-FL) and Ranking Member Olympia Snowe (R-ME) wrote to President George H. W. Bush urging the US to "totally rethink" its approach to international broadcasting. Bush and

NSC Advisor Brent Scowcroft agreed "the dramatic opening of Eastern Europe and the Soviet Union requires us to look afresh at all our broadcasting activities, including VOA and RFE/RL."[66] The total rethink acquired concrete meaning when a US Advisory Commission on Public Diplomacy report recommended the US "should start planning now for the termination of Radio Free Europe's language services when their goals have been achieved, and the transfer of assets as appropriate to the Voice of America."[67] This put the cat squarely among the pigeons. "Far from being a relic," declared outraged *Forbes* magazine publisher Malcolm "Steve" Forbes, Jr., chair of RFE/RL's board, "RFE/RL can be a model for the future." Its independence from government gives it credibility, and it's a "valuable trademark that must be preserved."[68]

The Commission replied it had not recommended termination of RFE/RL. Rather it had called for phasing out some RFE broadcasts, in Polish and Hungarian for example, "based on clear criteria: well-established democratic institutions and free media alternatives in Eastern Europe and demonstrable Voice of America/Radio Free Europe audience and program duplication." The US "does not need two government funded radio networks doing the same thing. Nor should we spend tax dollars to compete with a free press in other countries."[69]

After nine months of acrimonious debate, the White House Task Force on US Government International Broadcasting convened public hearings. They were a forum for the divergent views of officials, broadcasters, diplomats, lawmakers, and the Advisory Commission on whether the US would engage in official and surrogate broadcasting in the post-Cold War world.[70]

RFE/RL pursued a three-pronged strategy. First, "We have an evolving mission," its President Gene Pell declared. "Our surrogate broadcasting role is diminishing; our rising role is that of an alternative domestic medium."[71] Second, RFE/RL emphasized its independence from government as a corporate entity. Fewer nations, Forbes argued, "rely on the instrument of traditional state broadcasting—journalism under the direct control of government." Third, RFE/RL would turn to other parts of the world starting with RFA.[72] Allies on the Task Force and in the media agreed. Neoconservative Michael Novak declared that putting RFE/RL "under State Department control" at USIA would "require adherence to an official U.S. point of view." Conservative *New York Times* columnist William Safire was typically blunt: "V.O.A. is the nice cop, speaking on our behalf, and R.F.E. the tough cop, speaking on the local people's behalf; they work well together provided they are kept apart, like Treasury and Federal Reserve."[73]

VOA's supporters opposed giving RFE/RL an alternative mission that risked confusing audiences. The Radios were unlikely to be viewed as objective sources of news and information. VOA's deputy director Robert Coonrod noted listenership for US government broadcasts was declining as Eastern European countries were developing more reliable media.[74] The Advisory Commission advocated keeping VOA, Radio/TV Marti, and Worldnet TV in USIA and a timetable to phase out RFE services that duplicated VOA's democracy-building content and media training for foreign journalists.[75]

The Task Force tried to please rival practitioners on all sides. Keep VOA, RFE/RL, and the Martis as separate entities. Change RFE/RL's mission from "surrogate" to "alternative" broadcasting for countries establishing free media and democratic institutions. Keep VOA in USIA. Create RFA. Co-locate RFA with RFE/RL under the existing Board for International Broadcasting.[76] The recommendations simmered for a year as an NSC Policy Committee deliberated on options for the incoming Clinton administration. In December 1992 Senator Biden, intent on achieving his RFA legislation and independence for surrogate broadcasting, pressured all concerned to get on with it.

"Consolidation"

As broadcasting's future moved from studies to legislation in 1993, Congressional interest and media coverage increased.[77] Senators Russell Feingold (D-WI) and John Kerry (D-MA) wanted to keep VOA in USIA and downsize RFE/RL. For Feingold it was an ambitious first-term Senator's top priority, a path to deficit reduction and cuts in federal spending. His supporters included the Clinton White House, USIA's leadership, and the Advisory Commission. VOA quietly pushed for independence from USIA. "The best approach to making VOA, and possibly

RFE-RL, the best medium imaginable is by taking these entities out of the federal framework," VOA's now retired Bernie Kamenske declared.[78] Biden championed "private corporate grantee status" for a well-funded RFE/RL kept separate from State Department and USIA interference. Otherwise, he declared, a surrogate broadcaster would become "a US government journalist"—"a heretofore unknown breed" and the very "definition of an oxymoron."[79]

President Clinton announced a plan in June 1993. It would abolish RFE/RL's existing board, the BIB, and place all broadcasters (VOA, RFE/RL, the Martis, RFA, and USIA's Worldnet TV/Film service) under a bipartisan presidentially appointed Broadcasting Board of Governors (BBG). The US would continue "to provide surrogate broadcasting to regions denied full access to free and open media." The BBG would be "independent" but "report to the President through" USIA and take "guidance on foreign policy issues" from the Agency.[80] All parties endorsed the compromise. It may have been "a shotgun marriage," *The New York Times* editorialized, but there was something for everyone. The "Radio Free" broadcasters were on a path to expand with the addition of RFA. VOA had greater independence and a stronger firewall. Feingold and other budget deficit hawks trumpeted potential savings.[81]

The White House and Congress negotiated implementing legislation for a year. On most issues there was common ground apart from a fight over whether RFE/RL would be federalized or remain corporate grantees. The administration argued for federalization. Feingold agreed, pointing to RFE/RL's lack of "real independence" as grantees and out of control spending. Biden opposed federalization and threatened a filibuster. The administration caved to Biden. RFE/RL remained non-profit grantees. Feingold won major funding cuts for the Radios, a plan to move them to rent-free studios in Prague, and an expressed sense of Congress that the private sector should assume all funding for the surrogate Radios by 1999.[82] When the dust settled, the International Broadcasting Act of 1994 had consolidated all nonmilitary US international broadcasting. The broadcasters had achieved their independence.[83]

The 1994 Act authorized goals, standards, and structures that today provide the basic architecture of US international broadcasting. It led to two outcomes. First, it validated US broadcasting's braided narrative.

When facts on the ground changed, Americans turned to both VOA and surrogate broadcasting. Second, the Act confirmed key elements in US broadcasting's modus operandi—a firewall to protect journalism norms, a channel for foreign policy guidance, a mix of grantee and federal entities, and an independent board responsible for overseeing all broadcasting operations.[84] Unsurprisingly, debate persisted on goals, methods, new technologies, and management structures in this community of practice.

In 2018 the BBG changed its name to the US Agency for Global Media (USAGM). The USAGM's 2022–2026 strategic plan states its mission is to "inform, engage, and connect people around the world in support of freedom and democracy." The protean words "freedom" and "democracy" are praiseworthy. But as essayist George Orwell observed, they are abstractions with multiple and conflicting meanings. They are claimed by every kind of government, and they allow users to insert whatever content works in the moment.[85] Mission statements are of little use in making cost/benefit decisions, and they mask a wide variety of policies, interests, and strategies. A better indication of USAGM's goals can be found in its budgets and operational priorities.

Notes

1. On the origins of international shortwave broadcasting by governments, see Philo C. Wasburn, *Broadcasting Propaganda: International Radio Broadcasting and the Construction of Political Reality* (Praeger, 1992), 1–31.
2. Hart, *Empire of Ideas*, 20.
3. For an overview of US international broadcasting initiatives during the 1930s, see Gregory, *Broadcasting Service*; Walter R. Roberts, "The Voice of America: Origins and Recollections—Part I," in *Dr. Walter R. Roberts: The Compleat Public Diplomat*, ed. Barry Fulton (CreateSpace, 2016), 82–97; and Holly C. Shulman, "The Voice of Victory: The Development of American Propaganda and the Voice of America," PhD diss., (University of Maryland, 1984).
4. Quoted in Heil, *Voice of America*, 32. On the date of VOA's first broadcast, see Chris Kern, "A Belated Correction: The *Real* First Broadcast of the Voice of America," *Chris Kern* (blog), September 2010, http://www.chriskern.net/essay/voaFirstBroadcast.html (accessed May 16, 2023).

5. On tensions between OWI and its VOA office in New York, see Graham, *Culture and Propaganda*, 101–109; Winkler, *Politics of Propaganda*, 73–111; and Heil, *Voice of America*, 42–44.

6. Barry Zorthian Oral History, interviewed by Cliff Groce, Foreign Affairs Oral History Collection, ADST, Arlington, VA.

7. Loomis Oral History, interviewed by "Cliff" Groce; Heil, *Voice of America*, 64–65.

8. Foreign Relations Authorization Act, Fiscal Year 1977, Pub. L. No. 94–350, 90 Stat. 823, Title II, Sec. 206 (1976).

9. Heil, *Voice of America*, 168–169. Nessen is quoted in Philomena Jurey, *A Basement Seat to History* (Linus Press, 1995), 89.

10. Quoted in Heil, *Voice of America*, 169.

11. Quoted in Heil, *Voice of America*, 174; Richard M. Weintraub, "Percy Says VOA Violated Charter," *Washington Post*, May 6, 1975.

12. Bill Kovach and Tom Rosenstiel, *Elements of Journalism* (Random House, 2001), 36–49, 70–93.

13. Based on a decision by VOA Director Mary Bitterman, VOA's news and current affairs staff distinguished between commentaries that required clearance and news analyses that did not. Chris Kern, email to author, July 25, 2018.

14. Charles Z. Wick to Senator Claiborne Pell, September 28, 1987, author's copy.

15. Richard M. Weintraub, "Seeking Credibility, VOA Limits Embassy Ties to Its Staff," *Washington Post*, July 6, 1978; *Report of the Panel to Study the Role of the Foreign Correspondents of the Voice of America* (March 9, 1978), author's copy; "Guidelines and Operating Procedures for VOA's Foreign Correspondents" (June 30, 1978), author's copy.

16. Paul G. Houston [Committee of Correspondents] to Senator Claiborne Pell, March 18, 1980, author's copy.

17. *Hearing Before the Committee on Rules and Administration*, 98th Cong. (1983) (statement of Edwin J. Feulner, Jr., Chairman, US Advisory Commission on Public Diplomacy), author's copy; Gene Gibbons [Committee of Correspondents] to VOA Director Kenneth Y. Tomlinson, June 16, 1983, author's copy.

18. Foreign Relations Authorization Act, Fiscal Years 1994 and 1995, Pub. L. No. 103–236, 108 Stat. 383 (1994). The Act's Title 3, "United States International Broadcasting Act," authorized the BBG's composition and authorities, created Radio Free Asia, and enumerated broadcasting standards and principles.

19. "Statement of Senator Joseph R. Biden, Jr., Hearing on USIA Budget," News Release, March 6, 1997, author's copy.

20. Phil Kuntz, "U.S. Officials Tried to Stop Broadcast of Wei into China," *Wall Street Journal*, December 17, 1997; M. R. Parris, US Embassy Ankara, "VOA as Mouthpiece for Terrorist Leader," telegram to the NSC, Secretary of State, VOA Director, and USIA Director, February 24, 1998, author's copy.

21. Ellen Nakashima, "Broadcast with Afghan Leader Halted: State Department Pressures Voice of America Not to Air 'Voice of the Taliban,'" *Washington Post*, September 23, 2001; Richard Boucher, "Daily Press Briefing—Department of State," September 24, 2001; Felicity Barringer, "State Dept. Protests Move by U.S. Radio," *New York Times*, September 26, 2001; James Warren, "Reporter Off Radio After Taliban Story," *Chicago Tribune*, February 6, 2002.

22. William Safire, "Equal Time for Hitler," *New York Times*, September 20, 2001; Jesse Helms, "Opposing View: Attacks Justify Using Agencies to Tell America's Story of Freedom," *USA Today*, November 8, 2001; "Pashto Comes to Shove," *New York Times*, November 1, 2001.

23. On the Mullah Omar interview, VOA explained it had only planned to use interview excerpts in a larger story on Afghan reaction to a speech by President George W. Bush. For an account of the interview from VOA's perspective, see Heil, *Voice of America*, 410–424.

24. Kate Swoger and Christopher P. Winner, "RFE Insists on Independence," *Prague Post Online*, October 3, 2001.

25. *Changing Minds Winning Peace: A New Strategic Direction for U.S. Public Diplomacy in the Arab & Muslim World* (2003), Advisory Group on Public Diplomacy in the Arab and Muslim World (Djerejian Report), 32; "Broadcasting Board of Governors (BBG) Statement on 'Changing Minds Winning Peace,'" October 9, 2003, US Agency for Global Media website.

26. John Erwin Ward, Ithiel de Sola Pool, and Richard J. Solomon, *A Study of Future Directions for the Voice of America in the Changing World of International Broadcasting* (MIT Research Program on Communications Policy, 1983).

27. *United States International Broadcasting, National Security Decision Directive Number 45* (July 15, 1982); *The Voice of America Should Address Existing Problems to Ensure High Performance* (US General Accounting Office, 1982).

28. *Voice of America: Management Actions Needed to Adjust to a Changing Environment* (US General Accounting Office, 1992).
29. *An Agenda for Action: A Report of the Engineering Planning Committee* (Voice of America, 1989) author's copy; *International Audio Broadcasting for the Twenty-First Century* (National Research Council, 1989) author's copy. Some VOA practitioners believed they could have done more with alternative technologies if even a small portion of the funding for short-wave modernization had been reallocated. Chris Kern, email to author, July 25, 2018.
30. John Lennon, email to author, January 18, 2019.
31. Chris Kern, "The Voice of America: First on the Internet," *Chris Kern* (blog), December 2006, http://www.chriskern.net/history/voaFirstOn-TheInternet.html.
32. My thanks to John Lennon for pointing this out. Email to author, April 26, 2023.
33. On changing technologies and government broadcasting, see Monroe Price, Susan Haas, and Drew Margolin, "New Technologies and International Broadcasting: Reflections on Adaptations and Transformations," *The Annals of the American Academy of Political and Social Science* 616, no. 1 (March 2008): 150–172.
34. Shawn Powers, "R.I.P., Broadcasting," *PD Magazine* (Summer 2011).
35. *International Audio Broadcasting*, National Research Council, 40.
36. Sherwood Demitz to Robert Coonrod and Joseph Bruns, memorandum, "A Strategic Plan of Research for Broadcasting," August 30, 1991, author's copy; Woody Demitz to Joe Bruns and Geoffrey Cowan, memorandum, "Let Them Fly Blind?" April 8, 1994, author's copy; Voice of America, "VOA Russian Branch Program Review Notes," September 20, 1994, author's copy.
37. *Voice of America: Management Actions*, General Accounting Office, 26.
38. Shawn Powers, Matthew Baum, and Erik Nisbit, "Broadcasting Board of Governors: Research and Evaluation," in *Data-Driven Public Diplomacy*, 41–52.
39. Price, et al., "New Technologies," 168–170.
40. John Reinhardt to NSC Advisor Zbigniew Brzezinski, memorandum, "VOA Language Priorities," March 7, 1979, author's copy; Department of State to USIA, fax, "Re: Sen. For. Relations Proposed New Kurdish Service," June 6, 1990, author's copy; Peter Galbraith Oral History,

interviewed by Charles Stuart Kennedy, Foreign Affairs Oral History Collection, ADST, Arlington, VA.

41. *Broadcasting Board of Governors Announces Results of 2000/2001 Strategic Language Service Review*, January 19, 2001, author's copy; US Embassy Bangkok, "Closure of VOA's Thai Language Service," February 2, 2001, author's copy; "America, Signing Off," *Wall Street Journal*, June 14, 2001. The joint Greek/Turkish caucus statement was quoted in the *Turkish Daily News*, July 1, 2006. VOA's Greek service was terminated in 2014 after 72 years on the air; the Turkish service continues to broadcast.

42. Quoted in John Lewis Gaddis, *George Kennan: An American Life* (Penguin Press, 2011), 354.

43. On the origins of Radio Free Europe and Radio Liberty, see Mark G. Pomar, *Cold War Radio: The Russian Broadcasts of the Voice of America and Radio Free Europe/Radio Liberty* (Potomac Books, 2022); Michael Nelson, *War of the Black Heavens: The Battles of Western Broadcasting in the Cold War* (Syracuse University Press, 1997), 39–45; Linda Risso, ed., *Radio Wars: Broadcasting During the Cold War* (Routledge, 2016); Paul B. Henze, "RFE's Early Years: Evolution of Broadcast Policy and Evidence of Broadcast Impact," in *Cold War Broadcasting: Impact on the Soviet Union and Eastern Europe*, eds. A. Ross Johnson and R. Eugene Parta (Central European University Press, 2010), 3–16; and A. Ross Johnson, *Radio Free Europe and Radio Liberty: The CIA Years and Beyond* (Stanford University Press, 2010).

44. A. Ross Johnson, "Setting the Record Straight: Role of Radio Free Europe in the Hungarian Revolution," working paper, Woodrow Wilson Center, 2006, 7–8.

45. Quoted in Wasburn, *Broadcasting Propaganda*, 27.

46. Nelson, *Black Heavens*, 50; Richard H. Cummings, *Cold War Frequencies: CIA Clandestine Radio Broadcasting to the Soviet Union* (McFarland and Company, 2021), 28.

47. Frank G. Wisner to Deputy Director of Central Intelligence, memorandum, "Radio Free Europe," November 22, 1950, in Richard H. Cummings, *Cold War Frequencies*, Appendix D, https://ebin.pub/cold-war-frequencies-cia-clandestine-radio-broadcasting-to-the-soviet-union-and-eastern-europe-1476678642-9781476678641.html.

48. Quoted in Bennett Kovrig, *Of Walls and Bridges: The United States and Eastern Europe* (New York University Press, 1991), 66.

49. Johnson, "Setting the Record Straight," 16; Kovrig, *Walls and Bridges*, 81–85; Wasburn, *Broadcasting Propaganda*, 35.
50. Cord Meyer, *Facing Reality: From World Federalism to the CIA* (Harper and Row, 1980), 130.
51. Charles E. Bohlen, *Witness to History, 1929–1969* (W. W. Norton, 1973), 423.
52. Johnson, "Setting the Record Straight," 5; Nelson, *Black Heavens*, 69–84.
53. Sol Stern, "A Short Account of International Student Politics & the Cold War With Particular Reference to the NSA, CIA, Etc.," *Ramparts* (March 1967): 29–39. On disclosure of CIA's funding of US civil society organizations, see Meyer, *Facing Reality*, 87–90; Arch Puddington, *Broadcasting Freedom: The Cold War Triumph of Radio Free Europe and Radio Liberty* (University Press of Kentucky, 2000), 188–189; E. W. Kenworthy, "Hobby Foundation of Houston Affirms C.I.A. Tie," *New York Times*, February 21, 1967; and Richard Harwood, "O What a Tangled Web the CIA Wove: This is How the Money Goes Round," *Washington Post*, February 26, 1967. On President Johnson's effort to terminate CIA's funding of RFE/RL, see Nelson, *Black Heavens*, 140–141.
54. "28. Memorandum for the 303 Committee," *Foreign Relations of the United States, 1969–1976, Volume XXIX, Eastern Europe; Eastern Mediterranean, 1969–1972*, Historical Documents, Department of State.
55. "36. Telegram from the Embassy in Germany to the Department of State;" "54. Telegram from the Embassy in Poland to the Department of State;" "37. Memorandum from Helmut Sonnenfeldt of the National Security Council Staff to the President's Assistant for National Security Affairs (Kissinger)." All in *Volume XXIX, Eastern Europe*.
56. "31. Paper Prepared for President's Press Secretary (Ziegler)," *Volume XXIX, Eastern Europe*.
57. Evans and Novak, "Financing of Radio Free Europe Leaves Nixon Sensitive Problem," *Washington Post*, December 5, 1968. For the quotes of Senators Case and Fulbright, see Nelson, *Black Heavens*, 142–144.
58. *The Right to Know: Report of the Presidential Study Commission on International Radio Broadcasting* (1973), iii–iv, author's copy.
59. *Right to Know*, 3, 37–43; Nelson, *Black Heavens*, 145–148.
60. Kim Andrew Elliott, "Too Many American Voices," *Foreign Policy* 77 (Winter 1989–1990): 113–131; *U.S. International Broadcasting:*

Background and Issues for Reform (Congressional Research Service, 2016); *International Broadcasting: Downsizing and Relocating Radio Free Europe/ Radio Liberty* (US General Accounting Office, 1995).

61. Pub. L. 98–111, 97 Stat. 749 (1983); Pub. L. 101–246, title II, part D, 104 Stat. 15 (1990); *Radio and Television Broadcasting to Cuba: Background and Current Issues* (Congressional Research Service, 1994).

62. *U.S. Information Agency: Issues Related to Reinvention Planning in the Office of Cuba Broadcasting* (US General Accounting Office, 1996); *Broadcasting to Cuba: Actions are Needed to Improve Strategy and Operations* (US Government Accountability Office, 2009).

63. *Report of the President's Task Force on U.S. Government International Broadcasting: Hearing Before the Subcomm. on International Operations*, 102nd Cong. (February 4, 1992); *Radio Free China, Broadcasting and Public Policy* (Center for Strategic and International Studies, 1991), author's copy; *The Commission on Broadcasting to the People's Republic of China* (September 1992), https://books.google.com/books?id=ZRa2AA AAIAAJ&printsec=frontcover&source=gbs_ge_ summary_r&cad=0#v=onepage&q&f=false (accessed June 13, 2023).

64. *Broadcasting to China: Applying the Lessons from European Freedom Radios, Hearing Before the Subcommittees on European Affairs and East Asian and Pacific Affairs*, 102nd Cong. (November 21, 1991); "Biden Introduces Legislation to Establish Radio Free China," News Release, July 2, 1992, author's copy.

65. David I. Hitchcock to USIA Deputy Director [Kopp], memorandum, "Strategy on Radio Free China/Radio Free Asia," April 29, 1992, author's copy; [USIA Director] Henry E. Catto to [RFE news director] Gene Mater, May 5, 1992, author's copy; Lawrence Eagleburger to John Hughes, July 20, 1992, author's copy; Tom C. Korologos, "Getting the Message to China," *Washington Post*, July 25, 1992; Hans N. Tuch, "The Case Against Radio Free China," *Foreign Service Journal* 69, no. 7 (July 1992): 23–28.

66. Dante B. Fascell to George H. W. Bush, February 12, 1990, author's copy; Olympia Snowe to George H. W. Bush, April 2, 1990, author's copy; *H.R. 4013, Establishing a Bipartisan Presidential Commission for the Board for International Broadcasting and the U.S. Information Agency: Hearing Before the Subcomm. on International Operations*, 101st Cong. (March 22, 1990) (statement of Dante B Fascell and letter from Brent Scowcroft).

67. *Public Diplomacy in a New Europe* (1990), US Advisory Commission on Public Diplomacy Reports, 3.
68. "Response of BIB Chairman Malcolm S. Forbes, Jr. to report of the United States Advisory Commission on Public Diplomacy: Public Diplomacy in a New Europe," May 16, 1990, author's copy; David Binder, "Anti-Communist Radios Endangered by Success," *New York Times*, August 5, 1990.
69. Edwin J. Feulner, Jr., "Radio Strategy," Letter to the Editor, *Baltimore Sun*, May 31, 1990, author's copy; David Binder, "As Cold War Recedes, Radio Services Face Cuts," *New York Times*, June 29, 1990.
70. *The Report of the President's Task Force on U.S. Government International Broadcasting* (1991), author's copy.
71. Quoted in Henry Kamm, "'Free' Europe Embraces That Radio and its Mate," *New York Times*, May 6, 1990.
72. "Statement by Malcolm S. Forbes, Jr., Chairman, Board for International Broadcasting," June 27, 1991, minutes of meeting of President's Task Force on U.S. Government International Broadcasting, author's copy.
73. Michael Novak, "The Voice of Hope," *Forbes Magazine* (August 5, 1991); William Safire, "The Raid on R.F.E.," *New York Times*, July 1, 1991.
74. Thomas B. Rosenstiel, "Listening to the World Change on Shortwave," *Los Angeles Times*, September 25, 1990.
75. "Statement of Dr. Edwin J. Feulner, Jr., United States Advisory Commission on Public Diplomacy, before the President's Task Force on U.S. Government International Broadcasting," June 27, 1991, author's copy.
76. *Report of the President's Task Force*, author's copy.
77. Steven A. Holmes, "Cuts Set Off a Fight for Federal Broadcasting," *New York Times*, February 28, 1993; Tom C. Korologos, "Let's Simplify Our World Radio Role," Letter to the Editor, *New York Times*, March 11, 1993; Mary G. F. Bitterman, "VOA Can Do the Job," *Washington Post*, April 5, 1993; Czeslaw Milosz, "I'd Hate to See Them Go," *New York Times*, March 3, 1993; Dick Kirschten, "Radio Wars," *National Journal* 25, no. 15 (April 10, 1993): 865–867.
78. Quoted in Siobhan McDonough, "U.S. May Phase Out Radio Free Europe," *Washington Times*, March 22, 1991.

79. Biden's remarks on a "US government journalist" occurred in Senate debate on the State Department's budget authorization, 103rd Cong. Rec. S1281 (daily ed. January 25, 1994), 16.

80. William J. Clinton, "Statement on International Broadcasting Programs," June 15, 1993, American Presidency Project.

81. "A Stronger Voice of America," *New York Times*, June 17, 1993; Dick Kirschten, "Finally, Less Static on Overseas Radio," *National Journal* 25, no. 26 (June 26, 1993).

82. Joe Biden to [USIA Director] Joe Duffey and [BIB Chair] Dan Mica, July 13, 1993, author's copy; Carroll J. Doherty, "Tempers Flare Over Plan to Revamp Overseas Broadcasting Programs," *Congressional Quarterly* (July 17, 1993): 1890–1891; Dick Kirschten, "Broadcast News," *National Journal* 26 (February 19, 1994): 422–426.

83. Pub. L No. 103–236, Title III, 108 Stat. 383 (1994); *International Broadcasting: Downsizing and Relocating Radio Free Europe/Radio Liberty* (US General Accounting Office, 1995).

84. For a balanced overview of the BBG, see *U.S. International Broadcasting*, Congressional Research Service.

85. *Truth Over Disinformation: Supporting Freedom and Democracy: USAGM Strategic Plan 2022–2026* (2022); George Orwell, "Politics and the English Language," in *George Orwell: Essays*, ed. John Carey (Alfred A. Knopf, 1968), 954–967.

10

Soldiers

Why treat soldiers as practitioners in diplomacy's public dimension? In war, groups seek to "impose" their will on an enemy. "The means to this end is the organized application of or threat of violence by military force." Armed forces are a coercive instrument of power. At the same time, war is "an interactive social process." Its object is political and soldiers serve policy ends.[1] Diplomacy and military force are interconnected. Diplomatic negotiations can be more effective in the context of potential or actual use of force. Public diplomacy can increase the effectiveness of military power. Soldiers manage international military exchanges, engage in media relations, and support civic action programs in ways that influence the thinking and behavior of governments and civilian populations.

US combatant commanders in some countries engage in communication and representation activities comparable to those of ambassadors. With more money and people than civilian agencies, they fill a vacuum in US foreign affairs. For journalist Dana Priest, these "proconsuls to the empire" wield *all* the instruments of power and accept responsibilities that come their way from "an indecisive White House, an atrophied State Department, and a distracted Congress." The US military, Rosa Brooks writes, is now an all-purpose instrument for diplomatic and other tasks civilian agencies are unable to perform on an appropriate scale.[2]

243
B. Gregory, *American Diplomacy's Public Dimension*, Palgrave Macmillan Series in Global Public Diplomacy, https://doi.org/10.1007/978-3-031-38917-7_10

Then and Now

Like diplomacy, armed conflict's public dimension has existed throughout history. Assyrian warriors in ancient Mesopotamia called on besieged
cities to surrender with threats and promises delivered in the vernacular
of the people. Greek and Roman commanders used words and images to
undermine enemy morale and maintain political will at home. Consider
Sun Tzu's *The Art of War*, Pericles' orations, Alexander the Great's images
on coins, and eagles as symbols of predatory power on the standards of
Rome's imperial legions. Soldiers wield information strategies and soft
power tools. Americans have used such means to influence enemy fight-
ers, allies, and civilian populations since the early 1600s. Colonial military officers worked to maintain alliances with native tribes. This called
for diplomacy and "a liberal expense account."[3] In the nineteenth and
twentieth centuries "gunboat diplomacy" connected displays of naval
power with foreign policy objectives. Just as there is an American way of
diplomacy, scholars write about an American way of war that includes
initial reluctance to engage followed by full mobilization, citizen soldiers,
and rapid post-conflict demobilization fueled by popular demand.[4]

In today's wars people anywhere can be "on the battlefield." Space and
cyberspace are warfighting domains. National security is no longer
defined only by time, distance, and borders, Philip Bobbitt writes,
"because both the links among societies and the attacks on them exist in
psychological and infrastructural dimensions."[5] Adversaries are not only
states and failed states. Often, they are entities with no fixed address—
hackers, guerrilla groups, terrorist networks, and criminal syndicates.
Gray zone conflict, counterterrorism, special operations forces, remote
precision munitions, cyber technologies, robotics, and artificial intelligence are hallmarks of modern warfare.[6] War is still about lethal force,
but it is also about languages and cultures, stories and mindsets, social
and traditional media, and relations with civil society. Defense secretaries, commanders, and soldiers in the ranks operate in a mediated world.

What's in a Name?

Since World War II, a word salad has described methods and organizations in the military's information domain. US armed forces institutionalized two rival practitioner communities: psychological operations/military information support operations (PSYOP/MISO) and public affairs (PA). They have distinct modus operandi and overlapping and often conflicting goals. In 1948 the Pentagon created an Office of Public Affairs led by an Assistant Secretary of Defense. After the Korean War Armistice in 1953, the Army made psychological operations a permanent military capability. Associated terms and capabilities include Information Operations (IO), Information Warfare (IW), Strategic Communication (SC), Political Warfare (PW), Civil Affairs (CA), Key Leader Engagement (KLE), and more.

Largely missing in official vocabulary is propaganda, a word that has rolled through centuries of political and religious conflicts. As communications scholar Philip M. Taylor observed, "yesterday's epic poem or painting is really no more than the equivalent of today's propaganda film or television broadcast."[7] Despite arguments that propaganda is simply information propagation, soldiers display the same aversion to the word as diplomats.[8] Military practitioners understand its negative connotations and that many Americans believe it to be incompatible with democratic values. Propaganda is a defined term in military doctrine, but it is used infrequently and usually to frame what adversaries say and do.[9]

America's armed forces value information as a source of power. Military services jumped on each new wave of communication technologies from the telegraph to the Internet. They use them for situational awareness, command and control, and to create political will and influence behavior. Doctrine writers and military colleges use "Information" as an umbrella term for one of four elements of national power—diplomatic, informational, military, and economic—grouped as DIME.[10] The acronym has categorical neatness and pedagogical value. The elements overlap and signify conceptual and operational differences.

DIME's "I" embraces the information *environment* military practitioners seek to exploit and the information *capabilities* they deploy. In the environment, they seek two kinds of competitive edge. The first is operationally useful knowledge. Advantages come from processing valuable open information (news, images, and data) and awareness of what opponents attempt to conceal about their capabilities and intentions. Second, they communicate in ways intended to influence or deceive. Soldiers benefit from credibility and persuasion. They also gain when they create confusion or mislead an adversary.

Information capabilities likewise have two meanings. One involves electronic warfare and cyber activities that defend against or disable an adversary's information systems. A second relates to tools and methods used to inform and influence perceptions and behavior. Here there is overlap between military practitioners and other communities in diplomacy's public dimension. Soldiers typically, but not always, create a conceptual and organizational separation between capabilities used to openly influence and covertly deceive. Diplomats also deceive on occasion, but unlike military services, deception in diplomacy is not the object of training, doctrine, and core missions.

PSYOP/MISO

The US military's first psychological warfare organizations, created in World War I, were the Psychologic Subsection in the War Department's Military Intelligence Branch and the Field Propaganda Section under G-2 (intelligence) in the General Headquarters of American Expeditionary Forces in France led by Captain Heber Blankenhorn and his deputy Walter Lippmann. At its peak their small staff numbered no more than thirty soldiers. Their primary tools were leaflets dropped from balloons designed to encourage enemy troops to surrender. Radio as a mass communication medium did not exist and loudspeakers were primitive. The Army's "combat propaganda" practitioners were "borrowed" from civil society. After the war, the Field Propaganda Section lasted until 1925. Blankenhorn went home to a career in organized labor until he returned to lead a US Army "psychological warfare" team in World War II. Lippmann pursued his career as a journalist and public intellectual.[11]

The absence of an Army psychological operations capability until 1941 paralleled the absence of institutionalized public diplomacy. Both rose and fell with America's involvement in armed conflict. Both encountered resistance. In the interwar period, no military officers were assigned to study propaganda, and no career diplomats studied public diplomacy. "The use of propaganda as a military weapon against the enemy in the field … was a new thing in American army history," Blankenhorn recalled. But no reports on its operations were retained, including his own. When he returned in World War II, Blankenhorn encountered "not merely indifference to the idea of combat propaganda leaflets but … marked hostility from skeptical G-2 officers."[12]

War had a mobilizing effect, however, and General Eisenhower established an Army Psychological Warfare Branch in November 1942. Prior to the invasion of Europe, a Psychological Warfare Division was created at the Supreme Headquarters of the Allied Expeditionary Force. Mobile Radio Broadcasting Companies in North Africa, Europe, and the Pacific were equipped with radios, loudspeakers, typewriters, and printing units. They were demobilized in 1946. A small Tactical Information Detachment retained at Fort Riley, Kansas, was the only unit available for deployment in Korea in 1950. In 1951 the Army deployed a "Loudspeaker and Leaflet Company," which produced millions of leaflets disseminated by aircraft and artillery shells, and managed a radio network known as the Voice of the United Nations. President Eisenhower's decision to maintain a permanent capability after the war led to creation of a Psychological Warfare Center at Fort Bragg (renamed Fort Liberty), North Carolina, where it became part of a new US Army Special Operations Command.[13] The military's interest in PSYOP remained intermittent. An uptick during the Vietnam war was followed by a decade of inattention.

Creating a Doctrine. Scholars and practitioners debate what to call this capability. NSC reviews during the Reagan administration led to a Defense Department PSYOP master plan and a joint doctrine for PSYOP in "peace and crisis and at all levels of conflict."[14] NSC advisor Carnes Lord argued first for "psychological-political warfare" and "psychological-political operations." The former described tools and methods used against enemies in armed conflict, the latter tools and methods used to advance political strategies in allied and neutral countries. He soon became an advocate of the umbrella term "strategic communication."[15]

PSYOP, however, gradually became the consensus choice for an instrument with multiple objectives other than tactical support on the battlefield. The Joint Staff settled on a multidimensional definition that lasted essentially unchanged for decades. Language in a Joint Staff publication in 1996 was typical: "Psychological operations (PSYOP) are operations planned to convey selected information and indicators to foreign audiences to influence their emotions, motives, objective reasoning, and ultimately the behavior of foreign governments, organizations, groups, and individuals."[16] The revised publication in January 2010 made no definitional change.

Within a few months, however, Defense Secretary Robert Gates directed the Army's Special Operations Command to replace the term "psychological operations" with "military information support operations" (MISO). PSYOP units would henceforth be named Mission Information Support Teams (MISTs). But as Rosa Brooks, then an official in the Office of the Under Secretary for Policy, explained in a memorandum:

> This is just a terminological change, not a substantive change. The term PSYOP was anachronistic and misleading; Military Information Support is a more accurate description of the activities and programs at issue. We already use the term 'Military Information Support Teams' to describe the PSYOP personnel who deploy to embassies and provide support to State Dept. public diplomacy efforts; this more thoroughgoing terminological shift will make our terminology consistent and help reduce misunderstandings.[17]

Vietnam/JUSPAO. As with public diplomacy, the operations of practitioners gave meaning to PSYOP's broad goals. In Vietnam PSYOP forces expanded to four battalions. They assisted commanders in the field, advised the South Vietnamese government, operated a 50,000-watt radio station and large printing presses, published a magazine, developed a research capability, deployed aerial leaflet and loudspeaker teams, air dropped pre-tuned transistor radios, and supported covert activities intended to manipulate and deceive. They targeted enemy forces and neutral and allied civilian populations.

Initially, the Army's PSYOP battalions operated under the direction of the Joint United States Public Affairs Office (JUSPAO), which brought together representatives from the State Department, USIA, USAID, and the CIA. USIA's Barry Zorthian was double-hatted as JUSPAO director and the US Embassy's Minister Counselor for Public Affairs in 1964. A year later, NSC Advisor McGeorge Bundy reaffirmed USIA's responsibility for all "psychological and informational programs in South Vietnam under the direction of the U.S. ambassador." JUSPAO was formed, Zorthian later recalled, "because the whole communications [effort] was disoriented, uncoordinated, and sometimes contradictory." His role was to bring order and direction to the chaos.[18] The Army strongly endorsed the arrangement.

JUSPAO's operations divided into four categories: media relations with foreign and American journalists, information and cultural operations in South Vietnam, support for the South Vietnamese information ministry, and direction of psychological operations. Zorthian, a former Marine with a record of accomplishment as Newsroom Chief and Program Manager at VOA and USIA's Deputy PAO in India, had a gruff, genial, and winning personality. Nicknamed "Zorro," he charmed journalists, ambassadors, military officers, and colleagues with his wit and ability to accentuate whatever was positive while not covering up bad news. General William Westmoreland, commander of US forces, later wrote, "I considered the psychological effort so important that I provided extensive support to Mr. Zorthian in the form of military personnel, units, and facilities."[19]

Zorthian soon realized, however, that civilian control of JUSPAO created formidable challenges. As US forces expanded, military control of PSYOP battalions increased. Some commanders and their South Vietnamese counterparts viewed PSYOP as marginal to combat objectives. The Civil Operations and Revolutionary Development Support (CORDS) pacification program carried out autonomous activities in the provinces beyond JUSPAO's control.

USIA's support for JUSPAO also began to waver.[20] For many public diplomacy officers, psychological operations were not part of the Agency's mission. Association with PSYOP tarnished the credibility of USIA's information and exchange operations. JUSPAO's priority focus on briefing American journalists and shaping US public opinion ran counter to the Agency's mission to engage foreign publics and legal restrictions on domestic dissemination. VOA's broadcasters objected to using their transmitters for "gray" propaganda broadcasts to North Vietnam. "Disclosure, which would be unavoidable," VOA Director Kenneth Giddens stated, "would open us to the charge, at home and abroad, that VOA was put temporarily to a covert 'Cold War' use."[21] JUSPAO's staff of over 200 and annual operating budget of $10 million far exceeded any USIA field operation elsewhere, creating rivalries and resentment.[22]

JUSPAO was not USIA's first experience with psychological operations. The Agency had partnered with CIA in the covert operations that led to the overthrow of Mohammad Mosaddeq's government in Iran in 1953. That same year, USIA assisted CIA in efforts to discredit democratically elected President Jacobo Arbenz in Guatemala. In 1961 USIA's Hewson Ryan provided "vigorous participation" in President Kennedy's covert Operation Mongoose aimed at overthrowing Fidel Castro's government in Cuba. When US troops entered the Dominican Republic in 1965, it was Ryan who assumed operational command of the First Psywar Battalion and led a task force that organized all psychological operations.[23] But JUSPAO was the apex of USIA's involvement in psychological operations. In the decades after the Vietnam War, USIA and PSYOP teams rarely coordinated in theater.[24] In 1978 the Carter administration's USIA mission statement made clear the Agency would not be involved in covert operations.

Balkans/South America/Middle East. The military's PSYOP capabilities declined in the 1970s, expanded during interventions in Grenada and Panama in the 1980s, declined in the early 1990s, and expanded again during armed conflict in Bosnia, Kosovo, Liberia, and Kuwait, and wars in Iraq and Afghanistan after 9/11.[25] Along the way, PSYOP's practitioners established military doctrine and adopted new tools and methods. After leaflets and loudspeakers came newspapers, comic books, magazines, and broadcasts from terrestrial and airborne platforms that included a fleet of EC-130 Commando Solo aircraft capable of transmitting AM/

FM, shortwave, and TV signals. Later came Internet streaming, social media, and mobile phones.

Colonel Jeffrey B. Jones, a West Point graduate who commanded the 8th PSYOP Battalion in the Persian Gulf War and later served on the NSC staff, was a pioneering practitioner and highly regarded analyst of PSYOP and strategic communication in the post-Cold War era. His paper "The Third Wave and the Fourth Dimension" was required reading for years in military colleges and the Joint Staff.[26] In 1995 he described PSYOP's modus operandi:

> For Panamanian soldiers during Just Cause, U.S. psychological operations (PSYOP) was the voice of reason. In the Gulf War, PSYOP was millions of leaflets delivered by conventional means (artillery and aircraft) as well as more unusual means (facsimile machines and bottles washed up on beaches). It meant 18 hours of daily Arabic broadcasts and 66 loudspeaker teams deployed at brigade level with coalition forces. For the Kurds in Provide Comfort, PSYOP was multifaceted media support of humanitarian relief. In Restore Hope, PSYOP was radio and press—known as *Rajo* (Hope)—that offered credible information to some 100,000 Somalis; and it was seven million leaflets that disseminated guidance on lessening anarchy and receiving aid. It was communication via tactical loudspeaker teams accompanying Army and Marine units as well as coalition forces. To U.S. diplomats in Central and South America and the Caribbean, PSYOP is an effective tool in drug interdiction and eradication, medical and engineer support, public information, disaster relief, the formation of professional armies, and promoting democracy. In former war-torn nations, it is an educational vehicle to publicize landmine awareness in schools and villages.[27]

Practitioners stress that most PSYOP activities are open, attributed, and intended to be truthful. Leaflets explain how enemy troops can safely surrender. Media messages support disaster relief. Increased global transparency and use of PSYOP/MISO in nation-building and post-combat operations strengthened the case for operational transparency. A leaflet handed out in Bosnia can be read as easily on CNN as in Sarajevo. PSYOP/MISO teams supported outreach by public diplomats in Iraq and Afghanistan.[28]

But PSYOP's writ also encapsulates falsehood and misattribution. For example, PSYOP practitioners placed false stories in Arab media that Iraqi tank commanders were defecting in large numbers during the Persian Gulf War in 1991. The stories soon spread to US media. Military PA practitioners faced a dilemma. If unaware, they risked exposing the deception. If aware, they risked being seen as complicit. Most concluded it is better to be knowledgeable so they can respect their obligation to be truthful, however difficult, without damaging a covert operation.[29]

Office of Strategic Influence. This issue came to a head in the intense reaction to creation of an Office of Strategic Influence (OSI) in the Department of Defense soon after 9/11. In a story widely believed to have been leaked by the Office of Public Affairs, *The New York Times* reported, "The Pentagon is developing plans to provide news items, possibly even false ones, to foreign media organizations as part of a new effort to influence public sentiment and policymakers in both friendly and unfriendly countries."[30] Officials later informed Congress OSI's mission was to give guidance to combatant commanders and "serve as the Department of Defense focal point for all issues relating to the strategic information campaign in support of the war on terrorism."[31] Headed by Air Force General Simon P. "Pete" Worden, OSI's plan was to work with military PSYOP units and private contractors to shape themes, send email messages to journalists and civic leaders, counter disinformation, and provide computers and distance learning courses to Pakistan's religious schools.

Within a week of its disclosure, public outcry that the Pentagon had created an "official lies bureau" led Defense Secretary Donald Rumsfeld to shutter the Office. OSI "has clearly been so damaged that it is pretty clear to me that it could not function effectively," he declared. Media reports portrayed Assistant Secretary for Public Affairs Torie Clarke as a leading force in its demise.[32] But Rumsfeld was unchastened. Speaking to the press months later, he recalled that at the time "I ... said 'Fine, if you want to savage this thing, fine, I'll give you the corpse. There's the name. You can have the name, but I'm gonna keep doing every single thing that needs to be done.' And I have."[33]

Names and organizations came and went. A short-lived Office of Special Plans implemented some of OSI's activities. An Office of Defense

Support for Public Diplomacy lasted until the Obama administration shut it down. The Pentagon then created a "Global Strategic Engagement Team." The term "strategic communication" had a short run until Joint Chiefs Chairman Admiral Michael G. Mullen denounced it as a "cottage industry" that had lost its value. "Frankly, I don't care for the term," he wrote. "By *organizing* to it—creating whole structures *around* it—we have allowed strategic communication to become a thing instead of ... an enabling function that guides and informs our decisions."[34]

How "white," "gray," and "black" PSYOP should be organized and de-conflicted is a continuing challenge. PSYOP teams have long emphasized that truthful and attributed "white" content is less susceptible to blow-back and more likely to win public support. But deception is often neces-sary in war. If a just war legitimizes lethal force, then it certainly legitimizes lying. PSYOP doctrine authorizes "gray" content, delayed attribution, unattributed information, and "black" content that can be false and misattributed. The purpose of "gray" and "black" is not just to mislead, PSYOP's advocates maintain, but to influence thinking and behavior that supports military goals. RAND's Christopher Paul advocates separating "white" and sequestered "gray" and "black" capabilities within PSYOP. "Don't have the same organizations and personnel conducting both truth-based and false messaging. Retain some kind of conduit or connection between those who deceive and manipulate ... but keep such black capabilities small and away from the light."[35]

Public Affairs

The Joint Staff defines public affairs with deceptive brevity as "Communication activities with external and internal audiences." Its guidance elaborates that proactive release of "accurate information to domestic and international audiences puts joint operations in context, facilitates informed perceptions about military operations, undermines adversarial propaganda, and helps achieve national, strategic, and opera-tional objectives." Most PA practitioners, however, understand their mis-sion is to influence as well as inform. They also know their mandate is "to communicate with international publics," not just to the defense community and the American people.[36] They are actors in diplomacy's public dimension by intent and as a consequence of the military's dominant role in US foreign affairs.

PA's stakeholders have very different goals. Journalists want unrestricted access to battlefields and freedom to report and tell a story. Commanders seek control of operational environments and the support of American and allied publics. Political leaders want to promote policies, define agendas, and frame positive images. PA's military and civilian practitioners try to manage and leverage the media to the extent possible. In World War II, military officers controlled the reports of journalists in combat units. When satellite technologies and the Internet made censorship impractical, generals turned to keeping journalists close through press pools, embedding practices, and media relations strategies.

These approaches raise important questions. Should journalists who cover war also voice opinions? How should they report on casualties? Underlying reporters' concerns are corporate impulses often at odds with good journalism. War boosts ratings. How should commanders frame messages that influence publics abroad and at home? What are appropriate ground rules for the Defense Department's long-standing ties with America's news and entertainment industries? Joint Chiefs Chairman Richard Myers summarized the problem: "Perhaps the most challenging piece of this is putting together what we call a strategic influence campaign quickly and with the right emphasis. That's everything from psychological operations to the public affairs piece to coordinating partners in this effort with us."[37]

Military PA practitioners give priority to home audiences because citizens vote, enlist, pay taxes, and often determine operational success or failure. Messages at home do not stay at home. During the 2003 Iraq War, a speech delivered by General William Boykin in uniform to Christian evangelicals in the US, holding that "my God was a real God, and his [Islamic God] was an idol," enraged Muslims.[38] Journalists with smart phones, reporting on satellite television and social media, reach foreign and domestic audiences simultaneously. As technologies changed, presidents, defense secretaries, military commanders, military PAOs, and civilian PA practitioners changed their modus operandi. Wars in the

Persian Gulf, Bosnia, and Kosovo in the 1990s and Afghanistan and Iraq in the 2000s are case studies.

Persian Gulf War (1990–1991). In the Gulf War, PA practitioners focused on leveraging the 24/7 coverage of CNN, managing press pools of US and international journalists, and supporting the media strategies of Washington officials and combatant commanders. Regular briefings were used to inform the press and communicate directly to publics at home and abroad. "The information function was extraordinarily important" recalled Defense Secretary Richard Cheney, a constant presence in Pentagon briefings and Sunday talk shows. "I did not have a lot of confidence that I could leave that to the press." The press was "a problem to be managed."[39] For Chairman Powell, the media were conduits to multiple audiences. "We knew that when you stood up in one of those press conferences, you weren't talking to reporters … you were talking to the American people, you were talking to a hundred and fifty capitals, you were talking to the enemy and you were talking to your troops. So you always had to have a message that would fit all five audiences and the fifth audience of course being the reporters themselves."[40]

Battlefield commander Norman Schwarzkopf's strategy was two pronged: tightly controlled combat press pools and televised briefings on CNN. He "embraced it [public affairs] totally," Charles J. Lewis at Hearst News explained, "but he embraced it so he could control it."[41] CBS correspondent Morley Safer put it more colorfully. "The most brilliant stroke ever in press/military relations," he declared, "was Norman Schwarzkopf and the briefings in Desert Storm." His briefings "made journalism redundant." For most American and foreign CNN viewers "knowledge of the Gulf War was Norman Schwarzkopf looking them in the eye, that huge mound of a man, addressing them just like that and then putting on only pictures of missiles that worked. No mistakes were broadcast. This was a coup d'état by the Pentagon of the American press, the world press, ably assisted by CNN."[42] Early concerns about a "CNN effect" determining government decisions and public opinion, however, gave way to more measured views among scholars that the media's impact correlates with whether or not policies are legitimate and clearly articulated.[43]

Balkan Wars (1990s). NATO's military campaigns in Serbia, Bosnia, and Kosovo were not a response to an invasion; they were humanitarian

interventions in non-member states. Ethnic cleansing and human trag-
edy, portrayed in graphic TV images, were drivers of diplomacy and military operations. Americans demanded something be done. CNN still
mattered, but new technologies had radically changed the media environment. Mobile phones were ubiquitous. The Internet was in its early
stages. Cameras were smaller and digitalization dramatically reduced
costs. Leaders, diplomats, generals, and journalists developed strategies
for a world in which "the instantaneous flow of news and especially imag-
ery could overwhelm the ability of governments to explain, investigate,
coordinate, and confirm."[44]

US diplomat Richard Holbrooke used "the media to drive diplomacy,"
which led to the 1995 Dayton Peace Agreement that ended the war in
Bosnia, recalled General Wesley K. Clark, then on his negotiating team.
Holbrooke "knew that all sides were watching his brief CNN statements."
The media were a "means to influence Milosevic" and "critical for getting
Washington policymakers on board."[45] In his account of the Kosovo war
that followed, Clark lamented lack of media coverage of Serbia's ethnic
cleansing and deplored Serbian leader Slobodan Milosevic's ability to
exploit televised images of civilian casualties when NATO's warplanes
mistakenly bombed a Serb passenger train, China's embassy in Belgrade,
and a convoy of Albanian refugees—images broadcast by CNN and BBC
journalists he had allowed to remain in Serbia. "In this war, a camera
inside Kosovo would have been worth a dozen strikes on Serb vehicles."[46]

Fragile political support in NATO countries and lack of consensus on
using ground troops created other public affairs challenges. Most journalists covered the war from NATO's capitals and its military command
center in Brussels where a small, undertrained NATO public affairs staff
struggled in reactive press briefings with insufficient information.
Realizing they lacked the "media and communications infrastructure"
required by a Kosovo campaign that was dominating global news, British
Prime Minister Tony Blair sent his communication advisor Alastair
Campbell and a Downing Street press team to Brussels to work "the
magic" of the media strategy that brought his Labor government to
power.[47]

With the enthusiastic approval of Clark, now NATO's Supreme Allied
Military Commander, Campbell and NATO spokesman Jamie Shea

proceeded to overhaul NATO's media operations using the "war room" model and campaign techniques of political candidates. Increased media monitoring. Framing appropriate messages for each day. Twice-daily conference calls between London, Washington, and other NATO capitals. Insistence on knowing targeting plans in advance so questions could be anticipated. Messages tailored for reporters, publics in NATO member states, publics in other countries, and the Serb opposition.[48] The strategy worked.

For Clark, however, there were personal consequences. Following a press conference in which headline writers' interpretations of his remarks caught the attention of Washington policymakers sensitive to references to ground troops, the Secretary of Defense ordered him to stop giving televised briefings. Subsequent guidance confined the restriction to his briefings in Brussels but not to troop visits. "I knew that for military men, dealing with the media can be like drinking from a poisoned chalice," Clark wrote. "However heady the wine, at some point you may get a fatal dose."[49]

NATO's methods had positive long-term consequences for PA practitioners. Conference calls with political leaders improved their ability to deal with breaking events and multiple narratives. As one Pentagon spokesperson observed, they "helped us mobilize ourselves to focus on various messages we wanted to get out in various capitals, so it wasn't just a question of us talking ... we could make sure this happened in London, it happened in Brussels, it happened in Paris, it happened in Bonn as well."[50] Shea's "golden rules" became fixtures in military doctrine and training manuals. Practitioners were advised to adopt a proactive approach, provide regular information to the press, avoid lies and "no comment" answers, coordinate messages, admit mistakes, seize opportunities in transient media spotlights, develop a set of "master messages" and repeat some in every interview, insist on access to principals, and leave comment on political issues to political leaders.[51]

Afghanistan/Iraq Wars. In the months after 9/11, Defense Secretary Rumsfeld and military service chiefs appeared frequently in the Pentagon's daily press briefings to make the Bush administration's case for a war against al Qaeda and "every terrorist group of global reach."[52] They signed opinion columns and appeared on Sunday talk shows, Al Jazeera, CNN,

BBC, and VOA. The State Department's Washington foreign press center organized briefings by military spokespersons. Generals regularly briefed the media at US Central Command and in Kabul. Military PA practitioners coordinated with counterparts in the White House, State Department, other US agencies, and allied governments.

A year later, the White House rolled out its "meticulously planned strategy to persuade the public, the Congress, and the allies of the need to confront the threat from Saddam Hussein."[53] It was a strategy of regime change and preemptive war. Rumsfeld, now a media rock star, and military commanders helped to make the case. As Defense spokesperson Torie Clarke put it, "He [Rumsfeld] and Chairman of the Joint Chiefs General Myers would regularly spend thirty to sixty minutes once or twice a week before the Pentagon press corps.[54] Retired military officers fanned out on cable news channels to make the case for "the liberation of Iraq."

Clarke and her deputy Bryan Whitman developed a communications plan "to flood the zone with information" by embedding journalists in air, ground, and naval forces. A majority of the embeds were American journalists. A substantial minority represented Al Jazeera, the BBC, China's Xinhua, and other international media organizations. The plan had two goals: to counter Iraq's news management by providing on the ground access to embedded journalists, and to "shape public perception of the national security environment" in the US, allied countries, and countries affected by US military operations.[55] Pentagon officials declared embedding to be a principled and "historic" shift in media relations—a pragmatic response in a world where journalists using video phones, night vision goggles, laptops, and an array of whiz-bang audio–visual tools were giving global audiences a safe view of armed combat. Some field commanders questioned negative reporting and coverage that was too quick to focus on civilian casualties.[56]

For many journalists, embedding was an imperfect improvement over their Vietnam experiences and the constrictive press pool policies of the first Gulf War. It was a reasonable price to pay for access. Embargoed stories could be released later, an option that was foreclosed if you weren't there. But critics such as CNN anchor Bernard Shaw argued that "journalists who agree to go with combat units effectively become hostages of the military."[57] Reporters close to troops could be co-opted. Others questioned a "soda straw" view of combat that provided little perspective in the fog of war. They remained wary of what Joseph Nye called "the weaponization of reporters."[58]

PA practitioners occasionally undermined their own credibility. Dramatic accounts of the rescue of Army private Jessica Lynch in Iraq in 2003, captured on military video and widely broadcast to American viewers, were subsequently called into question. The press blamed the Pentagon for hyping the story. The Pentagon blamed the press for speculative reporting. The Lynch episode and the military's early misleading information about NFL football star Pat Tillman's death from "friendly fire" in Afghanistan provoked criticism and Congressional hearings. A House oversight committee concluded in both cases that "fictional accounts" became compelling public narratives in which the Defense Department did not meet its basic obligation to share accurate information with the public.[59]

In 2005 PA practitioners were confronted by outraged news organizations reporting on the Lincoln Group, a Washington-based public relations firm hired by the Pentagon to pay Iraqi journalists to publish positive news stories. White House officials stated they were "very concerned." Senators held hearings to deplore the damage to US credibility. Pentagon spokesman Whitman at first tried to deflect by describing an Iraq where "adversaries make it a practice to misinform, to deceive, and to lie," while the military seeks to give "good, accurate and timely information." But when an opinion poll showed 72 percent of Americans opposed paying Iraqi newspapers, he expressed understanding of the public's concern and said a review of the issue was ongoing.[60]

For decades USIA, State, USAID, and US broadcasters had trained foreign journalists on the norms and methods of a free press. Secret payments for stories did not fit the mold. Planting stories is "ineffective and counter-productive," National Defense University professor Dan Kuehl explained. "[T]he use of deception to print even factual and accurate information simply assures that the credibility and veracity of ALL information will eventually be damaged or discredited."[61] PA practitioners were caught in the middle. They were committed to open, credible communication. Officials and commanders sanctioned covert practices. All were forced to deal with the consequences of exposure.

Photos of US soldiers abusing naked detainees in Iraq's Abu Ghraib prison created another massive public affairs problem. President Bush condemned the actions on Arabic-language TV networks. Military officers apologized profusely. "My Army's been shamed by this," General Mark Kimmitt declared, "I apologize for what those soldiers did to your citizens. It was reprehensible, and it was unacceptable." State Department research reports documented "a global outpouring of revulsion, contempt and anger towards the 'barbaric idiocy' and 'sadistic abuse' shown by the U.S. troops." Commentators debated whether it was an isolated case of "mistreatment" by low level solders (argued by the Bush administration) or evidence of a policy of torture (argued by journalist Seymour Hersh and other critics). Scholars studied the implications of event-driven news, whether "abuse" or "torture" was the appropriate term in their reporting, and whether media organizations had a responsibility to frame an alternative to the administration's claims.[62]

Military Diplomacy

Soldiers partner with civilian diplomats and at times carry out ambassadorial functions and other diplomatic responsibilities such as negotiations on overseas bases and overflight rights.[63] State Department political and public diplomacy officers have long served as advisors at NATO, combatant commands, and the Army's PSYOP headquarters at Fort Liberty.[64] Diplomats study and teach at the National Defense University and military service colleges. Military officers are assigned to the NSC and State. Soldiers support and collaborate with diplomats in high-risk environments. US broadcasters partnered with the military in the construction of shortwave relay stations. Commando Solo EC-130 aircraft transmitted VOA and RFE/RL broadcasts in the Balkans, Kosovo, the Persian Gulf, Haiti, Nicaragua, Afghanistan, and Iraq.[65]

Nation Building. Soldiers throughout history have been diplomatic go-betweens, typically in occupied territories and colonies at outposts of empire. The US Army engaged in nation building in the Philippines,

Germany, Austria, and Japan, and later in Vietnam, Iraq, and Afghanistan. Its role as an autonomous diplomatic actor in Germany and Japan is a clarifying case. "Bring the boys home," Americans said loudly in 1945, and the military was quick to agree. Generals MacArthur and Eisenhower "are in favor of getting out of Government in Germany as soon as possible," Secretary of War Robert P. Patterson declared, "and they feel the Government of Germany should be turned over to … the State Department." This would be a "great mistake," Secretary of State James Byrnes replied. State is "not geared for this … [T]he Army has the best organization" and should remain "for some time to come."[66] Six months later it was agreed: State "will be responsible for formulation of governmental policy." The War Department "will be responsible for execution and administration of policy … in the occupation and government of these occupied areas."[67]

The Office of the Military Government, United States (OMGUS) assumed control of Germany's "political, economic, and cultural life," including its "communications, press, propaganda, and education." It engaged in negotiations with local governments and other occupying powers. Eventually its diplomacy with national political leaders led to elections and formation of the Federal Republic of Germany under the leadership of Chancellor Konrad Adenauer.[68]

As US representatives in German cities and states, America's "military governors" funded and conducted a wide range of public diplomacy activities. They distributed books and pamphlets, established and supervised German newspapers and radio stations, toured the country in jeeps with film projectors, built and directed a network of American Libraries (America Houses), and encouraged support for democracy through the OMGUS Reorientation Program. Over time they recruited American civilians to serve as a second generation of representatives called Resident Officers. One was a young Yale Richmond, who went on to a career as a cultural diplomat and scholar. It was "Public Diplomacy at the grassroots level," Richmond later wrote, "as we talked with mayors about US policy, promoted reforms in Germany, attended the town meetings we encouraged the Germans to hold, and showed the flag in a Germany we had been at war with only five years earlier."[69]

In Germany, the mission was to promote denazification and create new institutions. In Japan, the Army chose to work through existing institutions to conserve resources and because fewer Americans had language and cultural skills. Operating through the US General Headquarters in Tokyo, the Army revised Japanese textbooks, distributed films, and encouraged distribution of books by indigenous Japanese publishers.[70] As military occupations drew to a close, the Army increased its partnership with Foreign Service officers. From the war's end to the 1950s, when diplomats resumed control of their traditional domains, the US military had been a governance and diplomatic actor, roles it played in subsequent conflicts.

Fast forward to Mosul, Iraq, in 2003. General David Petraeus and the Army's 101st Airborne Division occupied the city, the hub of northern Iraq's Nineveh province. The task was nation building—restore basic services, rebuild civil government, open schools, provide humanitarian assistance, support economic development, rebuild media outlets, and importantly negotiate with local leaders to construct viable political governance. In his public diplomacy, Petraeus worked to reopen Mosul University, create public service announcements, and fund television programs including a Mosul talent show on the model of "American Idol." He and other Army officers became talk-show hosts. Within months, Mosul had 52 political parties, 24 newspapers, and a radio and TV station. There were no State Department diplomats to assist. Local Iraqis had no contact with the US Coalition Provisional Authority in Baghdad. The Army again was a governance and diplomatic actor.[71]

Mission Creep. America's military services have acquired responsibilities, authorities, and funding for activities previously the work of diplomacy practitioners. This "mission creep," analysts argue, "has been accommodated, and sometimes accelerated, by the choices made by senior policy officials and congressional representatives, and by the weaknesses and culture of the civilian foreign policy institutions themselves."[72] Defense Secretary Gates attributed it to America's lack of understanding and appreciation of the value of "core diplomatic operations," a strong political constituency for major weapons programs, and a blurring of the lines separating war, peace, diplomacy, and development.[73] CENTCOM Commander Anthony Zinni observed he "was asked to carry out presidential and other diplomatic missions that would normally have fallen to diplomats."[74] With huge budgets, personnel in the thousands, and open-ended mandates, US regional commands engage in activities that far exceed the State Department's bandwidth.

Defense officials occasionally express reservations about mission creep. "America's civilian institutions of diplomacy and development," Gates observed, "have been chronically undermanned and underfunded for far too long." He talked the talk but found change difficult. "[U]ntil our government decides to plus up our civilian agencies, these so-called 'non-traditional capabilities' have moved into the mainstream of military thinking, planning and strategy—where they must stay."[75] Even if civilian agencies are "plussed up," analysts argue, the military will still need a diplomacy capability. Soldiers engaged in armed combat, counter-terrorism, and responses to natural disasters and other emergencies need to explain and build support for their actions in civilian populations.[76]

Diplomats are conflicted. "Carrying out civil administration and police functions is simply going to degrade the American capability to do the things America has to do," former Secretary of State Condoleezza Rice declared. "We don't need to have the 82nd Airborne escorting kids to kindergarten."[77] Diplomats also complain military practitioners have unfair resource advantages and short-term attitudes. They waste money. They don't do public diplomacy well. They focus too much on quick unsophisticated messaging and less on building relationships through listening and dialogue. They generate public support for entering or prolonging unnecessary wars. Soldiers who fund concerts, television ads, school essay contests, and news websites are intruding on diplomacy's turf.[78]

Most soldiers would be delighted if diplomats and broadcasters took over these activities. When they ask diplomats to specify which Pentagon programs should be cut, improved, or transferred to the State Department, they seldom get answers.[79] Many ambassadors, however, find ways to leverage military resources to advantage. Interviews with more than two dozen ambassadors in one study reflected strong commitment to their Chief of Mission authority, but also a regard for combatant commanders as cooperative and respectful of their opinions and authority.[80] Rare is the diplomat who—after spending time with soldiers in a hostile foreign environment, as an advisor to a combatant command, or at a military service college—fails to appreciate their skills and dedication as well as their advantages in resources, staff, planning, training, and attention to professional education.

Embassies and exchanges. In most embassies, military attachés advise ambassadors, report on foreign military issues and conditions, engage host nation counterparts, and manage security cooperation programs.[81] Soldiers and Defense Department civilians negotiate joint military exercises with other countries. Navy ship visits support people-to-people interaction. Civil Military Affairs practitioners and the Army Corps of Engineers build roads and schools, provide health services, promote democratization and rule of law, protect cultural property in war zones, and support national and local governance entities. These civil-military operations are intended to "establish, maintain, influence, or exploit" relations with foreign governments, non-governmental organizations, and publics in friendly, neutral, and hostile countries. Joint doctrine provides extensive guidance on negotiation skills, language proficiency, effective communication, and cultural expertise.[82]

Military practitioners also manage an array of exchanges and visitor programs. The International Military Education and Training (IMET) program funds military-to-military exchanges to support combined operations, promote democracy and human rights, and develop English language and professional skills. The Professional Military Education (PME) program supports yearlong academic study and training by US and foreign military officers in military colleges abroad and in the United States. A lot of public diplomacy's "last three feet" occurs in seminar rooms at the National War College, military service colleges, and civilian universities.[83]

In some embassies, an Office of Defense Cooperation (ODC) manages training activities related to equipment purchases by foreign militaries.[84] The Pentagon funds regional education centers for security studies, research, and outreach: the Africa Center for Strategic Studies, Daniel K. Inouye Asia Pacific Center for Security Studies, George C. Marshall European Center for Security Studies, Near East-South Asia Center for Strategic Studies, and William J. Perry Center for Hemispheric Defense Studies. AFRICOM, the US military command initiated for Africa in

2007, was established to shift the focus from combat operations to activities intended to build relations with soldiers and security elites in partner nations. In AFRICOM's unique command structure, the Deputy Commander for Civil Military Engagement is a career ambassador.[85]

Soldiers and diplomats share vast areas of common ground. They engage civilian populations before, during, and after armed conflict. They operate in 24/7 news streams, medium-term campaigns, and engagement over years and decades. They value credibility in a world where attention, not information, is scarce. They view diplomacy and military force through a whole of government lens. They advise leaders on policy formulation and communication, engage in dialogue with others, inform and influence through words, images, and actions, and evaluate outcomes.[86] Soldiers are warriors first, but they also are actors in diplomacy's public dimension. With institutional footprints larger than those of embassies, corporations, and intelligence services, they have an outsized influence in America's foreign affairs. Americans have decided their military will have a front seat in representing them to the world, which means inevitably soldiers are diplomacy practitioners.

Notes

1. US Marine Corps, *Warfighting*, MCPD1 (June 20, 1997), 3–4, https://www.marines.mil/Portals/1/Publications/MCDP%201%20Warfighting.pdf; Scott K. Thomson and Christopher E. Paul, "Paradigm Change: Operational Art and the Information Joint Function," *Joint Force Quarterly* 89, 2nd Quarter (2018): 8–14.
2. Dana Priest, *The Mission: Waging War and Keeping Peace with America's Military* (W. W. Norton, 2003), 14, 61–77; Rosa Brooks, *How Everything Became War and the Military Became Everything: Tales from the Pentagon* (Simon & Schuster, 2016), 9, 357–358.
3. Richard R. Johnson, "The Search for a Usable Indian: An Aspect of the Defense of Colonial New England," *The Journal of American History* 64, no. 3 (December, 1977): 630.
4. Russell F. Weigley, *The American Way of War: A History of United States Military Strategy and Policy* (Macmillan, 1973).

5. Philip Bobbitt, *The Shield of Achilles: War, Peace and the Course of History* (Anchor Books, 2003), 813.

6. In the literature on modern warfare, see Rupert Smith, *The Utility of Force: The Art of War in the Modern World* (Alfred A. Knopf, 2007); Michael Ignatieff, *Virtual War: Kosovo and Beyond* (Metropolitan Books, 2000); David Kilkullen, *The Accidental Guerrilla* (Oxford University Press, 2009); and Wesley K. Clark, *Waging Modern War* (PublicAffairs, 2001).

7. Philip M. Taylor, *Munitions of the Mind: A History of Propaganda from the Ancient World to the Present Day*, 3rd ed. (Manchester University Press, 2003), 5.

8. Douglas Walton, "What is Propaganda, and What Exactly is Wrong with It?" *Public Affairs Quarterly* 11, no. 4 (October 1997): 383–413.

9. On the evolution of the term propaganda, see Paul A. Smith, Jr., *On Political War* (National Defense University Press, 1989), 1–8; Taylor, *Munitions of the Mind*, 1–16; and Nicholas J. Cull, "Roof for a House Divided: How U.S. Propaganda Evolved into Public Diplomacy," in *The Oxford Handbook of Propaganda Studies*, eds. Jonathan Auerbach and Russ Castronovo (Oxford University Press, 2013), 131–146. In 2010 the US Joint Staff "redefined the term 'propaganda' to clarify employment by the adversary." Joint Chiefs of Staff, *Psychological Operations*, JP 3–13.2 (2010), iii, B-9, https://irp.fas.org/doddir/dod/jp3-13-2.pdf.

10. On "DIME," see Joint Chiefs of Staff, *Strategy*, Joint Doctrine Note 1–18 (2018). https://www.jcs.mil/Portals/36/Documents/Doctrine/jdn_jg/jdn1_18.pdf; Catherine A. Theohary, *Information Warfare: Issues for Congress* (Congressional Research Service, 2018).

11. Hamilton, *Manipulating the Masses*, 318–321.

12. Quoted in Hamilton, *Manipulating the Masses*, 318.

13. On the history of PSYOP, see Alfred H. Paddock, Jr., "Military Psychological Operations," in *Political Warfare and Psychological Operations: Rethinking the US Approach*, eds. Frank R. Barnett and Carnes Lord (NDU Press, 1989), 45–50 and Major Ed Rouse (Ret), "Psychological Operations/Warfare," http://www.psywarrior.com/psyhist.html.

14. Paddock, "Military Psychological Operations," 50.

15. Carnes Lord, "The Psychological Dimension in National Strategy," in Barnett and Lord, *Political Warfare*, 13–20; Carnes Lord, *Losing Hearts*

and Minds: Public Diplomacy and Strategic Influence in the Age of Terror (Praeger Security International, 2006).

16. Joint Chiefs of Staff, *Doctrine for Joint Psychological Operations*, JP 3–53 (1996), v, https://nsarchive2.gwu.edu/NSAEBB/NSAEBB177/02_psyop-jp-3-53.pdf.

17. Quoted in Marc Ambinder, "Original Document: Making PSYOPS Less Sinister," *The Atlantic* (June 30, 2010); David Cowan and Chaveso Cook, "Psychological Operations Versus Military Information Support Operations and an Analysis of Organizational Change," *Military Review* (March 6, 2018). The Army's PSYOP teams resisted the name change to MISO with some success at tactical levels. Soldiers and their formations are called PSYOP; their activities are called MISO. The UK and other US allies continued to use PSYOP. Christopher Paul, email to author, March 21, 2020.

18. *National Security Action Memorandum No. 330, Intensified and Expanded Psychological Operation Activities in Vietnam*, (April 9, 1965)," Discover LBJ, https://www.discoverlbj.org/item/nsf-nsam330. On Zorthian's role and the origins of JUSPAO, see Zorthian Oral History, interviewed by Cliff Groce; Dan Oleksiw Oral History, interviewed by Hans N. Tuch, Foreign Affairs Oral History Collection, ADST, Arlington, VA; and Cull, *United States Information Agency*, 245–254.

19. Quoted in John Morello, "Open Arms, Closed Minds and Eyes: Chieu Hoi, Psyop, and the Intelligence Failures in the 1968 Tet Offensive," War History Online (October 20, 2017), https://www.warhistoryonline.com/vietnam-war/intelligence-failures1968-tet-offensivex.html; Alfred H. Paddock, Jr., "Legitimizing Army Psychological Operations," *Joint Force Quarterly* 56, 1st Quarter (2010): 89–93.

20. Zorthian Oral History, interviewed by Cliff Groce, 35–36.

21. Quoted in Cull, *United States Information Agency*, 311.

22. On JUSPAO's operational role and views within USIA and its impact on Agency operations and morale, see Oleksiw Oral History, interviewed by Hans N. Tuch; Zorthian Oral History, interviewed by Cliff Groce; Lawrence J. Hall Oral History, interviewed by Hans Tuch, Foreign Affairs Oral History Collection, ADST, Arlington, VA; and Sorenson, *Word War*, 281–292.

23. On USIA's psychological operations in Iran and Guatemala, see Osgood, *Total Cold War*, 136–138, 146–149. On USIA's psychological operations in Cuba and the Dominican Republic, see Hewson Ryan Oral History,

interviewed by Richard Nethercut, Foreign Affairs Oral History Collection, ADST, Arlington, VA and Cull, *United States Information Agency*, 198–199, 240–244.

24. Jack N. Summe, "Information Warfare, Psychological Operations, and a Policy for the Future," US Army War College, 1999, https://www.hsdl.org/?view&did=450860, (accessed May 17, 2023).

25. Philip M. Taylor, *Global Communications, International Affairs and the Media Since 1945* (Routledge, 1997), 145–192; Jeffrey B. Jones and Jack N. Summe, "Psychological Operations in Desert Shield, Desert Storm and Urban Freedom" (1997), Landpower Essay Series, https://www.ausa.org/sites/default/files/LPE-97-3-Psychological-Operations-in-Desert-Shield-Desert-Storm-and-Urban-Freedom.pdf (accessed May 17, 2023); Mark Kilbane, "Military Psychological Operations as Public Diplomacy," in *Routledge Handbook of Public Diplomacy*, eds. Nancy Snow and Philip M. Taylor (Routledge, 2009), 187–192.

26. Jeffrey B. Jones, "The Third Wave and the Fourth Dimension," in *Special Operations Forces: Roles and Missions in the Aftermath of the Cold War*, eds. Richard H. Schultz, Robert L. Pfaltzgraff, and W. Bradley Stock (Diane Publishing, 1996), 225–239; Jeffrey B. Jones, "Strategic Communication: A Mandate for the United States," *Joint Force Quarterly* 39, 4th Quarter (2005): 108–114.

27. Jeffrey B. Jones and Michael P. Mathews, "PSYOP and the Warfighting CINC," *Joint Force Quarterly*, no. 8 (Summer 1995): 29.

28. On MISO, the role of Military Information Support Teams (MISTs), and how strategic communication and public diplomacy bridge military and civilian domains, see Brian E. Carlson, "Who Tells America's Story Abroad? State's Public Diplomacy or DoD's Strategic Communication?" in *Mission Creep: The Militarization of US Foreign Policy*, eds. Gordon Adams and Shoon Murray (Georgetown University Press, 2014), 145–165.

29. Christopher Paul, email to author, March 23, 2020.

30. James Dao and Eric Schmidt, "A Nation Challenged: Hearts and Minds; Pentagon Readies Efforts to Sway Sentiment Abroad," *New York Times*, February 19, 2002.

31. Douglas J. Feith to Senator Carl Levin, April 6, 2002, author's copy.

32. Department of Defense, "Rumsfeld Addresses Strategic Influence Criticism," News Release, February 20, 2002; Thomas L. Ricks, "Defense Dept. Divided Over Propaganda Plan," *Washington Post*, February 20,

2002; Department of State, "Pentagon's OSI Plans Unleash Indignation in Overseas Media," Foreign Media Reaction, Issue Focus, February 22, 2002, author's copy; Mike Allen, "White House Angered at Plan for Pentagon Disinformation," *Washington Post*, February 25, 2002; Eric Schmidt and James Dao, "A 'Damaged' Information Office Is Declared Closed by Rumsfeld," *New York Times*, February 27, 2002; Franklin Foer, "Flacks Americana," *The New Republic* (May 20, 2002).

33. Quoted in Brooks, *Military Became Everything*, 87–88.

34. Michael G. Mullen, "Strategic Communication: Getting Back to Basics," *Joint Force Quarterly* 55, 4th Quarter, (2009): 2–4.

35. Christopher Paul, *Strategic Communication: Origins, Concepts, and Current Debates* (Praeger, 2011), 38–39, 181; Todd Helmus, Christopher Paul, and Russell W. Glenn, *Enlisting Madison Avenue: The Marketing Approach to Earning Popular Support in Theaters of Operation* (RAND, 2007), 26–55.

36. Joint Chiefs of Staff, *Public Affairs*, JP 3–61 (2015), vii, GL-5.

37. Quoted in Dao and Schmidt, "A Nation Challenged."

38. Bradley Graham, "Pentagon to Probe Remarks Made by General," *Washington Post*, October 22, 2003.

39. Quoted in Frank Aukofer and William Lawrence, *America's Team, the Odd Couple: A Report on the Relationship Between the Media and the Military* (Freedom Forum First Amendment Center, Vanderbilt University, 1995), 13.

40. "Oral History: Colin Powell," PBS Frontline, January 9, 1996, https:// www.pbs.org/wgbh/pages/frontline/gulf/oral/powell/1.html.

41. Aukofer and Lawrence, *America's Team*, 13–15.

42. Quoted in Michelle Ferrari and James Tobin, *Reporting America at War: An Oral History* (Hachette Books, 2003), 145.

43. On the role of the media and military public affairs strategists during the Gulf War and "CNN Effect" scholarship, see Steven Livingston, *Clarifying the CNN Effect: On Examining Media Effects According to Type of Military Intervention* (Joan Shorenstein Center, Harvard University, 1997) and Warren P. Strobel, *Late Breaking Foreign Policy: The News Media's Influence on Peace Operations* (United States Institute of Peace, 1997), 47.

44. Clark, *Waging Modern War*, 8.

45. Clark, *Waging Modern War*, 60. On Holbrooke's relations with the media, see Richard Holbrooke, *To End a War* (Random House, 1998)

and Christopher R. Hill, *Outpost: Life on the Frontlines of American Diplomacy* (Simon & Schuster, 2014).

46. Clark, *Waging Modern War*, 443.

47. Tony Blair, *A Journey: My Political Life* (Alfred A. Knopf, 2010), 236–237.

48. Rhiannon Vickers, "The Kosovo Campaign Political Communications, the Battle for Public Opinion," paper presented at the International Studies Association, Los Angeles, CA, March 2000, https://ciaotest.cc.columbia.edu/isa/vir01/, (accessed May 17, 2023); Clark, *Waging Modern War*, 271–274; Blair, *A Journey*, 236–240.

49. Clark, *Waging Modern War*, 273.

50. Quoted in Vickers, "Kosovo Campaign," 11.

51. Jamie Shea, *Dealing with the Media During Crises and Peacekeeping Missions* (NATO Defense College, 1999), author's copy.

52. George W. Bush, "Address Before a Joint Session of the Congress on the United States Response to the Terrorist Attacks of September 11," September 20, 2001, American Presidency Project.

53. Elisabeth Bumiller, "Bush Aides Set Strategy to Sell Policy on Iraq," *New York Times*, September 7, 2002.

54. Torie Clarke, *Lipstick on a Pig: Winning in the No-Spin Era with Someone Who Knows the Game* (Free Press, 2006), 58.

55. Clarke, *Lipstick on a Pig*, 53–85; Ralph Blumenthal and Jim Ruttenberg, "Journalists Are Assigned to Accompany U.S. Troops," *New York Times*, February 18, 2003; Department of Defense, "Public Affairs Guidance (PAG) on Embedding Media During Possible Future Operations/Deployments in the U.S. Central Command's (Centcom) Area of Responsibility (AOR)," February 2003, https://fas.org/sgp/othergov/dod/embed.pdf, (accessed May 17, 2023).

56. Howard Kurtz, "For Media After Iraq, A Case of Shell Shock," *Washington Post*, April 28, 2003; John Cook, "Military, Media Meet Off Battlefield to Debate War Coverage," *Chicago Tribune*, August 18, 2003; Terence Smith, "The Real-Time War: Defining News in the Middle East," *Columbia Journalism Review* 42, no. 1 (May/June 2003): 26–28.

57. Quoted in "'Boys of Baghdad' Relive Gulf War Broadcast," CNNAccess, January 17, 2003, https://www.cnn.com/2003/US/01/16/cnna.shaw.arnett/, (accessed May 17, 2023).

58. Nye, *Soft Power*, 116.

59. Esther Scott, *Reporting in the 'Fog of War': The Story of Jessica Lynch* (Harvard Kennedy School Case Program, 2004); *Misleading Information from the Battlefield: The Tillman and Lynch Episodes, Hearing Before the Committee on Oversight and Government Reform*, 110th Cong. 2008.
60. Whitman is quoted in Mark Memmott, "Most Think Propaganda Campaign in Iraq Wrong," *USA Today*, November 23, 2005. See also Mark Mazzetti and Borzou Daragahi, "U.S. Military Covertly Pays to Run Stories in Iraqi Press," *Los Angeles Times*, November 30, 2005; Eric Schmidt and David S. Cloud, "Senate Summons Pentagon to Explain Effort to Plant News Stories in Iraqi Media," *New York Times*, December 2, 2005; and David S. Cloud, "U.S. Urged to Stop Paying Iraqi Reporters," *New York Times*, May 24, 2006.
61. Dan Kuehl, "Iraq and the Information War," draft op-ed for the *Los Angeles Times*, n.d. [circa 2005], author's copy.
62. Maura Reynolds and Alissa J. Rubin, "U.S. 'Appalled,' Bush Tells Arabs; Lawmakers Seek Abuse Hearings," *Los Angeles Times*, May 6, 2004; Department of State, "Iraq: Global Media Say Prisoner Abuse Damages U.S. Credibility," Office of Research, May 7, 2004, author's copy; Seymour M. Hersh, "Torture at Abu Ghraib," *The New Yorker*, May 10, 2004; Sherry Ricchiardi, "Missed Signals," *American Journalism Review*, (August/September 2004); W. Lance Bennett, Regina G. Lawrence, and Steven Livingston, "None Dare Call It Torture: Indexing and the Limits of Press Independence in the Abu Ghraib Scandal," *Journal of Communication* 56, no. 3 (2006): 467–485.
63. Miriam Krieger, Shannon L. C. Souma, and Daniel H. Nexon, "US Military Diplomacy in Practice," in *Diplomacy and the Making of World Politics*, eds. Ole Jacob Sending, Vincent Pouliot, and Iver B. Neumann (Cambridge University Press, 2015), 220–255; Goran Swistek, "The Nexus Between Public Diplomacy and Military Diplomacy in Foreign Affairs and Defense Policy," *Connections, The Quarterly Journal* 11, no. 2 (Spring 2012): 79–86.
64. Kenneth Yates Oral History, interviewed by Charles Stuart Kennedy, Foreign Affairs Oral History Collection, ADST, Arlington, VA.
65. Broadcasting Board of Governors, *To Be Where the Audience Is, Report of the Special Committee on the Future of Shortwave Broadcasting* (2014); Department of Defense, *The Creation and Dissemination of All Forms of Information in Support of the Psychological Operations (PSYOP) in Time of Military Conflict* (Defense Science Board Task Force, 2000).

66. "732. Minutes of Meeting of the Secretaries of State, War, and the Navy, Held at Washington, October 23, 1945," *Foreign Relations of the United States: Diplomatic Papers, 1945, European Advisory Commission, Austria, Germany, Volume III*, Historical Documents, Department of State.

67. "[441] Memorandum by the Secretary of State, the Secretary of War (Patterson) and the Secretary of the Navy (Forrestal)," *Foreign Relations of the United States, 1946, The British Commonwealth, Western and Central Europe, Volume V*, Historical Documents, Department of State.

68. James Dobbins, et al., *America's Role in Nation-Building: From Germany to Iraq* (RAND, 2003).

69. Yale Richmond, *Practicing Public Diplomacy: A Cold War Odyssey* (Berghahn Books, 2008), 14.

70. Cull, *United States Information Agency*, 26–27, 38–39; Graham, *Culture and Propaganda*, 138–142; Richmond, *Practicing Public Diplomacy*, 5–20; Hench, *Books as Weapons*, 225–256; Arthur A. Bardos Oral History, interviewed by Hans N. Tuch, Foreign Affairs Oral History Collection, ADST, Arlington, VA.

71. Kirsten Lundberg, *The Accidental Statesman: General Petraeus and the City of Mosul, Iraq* (Harvard Kennedy School Case Program, 2006); Michael R. Gordon, "The Struggle for Iraq: Reconstruction; 101st Airborne Scores Success in Northern Iraq," *New York Times*, September 4, 2003; David Petraeus, "For Mosul, Learning From 2003," *Stars and Stripes*, August 13, 2016.

72. Adams and Murray, *Mission Creep*, 3.

73. Robert M. Gates, "Remarks by Secretary of Defense Robert M. Gates at USGLC Tribute Dinner," US Global Leadership Campaign, July 15, 2008.

74. Quoted in Adams and Murray, *Mission Creep*, 168–169.

75. Quoted in Adams and Murray, *Mission Creep*, 4, 100.

76. Christopher Paul, "Find the Right Balance Between Civilian and Military: Just Don't Strip the DOD of Capabilities to Inform, Influence, and Persuade," TheRANDBlog, October 31, 2010; Abiodun Williams, "The U.S. Military and Public Diplomacy," in Seib, *Toward a New Public Diplomacy*, 217–237.

77. Quoted in Michael R. Gordon, "The 2000 Campaign, The Military; Bush Would Stop U.S. Peacekeeping in Balkan Fights," *New York Times*, October 21, 2000.

78. Russell Rumbaugh and Matthew Leatherman, *The Pentagon as Pitchman: Perception and Reality of Public Diplomacy* (Stimson, 2012); Rugh, *Front Line Public Diplomacy*, 181–218.
79. Brooks, *Military Became Everything*, 89–91.
80. Adams and Murray, *Mission Creep*, 166–191.
81. Timothy C. Shea, "Transforming Military Diplomacy," *Joint Force Quarterly* 38, 3rd Quarter (July 2005): 49–52.
82. Joint Chiefs of Staff, *Civil-Military Operations*, JP 3–57 (2018), v–xi.
83. Department of State, *Annual Report on FY 2019 Data*, Interagency Working Group on U.S. Government-Sponsored International Exchanges and Training; Matthew Wallin, *Military Public Diplomacy: How the Military Influences Foreign Audiences* (American Security Project, 2015).
84. Often this office is dominant in the bilateral relationship leading to the suggestion that the "defense attaché is for show, the ODC is for the dough." Brian E. Carlson, email to author, August 2020.
85. Philip Seib, *America's New Approach to Africa: AFRICOM and Public Diplomacy* (Figueroa Press, 2009).
86. Department of Defense, *Report of the Defense Science Board Task Force on Strategic Communication* (2007), 10–20; Bruce Gregory, "Mapping Smart Power in Multi-stakeholder Public Diplomacy/Strategic Communication," paper presented at Institute for Public Diplomacy and Global Communication conference, George Washington University, October 5, 2009, https://pdaa-online.org/?p=52.

11

Covert Operatives and Front Groups

Relationships based on truth, openness, and trust are a bedrock of public diplomacy, yet covert intelligence operatives and civil society front groups play intermittent but significant roles in diplomacy's public dimension.[1] Earlier chapters examined instances of covert support for information, cultural, broadcasting, and military activities. This chapter looks at covert practitioners in the CIA and the citizen front groups they created and funded. Some participants were witting about the CIA's role; many were unwitting. It was covert sponsorship and funding that set them apart. Otherwise, they operated in ways comparable to civil society organizations that partner openly with government agencies in furtherance of public diplomacy.

US officials turn to covert methods when external threats lead to calculations that potential benefits outweigh their limitations. Covert actions can be wielded quickly, circumventing slower democratic processes required by overt means. Secrecy enables flexibility in dispersing funds and choices of activities and media products, especially those that might be constrained by domestic politics if made public. Unattributed publications, forged documents, and secret subsidies to commercial publishers are methods not generally available to overt practitioners. Covert operations can create the appearance of independence from government

© The Author(s), under exclusive license to Springer Nature Switzerland AG 2024   **275**
B. Gregory, *American Diplomacy's Public Dimension*, Palgrave Macmillan Series in
Global Public Diplomacy, https://doi.org/10.1007/978-3-031-38917-7_11

in the eyes of target populations and afford protection from Congressional and media critics.

Covert cultural practitioners during the first two decades of the Cold War came from a cross section of American life: intellectuals, professors, students, writers, publishers, artists, musicians, film makers, scientists, trade unionists, journalists, feminists, civil rights activists, refugees, peace activists, and religious leaders. Secrecy allowed the CIA to tailor tools and methods to different geopolitical circumstances. Some worked best for anti-communism, others for activities designed to engage the anti-colonialism and economic aspirations of the Global South. But covert means have limits. Individuals and front groups at times use covert funds in unintended ways.

Front groups appear to be independent, but they are partially or fully controlled by parent organizations. Intelligence services, political organizations, corporations, and crime syndicates use them in situations where a hidden hand is beneficial. In the 1920s Russia's Bolsheviks worked to spread communism internationally by using front groups to control youth organizations, trade unions, peace groups, and professional associations. After World War II the Soviet Union worked to subvert Western civil society organizations. Alarmed US officials responded by creating their own front groups. Secretary of Defense James Forrestal urged the State Department to take the lead, but Secretary of State George C. Marshall refused, fearing American diplomacy would lose credibility if a covert operation was revealed. An NSC directive in 1948 put the CIA in charge.[2]

Frank Wisner, Cord Meyer, Tom Braden

The CIA's first director Allen Dulles placed its covert political operations in an innocuously named Office for Policy Coordination (OPC) with a country desk structure and geographic regions similar to those in the Department of State. Its director was Frank Wisner, a hard charging former OSS operative. They recruited two practitioners who would become legendary: Cord Meyer, a Yale graduate and US Marine who fought in the Pacific in World War II, and Tom Braden, a Dartmouth graduate and former OSS operative. After a short postwar stint as leader of the United World Federalists, Meyer began a long CIA career that included policy guidance to RFE/RL and management of numerous covert political and information operations. Braden managed the OPC's front groups in Europe, reporting directly to Dulles, until he left in 1954 to pursue a career in journalism and Democratic Party politics.

Prominent among the CIA's front groups was the Congress for Cultural Freedom (CCF), an organization of anti-communist intellectuals that operated in more than thirty countries. Separately the CIA provided covert funding for programs sponsored by a variety of civil society organizations. Together these efforts became known as a "Mighty Wurlitzer" organ, the term Wisner used to describe, in British historian Hugh Wilford's words, an instrument "capable of playing any propaganda tune he desired."[3]

Diplomat George Kennan was an advocate of using covert methods to mobilize American citizens in a national response to Soviet political warfare. "Throughout our history, private American citizens have banded together to champion the cause of freedom for people suffering under oppression," he wrote in a 1948 State Department planning paper. "Our proposal is that this tradition be revived specifically to further American national interests in the present crisis."[4] The CIA's secret relations with civil society groups paralleled what State and later USIA were doing openly to leverage American volunteerism and cultural pluralism.

Wisner, Braden, Meyer, and the practitioners they recruited were imaginative, sophisticated, competitive, street savvy, risk tolerant, and supremely confident. They had vivid memories of the fight against fascism; now they sought to contain and confront authoritarian communist regimes. Secrecy gave them greater flexibility, but it also made them vulnerable when their practices were disclosed.

US National Student Association

The US National Student Association (NSA) was established in 1947. It was a liberal organization that became active locally in campus governance; nationally in the civil rights movement, women's rights issues, and anti-Vietnam war protests; and internationally in student conferences and regional political activities that would come to include support for revolutionary movements in Algeria, Cuba, Angola, Mozambique, and Iran. Its domestic operations were run from Madison, Wisconsin. Its International Commission was located and directed separately in Cambridge, Massachusetts. Student leaders at Harvard University, including some OSS and military intelligence veterans, also developed ties with Harvard's International Affairs Committee (HIACOM), which helped to create the Salzburg Seminar, a forum for global exchanges, and other projects. HIACOM and the NSA's International Commission had connections with Dulles, Wisner, and Meyer, and a number of Ivy League professors, notably William Y. Elliott at Harvard (and his protégé, the young Henry Kissinger) and Arnold Wolfers at Yale.[5]

What began as a small number of CIA "denial operations" with a few witting students sworn to secrecy broadened over the years. One of the NSA's early activities was to represent the United States at the Prague-based International Union of Students led then by Czech communists. Covert funds were channeled to numerous unwitting students through the Foundation for Youth and Student Affairs, other CIA "cutout organizations," and independent groups such as the Council on Foreign Relations, the YMCA, and the Asia Foundation. These organizations supported politically engaged US students who were projecting American ideas and values in international student conferences. The students also engaged in talent spotting and reporting on personalities and activities of potential future foreign leaders. Later some would channel CIA funds to revolutionaries seeking to topple governments and overthrow dictators.[6]

Congress for Cultural Freedom

Arts and Letters. On June 26, 1950, the CCF was incorporated at an international gathering of intellectuals and artists in Berlin. The lead organizer was Melvin Lasky, a New York intellectual and freelance journalist who at the time was editing *Der Monat*, a literary journal published by the US military government in Germany. Organizers included Arthur Koestler, the Hungarian-British author of *Darkness at Noon*, the Italian novelist Ignazio Silone, American philosopher and left-wing activist Sidney Hook, and American philosopher and conservative activist James Burnham.

Among other intellectuals who supported the effort were Britain's Bertrand Russell and Hugh Trevor-Roper, France's Raymond Aron and Jacque Maritain, Germany's Karl Jaspers, Italy's Benedetto Croce, and America's John Dewey, Tennessee Williams, Reinhold Niebuhr, and Arthur Schlesinger, Jr. Their goals were to advance freedom of thought, challenge pro-communist sympathies of many Western intellectuals, and give voice to ideas intended to counter totalitarianism on the left and the right.

Inevitably there were spirited debates on tactics. Should they be strongly confrontational toward Moscow? Or should they seek to co-opt communism's influence with a more measured tone? Lasky divided the conference into two main "tendencies." Koestler and Burnham "put main emphasis on the drive of Soviet imperialism toward world-conquest." Silone and other Europeans "concentrated on the strengthening of the Western European unity idea, social and economic reforms … and a less polemical attitude toward Moscow."[7] "More than anything," Giles Scott-Smith writes, "the Congress epitomized this attempt to create a unitary cultural community between the two continents."[8]

The CCF's headquarters was in Paris. Wisner appointed CIA agent Michael Josselson to be its director and Irving Brown, a trade unionist who worked for both the CIA and the American Federation of Labor (AFL), to serve on its steering committee. They channeled millions of dollars provided by Wisner, Braden, and Meyer to dozens of CIA-created foundations.[9] In Lasky's founding vision, the CCF was "not an official body, but a free association of men and women … the initial attempt of the intelligentsia of the civilized world—poets and scientists, philosophers and journalists, socialists and conservatives, churchmen and trade-unionists, painters and publishers—to join together freely, to discuss, to criticize, to formulate an independent program for the defense of their common democratic ideal."[10]

The Paris-based literary journal *Encounter*, edited by the poet Stephen Spender and journalist Irving Kristol, became the CCF's best-known publication. Contributors included such luminaries as Albert Camus,

Edith Sitwell, Czeslaw Milosz, Isaiah Berlin, Lionel Trilling, Alan Tate, James Farrell, W. H. Auden, Katherine Anne Porter, William Faulkner, Diana Trilling, Mary McCarthy, Dwight Macdonald, Robert Lowell, Gertrude Stein, and T.S. Eliot.

A typical CCF venture was its collaboration with New York's Museum of Modern Art in sponsoring the "Masterpieces of the Twentieth Century" art exhibit in Paris in 1952. A Paris performance of Stravinsky's *The Rite of Spring* by the Boston Symphony Orchestra was funded through a CIA grant arranged by Tom Braden and C.D. Jackson, Eisenhower's advisor on psychological warfare and a Symphony trustee. CCF records showed it only as a "donation from prominent individuals and associations." For Braden, the Symphony's performance "won more acclaim for the U.S. in Paris than John Foster Dulles or Dwight D. Eisenhower could have brought with a hundred speeches."[11]

During a span of three decades, the CCF operated a global network of branch offices, published some 20 reputable intellectual journals, managed a news and features service, sponsored art exhibitions, and offered prizes and performing opportunities to artists and musicians. When its covert funding was revealed in 1967, it was renamed the Association for Cultural Freedom and operated openly until 1979 with support from the Ford Foundation.

Defenders contend the CCF's impact came from the thinkers, writers, and artists who believed in individualism and freedom, not from its top-down paymasters. Critics find a connection between money and control. Frances Stonor Saunders argues the CIA "paid the piper" and therefore called the tune. But in Scott-Smith's studied conclusion, truth included a mix of both. Some writers and artists had deep concerns well before disclosure of the CIA connection, but they tolerated covert funding as necessary to achieve an organization with the CCF's capacities and scale. As Greg Barnhisel observes, some in the CIA may have wanted to call the tune, "but the pipers often refused to comply."[12]

Labor Unions. The American Federation of Labor, founded by Samuel Gompers in the 1880s, represented craft unions—bricklayers, carpenters, printers, and garment workers. Its rival, the Congress of Industrial Organizations (CIO), founded by United Mineworkers President John L. Lewis in 1935, organized machinists, auto workers, steel workers, and other industrial workers. Each had leaders and international affiliates who had engaged in clandestine operations against the Nazis. They were allied for a time with the Soviets and communist parties in Europe, but most soon severed these ties and became passionate anti-communists. Key AFL figures with close ties to Wisner were Jay Lovestone, Irving Brown, and George Meany. United Auto Workers president Walter Reuther and his brother Victor, who ran the CIO's Paris office, maintained connections with Wisner and later Tom Braden.

For the CIA, the labor leaders brought connections with foreign anti-communist unions, many more politically active than their American counterparts, knowledge of Stalin's communist parties and front organizations, and a passion for building free market economies in which democratic labor unions would play a pivotal role. For the unions, the CIA provided a steady stream of funding for their international activities. As Hugh Wilford summarized: "On one side were professional spies wanting to exert the maximum degree of control possible over the activities they were financing ... On the other were representatives of the American labor movement entirely confident of their own ability to carry out covert operations, indeed positively jealous of their independence in the field, yet bound to the CIA by the purse strings of covert patronage."[13] America's unions focused much of their attention on fascism and communism in Europe. They also established independent free trade unions in Asia, Africa, and Latin America, which connected them with national liberation movements, anti-apartheid efforts in South Africa, and groups opposed to military dictatorships in the Western Hemisphere.[14]

Covert funding of America's unions continued until disclosure of the CIA's role. Victor Reuther responded by describing his resistance to Tom Braden's attempt to recruit him as an agent. George Meany began by claiming he was unwitting, but soon held a press conference to declare his "pride in the work we have done overseas" and concern that "the CIA was trying to horn in on it."[15] The government's open partnership with organized labor continued. It had begun with the State Department's creation of a small labor attaché program in the 1940s and USIA's creation of a labor information officer program in association with the Alliance for Progress in the 1960s. In the 1980s Congress and the Reagan administration created the National Endowment for Democracy and through it a dedicated overt funding stream of annual grants for the AFL-CIO's overseas activities.

Scientists. America's scientists, central figures in international debates on science in free and authoritarian societies, were witting and unwitting partners with government. The CCF's organizers included the American geneticist H. J. Muller, physicists J. Robert Oppenheimer and Henry Margenau, and sociologist Edward Shils; Hungarian chemist Michael Polanyi; and Austrian physicist Hans Thirring. The role science had played in Nazi atrocities and contested views on scientific freedom in the Soviet Union colored proceedings at the CCF's founding conference in Berlin. At a large conference on "Science and Freedom" in Hamburg in 1953, Polanyi took the lead and called on scientists to speak out against the treatment of scholars and research under totalitarian rule. He went on to chair a permanent CCF Committee for Science and Freedom and secure a Rockefeller Foundation grant to fund the Committee's *Bulletin*, which appeared periodically between 1954–1961 for a small readership that reached 5500 at its peak.

The CCF adopted a more robust science strategy in 1961when Shils initiated the journal *Minerva*, a quarterly academic review devoted to scientific learning and policy. It continues to publish more than a half century later. In the 1960s, the CCF subsidized conferences of the American Association of Arts and Sciences, its journal *Daedalus*, and numerous other international conferences and seminars. The efforts were supported by CIA funds channeled through its Fairfield Foundation, the Ford and Rockefeller Foundations, and other entities.[16]

Covert operations in the sciences went well beyond the CCF. The CIA created an Office of Scientific Intelligence in 1949, which, among other responsibilities, managed exchanges of experts with non-governmental scientific communities. In 1950 the State Department established a science attaché program. Attachés were to focus on reporting, exchanges, and cooperation with foreign scientists and laboratories willing to share their research in the international arena.[17] Collecting intelligence on weapons development was more difficult. State's attachés and CIA's agents faced conflicting pressures for results and domestic criticism of any involvement with communists. They developed working relations, publicly at arm's length and privately productive. The CIA funded most of the Asia Foundation's activities between its founding in 1954 and 1967 when the connection was disclosed. These included science textbooks in Asian languages, science faculty training, and research awards. The Foundation's goals were to bring China and other Asian countries "into a Western modernity" through assistance to Asian technocrats and support for scientific inquiry based on learning instead of rote memory.[18]

The CIA also funded partnerships with social scientists, notably in the field of anthropology. Margaret Mead, who had advised the OSS, OWI, and State during World War II, Clyde Kluckhohn, who held leadership positions in the American Anthropological Association (AAA) during the early Cold War, and other scholars advised the government on how anthropological research could inform its policies and operations. The AAA secretly channeled funds to social science research projects of interest to US intelligence and military agencies. In the 1950s it provided the CIA with its membership lists and areas of specialization. The Asia Foundation funded visits by Asian anthropologists to the US and provided their names and contact information. The CIA's support for MIT's Center for International Studies helped create Project Modjukuto, a multisite ethnography project in Indonesia that funded the fieldwork of anthropologist Clifford Geertz.[19] When these relationships were disclosed, the AAA adopted numerous professional responsibility resolutions calling on anthropologists to be clear and open regarding the purpose, methods, results, and sponsors of their research.

Civil society domains associated with government operations maintain norms and professional standards of practice, and science is no exception. Many US scientists view their work as apolitical. They are dedicated to the principles of free inquiry and to following observed reality wherever it leads. Government diplomacy practitioners voice these norms as well. "Scientific research is conducted for its own sake simply to increase man's knowledge of himself and his environment," USIA's science advisor Harold Goodwin wrote in 1958.[20] Devotees of science diplomacy then and now emphasize the principles and political neutrality of science in democracies while attributing politically driven scientific research to authoritarian countries. But reality is more complex. Science and power are connected in all countries. American scientists during the Cold War and since have partnered with government as advisors, as diplomats, and as practitioners in military and intelligence services.

Journalists. Reporters too were part of the "Mighty Wurlitzer." Estimates of the number of US journalists who had working relationships with the CIA vary widely. *The Washington Post's* Carl Bernstein calculated more than 400 reporters had arrangements with the CIA between 1952 and 1977. A Congressional committee estimated the number as closer to 50. A series of *New York Times* articles put the total between 30 and 100. Accurate numbers are beyond reach given the varieties of relationships. Some were explicit; some were tacit. Some reporters simply shared information; others served as intelligence gatherers and intermediaries between spies and citizens in other countries. Some were CIA operatives using journalistic covers. In their associations with the CIA, many journalists had the approval of *The New York Times*, CBS News, TIME magazine, the Associated Press, and other media organizations.[21]

The views of journalists varied considerably. *Chicago Sun-Times* correspondent Stuart Loory considered CIA operatives to be very good sources of information, but he stated he had never been compensated by the CIA and called for a thorough public airing of past relations between the CIA and the press. The CIA, he declared, had "functioned as a propaganda machine aimed largely at affecting public opinion in the United States." *Washington Post* reporter turned novelist Ward Just thought any association between journalists and spies to be a mistake, because the reader or viewer does not know where the news is coming from.[22]

Some journalists worked directly with the CIA. Wilford portrays syndicated columnists Joseph and Stewart Alsop as close to CIA director Allen Dulles and often willing to publish stories and opinions favorable to US interests and the Agency. Citing Carl Bernstein, Wilford asserts that *New York Times* publisher Arthur Hays Sulzberger, also a friend of Dulles, signed a secrecy agreement with the CIA and provided some of its operatives with cover as reporters or clerical staff in its foreign bureaus. CBS President William Paley channeled CIA funds through the William S. Paley Foundation. The international staff of the American Newspaper Guild transferred funds from the CIA through the Asia Foundation and other front organizations to support technical assistance and training seminars for journalists in communist countries in Europe and the Global

South. Subsidies for news and opinion magazines spanned the political spectrum from the *New Leader* on the left, to the *Reporter* in the center, to Henry Luce's TIME magazine on the right.[23]

Ramparts magazine's exposure of CIA ties to the National Student Association in 1967 led to an about face by news organizations. Articles in *The New York Times, The Washington Post*, and the wire services now provided detailed accounts of the Agency's covert operations.[24] Appalled reporters rose to defend freedom of the press. Members of Congress voiced outrage. The Johnson administration worried it would erode support for the war in Vietnam. USIA's foreign media reports documented outcries in the foreign press that fueled anti-Americanism and tarnished the nation's image. The CIA feared it would become a scapegoat. As Cord Meyer recalled, the "drumfire of editorial denunciation and cartoon excoriation that swept across the country" included the false charge that CIA carried out these initiatives without policy approval or Congressional authorization. This ended when Senator Robert Kennedy (D-NY) stated the CIA should not "'take the rap' for programs that had been approved by high officials of three successive administrations."[25]

The issue simmered for decades. CIA regulations adopted in 1977 barred the practice of using journalistic cover, but a waiver permitted exceptions "with the specific approval of the CIA director." Intelligence officials on background stated exceptions were "extraordinarily rare." In 1996, responding to public concerns about the covert use of journalists, clergy, and Peace Corps volunteers, a Council on Foreign Relations task force recommended the rule be reexamined.[26]

Senate hearings on July 17 displayed a wide range of views. Senators Robert Kerrey (D-NE) and John Glenn (R-OH) opposed a legal prohibition that would exclude any American regardless of profession from working with the CIA if lives and vital national interests were at risk. Collaboration should be a matter of individual choice. CIA Director John Deutch managed to claim simultaneously (1) a nineteen-year CIA policy not to use American journalists for intelligence purposes, (2) strong personal sympathy for no intelligence use of journalists and his intent not to do so, and (3) freedom for the CIA to use journalists in exceptional circumstances such as terrorist groups threatening to use weapons of mass destruction in urban areas.

The Committee to Protect Journalists called for a no exceptions ban on any CIA collaboration with journalists. ABC's Ted Koppel agreed, arguing the prohibition should be in law to avoid greater strain on journalists' "worn thread of credibility." But he recognized the CIA would likely break the law in the face of extreme threats. *US News and World Report's* Mort Zuckerman asserted that any association by journalists with any government agency undermines the greater good that can be achieved by untainted journalism.[27]

Books. Collaboration between the government and American publishers began during World War II, expanded during the occupations of Germany and Japan, and continued in the following decades as a tool in the nation's public diplomacy. W. W. Norton, Alfred A. Knopf, Simon & Schuster, Random House, and other publishers formed a nonprofit Council on Books in Wartime to build morale at home and among troops abroad. When Franklin Roosevelt adopted W.W. Norton's slogan, "Books are weapons in the war of ideas," he foreshadowed years of mutually advantageous partnership.[28] The Army distributed American books to prisoners of war and liberated populations in Europe and Asia. Books were used in "denazification" programs and to support re-establishing local publishing industries. The Marshall Plan funded an International Media Guarantee program that enabled some countries to pay for books with local currency instead of scarce dollar reserves.

USIA conducted numerous book development, translation, and donation programs that ebbed and flowed with changing diplomatic priorities, currency fluctuations, and competition from foreign publishers. It was a win/win arrangement. US public diplomacy gained from distributing books by American authors that were not obviously propagandistic. Publishers benefited commercially and built goodwill with officials whose export regulations, tax credits, and financial support were vital to their growth in international markets.[29]

The CIA covertly funded book programs through front groups and arrangements with publishers. It channeled funds for fellowships and literary prizes to authors through its Fairfield Foundation; its board included Cass Canfield, the president of Harper & Row. Book contracts were given directly to some authors and indirectly through advances or book purchase guarantees to publishers such as Frederic A. Praeger, a firm with strong ties to the CIA, Arlington Press, and Chekhov Publishing Company. Subsidies were intended to fill gaps in the "ideological literature." Although the CIA made "editorial contributions" to some books, there is no evidence, historian Kenneth Osgood writes, that the CIA attempted to control the content. Rather, the government's influence turned on the selection of authors whose views were known to be compatible with US policy. Books were a high priority for the CIA. As one covert operations head put it, "Books differ from all other propaganda media primarily because one single book can significantly change the reader's attitude and action to an extent unmatched by the impact of any other single medium."[30]

The efforts of George C. Minden stand out. During a 37-year career with Free Europe Press, an affiliate of the CIA-funded Radio Free Europe, he facilitated distribution of millions of books and magazines to professionals and intellectuals in Eastern Europe and the Soviet Union. Minden's operating principles, stated in a 1956 plan, were subtle and pragmatic. All publications were to be distributed by a cover organization. They should not be direct attacks on communism. Instead, they "should favor 'revisionist' trends among the new elites." They should provide "[p]ractical alternatives to doctrinaire Marxist principles" and "cross reporting" on what was going on in other countries. Priority went to materials intended "to weaken confidence in the *bonafides* of their government" and "demonstrate the superior achievements of the West."

Mailings were sent from front groups in New York and cities in Western Europe. Communist censors attempted to defeat the project, but soon George Orwell's *1984*, Albert Camus' *The Rebel*, and books by American authors such as *The Portable Faulkner* and *Three Hundred Years of American Painting* were reaching readers behind the Iron Curtain. There were advantages to a covert program. Mailings could include a large proportion of European titles fit for purpose, whereas USIA's book programs were limited to American authors. Minden could avoid books with strident anti-communist political arguments, more to the taste of a McCarthy-era Congress, in favor of publications that appealed to appetites for Western values as portrayed in "psychology, literature, the theatre, and the visual arts." Such books, he explained, helped to create open societies and showed an interest in the cultural life of East European and Soviet readers.[31]

By 1962 an estimated 500 publishers and front groups in Europe and America were participating in a covert program funded largely by the CIA. Many American publishers were aware of the government funding. But they could maintain an arm's-length posture because distribution originated from the International Advisory Council and Bedford Publications (CIA front organizations merged into the New York-based International Literary Center in 1974), the Asia Foundation, and other cutouts. Unlike other covert operations that ceased or changed with *Ramparts'* disclosures, the CIA's book program under Minden continued until 1993. Expenditures at the end were approaching $2 million annually in a program estimated to have distributed ten million books and magazines.[32]

There was a gray area between the CIA and USIA book programs. Some USIA book development programs were "attributable." It meant USIA did not put its name on the books, but it made no attempt to conceal its association with programs that were openly funded by Congress. These included "Ladder Books" and "Current Thought Series," abridged adaptations of American books in high frequency vocabularies of 1000 words and higher for readers of English as a second language. "Ladder Books" included Mark Twain's novels, a compilation of Edgar Allen Poe stories, and a biography of the architect Frank Lloyd Wright. Books in the "Current Thought Series" were 5000-word adaptations of selected social science books such as Seymour Martin Lipset's *Political Man* and Simon Kuznets' *Modern Economic Growth*. USIA secured rights from publishers, contracted with professional adapters, edited their adaptations in-house, and sold them to readers in the Global South. A nominal price rather than a gift was believed to enhance their value in the eyes of the reader. The books were published in India using excess rupees in USAID's P.L. 480 Food for Peace Program. Feffer and Simons, Inc., a New York based publisher, sold the books internationally for 50 cents. USIA's Books in Translation program also was attributable. Publishers and the Agency collaborated to ensure that the books when published did "not attest to the US government's midwifing."[33]

Exposure and Assessments

Unlike overt public diplomacy practitioners who welcome public attention and support for their work, covert practitioners face outrage and often termination of funding when their work is disclosed. Exposure leads Americans to protest that secrecy is unsuited to a nation dedicated to freedom and openness, and it can damage the natural course of intellectual inquiry. America's intellectuals made a bad bargain, publisher Jason Epstein declared. "[I]t could never have been in the interest of art or literature, of serious speculation of any kind, or even of humanity itself, for them to serve the will of any nation." Others protested similarly. "Do you think I would have gone on the *Encounter* [magazine] payroll in 1956–1957 had I known there was secret U.S. government money behind it?" essayist Dwight Macdonald asked. "I think I've been played for a sucker."[34]

But other reactions were positive. Violinist Yehudi Menuhin praised the CIA for associating "with people like us." Polanyi, Koestler, and other intellectuals expressed no concern about revelations of covert support. The case for covert funding of students and other "Wurlitzer" operations turned on the urgency of the Cold War threat. "Sometimes you had to play hardball," Carnegie Corporation director John Gardner observed. A Congress seized with McCarthyism was not about to provide open funding for the liberal National Student Association, modern art exhibits, left wing intellectuals, journalists, and books by European authors. In a *Saturday Evening Post* interview, Tom Braden observed, "The idea that Congress would have approved many of our projects was as likely as the John Birch Society's approving Medicare."[35]

As Kennan summarized at the time, "This country has no Ministry of Culture, and CIA was obliged to do what it could to try to fill the gap. It should be praised for having done so, and not criticized."[36] But Kennan later reversed his position. "Operations of this nature are not in character for this country," he stated. "I regret today, in light of the experience of the intervening years, that the decision was taken."[37] Public diplomats generally maintain a live and let live posture toward covert operations as long as their secrecy is maintained. But they deplore being tarred with the brush of covert political operations and activities that seek to overthrow foreign governments and assassinate foreign leaders.

The CIA's "Mighty Wurlitzer" brought together an improbable mix of Cold War government hardliners, Republican anti-communists, and liberal Democrats who despised the Soviet Union's mockery of their progressive principles. After the reckoning brought about by *Ramparts*, "work arounds" emerged though open funding by the Board for International Broadcasting, the National Endowment for Democracy, the Asia Foundation, and other grant-making organizations.

Covert information operations after the Cold War are hard to assess. There are fewer open archives and disclosures by former practitioners. Greater transparency in the twenty-first century makes covert options less attractive given the potential for quicker blowback. It took two decades to expose the "Wurlitzer," a time frame unlikely to be repeated today. Sunlight proved damaging within weeks to the Pentagon's Office of Strategic Influence after 9/11 and the covert press operations of its Lincoln Group in Iraq in 2005. Threats posed by Al Qaeda and the Islamic State led some to renew the case for covert information operations. Journalism and public diplomacy scholar Philip Seib argues the State Department's open programs are constrained by limited funds and rules requiring attribution to the US government. A better approach, he contends, would be a "bare knuckles operation" in "a home where different rules would apply: the Central Intelligence Agency."[38]

Two arguments in particular are relevant to the use of deceptive intelligence service practices by a democracy committed to freedom and openness. First, rules and ethical standards are different in international society, which is more anarchic and lacks a democratic state's domestic constitutional order. The need to protect vital interests creates a rationale for more permissive means. Both liberals and conservatives adopt this argument, not to the extent that anything goes, but to legitimize secret measures abroad they would oppose at home. Second, once these political and moral requirements are satisfied, the standards for deceptive actions become pragmatic. Can the covert operation succeed? What are the prospects for plausible deniability? What are the risks of short-term blowback? Are decisions made with proper authority? Can open operations do the job as well or better?[39]

Assessments of the CIA's covert operations vary with circumstances and tolerance for their use when they were not exposed. Disclosures led to second-guessing, revisionist history, and critiques based on short- and long-term calculations. Covert manipulation of students was a bridge too far. The CIA's funding of book programs and surrogate broadcasting was acceptable and continued well beyond disclosure. Frances Stonor Saunders and other historians provide new and useful archival evidence, but their portrayals of a highly efficient CIA puppeteer pulling the strings of duped Americans is problematic.[40]

Reality is not clear cut. David Caute in *The Dancer Defects*, his monumental book on US-Soviet Cold War struggles for cultural supremacy, warns against assuming "the promotion explains the product; that all we need to know is who paid for the ink, for the acrylic and the auditorium."[41] Rather, Cold War tensions can best be understood by careful attention to the achievements of the writers, artists, musicians, playwrights, and film directors on both sides.

Louis Menand acknowledges that officials occasionally censored negative opinions about the US, but the most important consideration is that "*of course* the CIA sponsored writers critical of U.S. policies … that dissent was tolerated in the United States was a major Cold War selling point." The Agency was calling the bluff of American intellectuals. Those who talked distance from US policies or capitalism or consumerism "were actually talking the party line." Menand offers a second conclusion. Writings by American intellectuals contributed to dissent in Soviet bloc countries. "But the world was not colonized by *Partisan Review* or the Museum of Modern Art. It was colonized by Pop Art and Hollywood … Very few people knew who Lionel Trilling was. Everyone had heard of Elvis Presley."[42]

Such nuanced arguments did not carry the day. Americans concluded covert funding of information and cultural programs is not worth the price of exposure and long-term damage to the reputations of individuals and the values of the nation. "Cultural diplomacy, the winning of hearts and minds," Wilford concluded in agreement with Kennan, "should be left to overt government agencies and genuine, nongovernment organizations."[43]

Categorical judgments oversimplify. Diplomacy's public dimension includes a complex variety of overlapping government agencies, tools, and methods as well as blurred boundaries between government and civil society. Impact is hard to evaluate. Many investments occur over the course of decades and may never succeed. Personal agendas and rivalries play out in different programs. Civil society actors do not automatically check their intellectual, professional, and artistic integrity at the door when they wittingly or unwittingly accept covert funding. Democracies should give priority to overt instruments in diplomacy's public dimension, but there is also situational space for covert instruments that satisfy moral, political, and pragmatic criteria.

Notes

1. John J. Mearsheimer, *Why Leaders Lie: The Truth About Lying in International Politics* (Oxford University Press, 2011), 1–14; Caitlin Byrne, "Truth, Lies, and Diplomacy," *Griffith Review* 67, (August 25, 2020).
2. "292. National Security Council Directive on Office of Special Projects," *Foreign Relations of the United States, 1945–1950, Emergence of the Intelligence Establishment*, Historical Documents, Department of State; Rhodri Jeffreys-Jones, *The CIA and American Democracy*, 3rd ed. (Yale University Press, 2003), 50–51.
3. Hugh Wilford, *The Mighty Wurlitzer: How the CIA Played America* (Harvard University Press, 2008), 7, 249–254.
4. "269. Policy Planning Staff Memorandum," *Intelligence Establishment*.
5. Karen M. Paget, *Patriotic Betrayal* (Yale University Press, 2015), 43–60.
6. Paget, *Patriotic Betrayal*; Wilford, *Mighty Wurlitzer*, 123–148; Cord Meyer, *Facing Reality*; Louis Menand, "A Friend of the Devil," *The New Yorker* (March 23, 2015).
7. Quoted in Barnhisel, *Cold War Modernists*, 142–143.
8. Giles Scott-Smith, "'A Radical Democratic Political Offensive': Melvyn J. Lasky, Der Monat, and the Congress for Cultural Freedom," *Journal of Contemporary History* 35, no. 2 (April 2000): 275.
9. On the Congress for Cultural Freedom, see Giles Scott-Smith, *The Politics of Apolitical Culture: The Congress for Cultural Freedom and the*

Political Economy of American Hegemony 1945–1955 (Routledge, 2002); Barnhisel, *Cold War Modernists*, 136–178; Wilford, *Mighty Wurlitzer*, 70–98; and Audra J. Wolfe, *Freedom's Laboratory: The Cold War Struggle for the Soul of Science* (Johns Hopkins University Press, 2018).

10. Quoted in Barnhisel, *Cold War Modernists*, 142.
11. Quoted in Wilford, *Mighty Wurlitzer*, 109–111.
12. Frances Stonor Saunders, *The Cultural Cold War: The CIA and the World of Arts and Letters* (New Press, 2000), originally published as *Who Paid the Piper?* (Granta Publications, 1999); Scott-Smith, "Radical Democratic Political Offensive;" Barnhisel, *Cold War Modernists*, 9.
13. Wilford, *Mighty Wurlitzer*, 64–65.
14. On relations between the AFL-CIO and the CIA, see Robert Anthony Waters, Jr. and Geert Van Goethem, eds., *American Labor's Global Ambassadors: The International History of the AFL-CIO During the Cold War* (Palgrave Macmillan, 2013); Wilford, *Mighty Wurlitzer*, 51–69; and Dan Kurzman, "Lovestone's Cold War: The AFL-CIO Has Its Own CIA," *The New Republic* (June 25, 1966).
15. Quoted in Wilford, *Mighty Wurlitzer*, 245.
16. Wolfe, *Freedom's Laboratory*, 78–90; "The Congress of Cultural Freedom (CCF) Connection," The Polanyi Society Papers, http://polanyisociety. org/Nashotah%20House/Papers/Polanyi&CCF-5-23-16-FINAL.pdf (accessed May 18, 2023).
17. Department of State, *Science and Foreign Relations: International Flow of Scientific and Technological Information* (Department of State Publication 3860, May 1950).
18. Wolfe, *Freedom's Laboratory*, 55, 154–155.
19. David H. Price, *Cold War Anthropology: The CIA, the Pentagon, and the Growth of 'Dual Use' Anthropology* (Duke University Press, 2016).
20. Quoted in Wolfe, *Freedom's Laboratory*, 101.
21. Carl Bernstein, "The CIA and the Media," *Rolling Stone* (October 20, 1977); John Crewdson and Joseph B. Treaster, "The CIA's Three-Decade Effort to Mold the World's Views," *New York Times*, December 25, 1977, "Worldwide Propaganda Network Built by the CIA," *New York Times*, December 26, 1977, and "CIA Established Many Links to Journalists in U.S. and Abroad," *New York Times*, December 27, 1977; Wilford, *Mighty Wurlitzer*, 225–248; *The CIA and the Media: Hearings Before the Subcomm. on Oversight*, 95th Cong. (1977, 1978).
22. *CIA and the Media: Hearings*, 102–103, 196–197.

23. Wilford, *Mighty Wurlitzer*, 226–232; Bernstein, "CIA and the Media."
24. Sol Stern, "A Short Account of International Student Politics & the Cold War With Particular Reference to the NSA, CIA, Etc.," *Ramparts* (March 1967): 29–39; Neil Sheehan, "A Student Group Concedes It Took Funds From C.I.A.," *New York Times*, February 14, 1967; Juan de Onis, "Ramparts Says C.I.A. Received Student Report: Magazine Declares Agency Turned Group It Financed Into an Arm of Policy," *New York Times*, February 16, 1967; Neil Sheehan, "5 New Groups Tied to CIA Conduits," *New York Times*, February 17, 1967; Jeffreys-Jones, *CIA and American Democracy*, 153–164.
25. Meyer, *Facing Reality*, 88–89.
26. Walter Pincus, "Loophole Revealed in Prohibition on CIA Use of Journalistic Cover," *Washington Post*, February 16, 1996.
27. *CIA's Use of Journalists and Clergy in Intelligence Operations: Hearing Before the Select Comm. on Intelligence*, 104th Cong. (1996).
28. Quoted in Hench, *Books as Weapons*, 4–5.
29. Henderson, *Information Agency*, 161, 228–231; Osgood, *Total Cold War*, 288–304; Cull, *United States Information Agency*, 45, 57, 73, 174–175, 239–240, 405; Hench, *Books as Weapons*.
30. Quoted in Osgood, *Total Cold War*, 297, 303; Crewdson and Treaster, "Worldwide Propaganda Network;" Saunders, *Cultural Cold War*, 244–251.
31. Quoted in John P. C. Matthews, "The West's Secret Marshall Plan for the Mind," *International Journal of Intelligence and Counter-Intelligence* 16 (2003), 409–427. See also Alfred A. Reisch, *Hot Books in the Cold War: The CIA-Funded Secret Western Book Distribution Program Behind the Iron Curtain* (Central European University Press, 2013).
32. Douglas Martin, "George C. Minden, 85, Dies; Led a Cold War of Words," *New York Times*, April 23, 2006.
33. Bruce Gregory Oral History, interviewed by Charles Stuart Kennedy, Foreign Affairs Oral History Collection, ADST, Arlington, VA; Cull, *United States Information Agency*, 239–240; Curtis G. Benjamin, *U.S. Books Abroad: Neglected Ambassadors* (Library of Congress, 1984), http://catdir.loc.gov/catdir/toc/becites/cfb/83022245.html. On USIA's Books in Translation program, see Barnhisel, *Cold War Modernists*, 109–112.

34. Jason Epstein, "The CIA and the Intellectuals," *New York Review* 8, no. 7 (April 20, 1967). Macdonald is quoted in Saunders, *Cultural Cold War*, 409.
35. Menuhin is quoted in Saunders, *Cultural Cold War*, 408. Gardner and Braden are quoted in Paget, *Patriotic Betrayal*, 398.
36. Quoted in Saunders, *Cultural Cold War*, 408–409.
37. Quoted in Wilford, *Mighty Wurlitzer*, 254.
38. Philip Seib, "Counterterrorism Messaging Needs to Move from State to CIA," *DefenseOne* (October 27, 2014).
39. James A. Barry, "Managing Covert Political Action," 1992, Homeland Security Digital Library, https://www.hsdl.org/?abstract&did=3607.
40. Saunders, *Cultural Cold War*.
41. Caute, *Dancer Defects*, 616–617.
42. Menand, *Free World*, 716–717.
43. Wilford, *Mighty Wurlitzer*, 254.

12

Democracy Builders

When American diplomat John Adams secured a loan from Dutch bankers in 1782 to replenish an exhausted US treasury, the Netherlands was in the grip of political uncertainty. The pro-American *Patriottenbewegin* ("Patriot Party") was gaining strength inspired by America's war for independence. Its enthusiasm put Adams in a quandary. He needed its support for the loan and a commercial treaty between the two countries, but he had no interest in becoming involved in the agendas of Dutch political factions.[1] He disagreed with the "Patriots" on issues of democratic governance just as he often disagreed with Thomas Jefferson and Ben Franklin at home. He did appreciate the passionate welcome of the Dutch people during his visits to Rotterdam, Amsterdam, and other cities. Their reception, his wife Abigail wrote, was "striking proof ... of the ideas they entertain with respect to the Revolution which gave birth to their connection with us." Similarly moved, Adams declared it to be the first fruit of the American Revolution in Europe.[2]

In contrast, America's Minister to France Thomas Jefferson devoted much of his time to French politics. In June 1789 he drafted a charter of rights and gave it to the Marquis de Lafayette. He followed with suggestions on Lafayette's drafts of a "general Declaration of the Rights of Man." In August Jefferson participated in a six-hour meeting at which Lafayette

© The Author(s), under exclusive license to Springer Nature Switzerland AG 2024
B. Gregory, *American Diplomacy's Public Dimension*, Palgrave Macmillan Series in
Global Public Diplomacy, https://doi.org/10.1007/978-3-031-38917-7_12

and a band of French revolutionaries adopted the founding document of the French Revolution, a document heavily influenced by the Declaration of Independence. Jefferson defended his "presumption" as a diplomat by declaring to Lafayette his "unmeasurable love for your nation" and "painful anxiety lest despotism … should seize you again with tenfold fury."[3] He sent a copy of the French "Declaration" to James Madison and urged its endorsement by America's leaders. Adams and Jefferson were prototypical practitioners of America's approaches to spreading democracy: *persuasion by example* and *active engagement*.

Democratization Models

These models of democratization played out in the geopolitics and policy preferences of America's early leaders. The Federalists urged restraint in support for Europe's democracy movements and revolutions. Presidents Washington and Adams appointed ministers to France (Gouverneur Morris) and the Netherlands (John Jay and John Quincy Adams) with explicit instructions not to assist Europe's radicals. On refusing to join a Dutch democratic club, Quincy Adams explained he had been instructed to avoid "every act that could be charged with partiality to the Patriots."[4]

America's influence on Europe's radicals was considerable, historian Jonathan Israel observes, but "less as a directly intervening force than inspirational motor, the primary model, for universal change." Democracy "activists"—Jefferson, Madison, and Paine—viewed the French and Dutch Revolutions as offsprings of the American experiment to be actively nurtured. Jeffersonian Republicans were democratizers abroad, "inspiring, mobilizing, and cajoling competing forces within other revolutionary upheavals."[5] At home, "Democratic-Republican Societies" were providing assistance to counterpart Jacobin societies in France and democratic radicals throughout the Atlantic world.[6] It was democratization by example, however, that dominated US diplomatic practice in the 1800s. Jefferson's democratization heirs would have their day in the twentieth century.

Pure democracy was not the goal of these moderates and activists. They had created a republican form of government based on representation.

Their framing terms were liberty, equality, and individual rights. They feared mob rule and demagogues who could inflame the passions of the people. The word democracy does not appear in the Declaration of Independence or the US Constitution. Over time, however, "democracy" came into use as a protean term that embraced rule of law, civil liberties, government accountability, freedom of speech and the press, freedom to associate, religious freedom, and structural prerequisites such as fair and frequent elections, peaceful transfers of power, checks and balances, and separation of church and state.[7]

America's founders also advanced the universal relevance of their claim that "all men are created equal" and possess certain "unalienable rights." The nation could not escape this universalism, Walter Russell Mead maintains, because it "rests on a set of assumptions about what world society should be like, how all human beings should live."[8] It was bred in the bone. It made America exceptional. Spreading democracy by example came easily to leaders and diplomats in a new nation that believed its "truths to be self-evident."

The American experience was "profoundly destabilizing to the rest of the world … a living thriving reproach to the political legitimacy of autocracies abroad."[9] Monarchists, autocrats, and church hierarchies rejected representative democracy and pointed to its inadequacies and hypocrisies. It was a contest of big ideas with consequences for friends and foes alike. Alexis de Tocqueville in his *Democracy in America* (1835) called it a "great experiment," an "attempt to construct society on a new basis." He came to America to find "the image of democracy itself … to learn what we have to fear or hope from its progress."[10]

US diplomats in the 1800s were largely content to let their "great experiment" illuminate by example. With a few notable exceptions, they dealt only with regimes in power, which placed constraints on their relations with citizen democratizers. They were instructed to report on local politics but steer clear of other countries' internal affairs. In South America, the State Department's policy was to keep its hands off rebellions against Europe's monarchies but welcome the results if colonial governments were overthrown. As Secretary James Monroe explained to Joel Poinsett, US Consul General in Chile, "the disposition shewn (sic) by most of the Spanish provinces to separate from Europe and erect themselves into independent States excites great interest here," but "the destiny of those provinces must depend on themselves." "All we ask," Secretary of State Edward Livingston wrote to US envoy Edmund Quincy Roberts in China in 1832, "is free liberty to come and go for the purpose of buying and selling."[11] Not until its War with Spain (1898) did the US begin to institutionalize democratization as a tool of diplomatic and military practice.

"The cause of America," Thomas Paine famously declared, became "in great measure the cause of all mankind." Historian Jon Meacham writes, "As a matter of observable fact, the United States, through its sporadic adherence to its finest aspirations, is the most durable experiment in pluralistic republicanism the world has known."[12] It is America's national narrative, a nation founded on devotion to the principles of liberty and self-government and sustained by each generation's renewed belief in their exceptional promise.

But America's narrative also masks greed, power, and what Jefferson called a natural right of "going in quest of new habitations."[13] Admiration for America's democratic republic was undermined when others looked at the cruelties and inconsistencies of enslavement, the harsh treatment and forced displacement of native populations, the denial of voting rights and equal treatment for women, and continuing shortfalls in providing justice for all. Episodes of nativism and chauvinism, vulgarities and violence, gave foreign critics plenty of ammunition. The "city on a hill" would disappoint when it failed to live up to its principles.

Support for Revolutions Abroad

Americans in the early 1800s provided assistance to insurrections throughout Spanish and Portuguese South America. Private funds were raised. Arms were shipped from US ports. Mercenaries joined rebel forces. Sailors embarked on privateering vessels. Simon Bolivar and other revolutionaries benefited from Spanish translations of the Declaration of Independence and other founding documents. When Spain's colonies and Brazil declared independence, the new republics adopted constitutions almost identical to the US Constitution. Building stable democratic institutions proved more difficult. Monroe's "Doctrine" closed the hemi-sphere to further colonization and declared Europe's political systems to be "essentially different from that of America." For Bolivar, the Doctrine was a mixed blessing: a shield against European intervention but no bar-rier to an American sphere of influence.[14]

Europe's revolutionaries also admired the American model. When Greek rebels rose up against four centuries of Ottoman rule in 1821, Americans responded with an outpouring of support for these heirs of Pericles, Aristotle, and Homer. Rallies were held. Sermons were preached. Theaters gave benefit performances and merchants a share of their profits. Workers donated wages. Greek-American committees sent money, weap-ons, and medical supplies. The American press, uniformly supportive, was quick to report Turkish atrocities and overlook those of the Greeks. Americans, including prominently Dr. Samuel Gridley Howe, the hus-band of Julia Ward Howe, sailed to Greece to provide their services.[15]

European Revolutions in the 1830s also drew American support. Writers and scholars—James Fennimore Cooper, Ralph Waldo Emerson, Walt Whitman—became the new voices of American democracy abroad, a successor generation to Jefferson, Franklin, and Paine. Polish-American societies supported revolution in Poland motivated in part by memories of Colonel Tadeusz Kosciuszko's contributions in the Continental Army. The US rejected direct involvement in Europe's political turmoil, but a roadmap now existed for America's democratization activists.

Most Americans had little enthusiasm for the anarchists, communists, and radical socialists who shaped Europe's 1848 revolutions. Nevertheless, US reaction to the French overthrow of Louis Philippe was positive. Richard Rush, the American minister in Paris, ignoring objections of the international diplomatic community, announced US recognition of the Second French Republic. President Polk congratulated the French for adopting a "future government on liberal institutions similar to our own." Horace Greeley declared the "emancipation of Europe had begun" in his *New York Daily Tribune*. An estimated crowd of one hundred thousand Irish, Italian, German, and Polish immigrants singing "La Marseillaise" gathered in New York to celebrate.[16]

"Adjunct" Democratizers

Democratization emerged as a state-based instrument of foreign affairs in the twentieth century.[17] Spreading democracy was used to support hot and cold war strategies, benefit economic and security interests, avoid and resolve conflicts, achieve humanitarian objectives, protect human rights, support refugees and diasporas, and strengthen the rule of law. The idea that governments should institutionalize democratization was endorsed by Republican and Democratic administrations and shaped by global democratic "waves" that followed World War II and the Cold War.[18] Underlying it all is the conviction, Anne-Marie Slaughter maintains, "that liberty, democracy, equality, and justice are birthrights for *all*—not just all Americans."[19]

Many US democracy practitioners are "adjuncts." That is, they operate in subunits of military and civilian government departments and agencies with larger missions. Others, beginning in the 1980s, staff government-funded non-profit organizations. Together, with their civil society partners, democratizers constitute a practitioner community with distinct professional norms, tools, and methods in diplomacy's public dimension.[20]

Defense Department. US armed forces played an early and continuing role in democratization. American commanders seeking to establish democratic electoral and judicial systems in Cuba and the Philippines after the War with Spain pressured local authorities to make governance choices "essential to the rule of law and individual freedom." Democratic practices, Secretary of War Elihu Root instructed, "must be established and maintained in their islands for the sake of their liberty and happiness, however much they may conflict with the customs or laws of procedure with which they are familiar."[21]

In the 1920s and 1930s, US forces intermittently sought to establish democratic governments in Haiti, Nicaragua, and the Dominican Republic. After World War II, US military governments in Germany, Austria, and Japan made democracy building central to their occupation strategies. US forces returned to Nicaragua and the Dominican Republic in the 1960s. They invaded Granada in 1983 and Panama in 1989.

Democratization figured prominently in each of these conflicts as it did later in Somalia and the Balkans in the 1990s and Iraq and Afghanistan in the 2000s.[22]

In the 1990s the Department increased its support for civil–military relations and achieving democratization through professional education. In the words of Defense Secretary William J. Perry, two assumptions drove the effort: (1) more democracy in more nations reduces conflict and is good for national security, and (2) the US military has a responsibility "to embed democratic values" in military and defense establishments around the world. The military is the most cohesive and well-funded institution in many countries. If "we can build trust and understanding between the militaries of two neighboring nations, we build trust and understanding between the two nations themselves."[23] It was a page out of the playbook of public diplomacy's Fulbright and people-to-people exchanges.

Prominent among the military's democratization tools and methods are exchanges funded by the International Military Education and Training Program (IMET), the education of foreign military officers at US service colleges, and teams of military and civilian experts sent to advise on building militaries under civilian control. The case made by Perry, Admiral Dennis Blair, and other commanders is that non-violent means can be more effective in building democracies than overthrowing regimes by force of arms.[24] US forces face distrust, however, based on past support for military dictatorships. In the Western hemisphere, memories of military and covert intervention remain strong, despite occasional US "good neighbor" policies. Civil–military relations programs had little effect on Turkey's abuses of its Kurdish minority and marginal impact in Indonesia, Egypt, and other countries where security forces commit human rights abuses. This history for democracy scholar/practitioner Thomas Carothers means claims regarding IMET's transformative effects must, "be greeted with considerable skepticism."[25]

USIA and the Department of State. USIA made democratization part of its modus operandi. Early in the Cold War, the Agency seasoned its more strident anti-communism with books, films, support for American studies, and English teaching materials that conveyed basic ideas about citizenship and democracy.[26] In the 1970s it determined "US political and social processes" would constitute one of its four overarching themes. The others were foreign policy and national security, economic affairs, and arts and culture. Speakers, printed materials, and visual products emphasized US democratic institutions and rule of law. Foreign press centers in Washington and New York enthusiastically facilitated foreign journalists' coverage of political campaigns and party conventions. Supreme Court Justices and federal judges welcomed foreign jurists visiting the US and engaged in numerous USIA-sponsored visits overseas.

Republican and Democratic presidents used democratization to advance their policies. Democracy building was central to Eisenhower's support for "captive nations" in Eastern Europe. Kennedy's Alliance for Progress put USIA and USAID in the forefront of democratization in Latin America though assistance to labor unions and civil society groups opposed to military regimes. Carter emphasized human rights. Reagan initiated the National Endowment for Democracy.[27] George H. W. Bush's "new world order" and Bill Clinton's "enlargement and engagement" policies expanded these efforts in the democracy wave that followed the Cold War.

The State Department's approach to democratization emphasizes government-wide policy direction, efforts to coordinate US agencies, and relations with international organizations. The Department created a Bureau of Democracy, Human Rights, and Labor in 1975. Democratization assistance is also a priority of State's Africa Bureau. Each bureau manages direct grants to non-profit democracy building organizations. In the field, ambassadors oversee democratization and rule of law activities of USAID, Justice, Commerce, Defense, and other US departments.

State pays considerable attention to local politicians, trending political issues, visitor programs, and election observer missions. "What the US government should focus on," one US ambassador told Carothers, "are key politicians with real influence. The embassy should send them on study tours to the United States to learn how democracy works and keep the pressure on them at pivotal junctures to make sure they do the right things politically, like not appointing weak or corrupt people to important posts."[28] This "democracy by light bulb" approach is typical of many ambassadors in Carothers' experience. It fits easily with State's priorities and avoids connections with democratizing NGOs that might irritate host governments. Decades of visitor grants and election monitoring have had positive effects, but whether they are transformative is a more difficult question. Successful democratization, he argues, is best achieved through slow processes of generational change in civil society and governance.[29]

Peace Corps and USAID. Peace Corps volunteers are Americans motivated to seek peace and friendship through collaboration on common global problems in communities abroad. They share knowledge and skills in education, health, nutrition, agriculture, business, community development, environmental protection, and other fields. Just as most nineteenth-century missionaries and humanitarians did not go abroad to promote democracy, neither do most Peace Corps volunteers. Yet democratic values inform their relationships with stakeholders.

USAID's early approach to democratization was similarly indirect. Foreign assistance practitioners prioritized improving economic conditions and public administration, Carothers explains. They were responding to Castro's revolution and efforts to spread communism in the hemisphere through socioeconomic reforms that could give rise to democracy. However, in the Reagan administration USAID initiated small democracy promotion programs. In 1984 it supported voter registration training, vote counting, and projects to train judges and prosecutors in El Salvador. Similar initiatives were launched elsewhere in Latin America and in Africa after the Agency gradually overcame its skepticism that African countries would turn to democracy.[30] Practitioners continued to prioritize the socioeconomic model, but they increasingly saw value in aligning with the administration's support for democracy promotion.[31]

In the 1990s USAID turned enthusiastically to "the worldwide democratic revolution." It announced a "Democracy Initiative," made democratization one of its four central goals, expanded democracy projects in Latin America and the Middle East, and created an African Electoral Assistance Fund. In 1993 Administrator Brian Atwood established a Center for Democracy and Governance. The Agency also initiated democracy programs in Asia over the opposition of practitioners who deferred to the "Asian values" arguments of countries that viewed collectivism as more appropriate for the region than Western democracy and human rights. USAID was now supporting free and fair elections, new constitutions, legislative and judicial reforms, anti-corruption programs, civic education, journalism training, human rights, legal aid, women's rights, and assisting civil society organizations in more than 100 countries. Its democracy budget grew from $165 million in 1991 to $637 million in 1999.[32]

USAID's democracy projects fill a gap between State's policy-oriented approach and the grassroots methods of non-profit organizations such as the Ford Foundation and League of Women Voters. Similar to most NGOs, the Agency favors democratization through "a long-term developmental process consisting of the gradual reform of major state institutions matched by the slow building up of civil society, often with an emphasis on NGO development at the local level."[33]

As a government agency, however, USAID takes foreign policy direction from State, and its programs fit policy priorities. Initiatives surge in countries where the US wants to promote democracy; efforts are less robust where US interests drive relations with autocratic rulers. In Carothers' comparative judgment, State needs to step back from a "who's out, who's in" political calculus and give greater recognition to democratization as a durable field of professional practice. USAID needs to reform practices that are slow and bureaucratic, recognize that democratization is inherently political, that politicians and election outcomes are part of the work, and be more willing to use political leverage.[34]

National Endowment for Democracy

In 1980 the Republican and Democratic National Committees, the AFL-CIO, and the US Chamber of Commerce, normally fierce competitors, banded together to form the American Political Foundation. Their goal was to create a government-funded entity to support democracy building. On June 8, 1982, President Reagan in his Westminster speech to the British Parliament promised a new US initiative "to foster the infrastructure of democracy—the system of a free press, unions, political parties, universities—which allows a people to choose their own way, to develop their own culture, to reconcile their own differences through peaceful means." The "bipartisan American Political Foundation," he declared, would study "how the United States can best contribute—as a nation— to the global campaign for democracy now gathering force."[35]

The influential Americans who persuaded Reagan to endorse the Foundation's agenda included US Trade Representative William Brock, a former Chair of the Republican National Committee, Democratic National Committee Chair Charles Manatt, Republican National Committee Chair Frank J. Fahrenkopf, public diplomacy champion Dante Fascell (D-FL), Senator Christopher Dodd (D-CT), and Senate Foreign Relations Committee Chairman Charles Percy (R-IL). The Foundation's advisory board included AFL-CIO President Lane Kirkland, Reagan's first NSC Advisor Richard V. Allen, neo-conservative activist Ben Wattenberg, Anthony Lake, later President Clinton's NSC Advisor, and Georgetown University professor and democracy activist Allen Weinstein. With this much political heft, positive results were not surprising.

The Foundation's study, "The Democracy Program," was supported by grants from USAID and a special White House fund. It recommended that Congress create a grant-making non-profit entity to promote free and democratic institutions. In the parlance of the day, it would be a "QUANGO," a quasi-autonomous non-governmental organization. The Foundation took as its model Germany's political party foundations (Stiftungs), private organizations funded by grants from Germany's Bundestag.[36]

In November 1983 Congress authorized the National Endowment for Democracy (NED). Stating it was not "an agency or establishment of the United States Government," lawmakers authorized an independent bipartisan board of directors, Congressional oversight, and grants from annual appropriations to USIA. The Endowment filed articles of incorporation with the District of Columbia and papers securing its tax-exempt status. Its corporate structure was analogous to the Tennessee Valley Authority and Corporation for Public Broadcasting. NED's goals: international support for democratic institutions, electoral processes, and civil society infrastructure. Its methods: grants to civil society groups in the US and abroad to support democracy training, exchanges, research, and evaluation.[37]

Powerful backers notwithstanding, NED's survival was not assured. Some liberals worried it would be an instrument of US hegemony and interference in the internal affairs of others. Some conservatives fretted that the lion's share of its grants went to the AFL-CIO and it was promoting a social democratic agenda. Labor's long history of international activities had given it a head start over the newly formed political party and US Chamber of Commerce democracy institutes. GAO reports found deficiencies in NED's operating processes and lack of an overall strategy.[38] But critics were outmatched by the lobbying of America's political parties, labor, and business, and the political savvy of NED's board members and staff.

NED's president was Carl Gershman, a politically astute neoconservative who had transitioned from executive director of the staunchly anticommunist Social Democrats, USA to become a senior counselor to Reagan's UN Ambassador Jeane Kirkpatrick. Gershman led the Endowment for four decades until his retirement in 2021. Marc Plattner, former editor of *The Public Interest*, and political scientists Seymour Martin Lipset and Larry Diamond were part of NED's informal brain trust. The Endowment's influential *Journal of Democracy*, founded in 1990 by Plattner and Diamond, continues as a forum for views on democratic theory and practice by scholars and practitioners.[39] Four core grantees received most of NED's funding: the AFL-CIO's Free Trade Union Institute, later renamed the Solidarity Center, the Center for International Private Enterprise, the National Democratic Institute for International Affairs (NDI), and the International Republican Institute (IRI). They worked separately but often collaboratively to strengthen free trade unions, business enterprise, and democratic processes and institutions.

The Endowment and its grantees were by design an overt network of non-government organizations comparable to the CIA's early Cold War front groups that had faced blowback when exposed. The democracy activists in the 1980s were successful precisely because their work was open, journalist David Ignatius wrote. When political action is done overtly "the flap potential is close to zero." He bestowed particular praise on the Endowment, which he called "the sugar daddy of overt operations."[40]

NED's grantees normally do not identify with the term public diplomacy, but they are a distinct community of practice in US diplomacy's public dimension. Global trends shaped their priorities. In the 1980s they focused on anti-communist efforts in Eastern Europe, particularly Poland's Solidarity movement and Czechoslovakia's Velvet Revolution, and democracy transitions in Haiti, Namibia, Zambia, and South Africa. In the 1990s they concentrated on pro-democracy groups in the former Soviet Union and activists advocating democratic practices in China and Burma. They prioritized activities in countries where their "non-government" and "multi-sectoral" character were advantageous and where USAID's and State's democratization projects encountered political resistance.

With substantial support from private foundations, NED created the International Forum for Democratic Studies in 1994, a center that hosts conferences, publishes books and reports, and seeks to bridge gaps between democratization study and practice. In the 2000s NED collaborated with a growing number of new counterpart organizations, the UK's Westminster Foundation, Australia's Center for Democratic Institutions, the United Nations Democracy Fund, the Arab Democracy Foundation, and the European Partnership for Democracy. Other initiatives included a Center for International Media Assistance and serving as secretariat for the World Movement for Democracy, a global network of civil society activists, scholars, journalists, and parliamentarians committed to advancing democracy.[41]

The Endowment's grantees occupy a distinctive place in US democracy promotion for several reasons. First, they are avowedly political. Not in a partisan sense; indeed, they are outspokenly bipartisan. But they are resolutely committed to the politics of building democratic institutions and supporting pluralism in countries that are struggling to become democratic. These practitioners thrive in politically tense environments.

Second, NED maintains transparency as a Congressionally funded organization, but emphasizes its "quasi-public" and "quasi-private" nonprofit corporate character. Apart from a small headquarters staff, most of its funding goes to the private US and foreign organizations that manage

grants and projects. In this, democracy building is functionally comparable to cultural diplomacy. Congress funds; private organizations do
most of the work. Both communities support international exchanges,
conferences, publications, training programs, and media engagement.
Democratizers supplement these tools with election monitoring and
attention to theoretical issues in democracy studies and practice.

Third, unlike USAID and the State Department, NED does not exist
to promote US foreign policy, although it is legally required to operate
"in a manner consistent with ... the broad concerns of United States
national interests and with the specific requirements of the democratic
groups in other countries which are aided by NED-supported programs."[42] NED's grantees value an arm's length relation with government,
and they object when democratization is used to justify US military
interventions and other policy goals. Concerns were raised, for example,
about the appearance of policy advocacy when President George W. Bush,
speaking at the Endowment on its twentieth anniversary, connected
armed force with support for democracy in Afghanistan, Iraq, and "a new
policy, a forward strategy of freedom in the Middle East."[43]

Democratization also suffers when the US soft pedals responses to
sham elections in some countries (Kazakhstan and Azerbaijan in 2005) to
win support from authoritarian leaders for military and economic objectives. And when the US takes sides in foreign elections through statements and assistance programs designed to make incumbents or
opposition candidates look good. Likewise, when the US fails to support
outcomes in generally fair elections as when the Islamic Salvation Front
party prevailed in Algeria's elections in 1991 and Hamas scored a victory
in Palestinian elections in 2006.[44]

Assessments

By the end of the twentieth century democracy promotion had become
an accepted instrument in US diplomacy. Budgets in the low millions in
the 1980s grew to more than $2 billion annually in the 2000s.[45] With the
establishment of NED, US democracy building evolved from "adjunct"
activities in government organizations to become a public–private

community of practice. Not only are partnerships with US-based NGOs critical to its success, increasingly important are partnerships with European foundations, transnational non-profit NGOs, for-profit consulting firms, and multilateral organizations.[46]

It was a journey filled with achievements, limitations, and ongoing challenges. Significantly, US democratizers had moved from an early one-size-fits-all model—the idea that democracy looked like America's elections, government institutions, and civil society—to more mature strategies. Surface knowledge and top-down emphasis on American experts gave way to deeper understanding of foreign political and cultural contexts. Practitioners learned by comparing their experiences. Sustained presence abroad led to increased knowledge of indigenous drivers of change and more networking with local groups. Practitioners became more open to non-western institutions and processes, and more aware of how their efforts could be exploited by anti-democratic regimes.[47] Their evolving modus operandi called for varied approaches. Their field operations improved over time as they learned to value planning and evaluation, albeit with methods that in Carothers' assessment ranged from the superficial to the excessively complex.[48] Today, historians, political scientists, international relations scholars—and practitioners—are bridging the gulf between study and practice with excellent scholarship on democratization.[49]

To a considerable extent, democratization's challenges are baked into powerful contextual realities. Between 1990 and 2005 Freedom House documented significant net gains of countries with greater democracy and pluralism. Between 2005 and 2022 it recorded 17 years of net democratic decline.[50] Democratizers tend to do better when liberalism is on the rise. They are less successful when hardened authoritarian regimes create obstacles.

Many limitations are operational, however, and can be overcome. For example, rule of law projects too often relied on strengthening judicial institutions using Western legal models—"hasty transplants" that lacked stakeholder buy-in and were unsuitable for political systems in transition.[51] Election monitors contribute to fair elections, but analysts have concerns about professional standards, contradictory judgments by different organizations, and occasional endorsements of flawed elections.

Monitors have limited resources and often put undue focus on election day practices. Many lack local knowledge and capacity to penetrate the deception of local politicians.[52] In some cases, Kenya and Haiti in 2009, for example, organizations funded by the US government faced allegations that monitoring results were withheld when they were at odds with the State Department's winner preferences.[53]

Other difficulties arise from choices driven by donor preferences and NGO priorities. As nonprofit democracy organizations became stronger over time, many made compromises to meet expectations of affluent patrons and maintain their standing in other countries. Clifford Bob argues costs for NGOs are often measured in the potential for lost trust and reputation and risks in selecting some partners over others. As an executive of the International Foundation for Electoral Systems, a partner of the Democratic and Republican Party Institutes, put it, "We consider our own reputation. We don't want to fail; we want to have some successes."[54]

Practitioners creating a work plan for an NDI parliamentary training program in Somalia faced choices between western democracy models and "local clan democracy." Our training, one participant observed, focused on parliamentarians rather than clan representatives in part because it would "be better for the paperwork NDI would submit to the donors."[55] NGOs are not motivated by profit, but even the best, Jessica Mathews observed, can have "tunnel vision, judging every public act by how it affects their particular interest ... [A]s they grow, the need to sustain growing budgets can compromise the independence of mind and approach that is their greatest asset."[56]

Political scientist Sarah Bush, a leading proponent of the view that democracy assistance has been "tamed," contends that when democracy building became a multibillion-dollar, multicountry industry, grantees often turned away from controversial programs that would disturb the status quo. "[O]rganizations in the democracy establishment started working harder to pursue programs that would succeed at getting government grants and gaining access to the countries where they did their work, rather than just pursuing democratization."[57] Some projects were counterproductive. "Dictators wishing to appear democratic, for example, increasingly adopted the institutions promoted by democracy promoters, such as quotas for women's representation in politics, in order to cultivate domestic and international legitimacy."[58] "It was the desire for international legitimacy," Eric Bjornlund argues, "that drove the governments of Ferdinand Marcos in the Philippines, Augusto Pinochet in Chile, Manuel Noriega in Panama, and Daniel Ortega in Nicaragua to invite election observers."[59]

Finally, democratizers face limitations born of tendencies to conflate democracy and governance. USAID's strategy documents, democracy scholar Lincoln A. Mitchell explains, often refer to "democratic governance," implying that good governance is good for democracy. This might be true in countries transitioning to democracy, but in countries hostile to democracy, the connections are more ambiguous. Anti-corruption projects might improve government accountability, but projects that help governments deliver services more efficiently or communicate more effectively might in fact strengthen repressive regimes. USAID's Turkmenistan Governance Strengthening Program in 2011 trained government officials to use online information sharing, Skype, and other digital tools. It may have made Turkmenistan's government more effective, "but how training representatives of one of the world's most repressive governments … to use Skype or e-mail better strengthens democracy is a question for which there is no answer."[60]

America's democracy practitioners face interconnected challenges in the twenty-first century: diminished enthusiasm for a liberal world order, changed perceptions of the US driven by wars in Iraq and Afghanistan, a rising generation of populist leaders, and political and governance dysfunction in the United States. These challenges cannot be met with tactical adjustments. Democratizers began responding with calls for an imaginative analysis of the changing nature of authoritarian influence, a reconceptualization of "soft power," debate on the meaning of "sharp power," and strategies centered on a reaffirmation of democratic values and ideals.[61]

Emerging concepts of stakeholder democracy are attractive alternatives to the Westphalian state-based model in dealing with global problems. Informal governance structures and multiconstituency coalitions of governments and civil society stakeholders now operate across geographic and political boundaries. These stakeholders focus on particular issues and decisions, on positive outcomes that legitimize their activities, and on people who influence outcomes or are affected by them. It is an environment that in principle contains opportunities for democracy practitioners who rely heavily on partnerships with nonstate actors.

Notes

1. Jonathan Israel, *The Expanding Blaze: How the American Revolution Ignited the World, 1775–1848* (Princeton University Press, 2017), 230–233.
2. McCullough, *John Adams*, 368.
3. Israel, *Expanding Blaze*, 255; Meacham, *Thomas Jefferson*, 222–223.
4. Israel, *Expanding Blaze*, 244.
5. Israel, *Expanding Blaze*, 17–18.
6. Robert M. Chesney, "Democratic-Republican Societies, Subversion, and the Limits of Legitimate Political Dissent in the Early Republic," *North Carolina Law Review* 85, no. 5 (June 2004): 1525–1580; Ron Chernow, *Washington: A Life* (Penguin Books, 2010), 694–699; Jarrett M. Walker, "Evolution of a Word: Democracy and the Democratic-Republican Societies, 1793–1796," MA thesis (Georgia State University, 2013).
7. Mandelbaum, *Ideas That Conquered the World*, 245–247; Danielle Allen, *Our Declaration: A Reading of the Declaration of Independence in Defense of Equality* (W. W. Norton, 2014), 21–22.
8. Walter Russell Mead, "The Paradox of American Democracy Promotion," *The American Interest* 10, no. 5 (April 9, 2015).
9. Mead, "American Democracy Promotion."
10. Quoted in Doyle, *Cause of All Nations*, 95.
11. Quoted in Eicher, *Raising the Flag*, 109, 112–113, 144.
12. Meacham, *Soul of America*, 258.
13. Grandin, *End of the Myth*, 3.
14. Israel, *Expanding Blaze*, 423–455, 472–485; Grandin, *End of the Myth*, 37–38; Alan Taylor, *American Republics: A Continental History of the United States, 1783–1850* (W. W. Norton, 2021), 296–300.

15. Edward Mead Earle, "American Interest in the Greek Cause, 1821–1827," *The American Historical Review* 33, no. 1 (October, 1927): 44–63; Israel, *Expanding Blaze*, 495–511.
16. Israel, *Expanding Blaze*, 568–573.
17. Tony Smith, *America's Mission: The United States and the Worldwide Struggle for Democracy* (Princeton University Press, 2012).
18. Samuel P. Huntington, "Democracy's Third Wave," *Journal of Democracy* 2, no. 2 (Spring 1991): 12–34.
19. Anne-Marie Slaughter, *The Idea That Is America* (Basic Books, 2007), 232.
20. The terms democratization, democracy promotion, and democracy assistance describe a whole of government instrument of practice. Some scholars distinguish between democracy promotion and democracy assistance. Sarah Sunn Bush argues "democracy promotion" can take the form of sanctions and rewards, diplomatic pressure, and military intervention. "Democracy assistance" is aid given with the defined goal of advancing democracy in other countries. Sarah Sunn Bush, *The Taming of Democracy Assistance: Why Democracy Promotion Does Not Confront Dictators* (Cambridge University Press, 2015).
21. Quoted in Jayne A. Carson, "Nation-Building, The American Way," US Army War College, 2003, 8.
22. Joshua Muravchik, *Exporting Democracy: Fulfilling America's Destiny* (AEI Press, 1992), 91–118.
23. William J. Perry, "Remarks as Prepared for Delivery," Harvard University, May 13, 1996.
24. Dennis C. Blair, *Military Engagement: Influencing Armed Forces Worldwide to Influence Democratic Transitions* (Brookings, 2013); Thomas Carothers, *Aiding Democracy Abroad: The Learning Curve* (Carnegie Endowment, 1999), 196–200; Larry Diamond and Marc F. Plattner, eds., *Civil-Military Relations and Democracy* (Johns Hopkins University Press, 1996).
25. Carothers, *Aiding Democracy Abroad*, 199–200.
26. Cull, *United States Information Agency*, 109, 127.
27. *Democracy Promotion: An Objective of US Foreign Assistance* (Congressional Research Service, 2019), 4–5; Muravchik, *Exporting Democracy*, 206–207; David Lowe, "Idea to Reality: NED at 30," National Endowment for Democracy, https://www.ned.org/about/history/; Cull, *United States Information Agency*, 421–423.
28. Quoted in Thomas Carothers, "Democracy, State and AID: A Tale of Two Cultures," *Foreign Service Journal* 76, no. 2 (February 2001): 22.

29. Carothers, *Aiding Democracy Abroad*, 276–278.
30. Carothers, *Aiding Democracy Abroad*, 20–29; Smith, *America's Mission*, 214–236.
31. Muravchik, *Exporting Democracy*, 182–183; Carothers, *Aiding Democracy Abroad*, 34–38.
32. Carothers, *Aiding Democracy Abroad*, 40–51; Larry Diamond, *Promoting Democracy in the 1990s* (Report to the Carnegie Commission on Preventing Deadly Conflict, 1995), 13–14; Thomas Carothers, *Critical Mission: Essays on Democracy Promotion* (Carnegie Endowment, 2004), 7–52.
33. Carothers, "Democracy, State and AID," 22.
34. Carothers, "Democracy, State and AID," 24.
35. Quoted in Lowe, "Idea to Reality."
36. Lowe, "Idea to Reality;" *Events Leading to the Establishment of the National Endowment for Democracy* (US General Accounting Office, 1984); Carothers, *Aiding Democracy Abroad*, 30–44; Muravchik, *Exporting Democracy*, 204–220.
37. 22 USC Chapter 54, Subchapter II, National Endowment for Democracy, https://uscode.house.gov/view.xhtml?path=/prelim@title22/chapter54/subchapter2&edition=prelim.
38. Lowe, "Idea to Reality;" *1986 Annual Report*, US Advisory Commission on Public Diplomacy Reports, 31; *Promoting Democracy: The National Endowment for Democracy's Management of Grants Overseas* (US General Accounting Office, 1986); *Promoting Democracy: National Endowment for Democracy's Management of Grants Needs Improvement* (US General Accounting Office, 1991).
39. Nicolas Guilhot, *The Democracy Makers: Human Rights and the Politics of Global Order* (Columbia University Press, 2005), 83–100; Robert Pee and William Michael Schmidli, eds., *The Reagan Administration, the Cold War, and the Transition to Democracy Promotion* (Palgrave Macmillan, 2018).
40. David Ignatius, "Innocence Abroad: The New World of Spyless Coups," *Washington Post*, September 22, 1991.
41. Lowe, "Idea to Reality."
42. 22 USC Chapter 54, Subchapter II, National Endowment for Democracy.

43. George W. Bush, "Remarks on the 20th Anniversary of the National Endowment for Democracy," November 6, 2003, American Presidency Project.

44. Thomas Carothers, "Responding to the Democracy Promotion Backlash" (Carnegie Endowment, June 8, 2006).

45. *Democracy Promotion*, Congressional Research Service, 12–16.

46. Larry Diamond, *Ill Winds: Saving Democracy from Russian Rage, Chinese Ambition, and American Complacency* (Penguin Press, 2019), 285–307.

47. Carothers, *Aiding Democracy Abroad*, 86–96, 331.

48. For case studies on Guatemala, Nepal, Zambia, and Romania, see Carothers, *Aiding Democracy Abroad*, 297–302. On Indonesia, see Eric Bjornlund, *Beyond Free and Fair: Monitoring Elections and Building Democracy* (Johns Hopkins University Press, 2004), 256–278.

49. Lincoln A. Mitchell, *The Democracy Promotion Paradox* (Brookings, 2016); Bush, *Taming of Democracy Assistance.*

50. *Freedom in the World 2023: Marking 50 Years in the Struggle for Democracy* (Freedom House, 2023).

51. Wade Channell, "Lessons Not Learned about Legal Reform," in *Promoting the Rule of Law Abroad: In Search of Knowledge*, ed. Thomas Carothers (Carnegie Endowment, 2006), 137–159; Thomas Carothers, "Democracy Aid at 25: Time to Choose," *Journal of Democracy* 26, no. 1 (January 2015): 59–73.

52. Judith Kelley, *Monitoring Democracy: When International Election Observation Works and Why it Often Fails* (Princeton University Press, 2012); Thomas Carothers, "The Rise of Election Monitoring: The Observers Observed," *Journal of Democracy* 8, no. 3 (July 1997): 17–31.

53. Mike McIntire and Jeffrey Gettleman, "Secrecy Surrounds Kenyan Election Poll," *New York Times*, January 31, 2009.

54. Clifford Bob, *The Marketing of Rebellion: Insurgents, Media, and International Activism* (Cambridge University Press, 2005), 37.

55. Nimmo Osman Elmi, "Making Democracy Work: Tools, Theories and Templates of Vernacular Democracy in Somalia's Rebuilding," MA thesis (University of Oslo, 2014), 54–56, https://core.ac.uk/download/pdf/30902447.pdf.

56. Jessica T. Mathews, "Power Shift," *Foreign Affairs* 78, no. 1 (January/February 1997): 50–66.

57. Bush, *Taming of Democracy Assistance*, 231.

58. Bush, *Taming of Democracy Assistance*, 5; Thomas Carothers, et al., "Roundtable Review of The Taming of Democracy Assistance" (Carnegie Endowment, July 25, 2016).
59. Bjornlund, *Beyond Free and Fair*, 192.
60. Mitchell, *Democracy Promotion Paradox*, 86–94.
61. Christopher Walker and Jessica Ludwig, *Sharp Power: Rising Authoritarian Influence* (National Endowment for Democracy, 2017); Diamond, *Ill Winds*.

13

Presidential Aides

Soon after the National Security Council's second meeting on December 9, 1947, executive secretary Admiral Sidney W. Souers sent a memorandum to all members. He asked them to approve "Coordination of Foreign Information Measures (NSC 4)," a draft NSC directive that stated: "The Secretary of State should be charged with formulating policies for and coordinating the implementation of all information measures designed to influence attitudes in foreign countries in a direction favorable to the attainment of US objectives and to counteract effects of anti-US propaganda." The Assistant Secretary of State for Public Affairs would exercise these functions on behalf of the Secretary assisted by a qualified interagency staff.

The task was broadly defined. "Appropriate departments and agencies should be directed to insure the most effective coordination and utilization of their appropriate facilities for the implementation of approved foreign information policies."[1] How exactly an assistant secretary could be expected to "coordinate" large government departments and military services was not spelled out. President Truman quickly approved NSC 4. The operational meanings of its abstractions were left to the situational conflicts and compromises of practitioners in the interagency process.

© The Author(s), under exclusive license to Springer Nature Switzerland AG 2024
B. Gregory, *American Diplomacy's Public Dimension*, Palgrave Macmillan Series in Global Public Diplomacy, https://doi.org/10.1007/978-3-031-38917-7_13

A primary goal of the National Security Act of 1947, which created the NSC, CIA, Joint Chiefs of Staff (JCS), and Department of Defense, was "effectively coordinating the policies and functions of the departments and agencies of Government concerned with national security."[2] Why now? A conventional answer is that global trends—containment of Soviet expansion, an ideological cold war, Soviet nuclear weapons, and memories of German and Japanese aggression—justified the creation and coordination of unprecedented national security organizations.

Another answer, national security scholar Amy Zegart argues persuasively, is "They arose from one of the most bitter bureaucratic battles in American history." Truman developed the NSC system as a way to check the fierce rivalries of the Navy, War, State, and Justice Departments and the intelligence bureaucracy. Each fought to protect its interests and independence. Each had champions in Congress. Few among those "present at the creation" wanted a fundamental reorganization. But facing White House pressure they compromised in the creation of national security organizations that were suboptimal and flawed throughout their long trajectories by structural choices made at birth.[3]

Containing communism and defending the "free world" called for robust deployment and coordination of "psychological tools," the parlance of the day. But these tools, weakened at the end of World War II, were scattered about the executive branch. NSC 4 was meant to solve the problem, but the coordinating mechanism led by the State Department proved unequal to the task. After three years of intense interagency discord, Truman assigned foreign information coordination responsibilities to the NSC in 1951.

These decisions foreshadowed decades of subsequent practice. Multiple structures were created in an effort to achieve interagency coordination of foreign information operations. Presidents occasionally acquiesced in State-led coordination, but most preferred centralized NSC structures. Accordingly, presidential aides became a community of practice in diplomacy's public dimension. This chapter examines their characteristics and methods, and compares NSC and State Department coordination models. By law, the NSC is directed to advise the President on "the integration of domestic, foreign, and military policies" and to "effectively" coordinate "policies and functions" on matters of "common interest."[4]

Many practitioners act as though interagency coordination's meaning is self-evident. Reality is more complicated.

Coordination at its most basic level involves *information* sharing—vetting White House policy proposals with government organizations and collecting their concurring and opposing views for analysis and resolution. Here, the NSC staff wields power less through substantive input than in the choices and timing of issues to be coordinated, management of paper flow, and "creative note-taking." Agencies tend to welcome information sharing. It is minimally intrusive, and it can be helpful. Too often, however, they act as if coordination is *only* information sharing.

Coordination as *information integration* occurs when NSC staffs summarize the pros and cons of issues and consolidate agency positions in papers that frame choices and strategies for presidential decisions. Clever phrasing and omitted or included language can affect perceptions of agency views. The NSC's role can put it at odds with a State Department jealous of its mandate to advise the President on foreign policy and a Defense Department protective of its military operations.

Once information is shared, choices are integrated, and decisions are made, interagency coordination becomes a process of *implementation and communication*. Presidential aides seek to harmonize and monitor the operations of civilian and military agencies and the communication of policies to domestic and global publics. Vague presidential intent, disputes between organizations, and unwillingness to carry out decisions can impede both. NSC staffs occasionally engage in operations, but they lack the mandate and resources, and they usually are rebuked when they do. Crisis management is a special category. Sudden events, tardy responses by bureaucracies, and public pressures "to do something" can make the White House the center of communication and operations.[5]

Presidential Aides as a Community of Practice

We begin with two assumptions. First, how government agencies are organized and interact affects operational outcomes. In the daily grind of governance and diplomacy, David Rothkopf writes, "decisions about who is on what committee, what committee makes what decision, who recommends, who implements, how they do it, and what is required to start or stop an action can have a profound impact on events."[6] Second, rivalries and compromises of officials and practitioners constitute the interagency process. For Graham Allison and Philip Zelikow, it is "the pulling and hauling that is politics"—a mélange of power agendas, personalities, organizational interests and capacities, established routines, timing, and luck.[7] In domestic politics, "pulling and hauling" takes place in the interactions of civil society stakeholders, government agencies, and Congress. In foreign affairs, "presidents and bureaucrats are the primary players, battling … far away from the Capitol steps."[8]

Presidential aides are chosen for their expertise and ability to perform under pressure. They are expected to provide information—just enough, just right, just in time—and accommodate presidential leadership styles. There are no structured recruitment processes. No entrance exams. No training courses. Congress funds their activities, but they are not subject to Congressional confirmation and oversight. Some are political operatives; many are career diplomats and military officers on temporary assignment. Their power derives from access to the president, actual and perceived, and detailed knowledge of complex issues. Skilled aides can steer government bureaucracies that circumvent presidential directives or slow walk implementation of policies.[9] Occasionally, when stakes are high, they resort to press leaks and resignations.

Interagency coordination of what White House officials often refer to as strategic communication is characterized by endless meetings, bureaucratic infighting, planning papers, and frequent reorganizations. Information sharing becomes a substitute for collaborative action. Process often becomes policy; meetings often substitute for action. Practitioners repeatedly devise coordination structures; repeatedly they fall short.

State/USIA Model

Presidents occasionally approved State Department coordination of foreign information activities at the initiative of Secretaries of State keen to protect their responsibility to formulate and implement US foreign policy. State welcomed coordination authority, but it was seldom interested in the hard work of actual "coordination." In theory, the model has advantages. State has institutional memory, skilled practitioners, and a larger budget than the NSC. Uniquely, diplomacy has crosscutting relevance to all other instruments of power. But cabinet departments are peers and rivals. They rarely have interagency tasking authority, and they typically look to their own interests first.

National Psychological Strategy Board (1950). The NSC's decision in 1947 to put the State Department in charge of coordinating "foreign information measures" set the stage for years of bureaucratic wrangling. As ideological conflict with the Soviet Union intensified, the NSC tried to strengthen State's role. In March 1950, it circulated NSC 59/1, a report on "The Foreign Information Program and Psychological Warfare Planning." It gave the Department sweeping responsibility for:

(1) "formulation of policies and plans for a national foreign information program in time of peace," (2) "formulation of national psychological warfare policy in time of national emergency and the initial stages of war," and (3) "coordination of policies and plans for the national foreign information program and for overt psychological warfare with the Department of Defense, with other appropriate departments and agencies of the U.S. Government, and with related planning under the NSC-10 series [covert activities of the CIA]."[10]

In August, shortly after the outbreak of war in Korea, Truman announced that State had established a National Psychological Strategy Board (NPSB) with representatives from Defense, the Joint Chiefs, and the CIA. The impossible task of making it work was given to Assistant Secretary of State for Public Affairs Edward W. Barrett, who was double-hatted as the NPSB's director.

Barrett was widely regarded as the perfect choice. Born into a wealthy Alabama newspaper family, he graduated from Princeton and became editor of *Newsweek* magazine. In World War II, he headed the allied forces' Psychological Warfare Branch in Europe, directed the Overseas Branch of OWI, and helped to create VOA. He went back to *Newsweek* after the war, but in February 1950 returned as an Assistant Secretary of State responsible for domestic public affairs, foreign information activities, and exchanges. The NPSB occasionally did "some good," he recalled, but it fell far short of what was needed. Most of his time was spent preventing the Pentagon and CIA from taking control away from State.

His principles were sound. "By its very nature, international persuasion is *inter*dependent with the other foreign programs and policies of government," Barrett argued. Information specialists should participate, not only in the top policy councils of State, they also "must be intimately tied in with the top policy-makers of government, including the President and the National Security Council." Presidents should have a senior "special assistant with the functions of 'persuader-in-chief'"—and a "coordinator-in-chief of government-wide psychological planning." This senior presidential aide should attend cabinet and NSC meetings and have the full confidence of the president. He also faulted "too much Washington masterminding of complex tactical problems that could best be solved by first-rate men in the field."[11]

Barrett, an assistant secretary outranked by generals, admirals, and senior officials, was unable to overcome the NPSB's structural shortcomings. The Defense Department opposed its sweeping mandate, and it was never formally approved by the NSC. Barrett was under no illusions about the board's authority. The NPSB "is a coordinating mechanism," he declared, "and does not have the authority or competence to command the component governmental elements represented on the board."[12]

Unhappy with the NPSB, Truman in June 1951 created a similarly named Psychological Strategy Board (PSB) that reported to the NSC. The US now had two coordinating mechanisms, which the Department tried to explain in a press release. Barrett's group would "continue in existence with responsibility for coordinating the execution of ... United States foreign information programs under the name 'Psychological Operations Coordinating Committee,'" (the new name for the NPSB). Other activities in State "will continue as presently organized under the broad guidance of the separate Psychological Strategy Board announced by the President."[13] This did little to clarify matters. After two years as assistant secretary, Barrett returned again to the private sector, where he founded a public relations firm and later served as dean of the Columbia School of Journalism.

International Information Administration (IIA). In January 1952 State established the IIA as a semi-autonomous entity within the Department to conduct and coordinate international information and exchange programs. It was led by an Administrator, Wilson Compton, a Republican, business executive, and later a college president, who was directly accountable to Secretary Dean Acheson. Compton also chaired the Department's interagency Psychological Operations Coordinating Committee. His formal powers were sweeping: direct all IIA programs "at home and abroad," with the "advice" of the regional bureaus, select and assign all IIA personnel, and chair the Coordinating Committee.[14]

A year later, Compton's report to Acheson was mixed. The expected autonomy to determine information policies and execute programs overseas had "materialized satisfactorily." However, "The planned 'semi-autonomy' with respect to (1) the selection, assignment and management of personnel and (2) the control of its own finances has not worked out satisfactorily." The reasons, he stated, were the Department's reluctance to change and IIA's lack of personnel authority and control of its funds.[15] IIA's difficulties with foreign information coordination derived from State's lack of enthusiasm and the gap between formal authority and operational capabilities.[16]

US Information Agency (1953–1978, 1982–1999). To expect USIA to coordinate government-wide information activities was a bridge way too far when it was created in 1953. The NPSB's failure was fresh in the minds of White House officials. The Eisenhower administration placed foreign information coordination in the White House. USIA was authorized to *advise* presidents and the NSC, but its biggest challenge was getting a seat at the table. Participation depended largely on personal relations between presidents and directors.

USIA's legal advisors made compelling arguments for the Agency's statutory advisory role. The US Advisory Commission on Public Diplomacy's reports for decades recommended that USIA "serve as a statutory advisor to the National Security Council and as the principal advisor to the President on foreign public opinion." It would ensure "that our government adequately understands foreign opinion and culture for policy-making purposes" and strengthen "the central role of the President in foreign communications." The GAO argued similarly that without an institutionalized role in the NSC, USIA could not "effectively fulfill its responsibility for providing advice on the implications of foreign opinion to U.S. foreign policymakers."[17]

US International Communication Agency (1978–1982). The closest USIA came to a statutory NSC advisory and coordination role occurred when "Reorganization Plan No. 2 of 1977" became law during the Carter Administration. The Plan, which consolidated USIA and State's Bureau of Educational and Cultural Affairs and changed USIA's name briefly to the US International Communication Agency (USICA), declared that the Director "shall serve as the principal advisor to the President, the National Security Council, and the Secretary of State *on the functions vested in the Director* [emphasis added]."[18]

USICA's director, Foreign Service officer John Reinhardt, believed the Agency was "indispensable" to the foreign policy process.[19] It could be of "unique service," he explained to NSC Advisor Zbigniew Brzezinski, by providing "1) direct access to foreign publics and opinion leaders, 2) insight into foreign public attitudes and likely public reaction to contemplated U.S. actions, and 3) systematic feedback on the effects of our actions or policies on foreign opinion."[20] In 1978 USICA's main tasks were codified in law. It would "assist in the development of a comprehensive national policy on international communications" at the highest levels of government, and "*coordinate* international informational, educational, or cultural activities conducted or planned by departments and agencies of the United States Government [emphasis added]."[21]

The authorities looked good on paper. In practice, Reinhardt met with Carter on two ceremonial occasions. Brzezinski's interest was largely in weekly foreign media reaction reports and international broadcasting. He invited Reinhardt to meetings of the NSC's Special Coordinating Committee as issues warranted, but the NSC had no interest in USICA acting as a "statutory advisor" in a manner comparable to the CIA and the Joint Chiefs of Staff.[22] Reinhardt and his deputy Charles Bray, also a career diplomat, were regarded as presidential appointees, but they lacked the personal ties that politically appointed agency heads usually possess. USICA's advisory participation in the formulation of policies was rare, and its interagency coordination of their communication rarer still.

Working Group on Public Diplomacy for Iraq (1991–1992). USIA
played brief coordinating roles in two wars. The first was JUSPAO in
Vietnam (see Chap. 10). The second occurred during the Persian Gulf
War in 1991. When Saddam Hussein's forces invaded Kuwait, President
George H. W. Bush and NSC Advisor Brent Scowcroft established an
Inter-agency Working Group on Public Diplomacy for Iraq. Its task was
"to plan a public diplomacy strategy, to develop themes supportive of
U.S. policies, to counter misperceptions and Iraqi disinformation and to
coordinate media and other public diplomacy activities." Ambassador
William Rugh, USIA's Director of Near East and South Asian Affairs,
co-chaired the Working Group with the State Department's Gerald
B. Helman.

Rugh was a key advisor in White House and interagency deliberations.
Relying on daily updates from PAOs in the region, he generated talking
points for US officials, briefed the president regularly, provided material
for his speeches, and advised him on a key interview with Arab media.
The Working Group drafted issues papers and leaflets. It monitored anti-
coalition demonstrations, relayed positive stories in Arab media, and
worked to separate Israel/Palestinian issues from the invasion of Kuwait.
The Advisory Commission on Public Diplomacy reported that USIA was
a "full partner 'at the table' in developing the Gulf public diplomacy
strategy and in carrying it out."[23]

State Department 9/11 Public Diplomacy Task Force (2001). On October
7, 2001, State created a Public Diplomacy Task Force in its Executive
Secretariat. Executive Secretary Maura Harty explained that it operates
24/7 and "monitors public diplomacy activity overseas, encourages additional activity, and coordinates the Department's participation in the
strategic information campaign." Its "mission is proving pivotal to leadership in the Department, White House, Pentagon, and other agencies,
reinforcing the need for factoring public diplomacy into our evolving
policy."[24]

David Arnett, a skilled and highly regarded public diplomacy officer,
was assigned to lead the Task Force. In this capacity, he represented State
at NSC meetings and attended daily briefings with Secretary of State
Colin Powell and other senior officials.[25] Teams assigned to daytime, evening, and overnight shifts were volunteers from public diplomacy offices

located throughout the Department following the merger of USIA and State two years earlier. Their primary responsibility was to prepare twice-daily Situation Reports (Sitreps) on "public diplomacy activities and concerns" for the Secretary and the Department's "seventh floor," other "foreign policy principals," and US missions abroad.[26] Sitreps contained "proposed PD themes of the day," summaries of foreign media broadcasts, analysis of Arab media trends, and "lessons learned" reported by US agencies and embassies. The Task Force also circulated interviews by cabinet secretaries and other US officials on Al Jazeera and other networks. At the request of Ambassador Francis Ricciardone, a team of Arabic language instructors at State's Foreign Service Institute monitored Al Jazeera's broadcasts as a supplement to the Foreign Broadcast Information Service's regular monitoring through its Jordan Bureau.

The Task Force was State's link to Coalition Information Centers (CIC), a network established by White House communications director Karen Hughes and Alastair Campbell, Prime Minister Tony Blair's communications advisor. The network connected the White House, State, the UK's No. 10 Downing Street, US Embassy London, and US Embassy Islamabad.[27] Senior public diplomacy officers—Greg Lagana at the White House, Lee McClenny in London, and Kenton Keith in Islamabad—responded to news events, media inquiries, and misinformation in real time. As Keith recalled, "we took the media field away from exclusive exploitation by the Taliban ambassador in Islamabad. We were able to refute his outlandish claims as soon as he made them, rather than waiting for many hours while London and Washington reacted."[28]

This was all quite extraordinary. A 24/7 public diplomacy task force in the State Department's seventh floor Operations Center was unprecedented. Secretary Powell and Political Affairs Under Secretary Marc Grossman created the Task Force, not Under Secretary for Public Diplomacy Charlotte Beers. Cabinet secretaries and senior officials lined up to do interviews on Al Jazeera, a network many had previously criticized. The Task Force demonstrated the value of a coalition information network, "just in time" guidance and media reporting, and timely circulation of "lessons learned." It showcased the effect of a flattened hierarchy in a department famous for its time-consuming clearances. Sitreps required only one clearance before distribution worldwide in Secretary

Powell's name. The Task Force had limitations. Most Department messages circulated on classified systems. Most public diplomacy messages were unclassified. In the early days, the bureaus sent their "A team" officers. Before long bureau priorities took precedence. It was a crisis response that lasted only a few months.

These instances of presidents and their aides turning to the State Department and USIA to coordinate strategic communication were short-lived exceptions. When Karen Hughes served as Under Secretary of State for Public Diplomacy and Public Affairs after her stint as White House communications director, she came to realize continuing her interagency coordination role would not be possible. Managing public diplomacy within the Department was difficult and all-consuming.[29]

NSC Model

The NSC benefits from presidential power and its central location. With White House backing, presidential aides can influence government agencies and the way the media frame issues and policies. The NSC "thinks" in interagency terms. Military practitioners prefer NSC coordination, and they rarely if ever call for Defense to take the lead. But the NSC's budgets are small, and its staffs have less continuity than department practitioners.[30] At the tactical level, spokespersons at the White House, State, and Defense coordinate talking points for daily press events. But this is not strategic level coordination. Six cases illustrate how the NSC model worked over time.

Psychological Strategy Board (1951–1953). When President Truman announced his Psychological Strategy Board (PSB) on June 20, 1951, he wanted to end the bureaucratic infighting that State's NPSB had failed to contain. As one Defense official colorfully stated, "Our psychological operating agencies are like bodies of troops without a commander and staff. Not having been told what to do or where to go, but too dynamic to stand still, the troops have marched in all directions."[31]

The PSB's origins lay in Project Troy, a study State had commissioned to examine "the broad problem of how to get information into Russia." It was the work of 21 MIT and Harvard scholars who convened to analyze communication theories, methods of psychological warfare, and technical capabilities.[32] Their report recommended a "single authority … with the capacity to design a comprehensive program and the power to obtain the execution of the program through the effective action of all the agencies and departments that are now engaged in waging political warfare."[33] The PSB provided that single authority under the NSC. Its executive director was presidentially appointed and its members were the Under Secretary of State, the Deputy Secretary of Defense, the CIA Director, and a representative of the JCS.

The PSB's mandate was to provide guidance to US departments and agencies on "over-all national psychological objectives, policies, and programs."[34] State's W. Phillips Davison defined this simply as "(a) National planning, (b) 'Wheel-greasing,' (c) Evaluation, and (d) Coordination." Infighting began immediately. The Defense Department's General John Magruder wanted a grand strategy for psychological operations comparable to the strategy of the Combined Chiefs of Staff in World War II. But this, objected Charles Burton Marshall, a member of State's Policy Planning Staff, would be a "fundamental—indeed, an implicitly revolutionary—shift in authority in the entire organization of the Executive Branch." The CIA's Frank Wisner opposed a PSB "'Charter' which would require departmental concurrence." Allen Dulles saw no need for regional specialists, since "they would be in competition with the existing agencies." The Joint Chiefs' Admiral Leslie C. Stevens opposed letting the PSB "interpret NSC papers into guidances for the departments." Rather, it "could give top direction by setting priorities and needling departments." All agreed the PSB's staff should do only what could not be done elsewhere or delegated.[35] Just what constituted effective coordination was left to practitioners to sort out.

The PSB's first executive director was Gordon Gray, Yale Law School, former Secretary of the Army, and University of North Carolina president. Truman's intent, he declared, is that psychological operations serve as "a cover name to describe those activities of the US in peace and in war through which all elements of national power are systematically brought to bear on other nations for the attainment of US foreign policy objectives."[36] Gray's assistant, Robert "Bobby" Cutler, a Harvard educated financier and later Eisenhower's national security advisor, was similarly expansive. The PSB is a "nerve center for initiating, receiving, coordinating, and evaluating psychological impulses." It was "more that of a command post than an information center."[37]

State was compelled to go along but remained emphatic about what the PSB should not do. When informed the PSB was trying to act as a "general staff" for "Cold War operations," Policy Planning Director Paul Nitze bluntly told Gray, "Look, you just forget about policy, that's not your business; we'll make the policy and then you can put it on your damn radio."[38] After more back and forth, Nitze informed Acheson the PSB had "capitulated on all fronts as regards the thesis that [it] should create a master plan for the overthrow of communism."[39] For Nitze and Marshall, psychological operations had an auxiliary place in warfare and in peacetime foreign policy when they were truthful. But efforts to deceive others were counterproductive in peacetime and overall "not worth a damn."[40]

With a staff of about 50, the PSB produced numerous assessments of psychological operations during the Korean War. It evaluated US Army leaflets and monitored VOA broadcasts. More broadly, it developed plans to support anti-communist groups in Europe, Asia, and the Middle East. Members argued over covert operations. CIA Director Walter Bedell Smith favored open advocacy of "liberation" and covert support for groups seeking to overthrow the Soviet Union's satellites. State's Under Secretary David Bruce, Soviet expert Charles Bohlen, and others disagreed. Favoring "containment," they allied with PSB planners who questioned support for uprisings and feared a Soviet military reaction.[41]

A definition of psychological strategy was unnecessary, Gray declared, because he "had no intention of barging unwanted into the jurisdictions of other agencies."[42] How a PSB that chose not to define its role or intervene in the activities of government organizations could act as the nation's psychological operations nerve center was not explained. Its recommendations were largely ignored.

Operations Coordinating Board (1953–1960). President Eisenhower replaced the PSB with the Operations Coordinating Board (OCB) on September 2, 1953. Its mission was largely identical, but unlike the PSB, OCB would "provide for integrated *implementation* of national security policies by the several agencies [emphasis added]" after they had been approved by the President.[43] The OCB's champions were Eisenhower's close advisors and others who would become senior officials in US public diplomacy. Most were white, male, affluent, and had attended Ivy League universities. Many had been journalists or public relations executives in large corporations, and most had served in the military, OSS, or OWI during World War II. Foremost among them was C. D. Jackson, Eisenhower's campaign speechwriter who became an OCB Board member.

The OCB was a "cooperative agreement" among government departments, its executive director Elmer Staats declared. It had no authority to direct their actions. It was a forum in which their operating heads could discuss plans developed by more than 40 working groups to implement national security policies. Unlike the PSB, he explained, the OCB "serves as an important working extension of the National Security Council machinery" and "receives the majority of its assignments directly from the President."[44] It identified diplomatic, economic, military, and psychological actions to be taken by departments and agencies on their own and in partnership with civil society organizations many of which were covertly funded front groups. It provided guidance on press releases, speeches, and media appearances by US officials. At regular Wednesday lunches, CIA director Allen Dulles and State's Walter Bedell Smith (a former CIA director) met without staffs to coordinate covert activities.[45]

Eisenhower's personal interest could compel integrated implementation at times, but departments and agencies in time-honored fashion could slow roll or ignore advice that didn't suit their interests. As Henry Loomis, a top VOA and USIA official, later recalled, "The theory was that the NSC prepared policy alternatives 'on the way up.' The president determined the policy. The OCB was meant to coordinate the implementation of the policy 'on the way down' which may sound all right on paper but was not that effective."[46] The OCB lasted until the Kennedy administration in 1960 when it was abolished as too ponderous. Kennedy and his NSC Advisor McGeorge Bundy preferred an informal process, a small NSC staff, and ad hoc groups of advisors. They valued public diplomacy, but left it largely to Edward R. Murrow and USIA. Presidents continued this approach throughout the 1960s and 1970s.

National Security Decision Directive 77 (1983–1987). The Reagan administration returned to a strong NSC coordination structure. On

January 14, 1983, President Reagan signed NSDD 77, "Management of Public Diplomacy Relative to National Security." It established a Special Planning Group (SPG) "under the National Security Council" to engage in "the overall planning, direction, coordination, and monitoring of the implementation of public diplomacy activities."[47] Unlike Truman's PSB and Eisenhower's OCB, the SPG was chaired by the National Security Advisor. Its members included the Secretary of State and Secretary of Defense, not their deputies. Other members were the directors of USIA and USAID, and the Assistant to the President for Communications. NSC staff managed its activities.

The SPG had four standing committees. (1) An *International Information Committee*, chaired by a USIA officer with a State Department officer as vice chair, to plan, coordinate, and implement public diplomacy activities. (2) An *International Political Committee*, chaired by a State officer with a USIA officer as vice chair, to plan, coordinate, and implement international "political" activities. These included support for foreign governments and private groups engaged in strengthening democratic institutions and countering Soviet political influence activities. (3) An *International Broadcasting Committee*, chaired by a representative of the NSC Advisor, to plan and coordinate activities of VOA and RFE/RL. (4) A *Public Affairs Committee*, co-chaired by the Assistant to the President for Communications and the Deputy NSC Advisor, to coordinate major speeches and media appearances by US officials. Departments and agencies were expected to provide resources for the committees. The SPG met several times in 1983; its standing committees met biweekly. It was a coordination structure unparalleled in its ambitious goals, high-level leadership, and complex architecture.

NSDD 130, issued in 1984, amplified the NSC's intent to treat "international information" and "other components of public diplomacy" as a "strategic instrument of US national policy, not a tactical instrument of US diplomacy." It spelled out functional objectives. Respect for "accuracy and objectivity." Knowledge of the "habits, interests, expectations, and level of understanding of foreign audiences." Programs differentiated to reach elites, key opinion sectors, and mass audiences. International broadcasting as "the most effective means of communicating the truth" to foreign publics. Partnerships with publishers to disseminate publications on American and Western institutions and principles. A PSYOP capability integrated in interagency plans. Public opinion research and media reaction. Enhanced public diplomacy training and career development tracks. Modernized broadcasting facilities and enhanced attention to television. Public diplomacy replaced psychological strategy as a term of art.[48]

These directives and interlocking committee structure were largely the work of a single individual, Carnes Lord, a gifted classics scholar whose career combined long periods of academic scholarship and government service. The holder of two PhDs, one from Yale and the other from Cornell, Lord held teaching positions at Dartmouth, Yale, the University of Virginia, the National Defense University, Tufts, and the Naval War College. He joined the Reagan administration's NSC staff to "revive the strategic approach to public diplomacy that had marked the early years of the Cold War."[49] For Lord, public diplomacy is not a euphemism for propaganda or an instrument to impose American values. Rather, it is the art of persuading others, using whole of government instruments of practice, through reasoned argument, dialogue, emotional appeal, and the character and images that leaders and diplomats project.[50]

Lord was the conceptual architect. Walt Raymond handled the SPG's operations. Educated at the College of William and Mary and Yale, Raymond served with the Army in Korea before joining the Defense Department as an intelligence analyst on Soviet bloc and West European Affairs. In 1960 he transferred to the State Department, and in 1970 he joined the CIA to work on covert media and political action operations. He was detailed to the NSC staff in 1982.

Raymond was a busy man. He directed planning and coordination on a wide range of issues: US–Soviet public diplomacy, political action in Afghanistan, Defense Department public diplomacy funding, military PSYOP programs, and international broadcasting. He worked with Oliver North on covert projects relating to anti-Sandinista campaigns, Carl Gershman on the National Endowment for Democracy's early funding decisions, USIA officials on "Project Truth," Otto Reich's State Department "Office of Public Diplomacy for Latin America and the Caribbean," and democracy building activities of the Asia Foundation and Freedom House.[51]

While at the NSC and after, Raymond repeatedly disavowed any CIA involvement with USIA's and NED's programs. But he chaired the NSC's Central America Public Diplomacy Task Force, which oversaw overt and covert programs. In 1987 he was a key witness in Congress's investigation of the Iran-Contra scandal, North's failed secret attempt to sell arms to Iran and use the proceeds to buy arms for anti-Sandinista rebels in Nicaragua. His deposition stated he had resigned from the CIA in 1983 so "there would be no question whatsoever of any contamination" of the public diplomacy and democracy building programs.[52] But his work on the Iran-Contra project raises a key question. How could they escape "contamination" when the NSC's co-located open and covert projects were exposed?

Other problems arose from the domestic influence activities of Reich's Public Diplomacy Office in State. It sponsored speakers, disseminated materials, engaged in media outreach, and used USIA's employees in a campaign to convince Americans to support the Reagan administration's Central America policies. Reich reported to Raymond outside the Department's normal chain of command. A GAO report, requested by House Democrats Jack Brooks and Dante Fascell, found these activities violated federal laws that prohibited using appropriations for unauthorized "publicity or propaganda purposes" and "covert propaganda activities."[53]

The NSDD 77 structure was disbanded following the Iran-Contra disclosure. As Lord recalled, NSC Advisor Frank Carlucci in January 1987 "essentially shut down the NSDD 77 apparatus as part of its effort to provide reassurance that the White House would no longer play an 'operational' role in national security affairs."[54] Raymond left the NSC in 1987 to join USIA where he served until 1992 as an assistant director responsible for liaison with Congress, the White House, and other government agencies. He later became USIA's senior coordinator for democracy promotion in Eastern Europe. The NSDD 77 structure was gone, but his enthusiasm for a centralized mechanism to connect public diplomacy and foreign policy in a "seamless web" continued. He urged reconstitution of the SPG under the Deputy NSC Advisor with a leaner structure and smaller executive secretariat to task agencies "to carry out or to coordinate all public diplomacy management and program issues."[55]

How successful was the NSDD 77 structure? Lord viewed it as "far from perfect in practice." But it provided an interagency framework that contributed to success against the Soviet Union in the end game of the Cold War.[56] The Advisory Commission saw it as evidence that public diplomacy had greater standing in US foreign affairs, although it lamented that USIA still was "rarely afforded the opportunity to participate in an advisory capacity when policies are being developed."[57] State diplomat Gifford Malone, who wrote a highly regarded book on the organization of public diplomacy, concluded that NSDD 77 brought needed focus, legitimized the public diplomacy of agencies other than USIA, and created "oversight that was probably needed" for a Defense Department "inclined to pursue its own course." But in practice, he concluded, NSDD 77 could not live up to its advocates' high expectations.[58] Five years later, career USIA diplomat David Hitchcock wrote that "almost everyone consulted believes NSDD 77 has not worked."[59] In the end, it was Iran Contra and partisan politics more than lack of effectiveness that brought it down.

President George H. W. Bush's NSC Advisor Brent Scowcroft and Secretary of State James Baker wanted no part of the NSC structure that produced Iran-Contra. Their first NSC directive featured a Principals Committee of NSC members and statutory advisors, a Deputies Committee of second ranking officials, and Policy Coordinating Committees (PCCs). A senior Director for International Programs handled public diplomacy as one element in a portfolio that spanned African affairs, security and economic assistance, counter-terrorism, counter-narcotics, refugee programs, and low-intensity conflicts.[60] The Defense Department abolished its public diplomacy support staff and military liaison position in USIA. Congressional Republicans launched their campaign to abolish USIA and other foreign affairs agencies.

The first Clinton administration likewise had no appetite for strong NSC coordination.[61] Clinton's Presidential Decision Directive/NSC 2 renamed the PCC policy committees as Interagency Working Groups (IWGs) and otherwise replicated the Bush/Scowcroft NSC model. There was no IWG for public diplomacy.[62] In 1997 a Presidential Decision Directive (PDD 56) on "Managing Complex Contingency Operations" created a process for political–military operations in "low intensity conflicts" in Haiti, Somalia, northern Iraq, Bangladesh, central Africa, and the former Yugoslavia. Committees of department representatives were formed to handle congressional consultation, diplomacy, funding, media coordination, military support, humanitarian services, human rights monitoring, social development, and public information.[63] PDD 56 made no mention of public diplomacy.

PDD 68 (1999–2000). Late in Clinton's second term, however, Jamie Metzl, the NSC's Director of Multilateral and Humanitarian Affairs, took a run at coordinating public diplomacy. An ironman triathlete with a high-quality education (Brown University BA, Oxford DPhil, and Harvard Law School JD), Metzl was motivated by the US failure to intervene in the Rwanda genocide. In the *American Journal of International Law*, he called for an exception to the US policy against radio jamming when broadcasts were used to incite ethnic tension and mass murder.[64] Metzl convened a group of representatives from USIA, State, Defense, Justice, Treasury, Commerce, and the FBI. Their task: create a sustained NSC capability to monitor foreign public opinion, plan strategies, and coordinate public diplomacy, public affairs, and overt military information activities.[65]

Clinton issued Presidential Decision Directive (PDD 68), "International Public Information (IPI)," on April 30, 1999. It authorized an IPI Core Group (ICG) under the NSC's Deputies Committee to coordinate open civilian and military activities targeted at "foreign audiences only." It directed agencies to partner with NGOs to develop civil society institutions, promote free exchange of ideas and information, assist media outlets, and work with military and civilian educational institutions to educate professionals on international public information planning and techniques. The ICG would not "mislead audiences" or "compromise in any way the integrity and independence of nongovernmental organizations."[66] Metzl favored NSC-led coordination, but he understood the politics that had recently put USIA's functions in the State Department. He agreed the Under Secretary of State for Public Diplomacy and Public Affairs would chair the ICG and direct its secretariat, leaving the NSC to appoint the Deputy Chair. Metzl became State's senior coordinator for international information. In the summer of 1999, the ICG began framing a public information strategy to support

NATO's military actions in Kosovo and UN peacekeeping operations in East Timor.

A barrage of criticism came quickly from voices on the right. Opinion columns by Ben Barber in the conservative-leaning *Washington Times* described PDD 68 as a "secret Clinton administration program" to influence American audiences. His articles made ominous references to "Orwellian" clauses in a directive that gave "the impression of a vast, coordinated propaganda operation." Gene Kopp, a former USIA deputy director and a strong opponent of the Agency's demise, was quoted as having deep concerns about PDD 68's potential for abuses and a probably irresistible "temptation to spin this stuff in a partisan way." *Washington Times* deputy editor Helle Bering [Dale] opined, "We really don't need pinstriped diplomats to feed us propaganda about administration policy."[67] It all was a bit rich coming from voices that had endorsed the Reagan administration's NSDD 77 coordinating structure and Otto Reich's State Department Public Diplomacy Office.

The usual barriers to coordination came into play. High level NSC attention was not forthcoming. A tiny staff of five in State's Bureau of International Information Programs meant the ICG's activities consisted mostly of information sharing in "fusion teams," a far cry from the senior level planning and coordination envisioned by Metzl's NSC working group. Metzl's high energy approach was not an enduring fit at State, and he left to join the staff of the Senate Foreign Relations Committee. The ICG "soon bogged down in the morass that was post-USIA American public diplomacy," Nicholas Cull concluded, "and an opportunity to rebuild the sort of coordinated structure of the era of Eisenhower and C. D. Jackson was lost."[68] The Defense Science Board concluded that PDD 68's ICG suffered from lack of strong leadership, location in a State Department bureau, the absence of tasking and contracting authorities, inadequate communication technologies, and insufficient staff and resources.[69]

Strategic Communication PCCs (2002–2008). When the US went to war in Afghanistan and Iraq, the NSC turned again to strategic communication coordination, but without much success. In June 2002 the White House created an Office of Global Communications (OGC) led by George W. Bush's campaign communications advisor Karen Hughes.[70]

The following September, NSC Advisor Condoleezza Rice created a PCC on "Strategic Communication," co-chaired by the chair of the NSC's PCC on Democracy, Human Rights and International Operations and the Under Secretary of State for Public Diplomacy and Public Affairs, the newly appointed Charlotte Beers. A Defense Science Board task force assessed that the OGC and PCC had overlapping authorities and neither came close to achieving its responsibilities in strategic communication planning, coordination, and evaluation.[71]

In 2007 NSC Advisor Stephen Hadley turned to Hughes, now Under Secretary of State for Public Diplomacy and Public Affairs, to lead a "new and enhanced" PCC and a "U.S. National Strategy on Public Diplomacy and Strategic Communication."[72] Hughes declared that "PD is back and is now a high priority at the highest levels of government." She went on to say, "Each agency—such as HUD—is now preparing an agency specific strategic communications plan," and "it's important for our messages to be coordinated."[73] But a GAO report found the PCC was not "adequately supported by agency-specific plans and country-level plans modeled on private-sector best practices" that could help coordinate "U.S. communication efforts that are distributed across major agencies, dozens of discrete programs, a diverse range of communication objectives, and assorted target audiences around the world." Other critics questioned putting interagency coordination in the hands of a State Department under secretary.[74]

NSC Strategic Communication 1055 Reports (2010–2015). Interest in strategic communication coordination during the Obama administrations came not from the NSC, but from the bipartisan efforts of Rep. Mark Thornberry (R-TX), Rep. Adam Smith (D-WA), and others on the House Armed Services committee with ties to the Defense Science Board. Section 1055 in the 2009 Defense Authorization Act required the President to issue a new "comprehensive interagency strategy on public diplomacy and strategic communication." The intent was to align strategic communication strategies with the NSC's periodic National Security Strategy reports.[75]

President Obama submitted his first 1055 report, "A National Framework for Strategic Communication," in March 2010. The 14-page report was ambitious in its intent. It defined strategic communication as "synchronization of our words and deeds" and "deliberate efforts to communicate and engage with intended audiences." It sought "an appropriate balance between civilian and military efforts." It identified a whole of government "communications community" and distinguished between public affairs, public diplomacy, military information operations, and defense support for public diplomacy. It identified roles and responsibilities of an array of government organizations. NSC Deputy National Security Advisor for Strategic Communications Ben Rhodes chaired a Strategic Communication Policy Coordinating Committee.[76] Obama's "National Framework" was conceptually elegant. Operationally, it rarely worked. There is little evidence Rhodes used the PCC to achieve interagency coordination. He devoted most of his attention during eight years in the NSC to speechwriting and advising the president on policy matters.[77]

The Trump administration, with its chaotic approach to governance and diplomacy, gave little thought to whole of government coordination of public diplomacy. There was one exception—its support for a State Department-led effort to counter the threat of disinformation. President Obama had established the Department's Global Engagement Center (GEC) in 2016 as a successor to several attempts to coordinate interagency efforts to counter violent extremism. Congress changed the GEC's mandate to give priority to countering foreign state propaganda and disinformation efforts. With bipartisan support in Congress and from Secretary of State Mike Pompeo, the GEC's budget expanded as concerns grew over disinformation from Russia, China, Iran, and other actors.[78]

For more than seventy years, presidents and senior aides have not wavered from the idea that harmonization of foreign strategic communication activities of departments and agencies is vital to America's interests. Yet they have repeatedly failed to create durable coordination structures. Their efforts constitute a pattern of hollow authorities, short-lived and largely ineffectual organizations, turf battles, occasional successes, and lack of sustained impact. This raises a question to be examined in the book's final chapter: should the 1947 National Security Act be amended to give the NSC the capability to provide strategic communication *direction* in addition to *coordination*?

In the twenty-first century, government, sub-state, and non-state actors have multiplied. Global issues have grown more abundant and complex. Technologies continue to transform governance and society. Yet the US approach to strategic communication remains the same—persistence in willing the ends of interagency "coordination" but not the means. Future threats will motivate renewed interest in coordination. Without fundamental changes in law, future presidents and their aides are destined to replicate some version of past NSC or State Department models.

Notes

1. "252. Memorandum from the Executive Secretary (Souers) to the Members of the National Security Council," *Foreign Relations of the United States, 1945–1950, Emergence of the Intelligence Establishment,* Historical Documents, Department of State.
2. National Security Act of 1947, Pub. L. No. 235, 61 Stat. 496 (1947).
3. Amy B. Zegart, *Flawed by Design: The Evolution of the CIA, JCS, and NSC* (Stanford University Press, 1999), 10, 54–75.
4. National Security Act of 1947.
5. Christopher C. Shoemaker, *The NSC Staff: Counseling the Council* (Westview Press, 1991), 21–48.
6. David Rothkopf, *Running the World: The Inside Story of the National Security Council and the Architects of American Power* (PublicAffairs, 2005), 15.
7. Allison and Zelikow, *Essence of Decision*, 255–313.
8. Zegart, *Flawed by Design*, 7.
9. Zegart, *Flawed by Design*, 54–108; Rothkopf, *Running the World*; R.D. Hooker, Jr., *The NSC Staff: New Choices for a New Administration* (National Defense University Press, 2016). On staff influence during policy implementation, I am indebted to Michael Schneider, email to author, November 2020.
10. "2. National Security Council Report," *Foreign Relations of the United States, 1950–1955, The Intelligence Community 1950–1955,* Historical Documents, Department of State; "17. Editorial Note," *Intelligence Community 1950–1955.*
11. Barrett, *Truth is Our Weapon*, 244–246, 301.

12. Notes on meeting of National Psychological Strategy Board, October 16, 1950, Freedom of Information Act Electronic Reading Room, CIA Library, https://www.cia.gov/readingroom/docs/CIA-RDP80-01065A000500130073-9.pdf.

13. "74. Department of State Press Release," *Intelligence Community 1950–1955.*

14. "294. State Department Announcement No. 4," *Foreign Relations of the United States, 1952–1954, National Security Affairs, Volume II, Part 2,* Historical Documents, Department of State.

15. "303. Extract From a 'Report on International Information Administration—1952' to the Secretary of State from the Administrator of IIA (Compton) December 31, 1952," *National Security Affairs, Volume II, Part 2.*

16. On the short and checkered history of IIA, see Cull, *United States Information Agency,* 71–80.

17. USIA's General Counsel, memorandum, "Arguments Supporting the Director's Participation in the NSC," n.d. [circa 1980], author's copy; *1973 Twenty-Sixth Report,* US Advisory Commission on Information, US Advisory Commission on Public Diplomacy Reports, 11; *1980 Annual Report,* US Advisory Commission on Public Diplomacy Reports, 17; *1982 Annual Report,* US Advisory Commission on Public Diplomacy Reports, 13; *Telling America's Story to the World: Problems and Issues* (US General Accounting Office, 1974), 2.

18. Reorganization Plan No. 2 of 1977, Section 2, 91 Stat. 1636 (1977).

19. "30. Memorandum From the Director of the United States Information Agency (Reinhardt) to all USIA Heads of Offices and Services," *Foreign Relations of the United States, 1977–1980, Volume XXX, Public Diplomacy,* Historical Documents, Department of State.

20. "35. Memorandum From the Director of the United States Information Agency (Reinhardt) to the President's Assistant for National Security (Brzezinski)," *Volume XXX, Public Diplomacy.*

21. "Mission of the International Communication Agency," Pub. L. No. 95–426, Sec. 202, October 7, 1978.

22. Cull, *United States Information Agency,* 362–363.

23. William Rugh Oral History, interviewed by Charles Stuart Kennedy, Foreign Affairs Oral History Collection, ADST, Arlington, VA, 82–83; Cull, *Decline and Fall,* 43–46; *1991 Annual Report,* US Advisory Commission on Public Diplomacy Reports, 14.

24. Maura Harty to Under Secretary [Charlotte] Beers, Assistant Secretary [William] Burns, and Assistant Secretary [Lincoln] Bloomfield, memorandum, "Task Forces Organized for War on Terrorism," with attachment, "Public Diplomacy Task Force," October 26, 2001, author's copy.

25. David Arnett, email to author, November 25, 2019.

26. Harty, "Task Forces Organized;" Janice Brambilla, "Public Diplomacy Task Force Needs Volunteers," email, October 12, 2001, author's copy; Maura Harty to Chiefs of Mission, "Task Forces Organized for War on Terrorism," October 26, 2001, author's copy.

27. "Public Diplomacy Annex to Situation Report Number 073, Overnight Issues from Abroad," n.d. [circa October 2001], author's copy; "Public Diplomacy Annex to Situation Report Number 089, Overnight Issues from Abroad," n.d. [circa October 2001], author's copy; Bruce Gregory, working paper, "Task Force 1 Public Diplomacy—Monitoring Al Jazeera 24/7," October 16, 2001, author's copy; Peter Baker, "In Pakistan, U.S. Joins Battle on Publicity Front," *Washington Post*, November 21, 2001.

28. Kenton Keith Oral History, interviewed by Charles Stuart Kennedy, Foreign Affairs Oral History Collection, ADST, Arlington, VA.

29. Hughes volunteered this point during a meeting with the Defense Science Board Task Force on Strategic Communication, September 6, 2007, author's recollection.

30. Department of Defense, *Report of the Defense Science Board Task Force on Strategic Communication* (2004), 60–62; Department of Defense, *Report of the Defense Science Board Task Force on Strategic Communication* (2007), xiii, xvii, 94–95.

31. Quoted in Walter L. Hixson, *Parting the Curtain: Propaganda, Culture, and the Cold War* (St. Martins, 1997), 19.

32. Hixson, *Parting the Curtain*, 16–17; Wolfe, *Freedom's Laboratory*, 66–68.

33. Quoted in "59. Memorandum from Robert J. Hooker of the Policy Planning Staff to the Director of the Policy Planning Staff (Nitze)," *Intelligence Community 1950–1955*.

34. Harry S. Truman, "Directive Establishing the Psychological Strategy Board," June 20, 1951, American Presidency Project.

35. Davison, Magruder, Wisner, and Stevens are quoted in "Psychological Strategy Board (PSB)," memorandum of conversation held in the CIA Conference Room, May 16, 1951, Freedom of Information Act Electronic Reading Room, CIA Library, https://www.cia.gov/reading-

room/docs/CIA-RDP80R01731R003400010025-1.pdf. Marshall is quoted in Gregory Mitrovitch, *Undermining the Kremlin: America's Strategy to Subvert the Soviet Bloc, 1947–1956* (Cornell University Press, 2009), 62.

36. Quoted in Scott Lucas, "Campaigns of Truth: The Psychological Strategy Board and American Ideology, 1951–1953," *The International History Review* 18, no. 2 (May, 1996): 288.
37. Quoted in Osgood, *Total Cold War*, 44.
38. Gordon Gray Oral History, interviewed by Richard D. McKinzie, Harry S. Truman Library.
39. Quoted in Mitrovitch, *Undermining the Kremlin*, 71–72.
40. Charles Burton Marshall Oral History, interviewed by Neil M. Johnson, Harry S. Truman Library.
41. Hart, *Empire of Ideas*, 161–163; Scott Lucas, *Freedom's War: The U.S. Crusade Against the Soviet Union* (Manchester University Press, 1999), 144–147; Lucas, "Campaigns of Truth," 289–294.
42. Quoted in Lucas, "Campaigns of Truth," 288–289.
43. "157. White House Press Release," *Intelligence Community 1950–1955*.
44. Elmer Staats, "Operations Coordinating Board: A Descriptive Statement of the Organization, Functions, and Procedures of the OCB," September 1955, Freedom of Information Act Electronic Reading Room, CIA Library, https://www.cia.gov/readingroom/docs/CIA-RDP80B01676R002700040035-3.pdf.
45. On the structure and activities of the OCB, see Osgood, *Total Cold War*, 85–88; Wolfe, *Freedom's Laboratory*, 93–94; and Shawn J. Parry-Giles, "The Eisenhower Administration's Conceptualization of the USIA: The Development of Overt and Covert Propaganda Strategies," *Presidential Studies Quarterly* 24, no. 2 (Spring, 1994): 263–276.
46. Loomis Oral History, interviewed by "Cliff" Groce.
47. *Management of Public Diplomacy Relative to National Security, National Security Decision Directive Number 77* (January 14, 1983).
48. *U.S. International Information Policy, National Security Decision Directive Number 130* (March 6, 1984).
49. Carnes Lord, "The Past and Future of Public Diplomacy," *Orbis* 42 (Winter 1998): 56.
50. On Lord's influence on public diplomacy, see Giles Scott-Smith, "Aristotle, US Public Diplomacy, and the Cold War: The Work of Carnes Lord," *Foundations of Science* 13 (2008): 251–264.

51. Walter Raymond, Jr. to National Security Advisor William C. Clark, memorandum, "The Asia Foundation," December 15, 1982, cited in Robert Parry, "Reagan Documents Shed Light on U.S. 'Meddling,'" *Consortium News*, September 13, 2017, https://consortiumnews.com/2017/09/13/reagan-documents-shed-light-on-u-s-meddling/. On Raymond's NSC activities, see Robert Parry and Peter Kornbluh, "Iran-Contra's Untold Story," *Foreign Policy*, No. 72 (Autumn, 1988): 3–30; Robert Parry and Peter Kornbluh, "Reagan's Pro-Contra Propaganda Machine," *Washington Post*, September 4, 1988; and Robert Parry, *America's Stolen Narrative: From Washington and Madison to Nixon, Reagan and the Bushes to Barack Obama* (The Media Consortium, 2012).

52. Parry, "Reagan Documents Shed Light."

53. Thomas Blanton, ed., *Public Diplomacy and Covert Propaganda: The Declassified Record of Ambassador Otto Juan Reich*, March 2, 2001, National Security Archive, George Washington University, https://nsarchive2.gwu.edu/NSAEBB/NSAEBB40/; Comptroller General of the United States to Jack Brooks and Dante Fascell, September 30, 1987, National Security Archive, George Washington University, https://nsarchive2.gwu.edu/NSAEBB/NSAEBB40/04287.pdf.

54. Lord, "Past and Future," 68, n. 40.

55. Walter Raymond, Jr., memorandum for the record, "Organization of Public Diplomacy," August 15, 1988, author's copy.

56. Lord, "Past and Future," 58.

57. *1983 Annual Report*, Advisory Commission on Public Diplomacy Reports, 14.

58. Malone, *Political Advocacy*, 74–76.

59. David I. Hitchcock, *U.S. Public Diplomacy* (Center for Strategic and International Studies, 1988), 20–26.

60. Richard A. Best, Jr., *The National Security Council: An Organizational Assessment* (Congressional Research Service, 2011), 20; Mary Ellen Connell, "Coordinating the Information Instrument of National Security Strategy," student paper, National War College, April 1992, author's copy; Michael Pistor to David C. Miller, February 28, 1990, author's copy.

61. Rothkopf, *Running the World*, 309–316; Best, *National Security Council*, 20–22.

62. *Organization of the National Security Council, Presidential Decision Directive/NSC-2* (January 20, 1993).

63. *Managing Complex Contingency Operations, Presidential Decision Directive/NSC 56* (May 1997).
64. Jamie Frederic Metzl, "Rwandan Genocide and the International Law of Radio Jamming," *American Journal of International Law* 91, no. 4 (October 1997): 628–651.
65. Department of Defense, *Report of the Defense Science Board Task Force on Managed Information Dissemination* (2001), 12–20; Nicholas J. Cull, "How We Got Here," in Seib, *Toward a New Public Diplomacy*, 38–42.
66. *International Public Information (IPI), Presidential Decision Directive/ NSC 68* (April 30, 1999).
67. Ben Barber, "Group Will Battle Propaganda Abroad," *Washington Times*, July 28, 1999; Ben Barber, "Information-control Plan Aimed at U.S., Insider Says," *Washington Times*, July 29, 1999; Ben Barber, "White House Says Information System Not Aimed at U.S." *Washington Times*, July 30, 1999; Helle Bering, "Professor Albright Goes Live," *Washington Times*, August 4, 1999.
68. Cull, "How We Got Here," 42.
69. Department of Defense, *Managed Information Dissemination*, 26.
70. George W. Bush, "Executive Order 13283—Establishing the Office of Global Communications," January 21, 2003, American Presidency Project.
71. Condoleezza Rice, memorandum, "Establishment of the Strategic Communication Policy Coordinating Committee," September 10, 2002, author's copy; Department of Defense, *Task Force on Strategic Communication* (2004), 25–26; *U.S. Public Diplomacy: Interagency Coordination Efforts Hampered by Lack of a National Communication Strategy* (US Government Accountability Office, 2005), 11–13.
72. Stephen J. Hadley, "Establishment of the Public Diplomacy and Strategic Communications Policy Coordination Committee (PCC), April 8, 2006, author's copy; *U.S. National Strategy for Public Diplomacy and Strategic Communication," Policy Coordinating Committee (PCC)* (June 2007), https://2001-2009.state.gov/documents/organization/87427.pdf (accessed May 19, 2023).
73. Karen Hughes, "Strategic Communication and Public Diplomacy: Interagency Coordination," remarks at Department of Defense Conference on Strategic Communication, July 11, 2007, US Department of State, Archive Websites.

74. *U.S. Public Diplomacy: Key Issues for Congressional Oversight* (US Government Accountability Office, 2009), 20–22; *U.S. Public Diplomacy: Background and Current Issues* (Congressional Research Service, 2009), 32–34; Department of Defense, *Task Force on Strategic Communication* (2007), 2–4.

75. Public Law 110-417, Sec.1055; Kristin M. Lord, *Voices of America: U.S. Public Diplomacy for the 21st Century* (Brookings, 2008), 32–33.

76. "National Framework for Strategic Communication," The White House, n.d. [circa March 2010], https://man.fas.org/eprint/pubdip.pdf; "Letter from the President to Congress Concerning a Strategic Communications Report," n.d. [circa March 2010], https://obamawhitehouse.archives.gov/realitycheck/the-press-office/letter-president-congress-concerning-a-strategic-communications-report; "Update to Congress on National Framework for Strategic Communication," n.d. [circa 2012], https://www.hsdl.org/?view&did=704809. Documents accessed May 8, 2023.

77. Ben Rhodes, *The World as It Is: A Memoir of the Obama White House* (Random House, 2018), 69. The term public diplomacy appears on the dust jacket of Rhodes' memoir, but nowhere in the book. Readers will look in vain for insights into how he carried out duties he fleetingly described as being "in charge of the sprawling ways the United States reaches foreign publics—from exchange programs to information operations."

78. Barack Obama, "Executive Order 13721—Developing an Integrated Global Engagement Center to Support Government-wide Counterterrorism Communications Activities Directed Abroad and Revoking Executive Order 13584," March 14, 2016, American Presidency Project; Mathew C. Weed, *Global Engagement Center: Background and Issues* (Congressional Research Service, 2017).

Part III

Twenty-First-Century US Diplomacy

14

Reinvention and Fragmentation

On September 21, 1993, a 13-page document circulated in USIA. It summarized an internal discussion about the Agency's future after the Cold War. Part mission statement, part budget reduction rationale, and part blueprint for reorganization, it proposed radical changes in the Agency's operations and structure to ensure it would "make an even greater contribution to furthering U.S. interests."[1] Like earlier planning papers at crucial times in public diplomacy, it reflected intense debate among practitioners. Senior USIA leaders quickly accepted its ideas, made a few changes, and owned it in the public square.

"American Foreign Policy in an Information Age"

The paper's author was USIA's Counselor Donna Oglesby, a self-described "Army-brat" who had grown up in Japan and Turkey. She joined the Foreign Service in 1970 with an MA from Columbia and rose through the ranks in cultural, press, and PAO assignments in Europe, Asia, and Latin America. In 1993 newly appointed USIA director Joe Duffey asked her to serve in the Agency's senior career position. She had just finished a

© The Author(s), under exclusive license to Springer Nature Switzerland AG 2024   **351**
B. Gregory, *American Diplomacy's Public Dimension*, Palgrave Macmillan Series in Global Public Diplomacy, https://doi.org/10.1007/978-3-031-38917-7_14

year at Tufts University's Fletcher School of Law and Diplomacy where she soaked up new ideas in the seminars, libraries, and bookstores of Boston. Oglesby challenged her colleagues to reckon with thought leaders trying to make sense of digital communication technologies, ascendant globalization, and changes in the world order.[2] In hallway conversations and brown bag lunches, they debated media scholar W. Russell Neuman's "future of the mass audience," Samuel Huntington's "clash of civilizations," Francis Fukuyama's "end of history," and Joseph Nye's "soft power." Big ideas were afoot.

USIA's new political leaders were an unlikely pair. Duffey, a coal miner's son from West Virginia, had degrees from Andover Theological School, Yale University, and Hartford Seminary before turning to a career in politics. He ran unsuccessfully for the Senate in Connecticut in 1970 as an anti-Vietnam War peace candidate; a young Bill Clinton worked in his campaign. Duffey went on to be president of Americans for Democratic Action, Assistant Secretary of State for Educational and Cultural Affairs, Chairman of the National Endowment for the Humanities, and president of the University of Massachusetts and American University. His deputy, Penn Kemble, was a lifelong Social Democrat, committed anti-Communist, and democracy advocate. Unlike Duffey whose political style was that of an academic given to endless conversations, Kemble was skilled in the cut and thrust of Washington's bureaucratic politics. The two resolved to make their USIA partnership work, and for the most part it did.[3]

Oglesby's paper was not USIA's first post-Cold War planning document. USIA director Henry Catto in 1991 had asked four groups of career officers to "take a fresh look" at the Agency's activities. Three offered largely unimaginative "now more than ever" recommendations— no cuts for field operations, enhanced cooperation with the private sector, more resources for Fulbright scholarships and arts programs.[4] Only the report on "Broadcasting in the New Information Era" framed an ambitious agenda: a new public diplomacy mission, phasedown of RFE/RL services, consolidation of US broadcasting entities, few or no VOA editorials, elimination of TV Marti, and modernized technologies.[5]

Clinton Democrats had campaigned to make government less expensive and more efficient. USIA was under pressure from Vice President Al

Gore's National Performance Review to rethink, restructure, and slim down. A White House Task Force and "Reinvention Teams" guided the process. As Oglesby recalled, "There was this kind of pincer movement from the left and from the right on the American political scene that wanted to find a peace dividend. Their motivation was very, very different, but USIA was under attack."[6]

Duffey and Kemble circulated Oglesby's paper largely unchanged. It was a clarion call for USIA to advance US interests with fewer resources in a changed world. First, public diplomacy has deep roots in the diplomacy of Franklin, Jefferson, and Lincoln. Second, new challenges are a new warrant for public diplomacy: violent extremism, ethnic cleansing, assaults on human rights, mercantilist economic agendas, wariness of immigration, and environmental threats. Third, "Dimes spent now will save (and yield) untold dollars in the future." Fourth, the line between "foreign" and "domestic" is no longer clear, and diplomats "increasingly share the stage with private individuals and non-governmental institutions that work across national borders." Finally, the paper focused on the "worldwide electronic and human information network." USIA will "try to piggyback wherever possible on existing online services, such as Internet."[7]

USIA's practitioners wanted to "do more than renovate and refurbish"; they wanted to "rebuild this Agency from the foundation up." They intended to make hard choices, not across-the-board cuts. Programs to be eliminated included worldwide and regional magazines; book exhibits, book fairs, and donated books; and USIA's Exhibits Service. They would consolidate all exchange and visitor programs in a single bureau. They called for an Office of Research and Media Reaction, division of the European Affairs Office, and a streamlined Bureau of Management. They rejected drastic reductions in USIA's posts because public diplomacy required working "where people live to have influence in their lives." Budget cuts were estimated to total $17.5 million; 210 positions were slated to be eliminated.[8]

Line managers voiced concerns. European hands objected to doing away with American libraries in Portugal, Spain, Greece, and Turkey. They should instead become "computer-based reference and documentation centers." The politically hazardous plan to create separate West and

East European offices ran counter to "American efforts to stitch together a 'Europe whole and free.'" Supporters of magazines argued they should be "phased out" rather than eliminated. They were fine, however, with eliminating the Exhibits Service. Exhibits professionals felt otherwise. An absence of cuts in USIA's Management Bureau brought complaints about fairness in the entire process.[9] "Reinvention" animated Agency practitioners, produced strong resistance, and over time led many to be glad the changes were made.

I Bureau Reinvention

The most consequential proposal was "a new, unified and technologically modernized Bureau of Information." The "I Bureau," as it became known, would be a hub that supported electronic networks with USIS posts and other foreign affairs agencies. It would integrate the information capabilities of the Agency's multilanguage press service, known as the Wireless File, online research networks replacing traditional overseas libraries, speaker programs, and foreign press centers in Washington, New York, and Los Angeles.

The effort was led by Barry Fulton, a Foreign Service officer with a PhD in communications from the University of Illinois and service in the Air Force, where he had managed four radio stations and established a TV station for US forces in Turkey. Like Oglesby, he enjoyed connecting academic ideas and professional practice. His rise through the ranks included tours in Islamabad, Karachi, Tokyo, Rome, and the US Mission in NATO. Elaine Kamarck, a Democratic party activist who would go on to teach public policy at Harvard, provided guidance from Gore's National Performance Review Task Force.

The way USIA went about creating the I Bureau was unique. Planners started from a "zero base" rather than a reconfiguration of existing organizational units. The process combined the perspectives of Foreign Service field officers and Civil Service writers, graphic artists, printers, video producers, and computer technicians. The Gore Task Force insisted on Partnership Councils with employee unions, which meant AFGE and AFSA co-chaired the effort. Two hundred practitioners met daily, argued intensely, and defended bureaucratic turf.[10] After five weeks, they had their reinvention. Three project management teams, directly responsive to field posts, replaced hierarchical structures: geographic, to craft regional and country-focused products and services; thematic, to address specific topics and broad issues; and service elements, that included administrative and computer support, printing and graphics, and the foreign press centers.

Then came the hard part—implementation. In a move rare for a career officer, Fulton was named to a presidentially appointed position as the I Bureau's director. During the next two years deputy and special assistant positions vanished. Team leader positions rotated. New job titles accompanied new responsibilities. Consultants were hired. Staff was reduced by 38 percent. Harsh critiques were plentiful. Gradually, however, came an acceptance that something creative was happening. VOA had experimented with the Internet a year earlier; now the I Bureau was adopting the Internet for officers in the field. The Bureau launched its first website on April 12, 1995. It distributed its renamed Washington File and other materials on the Web and developed the first embassy websites. Howard Cincotta, one of many print media specialists who migrated successfully to digital technologies, wrote they had introduced "a generation of public diplomacy officers to the promise and perils of Web work."[11]

"We all of a sudden had a different organization," Fulton recalled. The Vice President's Task Force bestowed one of its "Hammer Awards," which the Bureau displayed with pride for years. Remarkably, for a government bureaucracy, they had radically changed their organizational structure and culture. When the I Bureau's professionals were basking in praise and he was widely credited with the reinvention's overall success, Fulton took exception to having originated the team-based approach. "[I]t wasn't my idea … It sort of came [up] spontaneously in one of these large and somewhat cantankerous meetings, and somebody said we should have a team approach. It was the one thing early on that leadership and the unions agreed on."[12]

USIA's practitioners made their case in diplomacy's new context. "Precisely because we no longer have the shadow of the Cold War," Foreign Service officer Kent Obee declared, "we have … a better shot at dealing with the many very real problems confronting our planet." For

Bruce Wharton and Robert Earle, achieving the North American Free
Trade agreement (NAFTA) would be easier with USIA "as a catalyst and
mediator for the … political leaders, universities, media enterprises,
museums, NGOs, environmentalists, and others" entering "a new phase
of cross border cooperation."[13] Oglesby talked about the "new Joycean
landscape of modern diplomacy." The days when diplomacy could be
done only by "a chosen few descendants of the Congress of Vienna" are
over, she told AFSA. "The doors of the foreign affairs cloister have been
blown open." Public diplomacy is essential in the hard politics of foreign
policy in a world with porous borders and new issues.[14]

But Congress, State, and the NSC had different priorities. Once again
public diplomats lacked a wartime rationale. USIA's reinvention did not
capture the national imagination. It became the focus of partisan divides,
practitioner rivalries, and intense fights over organization charts, solid
lines, and dotted lines. This was not just a debate over another blue-
ribbon commission's recommendations. It was a nearly decade long
struggle involving two presidents, three secretaries of state, and powerful
lawmakers who made foreign affairs downsizing and reorganization a
priority.

Consolidation "Doesn't Solve a Problem and It Doesn't Save Money"

Secretary of State James Baker III commissioned a study on managing
foreign affairs in 1992. It recommended merging the Arms Control and
Disarmament Agency (ACDA) into State in a reorganization model that
could include USAID and USIA.[15] Two years later, when the White
House called for "reinvention" options, then Secretary Warren Christopher
responded with a plan to merge USIA, USAID, and ACDA into the
Department.[16] Others chimed in. Former Ambassador to Germany
Robert Kimmitt, who had described USIA as "our most effective means
of developing long-term relationships with countries crucial to U.S. inter-
ests," now claimed the Agency would be stronger in State. "There is no
Soviet propaganda machine to counter now," former Republican NSC

Advisor Brent Scowcroft opined. "In its place we have CNN Worldwide and Sky Television. The world is deluged with information. We no longer need to have a government network, if you will, to argue our case."[17]

Conservative Senator Jesse Helms (R-NC), the powerful Chairman of the Senate Foreign Relations Committee, was consolidation's strongest advocate. In a jocular *Washington Post* op-ed labeled "Christopher is Right," he drove a wedge between the Secretary and the White House, which opposed consolidation. It is "time to close down some of these agencies and create a single, unified department to conduct U.S. foreign policy," he declared. After years of hostility toward "cookie pushers" and a "striped pants set" that failed to put America's interests first, he enjoyed trumpeting that former Secretaries of State supported his plan. They included Lawrence Eagleburger, George Shultz, and James Baker.[18] On June 9, 1995, Helms introduced his "Foreign Relations Revitalization Act." Consolidation of ACDA, USAID, and USIA into State, he claimed, would eliminate redundant functions and result in "tremendous resource savings."[19] House Foreign Affairs Committee Chairman Ben Gilman (R-NY) introduced a similar bill in the House.

Opposition was immediate and strong. The White House press office responded: "USIA, AID, and ACDA should continue to pursue their missions as independent agencies under the foreign policy direction of the Secretary of State."[20] A week later Gore sent a letter to lawmakers. Presidents need "agencies that permit a clear conceptual and managerial focus on arms control, developmental assistance, and public diplomacy," he wrote. Consolidation in "a large foreign affairs super-department risked creating a super-bureaucracy." It would strain State's management capacity and undermine agency reinventions already underway. Real savings come "from hard decisions about what we no longer need to do, what can be eliminated, what can be privatized ... In short, moving boxes is no substitute for real change." Elaine Kamarck was blunt: "It doesn't solve a problem, and it doesn't save money."[21]

USIA and its supporters agreed. Joe Duffey issued a press release stating his opposition to Helms' plan. The US Advisory Commission on Public Diplomacy pointed to a State Department culture that "reflects 200 years of dealing with foreign governments, not foreign publics" and a tradition of "policy, not program management—secret negotiations, not open communication." Other critics included NSC advisors McGeorge Bundy and Zbigniew Brzezinski, and numerous NGOs. Even the conservative Heritage Foundation concluded "it does not make sense as Helms proposes, to fold the United States Information Agency (USIA) into the State Department." State's "bureaucrats lack the necessary expertise, understanding, and interest to make public diplomacy work."[22]

Actions followed words. In an about face, Secretary Christopher voiced a full-throated critique of legislation that "wages an extraordinary assault on this and every future President's constitutional authority to manage foreign policy." The White House issued a veto threat.[23] Duffey and Kemble mobilized "friends of public diplomacy." They requested a database, broken down by ZIP codes, that showed spending by Fulbright and other exchange programs in Congressional districts, VOA programs about Americans, grants to US universities, and Foreign Press Center-sponsored trips in the United States. Freedom House published a bipartisan list of prominent Americans opposed to elimination of USIA. Clinton vetoed the legislation. Helms responded by placing holds on ambassadorial nominations and putting his plan in the foreign affairs authorization bill for 1996.[24]

The consolidation fracas gave traction to three arguments. First, State's dominant role in foreign affairs was eroding as domestic agencies and economic, trade, health, and environmental issues gained prominence. USIA's practitioners circulated a pie chart based on a GAO report that showed State barely led government staffing in US embassies at 38 percent. Defense, Justice, Transportation, Treasury, Agriculture, Commerce, USAID, and other agencies constituted the rest.[25] USIA could not serve whole of government diplomacy well if it were absorbed by the Department.

Second, State and USIA had different cultures and communication technologies. State had "the dubious distinction of being almost *the* model of bureaucratization in the U.S. federal executive system," sociologist Donald Warwick wrote years earlier, "[c]aught in an incredible tangle of hierarchy, rules, clearances, interdependencies, internal wars, and external constraints."[26] Consolidation would dilute USIA's flexibility and effectiveness.

Third, USIA's supporters saw value in a degree of separation from foreign policy. It allowed State to maintain relations with governments, while the Agency engaged independent and opposition voices in civil societies. Separate appropriations also protected USIA from Department predators. State's quiet support for consolidation, Oglesby informed the Advisory Commission, came from its unwillingness to reform and accept budget reductions. It was easier to "enlarge the pie" by absorbing agencies. And should consolidation occur, it must be contingent on protections for USIA's budget.[27]

Winning the Battle, Losing the War

Clinton was inaugurated for a second term in January 1997. Madeleine Albright was nominated to be Secretary of State. Duffey and Kemble remained at USIA. Helms still chaired the Foreign Relations Committee. There was little discussion of foreign affairs reorganization during the campaign. Now it was time for a political reset with the Senator. Ambassadorial nominations were still on hold. The administration wanted Senate ratification of a Chemical Weapons Treaty, payment of UN dues, smooth sailing on NATO enlargement and other policy initiatives. A fight over three small agencies that few Americans had ever heard of was no longer worth it.

Albright played to Helms' vanity. Traveling to North Carolina, she gave him a nightshirt with the inscription, "Someone at the State Department Loves You." The administration agreed to his consolidation plan. In return, Helms agreed not to block the Chemical Weapons Treaty. Albright neglected to mention the trade-off in her memoir. But Clinton did. "I spent most of the month [April 1997]," he wrote, "in an intense effort to convince the Senate to ratify the Chemical Weapons Convention: calling and meeting with members of Congress; agreeing with Jesse Helms to move the Arms Control and Disarmament Agency and the U.S. Information Agency into the State Department in return for his allowing a vote on the CWC."[28]

On April 18, 1997, Gore announced the reorganization. "President Clinton's plan brings an end to bureaucracies originally designed for the

Cold War, streamlines the Executive Branch's policy-making process, and enhances our nation's ability to meet the growing foreign policy challenges of the twenty-first century," he stated. It put "arms control, sustainable development, and public diplomacy where they belong, at the heart of our foreign policy within a reinvented Department of State." Gone was the idea that consolidation would not save money or solve a problem.[29] At the White House, press Secretary Mike McCurry took questions. Why was consolidation such a "bum idea the last two years" and such a "great idea" now? It's never been a "bum idea," McCurry replied, "but the time is right now, and the time wasn't exactly right then." Then after much chuckling, he turned the mic over to Kamarck to "tell you why." After talking about consolidation as a natural extension of reinvention, she made a key point: "Reinvention in the State Department is an *a priori* qualification for doing any other consolidations of other agencies."[30]

The agencies had no choice but to agree. In a State Department town meeting, Duffey stated, "USIA comes to the table with a commitment to the task … [but] I would not be candid today if I did not say that USIA approaches the process with some concerns." Previously, in a private memorandum to Clinton, Gore, and NSC Advisor Anthony Lake, he had said he could "accept the notion that, within two years, USIA would disappear as a separate independent agency; my commitment is not to the preservation of USIA itself." But he also raised arguments about the threat to USIA's "capacity for public outreach," the prospect that State would "plunder" the Agency's resources, and fears that consolidation would weaken needed reform of the Department's "edifice complex" and "fascination with palatial fortress-embassies."[31]

Planning for Consolidation. The White House announcement framed an overall plan. State was directed to "undertake a new round of internal reinvention to incorporate new organizations and to manage new responsibilities." USIA would be integrated in two-years; its director would become the Under Secretary of State for Public Diplomacy. ACDA's director would become Under Secretary of State for Arms Control and International Security Affairs. USAID was to "remain a distinct agency, but [it] will share certain administrative functions with State and will report to and be under the direct authority and foreign policy guidance of the Secretary of State."[32] Details were left to State and the agencies.

State's planning structure consisted of a top-level steering committee of agency directors led by Secretary Albright and Deputy Secretary Strobe Talbot, a core team led by State's Under Secretary for Management Patrick Kennedy that included Kemble and other deputy directors, and planning groups of senior career officers. Veteran USIA diplomat Ambassador Kenton Keith was the Agency's lead negotiator.

USIA's negotiators had clear priorities. First, they insisted on simultaneous reforms in State. These included putting public diplomacy in the Department's mission, mandated public diplomacy impact statements for major policy decisions, a global, high-speed digital network separate from State's classified network, public diplomacy proficiency standards in performance evaluations and promotion precepts, changes in the Department's training, and a streamlined clearance process. Second, they urged organizational separation between public diplomacy and domestic public affairs, and a firewall to protect public diplomacy appropriations in the Department's budget. Third, they argued for a public diplomacy undersecretary with strong budget and program authorities, a senior deputy, and four assistant secretaries directing four bureaus (Information, Exchanges, Field Liaison/International Public Affairs, and Broadcasting).[33]

Throughout the summer of 1997 the agencies negotiated a plan that reached the Secretary's desk in September with only a few unresolved issues. There it sat until April 1998, a year after the Clinton/Gore announcement.[34]

Broadcasters Escape Helms' Net. US broadcasters had achieved their own consolidation in the International Broadcasting Act of 1994. The Act appeared to settle matters, but in June 1997 divisive issues reappeared when Helms, in a strange bedfellow's alliance with Senator Joe Biden, excluded broadcasting from USIA's consolidation with State. The Broadcasting Board of Governors, they argued, would become a fully independent agency in the executive branch. Senator Russell Feingold (D-WI) took to the Senate floor with an amendment to keep broadcasting services in USIA and part of the consolidation. It is "extraordinary," he declared, that in legislation to consolidate foreign affairs agencies "we find language to create a new independent Federal agency to administer the U.S. international broadcasting program." Biden insisted on full independence for all US broadcasters. Helms stated artfully his legislation "does not create a new Government agency. What it does is simply keep a current function of USIA and move the rest of them out. It is the only thing left." Biden and Helms prevailed by a vote of 74 to 21.[35]

Exchanges—Going Home. Broadcasters had never been part of State's DNA. USIA's Educational and Cultural Exchanges Bureau (ECA) had a different history. As Michael Schneider, a senior advisor to USIA's director, explained, "Consolidation will return the program to State, its original home, from its inception [1938] until 1977–1978. The new Bureau will undoubtedly be seen as the old State/CU (Bureau of Cultural and Educational Affairs) redux." Consolidation offered advantages and disadvantages in Schneider's view. Pluses included greater recognition and more institutional clout. State was better known than USIA and had more influence and longevity. Disadvantages were possible raids on the exchanges budget, State's hierarchy and clearance processes, and its tradition as a policymaking rather than program management organization.[36] Michael McCarry, executive director of the Alliance for International Educational and Cultural Exchange, recalled that when exchanges were in the Department, "They were respected, and the integrity was preserved." However, "We want to see some sort of legislative firewall so funds for exchanges can't be used for other purposes." At the American Council of Teachers of Russian, Carl Herrin wanted assurances that policy disagreements would not "hold up exchanges" in countries such as China and Russia. Going back to State was fine as long as exchanges were protected and well-funded.[37]

Consolidation planning teams listed no major exchange issues to be decided. "USIA's current E Bureau with its mission of managing a variety of exchange programs would continue as at present," Kennedy's Core Team stated in a report to Secretary Albright in the summer of 1997.[38] Educational and cultural affairs would continue in a single bureau with a protected budget and be led by an assistant secretary. There would be no changes in the Fulbright Foreign Scholarship Board and the Advisory Committee on Cultural Property. In subsequent months, exchange practitioners kept a wary eye on the merger, but they were assured when State's negotiators never wavered.

Then a problem occurred. On December 30, 1998, Clinton submitted the reorganization plan to Congress. It downgraded exchanges and combined them with USIA's information programs in a Bureau of Information Programs and International Exchanges. There would be two deputy assistant secretaries for exchanges and one for information programs reporting to an assistant secretary.[39] The Alliance and its allies in Congress made short work of the sudden change. McCarry explained the situation to Dr. William C. "Bill" Friday, a Fulbright enthusiast and former president of the University of North Carolina. As McCarry remembers, Friday said, "Michael, do you mean to tell me they want to have our Fulbright program cheek by jowl with the propaganda activities? I'm going to call Jesse."[40]

A few weeks later Helms and Biden conveyed their strong objection in a joint letter to President Clinton. Legally, they argued, it violated the terms of the Fulbright-Hays Act, which created a "statutory command" for a bureau to carry out educational and cultural affairs programs. As a policy matter, exchanges were too important to be relegated to the deputy assistant secretary level. Merging them with "information" would "cause grave damage to the reputation our exchange programs now enjoy." They would be "perceived by foreign publics and students as little more than a 'propaganda' exercise rather than … an investment in mutual understanding."[41]

The Department submitted a revised plan a few weeks later. It stated exchanges and academic programs would transfer to a single bureau with an assistant secretary and "will continue to have their own appropriations" unlike the rest of the public diplomacy budget, which was incorporated in appropriations for State's Diplomatic and Consular Programs Abroad.[42] What caused this last-minute uproar? "It still bewilders me," Kenton Keith recalled. "I cannot understand why they decided to downgrade that position. I believe nobody at my level and nobody that I dealt with, including Patrick Kennedy, could explain what was happening except that it was a decision made by Madeline Albright herself."[43] When it was over, cultural diplomacy practitioners had simply changed landlords and as a bonus gained protection against raids on their budget. The exchanges bureau would play a strong and largely independent role in the Department in the decades that followed.

Ambassador Pickering's "Corporate Board." Undersecretary of State for Political Affairs Thomas Pickering, State's senior career diplomat, and a small team led by Nancy Ely-Raphel, managed the long game. "We are not here to reinvent what you have been doing," she told the agencies, "but to benefit from it." Their goals were to build a more agile and creative Department, replicate the embassy country team model in Washington, push decisions "down to the Assistant Secretaries," and "empower office directors in a way they've not been empowered before."[44] Lofty rhetoric about State's reinvention was all well and good, but as the straight-talking AFSA president F. Allen "Tex" Harris asked, would it "be an eye wash exercise or an exercise in real change?" He was betting on the former. Would Albright make hard decisions about pushing power down or let it migrate up? And who would control the money? "Stay tuned," he told his members, "the years' long game has just begun."[45]

Secretary Albright sent a memorandum to all foreign affairs employees on August 8, 1997, that channeled Pickering's and Ely-Raphel's ideas. Regional and functional assistant secretaries would be "the Department's main sources of policy leadership and operational strength." They would have the lead on issues and direct access to the Secretary. Undersecretaries would serve as her "advisers" and act as a "corporate board" responsible for determining "international affairs priorities at key stages in the budgetary and strategic planning processes."[46]

In a meeting with the US Advisory Commission on Public Diplomacy on August 11, Pickering explained his thinking. Pushing resources and operational control down to the regional and functional assistant secretaries would give them real power and reduce bureaucratic layers. Desk officers would be issue managers, which could mean doing away with office directors. Undersecretaries would have "a tie breaking" role on major disputes, but they would not engage in day-to-day decision-making. Pickering emphasized that public diplomacy was vital to US interests. Structurally, he inclined to a foreign policy connection between the Secretary and broadcasters, an independent bureau for exchanges, integration of USIA's geographic area offices in State's regional bureaus, and separation between public diplomacy's information programs and domestic public affairs.[47]

This was the extent of State's thinking on reinvention. Its consolidation task force "was never staffed and never met," Keith recalled. The pervasive view in the Department was it did not need to make substantial changes or be part of the process.[48] The "corporate board" model did have a long-term impact on public diplomacy. It weakened the authorities and responsibilities of the Undersecretary for Public Diplomacy and Public Affairs. Legislated ceilings on the number of assistant secretaries meant less influence for USIA's information programs, which were denied an assistant secretary. Fifteen years later, Pickering agreed with those who believed the merger had been a mistake, and he appeared to disavow his role in originating the "corporate board" idea. When queried during his Walter R. Roberts Endowment lecture in 2013, he stated he was thinking about the Defense Department as an organizational model at the time. "I don't think you can stick me with the corporate board," he said, adding that "perhaps my memory is faulty."[49]

Area Offices, Information Programs, PAOs, Cones, and Opinion Research. With broadcasting and exchanges resolved, consolidation decisions turned on USIA's field operations, management, information programs, and other issues. USIA's geographic area directors were powerful senior Foreign Service officers who set budget priorities, approved country plans, coordinated distribution of media and program resources, and evaluated (jointly with ambassadors) the performance of PAOs. USIA argued they should be deputy assistant secretaries (DASs) in State's regional bureaus. State decided they would be office directors, which reduced their authority over field operations. It remained a contentious issue until State appointed regional DASs for public diplomacy a decade later.[50]

A second issue was the location of USIA's I Bureau. The Agency proposed an Information Bureau led by an assistant secretary separate from State's Bureau of Public Affairs. The final reorganization plan, however, designated the I Bureau as an Office of International Information Programs (IIP) led by a "Coordinator," a rank with less prestige and influence than an assistant secretary and not Senate-confirmed. IIP's status was another divisive issue that lasted for years.[51] State transferred USIA's foreign press centers and Worldnet television programs to its Public

Affairs Bureau, which undercut the distinction between public diplomacy and public affairs.

Control over priorities and resources in the field was a third issue.
Traditionally, PAOs reported to ambassadors and USIA. The Agency was
concerned that ambassadors too often confused public diplomacy with
publicity for themselves and might favor policy-oriented information
programs over long-term exchanges, problems that could increase if they
controlled the PAO's budget. Consolidation made life more difficult for
PAOs, Keith observed. Without separate administrative services, they
had to rely on State's consolidated transportation, financial, security, and
human resources support. Added paperwork kept them away from their
audiences. A GAO survey of PAOs in 2003 found a widespread view that
State's administrative services were "often too slow and inflexible to handle the logistics and timing required to set up media and cultural events
and other program activities."[52]

With consolidation, USIA's Foreign Service officers became a career
track known as the "PD cone," separate from State's political, economic,
consular, and administrative "cones." A fourth issue concerned the extent
to which "PD cone" officers would be viewed as "second class" citizens in
a department where political officers reigned. USIA argued they should
be competitive for deputy chief of mission and ambassadorial assignments, and for cross-cone assignments with political and economic officers whose work increasingly involved public outreach and advocacy.[53]

A final decision concerned USIA's opinion and media research offices.
The Agency wanted them in the office of the Undersecretary for Public
Diplomacy. Polling and media analysis were essential in advising the
Secretary and other policymakers. In a decision on which until recently
there was little documentation, they were placed in State's Bureau of
Intelligence and Research (INR). The decision, former INR director
Thomas Fingar writes, was made after a chance conversation with Patrick
Kennedy in State's cafeteria. Kennedy said he planned to assign USIA's
research staff to INR, "because they were analysts." Fingar agreed. For
INR it was a good decision. They were appreciated for their contributions to intelligence products and the INR Assistant Secretary's briefings
of the Secretary. It meant, however, that foreign opinion research lost
some of its connectivity to public diplomacy operations.[54]

"Done as Well as Possible"

Kenton Keith "hated the idea of consolidation." But once the decision was made, he stated, "I felt it was my obligation to try to make sure it was done as well as possible with as little harm to the function as possible." This was the view of most practitioners. They had few cards to play. Albright's unwillingness to reform State and lack of interest in genuine integration created a hostile environment. A few optimists had forecast they would bring transformation with them. Some had even talked of a "leveraged buyout." In a speech at USIA's headquarters on its last day, Albright tried to assure skeptical employees in "the finest institution of public diplomacy the world has ever known" that "public diplomacy must be and will be an integral part of our foreign policy initiatives from the day those policies are conceived." Unconvincingly to most, she declared that "In joining the Department of State, you change it forever."[55]

How did it work out? USIA was abolished on October 1, 1999, and its 4025 non-broadcasting employees (including foreign nationals) were transferred to the Department of State. In the early going, inequities were the norm. Practitioners found much to deplore. Public diplomacy is considered "second tier" at State and their morale is "worryingly low," the Advisory Commission stated a year later. "Public diplomacy, largely driven by the needs of posts overseas and revolving around programs such as exchanges and information dissemination, stands in contrast to the policy-driven State Department, a highly centralized and hierarchical institution driven by the needs of the Secretary of State and other top officials in Washington, D.C."[56]

Consolidation is used to describe what happened, but fragmentation is a more apt term. Pieces of USIA were scattered throughout State's regional, functional, and management bureaus. Many employees in USIA's area offices were not co-located in their assigned regional bureaus. ECA and IIP remained several miles away in the former USIA headquarters building, now a State Department annex. Evelyn Lieberman, the first Undersecretary for Public Diplomacy and Public Affairs, had an office in State and attended the Secretary's morning meetings. But she was cautious about involvement in the public diplomacy activities of regional bureaus that reported to the Undersecretary for Political Affairs and functional bureaus that reported to the Undersecretary for Global Affairs. USIA's administrative, training, and security staffs were merged with counterpart offices in State, which reported to the Undersecretary for Management. Non-profit organizations that worked with ECA complained they faced on average four more layers of clearance on grant decisions than in USIA.[57]

Practitioners adapted. The best, such as Rick Ruth in Lieberman's office, David Arnett and Renee Earle in the Bureau of European Affairs, and Betsy Whitaker and Linda Jewell in the Bureau of Western Hemisphere Affairs, soon learned to navigate the folkways of their new home. Public diplomacy benefited from legislated budget protection, thanks to the efforts of USIA's able Comptroller Stanley Silverman and actions of sympathetic lawmakers on the House Appropriations Committee. A floor colloquy between House Republicans Christopher Smith and Benjamin Gilman paved the way. Referring to a bipartisan consensus, the lawmakers made it clear consolidation was contingent "on the understanding that the integrity of all USIA functions will be preserved." This also meant its resources were not to be used for "a massive domestic State Department public relations operation."[58] A budget firewall for public diplomacy programs, monitored closely by House appropriators, became a durable consequence of the consolidation.

Restoration or Transformation?

In the years that followed, retirees lamented USIA's demise and criticized State's handling of public diplomacy. Many were members of the USIA Alumni Association and the Public Diplomacy Council, a nonprofit organization affiliated with George Washington University that focused on teaching, advocacy, and practice. Former VOA director Geoffrey Cowan launched the Center on Public Diplomacy at the University of Southern California; it soon was a leading institution for public diplomacy study and practice. Retired Foreign Service officers Leonard Baldyga and John H. Brown published widely read online updates of news and opinion items on US public diplomacy. Some retirees taught university courses, curated literature reviews, wrote articles in academic journals, and presented papers at the International Studies Association and other professional organizations.[59]

For retired practitioners, USIA had seen some of its best days in the 1980s when the Cold War that gave it birth was coming to an end. Public diplomacy and promoting democracy mattered to the Reagan administration and its allied tribes of free market conservatives and anti-communist neoconservatives. USIA Director Charles Z. Wick had significantly increased the Agency's budget. When the Berlin Wall collapsed in 1989, many gave substantial credit to USIA. The loss of the Agency signified a deplorable lack of appreciation for their skills and contributions.

There was a consensus about what needed to be fixed in State: upgraded digital telecommunications, appointment of public diplomacy DASs in regional and functional bureaus, more authority for the Undersecretary of Public Diplomacy and Public Affairs, and greater regard for public diplomacy. USIA veteran Dell Pendergrast spoke for many when he wrote that "So far, all that has happened to integrate USIA with State is that the organizational chart has been redrawn, lines of authority have been established and a new letterhead has been printed. The cultural changes needed to assimilate USIA's public diplomacy function into State are, however, barely visible." He quoted Lieberman, who described her role "as a 'missionary' to State because many colleagues … do not understand public diplomacy or value USIA professionals' expertise."[60] Practitioners came to hold two very different visions of public diplomacy's future: restoration and transformation.

Traditionalists favored restoration. Fifteen years after the merger, former USIA officer William Rugh continued to make their case. "The skills an FSO should have in a public diplomacy assignment differ in several respects from the skills required in non-PD assignments." They include program and personnel management, interpersonal and communication skills, language fluency, empathy, and cultural curiosity. Rugh opposed public diplomacy assignments for political and economic officers. What was lost "because of the merger, and because of the notion that 'every FSO must do PD,'" he argued, "is the professionalism and efficiency that came with the specialization of the PD officers."[61]

With a restored USIA politically out of reach, the traditionalists' solution was to create an autonomous USIA-like structure in State. In October 2005, the non-profit Public Diplomacy Council issued a report calling for "an agency within the Department of State and the National Security Council process, the US Agency for Public Diplomacy (USAPD), to manage the U.S. government's civilian information and exchanges functions and to coordinate all U.S. government public diplomacy efforts." It emphasized a threat-based rationale and other arguments used in the past. Public diplomacy was "an effective weapon in the war against terrorism." Favorability ratings of the US had fallen dramatically. More democracies meant foreign public opinion mattered more. "By remaining silent, we allow an information vacuum to be filled by those who hate the United States." The report recommended a cabinet level interagency coordinating committee co-chaired by a Deputy National Security Advisor for Communication and the USAPD director, and a "public-private partnership 'Foundation for the Global Future' to provide permanent off-budget funding for the government's international civilian and military exchanges."[62]

A different vision focused on transformation. In a dissent to the Council's report, advocates called for public diplomacy's integration into the conduct of diplomacy. The Council had failed to address global challenges that were "wholly different from the Cold War." Swapping out communism for terrorism as a justification for public diplomacy would not work in a world where "every major strategy, policy, or diplomatic initiative must have public support in order to succeed." An autonomous agency in State was impractical. It would undermine efforts to change State's culture, separate public diplomacy from policy *formulation* and *implementation*, and put distance between exchanges and "a national strategy for engaging international publics on both policy and socio-cultural issues."[63]

Their dissent was an early indicator of a growing conversation among practitioners about diplomatic practice in the twenty-first century. Michael McClellan, an experienced PAO, argued that "public diplomacy has never been the sole purview of one government agency or one embassy section." Rather, it is the cumulative result of activities and programs that "should be carried out across *all* areas of U.S. engagement abroad."

Reflecting on his career in public diplomacy, Joe B. Johnson recognized what was happening. "Looking back, it is clear that a new landscape has emerged over the past decade to reshape diplomacy itself. In 1999, the State Department approached USIA as an add-on, indicated by the shorthand "public diplomacy," he wrote. "Now terms like 'engagement' and 'three-D diplomacy' [diplomacy, development, and defense] may begin to replace the old paradigm and recast press and cultural affairs as a truly integral part of diplomacy."[64]

Global Trends

What was happening in this new landscape? Scholars and practitioners examined global trends and their impact on diplomatic practice. It was another turning point in diplomacy.

First, borders were more permeable. "In today's global world, there is no longer anything foreign about foreign policy," John Kerry declared in his first major speech as Secretary of State. What was new was "thick globalism" and the accelerating pace of globalization.[65] Also new was a power shift from states to other governance and diplomacy actors. States will remain dominant, Joseph Nye argued, but "an increase in the diffusion of power to non-state actors and network centrality" will be "a key dimension of power in the twenty-first century." For Manuel Castells, the terrain in which power relationships occur "is primarily ... between the global and the local ... [and] primarily organized around networks, not single units."[66]

As early as 1991, Canada's ambassador to the United States Allan Gotlieb wrote about his surprise at finding on arrival in Washington he spent most of his time, not at the State Department with diplomats, but with lawmakers, lobbyists, business executives, think tanks, the media, and state governors.[67] For India's scholar/diplomat Kishan Rana, two decades later, "diplomacy has become multifaceted, pluri-directional, volatile, and intensive."[68] Diplomacy scholar Brian Hocking argues this "boundary erosion" means diplomacy between states coexists with diplomacy in policy networks where non-state actors are diplomatic actors. As state power interacts more with societal power, certain processes become more important: issue framing, agenda setting, norm advocacy, and actor credibility. Diplomats are motivated increasingly "by the logic of mutual interference in each other's domestic affairs."[69]

Second, global population levels that took all of human history to reach three billion, more than doubled in less than a lifetime to reach eight billion in 2022. Nearly two-thirds of the world's population is projected to be urban by 2040.[70] These quantitative changes are creating qualitative changes in diplomacy. Today there are more diplomatic actors *above* the state in global and regional associations, *within* the state in government departments other than foreign ministries, *below* the state in subnational authorities, and *beyond* the state in civil society. City diplomacy is trending as urban networks become major global actors in multiple policy domains.[71] Diplomats derive authority and legitimacy not only from those they represent (state sponsored diplomats), but from their effectiveness in achieving objectives in global policy networks (nonstate diplomatic actors).[72]

Third, "wicked problems"—challenges with no generally agreed upon definitions, resolutions, and visible end points—dominate global agendas. Climate change, pandemic disease, inequality, migration, nanotechnology weapons, out-of-control artificial intelligence, and other transborder threats are characterized by intense disagreements, insufficient knowledge, and global impact on multiple stakeholders. They create emotional contagion. Coping with them separately can compound rather than mitigate their effects.[73] The political will to act is often unachievable even when agreements are reached on what needs to be done. Short-term costs outweigh the potential for long-term gains.[74]

Fourth, global problems create policy agendas that exceed the capacities of foreign ministries and "cut across national governmental structures and designated roles and responsibilities." Almost every government department now engages in activities beyond national borders, Hocking writes. Together, they constitute what he calls the "national diplomatic system."[75] Ambassadors are CEOs in "an institutionalized, 'whole of government,' all-agency operation … each with its own mandate, culture, and place in executing US foreign policy goals."[76] Government specialists also are diplomatic actors in what Anne-Marie Slaughter calls the "disaggregated state." They perform governance and diplomacy functions in banking, law enforcement, global health, civil aviation, Internet governance, and other domains.[77] They represent state interests, but they wear their national identities lightly. The line between diplomacy and governance is blurred, because they are simultaneously engaged in representing principals at home and creating global governance rules and regulations.

Foreign ministries are still respected for their functions and comparative advantages, but not for their "notional primacy in foreign affairs," Rana declares.[78] As other diplomacy scholars observed, "No one seriously doubts the future of diplomats or diplomacy." But when "domestic ministries contribute more to foreign policy, which itself becomes more domestic," diplomats and foreign ministries need to decode the new environment and adapt.[79]

Fifth, the digital revolution that defines the modern era continues to transform diplomatic practice. Computers, social media, mobile devices, big data, and artificial intelligence have radically changed the speed, quantity, and cost of information creation, processing, and transmission.[80] Diplomats are using digital tools to gain attention, build networks, amplify messages of others, humanize ambassadors, pressure adversaries, and evaluate successes and failures. As Danish scholars Rebecca Adler-Nissen and Kristin Anabel Eggeling argue, the analog and digital ways of doing things have now become "deeply intertwined in everyday diplomatic life."[81] Practitioner communities are adapting their modus operandi, and scholars are reimagining diplomacy studies. The literature is enormous.[82]

Three propositions help frame ways of thinking about digitalized diplomacy. (1) Digital technologies are integral to all aspects of diplomacy. Diplomats in hybrid combinations of state and non-state organizations are "interacting to produce more diverse and complex diplomatic scenarios."[83] (2) Connections take place in geographical and sociopsychological contexts. Geographic proximity is still important, Ethan Zuckerman argues, because people are constrained by interests and limited attention, language, fondness for domestic news sources, and views of the world that are "local, incomplete, and inevitably biased."[84] (3) Not everything is digital; much that matters occurs offline. In the words of US Ambassador Christopher Hill, "tools alone cannot solve or build anything."[85]

The next chapter examines changes in US practitioner communities in the aftermath of 9/11 and armed conflict in Afghanistan and Iraq. Americans again "discovered" public diplomacy in response to an external attack. Global trends continued to shape diplomatic practice compounded by the weakening of democracy abroad and at home.

Notes

1. Donna Oglesby, working paper, "American Foreign Policy in an Information Age," September 21, 1993, author's copy. The paper was drafted for internal USIA discussion purposes.
2. Donna Oglesby Oral History, interviewed by Charles Stuart Kennedy, Foreign Affairs Oral History Collection, ADST, Arlington, VA.
3. Cull, *Decline and Fall*, 67–73.
4. "Final Report," The [USIA] Director's Study Groups, October 30, 1992, author's copy.
5. "Broadcasting in the New Information Era," report of a USIA study group, November 5, 1992, author's copy.
6. Oglesby Oral History, interviewed by Charles Stuart Kennedy.
7. Joseph Duffey and Penn Kemble, "Dear Colleague" letter transmitting the final version of "American Foreign Policy in an Information Age," October 22, 1993, author's copy.
8. Duffey and Kemble, "Information Age," 5–12; Penn Kemble, memorandum, "Outline of Projected USIA Restructuring," September 21, 1993, author's copy; Cull, *Decline and Fall*, 72–73.
9. Jack Harrod to Acting Director [Kemble], memorandum, September 21, 1993; Robert A. Powers to Acting Director [Kemble], memorandum, September 23, 1993, author's copies.
10. Barry Fulton Oral History, interviewed by Charles Stuart Kennedy, Foreign Affairs Oral History Collection, ADST, Arlington, VA.
11. Howard Cincotta, "Wireless File to Web: State Department's Print and Electronic Media in the Arab World," in *Engaging the Arab & Islamic World Through Public Diplomacy*, ed. William A. Rugh (Public Diplomacy Council, 2004), 139, 141–142.
12. Fulton Oral History, interviewed by Charles Stuart Kennedy.
13. Kent Obee, "South Africa: Where Public Diplomacy Made a Difference" and Bruce Wharton and Robert Earle, "USIA and NAFTA: Building the

Foundation for Success," papers delivered at the Center for Strategic and International Studies, June 7–8, 1994, author's copies.

14. Donna Oglesby, "The New Foreign Affairs Agenda: The USIA Perspective," speech, American Foreign Service Association, March 17, 1994, author's copy.

15. US Department of State Management Task Force, *State 2000: A New Model for Managing Foreign Affairs*, December 1992, 73–74, author's copy.

16. Susan B. Epstein, Larry Q. Nowels, and Steven A. Hildreth, *Foreign Policy Reorganization in the 105th Congress* (Congressional Research Service, 1998), 2.

17. Kimmett and Scowcroft are quoted in Dick Kirschten, "Restive Relic," *National Journal* 27, no. 16 (April 22, 1995): 976–977.

18. Jesse Helms, "Christopher is Right," *Washington Post*, February 14, 1995; Thomas W. Lippman, "3-Ex-Secretaries of State Back Demise of Cold War-era Agencies," *Washington Post*, March 24, 1995.

19. *Foreign Relations Revitalization Act of 1995, Report of the Committee on Foreign Relations to Accompany S. 908*, 104th Cong. (1995).

20. White House, "Statement by the Press Secretary [Mike McCurry]," February 15, 1995.

21. Vice President Al Gore to Senator Olympia J. Snowe, February 21, 1995, author's copy; Kamarck comment, author's recollection.

22. "Statement by USIA Director Joseph Duffey on Senate Foreign Relations Committee Plan to Restructure U.S. Foreign Affairs Agencies," USIA News Release, March 16, 1995; [Advisory Commission] Chairman Lewis Manilow to Gore, Secretary of State Warren Christopher, and Office of Management and Budget, memorandum, January 19, 1995; "A Foreign and Defense Policy Agenda for the Post-100 Days" (The Heritage Foundation, April 17, 1995), all author's copies.

23. Secretary of State Warren Christopher to House Speaker Newt Gingrich, May 22, 1995, author's copy; William J. Clinton, *Statement of Administration Policy: H.R. 1561—American Overseas Interest Act of 1995*, May 22, 1995, American Presidency Project.

24. "USAID and USIA Man the Ramparts," *Washington Times*, May 16, 1995; "Bipartisan Group Opposes USIA Elimination," Freedom House News, April 19, 1995; Cull, *Decline and Fall*, 105–106.

25. *Overseas Presence: Staffing at U.S. Diplomatic Posts* (US General Accounting Office, 1995).

26. Donald Warwick, *A Theory of Public Bureaucracy: Politics, Personality, and Organization in the State Department* (Harvard University Press, 1975), 9.
27. "Minutes of the Meeting of March 14–15, 1995," US Advisory Commission on Public Diplomacy, author's copy.
28. Madeleine Albright, *Madam Secretary* (Miramax Books, 2003), 231; Bill Clinton, *My Life* (Alfred A. Knopf, 2004), 753.
29. White House, "Fact Sheet Re: Reorganization," Office of the Press Secretary, April 18, 1997.
30. White House, "Press Briefing by Mike McCurry," April 18, 1997, American Presidency Project.
31. Joseph Duffey, statement at Town Hall Meeting, Department of State, April 29, 1997; Joe Duffey to the President, Vice President, and National Security Advisor, memorandum, "Re: Reorganizing Foreign Affairs Agencies: Opting for Option C—With Some Major Disclaimers," April 16, 1997, author's copies.
32. White House, "Fact Sheet Re: Reorganization."
33. "Status Report on Foreign Affairs Agencies Reorganization," USIA Commteam Message Number 3, May 22, 1997; Bruce Gregory to US Advisory Commission on Public Diplomacy, memorandum, "Consolidation of U.S. Foreign Affairs Agencies," May 7, 1997, author's copies.
34. Kenton Keith, "Troubled Takeover: The Demise of USIA," *Foreign Service Journal* 76, no. 9 (September 1999): 18–23.
35. 105 Cong. Rec. S5742 (daily ed. June 17, 1997) (statement of Sen. Feingold); 105 Cong. Rec. S5749 (daily ed. June 17, 1997) (statement of Sen. Helms); Cull, *Decline and Fall*, 90–93.
36. Michael Schneider to Fulbright Study Steering Committee, memorandum, "Consolidation of U.S. Foreign Affairs Agencies," April 30, 1997, author's copy.
37. Quotes are in Amy Magard Rubin, "Clinton Agrees to Fold USIA and Its Exchange Programs into the State Department," *Chronicle of Higher Education*, May 2, 1997.
38. Core Team to Secretary of State Albright and Reorganization Steering Committee, "Draft Report on Reorganization," September 1997, author's copy.

39. William J. Clinton to the Congress, "Reorganization Plan and Report," December 30, 1998, Department of State, https://1997-2001.state.gov/global/general_foreign_policy/rpt_981230_reorg3.html.

40. Michael McCarry, email to author, July 7, 2021.

41. *Fiscal Year 2000 Foreign Affairs Budget and Embassy Security for a New Millennium, Hearings Before the Subcommittee on International Operations*, 106th Cong. (1999) (letter from Senators Jesse Helms and Joseph R. Biden Jr. to President Bill Clinton, February 24, 1999), 2–3.

42. "Reorganization Plan and Report, (revised March 1999)," Department of State, https://1997-2001.state.gov/global/general_foreign_policy/rpt_990331_reorg.html.

43. Keith, "Troubled Takeover," 22; Keith Oral History, interviewed by Charles Stuart Kennedy.

44. Quoted in Reorganization Steering Committee, "The Reorganization Daily," July 17, 1997, author's copy.

45. F. A. "Tex" Harris, "Metaphor for State: To Rebuild or Remodel," *Foreign Service Journal* 74, no. 6 (June-July, 1997): 5; "Foreign Affairs Reorganization: Notes from American Foreign Service Association President Tex Harris," May 7, 1997, author's copy.

46. Secretary of State Madeleine Albright to employees of ACDA, State, USAID, and USIA, memorandum, "First Steps in Reorganizing the Department: The Roles of Assistant Secretaries and Under Secretaries," August 8, 1997, author's copy.

47. Bruce Gregory, "Memorandum of Conversation," meeting of US Advisory Commission on Public Diplomacy Chairman Lewis Manilow, Commissioner Walter Roberts, and Under Secretary of State Thomas Pickering, August 11, 1997, author's copy.

48. Keith Oral History, interviewed by Charles Stuart Kennedy.

49. "2013 WR Annual Lecture: Thomas Pickering," George Washington University, November 5, 2013, (video), https://ipdgc.gwu.edu/2013/11/05/2013-wr-annual-lecture-thomas-pickering/. Kenton Keith and William Rugh confirmed Pickering's leading role in establishing the "corporate board" model. Emails to author, November 7–8, 2013.

50. Keith Oral History, interviewed by Charles Stuart Kennedy.

51. Eventually State changed IIP from an office to a bureau but it failed to convert the rank of coordinator to assistant secretary. In 2019, two decades after consolidation, IIP and Public Affairs were merged into a Global Public Affairs Bureau led by an assistant secretary.

52. Keith Oral History, interviewed by Charles Stuart Kennedy; James Bullock, "The Role of the Embassy Public Affairs Officer After 9/11," in Rugh, *Arab & Islamic Worlds*, 44–45; *US Public Diplomacy: State Department Expands Efforts but Faces Significant Challenges* (US General Accounting Office, 2003), 26.

53. Keith, "Troubled Takeover," 23.

54. Thomas Fingar, *From Mandate to Blueprint: Lessons from Intelligence Reform* (Stanford University Press, 2021), 218, n. 11; *Consolidation of USIA Into the State Department: An Assessment After One Year (2000)*, US Advisory Commission on Public Diplomacy Reports, 14.

55. Madeleine Albright, "Remarks at Ceremony Commemorating the Consolidation of the Department of State and the U.S. Information Agency," October 1, 1999, US Department of State, Archive Websites.

56. *Consolidation of USIA*, US Advisory Commission, 3, 6, 15.

57. Cull, *Decline and Fall*, 163–178; William P. Kiehl, "Unfinished Business: Foreign Affairs Consolidation Was Only the Beginning," *National Security Studies Quarterly* 7, no. 1 (Winter 2001): 117–129.

58. 105 Cong. Rec. H1583 (daily ed. March 26, 1998) (floor colloquy of Reps. Smith and Gilman).

59. See, for example, the author's bimonthly *Diplomacy's Public Dimension: Books, Articles, Websites*, archived at George Washington University, https://ipdgc.gwu.edu/bruce-gregorys-resources-on-diplomacys-public-dimension/.

60. Dell Pendergrast, "Speaking Out: State and USIA: Blending a Dysfunctional Family," *Foreign Service Journal* 86, no. 10 (October 2009): 19.

61. Rugh, *Front Line Diplomacy*, 25–39; William A. Rugh, "PD Practitioners: Still Second-Class Citizens," *Foreign Service Journal* 86, no. 10 (October 2009): 29–34.

62. "A Call for Action on Public Diplomacy: Public Diplomacy in Crisis, October 2005," in *America's Dialogue with the World*, ed. William P. Kiehl (Public Diplomacy Council, 2006), 171–185.

63. Barry Fulton, Bruce Gregory, Donna Marie Oglesby, Walter Roberts, and Barry Zorthian, "Public Diplomacy A Dissent: Transformation Not Restoration," in Kiehl, *America's Dialogue*, 186–192.

64. Michael McClellan, "A Holistic Approach," *Foreign Service Journal* 86, no. 10 (October 2009): 35; Joe B. Johnson, "The Next Generation," *Foreign Service Journal* 86, no. 10 (October 2009): 28.

65. John Kerry, "Address at the University of Virginia," February 20, 2013, US Department of State, Archive Websites; Robert O. Keohane and Joseph S. Nye, Jr., "Governance in a Globalizing World," in *Power and Governance in a Partially Globalized World*, ed. Robert O. Keohane (Routledge, 2002), 193–218.

66. Nye, *Future of Power*, xv, 118–122, 150–151; Castells, *Communication Power*, 50.

67. Allan Gotlieb, *'I'll be with you in a minute, Mr. Ambassador': The Education of a Canadian Diplomat in Washington* (University of Toronto Press, 1991).

68. Kishan S. Rana, *21st Century Diplomacy: A Practitioner's Guide* (Continuum International, 2011), 14.

69. Brian Hocking, "Diplomacy and Foreign Policy," in *The Sage Handbook of Diplomacy*, eds. Costas M. Constantinou, Pauline Kerr, and Paul Sharp (Sage, 2016), 69–73; Brian Hocking, et al., *Futures for Diplomacy: Integrative Diplomacy in the 21st Century* (Netherlands Institute of International Relations, 2012), 19.

70. National Intelligence Council, *Global Trends: A More Contested World*, 2021.

71. Sohaela Amiri and Efe Sevin, eds., *City Diplomacy: Current Trends and Future Prospects* (Palgrave Macmillan, 2020).

72. Teresa La Porte, "The Impact of 'Intermestic' Non-State Actors on the Conceptual Framework of Public Diplomacy," *The Hague Journal of Diplomacy* 7, no. 4 (2012): 441–458.

73. Allan McConnell, "Rethinking Wicked Problems as Political Problems and Policy Problems," *Policy & Politics* 46, no. 1 (January 2017): 165–180; Brian Head and John Alford, "Wicked Problems: Implications for Policy Management," *Administration & Society* 47, no. 6 (2015): 711–739.

74. Hocking et al., *Futures for Diplomacy*, 6, 16–20. On "wicked problems" and public diplomacy, see Ali Fisher and Scott Lucas, eds., *Trials of Engagement: The Future of US Public Diplomacy* (Martinus Nijhoff, 2011), 1–2.

75. Brian Hocking, "The Ministry of Foreign Affairs and the National Diplomatic System," in Kerr and Wiseman, *Diplomacy in a Globalizing World*, 129–149.

76. *Forging a 21st Century Diplomatic Service for the United States Through Professional Education and Training* (Stimson Center and The American Academy of Diplomacy, 2011), 19.
77. Anne Marie Slaughter, *A New World Order* (Princeton University Press, 2004), 12–64.
78. Rana, *21st Century Diplomacy*, 16.
79. Brian Hocking, et al., *Whither Foreign Ministries in a Post-Western World?* (Clingendael Institute Policy Brief, April 2013), 1.
80. James Glieck, *The Information: A History, A Theory, A Flood* (Pantheon Books, 2011); Clay Shirky, *Here Comes Everybody* (Penguin Books, 2008); Ethan Zuckerman, *Rewire: Digital Cosmopolitans in the Age of Connection* (W. W. Norton, 2013).
81. Rebecca Adler-Nissen and Kristin Anabel Eggeling, "Blended Diplomacy: The Entanglement and Contestation of Digital Technologies in Everyday Diplomatic Practice," *European Journal of International Relations* 28, no. 3 (2022): 640–666.
82. Corneliu Bjola and Marcus Holmes, eds., *Digital Diplomacy: Theory and Practice* (Routledge, 2018); Brian Hocking and Jan Melissen, *Diplomacy in the Digital Age* (Clingendael, Netherlands Institute of International Relations, 2015); Ilan Manor, *The Digitalization of Public Diplomacy* (Palgrave Macmillan, 2019); Craig Hayden, "Digital Diplomacy" in *The Encyclopedia of Diplomacy* (John Wiley, March 2018), 1–13. Examples from a very long list.
83. Hocking and Melissen, *Diplomacy in the Digital Age*, 11–12, 22, 54.
84. Zuckerman, *Rewire*, 73.
85. Christopher R. Hill, "The Limits of Twitter Diplomacy," *Project Syndicate*, August 20, 2013.

15

A Failure to Communicate?

Three weeks after the attacks of 9/11, House International Relations Committee Chairman Henry J. Hyde (R-IL) and Senate Foreign Relations Committee Chairman Joe Biden (D-DE) appeared together on NBC's "Meet the Press." "[T]he United States has a proud record of humanitarian aid to people and to Islam around the world, and that story needs to be told," Hyde told moderator Tim Russert. "We don't blow our own horn very well," Biden added … We've [got] to make our case in a way we haven't before."[1]

"How is it," Hyde asked several weeks later, "that the country that invented Hollywood and Madison Avenue has such trouble promoting a positive image of itself overseas?" What it comes down to, House Democrat Tom Lantos answered, is "our appalling failure to conduct public diplomacy with the seriousness and with the resources that this very important function desperately calls for."[2] Americans were puzzled. Many believed no country had been a greater force for good in the world, and they coveted no territory. Why do they hate us? It must be a failure to communicate.

Diplomats agreed. "How can a man in a cave out-communicate the world's leading communications society?" asked Richard Holbrooke. "Call it public diplomacy, or public affairs, or psychological warfare

© The Author(s), under exclusive license to Springer Nature Switzerland AG 2024   **381**
B. Gregory, *American Diplomacy's Public Dimension*, Palgrave Macmillan Series in
Global Public Diplomacy, https://doi.org/10.1007/978-3-031-38917-7_15

or—if you really want to be blunt—propaganda. But whatever it is called, defining what this war is really about in the minds of the one billion Muslims in the world will be of decisive and historic importance."[3] We will be convincing, however, cautioned Ambassador Edward P. Djerejian, if we are "not only talking the talk, but walking the walk. By that I mean implementing policies that carry out [our] ideals."[4]

Terrorism filled America's field of vision in the decade that followed. An attack that killed nearly 3000 Americans meant, unambiguously, a military response came first. The US spent large sums on a militarized strategy: counterterrorism, armed conflict, and episodes of nation building. The US also turned again to public diplomacy. The White House created an Office of Global Communications. Advisory panels and think tanks wrote reports. Lawmakers debated how *more* resources should be spent. Hyde introduced a Freedom Promotion Act to elevate State's attention to public diplomacy, increase contacts between Muslim populations and the American people, and reform international broadcasting's organizational structure.[5]

The bipartisan 9/11 Commission issued a report in 2004 that wielded enormous influence. Its long list of public diplomacy recommendations updated the Cold War playbook for another long-term struggle of ideas. Officials and diplomats should communicate America's vision of hope, opportunity, freedom, and democracy to the large majority of Arabs and Muslims opposed to violence. Cultural diplomats should prioritize exchanges for young people in the Islamic world. The US should support an International Youth Opportunity Fund to build primary, secondary, and vocational schools in Muslim states. Broadcasters should launch television and radio initiatives in the Arab world, Iran, and Afghanistan. Soldiers and civilians should restore the rule of law, build infrastructures, and extend public services in conflict zones. America could not win "the war on terrorism" unless it could win "hearts and minds across the great swath of the globe."[6]

Diplomacy practitioners set about reimagining their profession. "The practice of public diplomacy by professionals, including U.S. ambassadors, has changed dramatically," diplomat Christopher Ross declared. "The U.S. government is by no means the only actor on the public diplomacy stage abroad … [and] the Department of State is in no way the only actor involved in public diplomacy." Ambassador Peter Galbraith had argued earlier that public diplomacy "cannot be thought of as [just] what USIA did but as a (and often THE) central preoccupation of top policymakers."[7] Ross and Galbraith were accurately forecasting twenty-first century changes in whole of government diplomacy.

State's struggle to adapt was reflected in a quarter-century-long revolving door of public diplomacy undersecretaries. Between USIA's merger in 1999 and the third year of the Biden administration in 2023, there were nine Senate-confirmed Undersecretaries of State for Public Diplomacy and Public Affairs. Most held office less than two years. Senior diplomats served in acting capacities during long vacancies.[8] It is "the least noticed, least respected and possibly most important job in the State Department," Anne Applebaum wrote in *The Washington Post*.[9] Writing about his experiences as undersecretary, Richard Stengel, *Time* magazine editor and Nelson Mandela biographer, voiced a sharp critique of State in his story of a journalist who came to government an "information idealist" and left an "information realist."[10] State's public diplomacy undersecretaries brought ideas, a will to succeed, and competence in journalism, advertising, and communications. But the position's limited authority and resources were formidable, and their impact overall was marginal.

Critics found problems with policies as well as process. Counterterrorism strategist Daniel Benjamin noted the gap between US rhetoric and actions.[11] A Defense Science Board report stated, "Muslims do not 'hate our freedom,' but rather, they hate our policies." It found many Muslims perceived US public diplomacy to be narcissistic, hypocritical, lacking in credibility, and too simplistic in its binary distinction between "good Muslims" and "bad Muslims."[12] Secretaries of State increasingly understood the importance of diplomacy's public dimension. Hillary Clinton declared "public diplomacy a core diplomatic mission" and "public engagement every diplomat's duty" in State's first Quadrennial Diplomacy and Development Review (2010).[13] Her words mattered, but it was practitioner communities of Foreign Service officers, cultural diplomats, broadcasters, soldiers, and democratizers who were changing diplomacy.

Next-Generation Country Teams

Field officers increasingly took the view that all diplomats serving abroad should engage in public diplomacy. Dan Sreebny, an officer with experience in the Middle East, Asia, and Europe, was clear. "Every United States diplomat—*every* one—must know and be able to effectively promote U.S. policies and priorities with individuals and audiences in their countries of assignment [emphasis in the original]."[14] Linda Jewell, a public diplomacy officer who became US ambassador to Ecuador, required her entire country team to engage in outreach activities. Scholar and longtime public diplomat Mary Thompson-Jones pointed to creative embassy projects on the environment, food security, and other topics that were changing a public diplomacy agenda, which for too long had been "standard issue … exchanges, cultural programming, and American speakers."[15] The job, declared Jim Bullock, who had served in six Arab countries, was to complete the 1999 merger "by getting State Department diplomats to buy into the notion of public diplomacy."[16]

In 2009 a group of mid-level officers convened a Public Diplomacy Front Line Working Group. They were a new generation of practitioners, open to change, "with no institutional memory of the U.S. Information Agency." Their white paper, which addressed skill sets, assignments, training, and professional education issues, was written to "start a conversation about the direction of public diplomacy" in the Department of State.[17]

State was making changes in assignments, performance evaluations, and promotions. Public diplomacy proficiency became a requirement in promotion panel precepts. Failure to engage in public diplomacy was documented in performance evaluations of political, economic, and consular Foreign Service officers. This was not because USIA had somehow "infected" the Department, reported Julie Gianelloni Connor after serving on a 2009 promotion panel for the Senior Foreign Service. It was happening because a younger generation of diplomats in all career tracks had digital skills and openness to a world where diplomacy was changing. They laid bare the myth that "only seasoned PD officers can adequately 'do PD.'" Performance evaluations showed "many officers from other cones getting rave reviews for their stints as PAOs, IOs and CAOs and for 'new technology' pilot projects."[18]

Bruce Wharton, who would go from public diplomacy assignments in USIA and State to become US Ambassador to Zimbabwe and Acting Undersecretary for Public Diplomacy and Public Affairs, profiled successful public diplomacy practitioners of the future. They would be strong leaders and managers in the interagency environment of US missions, social entrepreneurs who would make strategic use of an embassy's convening power, and effective users of technologies and social media. "The next generation of PDOs will make PD programs such a natural and integral part of an embassy's exercise of smart power that we will stop thinking about public diplomacy as a separate diplomatic function."[19]

"Ambassadors Are the New PAOs"

The distinguished US diplomat Walter Roberts would say this often in the 1990s when in retirement he taught courses on public diplomacy. His evidence was a European foreign ministry where the choice between two equally qualified envoys to Washington turned on how well they handled television interviews. Or he would point to "Public Diplomacy Was His Forte," a newspaper headline on a German ambassador's departure from Washington. Roberts confidently predicted America would catch up.[20]

Christopher Hill. In a Foreign Service career that bridged diplomacy's pre-digital and digital eras, Hill learned from two mentors who understood the role of the media and public outreach: Lawrence Eagleburger, his ambassador in Yugoslavia, and Richard Holbrooke, a "force of nature" in the shuttle diplomacy leading to the Dayton Peace accords in 1995. Holbrooke used CNN to send messages to Bosnians, Croats, Serbs, and Washington. "Yes, I saw your report on CNN," Serb leader Slobodan Milosevic would say as a meeting began. The media helped build momentum in negotiations.[21] Hill used lessons learned as Holbrooke's deputy in later assignments as ambassador to Macedonia, Poland, South Korea, and Iraq. He developed rules for using speeches and media interviews to advance diplomatic agendas. Treat ambush journalists as an opportunity. Walking past them is unnecessary. It's always possible to say something friendly, general, and responsive. He adopted Holbrooke's belief that "on the record" is better than unidentified backgrounders. There are fewer chances of being misquoted. He insisted on more public diplomacy, a lot of listening, and diplomats who would do "a better job of reaching out to non-traditional audiences."

Hill also knew when to call "a diplomatic audible." His instruction from Secretary Rice was not to meet alone with the North Koreans in the Six Party talks; negotiations were to be held in a Chinese facility with the Chinese present. On one occasion a promising meeting with North Koreans, who had been avoiding the talks, was about to be cancelled because the Chinese were absent. What would Eagleburger and Holbrooke do, Hill recalled thinking before deciding to proceed with the one-on-one. Press coverage followed with comments about a "diplomat gone rogue." The North Koreans, however, had participated. The audible worked. "The outcome was good," Rice grumbled, "but the process was bad." In the end, she resolved matters with the Chinese and backed up her negotiator. Diplomatic risk taking is a matter of judgment, timing, and luck.[22]

Michael McFaul. "I tackled everything from my views on missile defense to my take on the best restaurants in Moscow, in 140 characters or less," recalled America's ambassador to Russia from 2012–2014. Social media gave him access to hundreds of thousands of Russians in a country where US diplomats are often denied access to traditional media. Russian language skills, willingness to take risks, apologies for mistakes, and the support of President Obama and Secretary Clinton were critical factors in McFaul's use of Twitter, Facebook, and a blog on LiveJournal. He called out a show trial of Russian opposition leader Alexei Navalny with a tweet hours before Washington could respond. In minutes it sparked close to a thousand retweets. His blog topics included the American foster care system, the role of NGOs in American politics, the evolution of LGBTQ rights in the US, his favorite vacation spots, and his respect for Russian sacrifices in World War II. His tweets and blogs reached Russians unfiltered by state media, but he also knew reach did "not translate neatly into impact."[23]

McFaul's public diplomacy is instructive in other ways. It was a whole of government effort. "[S]o I told my entire embassy team—State Department diplomats as well as representatives from all other agencies at our embassy—that they were all deputized as 'public affairs officers' charged with identifying and formulating positive public messages about their work," he wrote. In time, diplomats from State, Commerce, Defense and other departments began reaching out to the Russian people on "win-win" issues, "be they doctors collaborating on tuberculosis prevention, astronauts living and working together on the International Space Station, or professors teaching side by side at Skoltech."

McFaul was quick to say digital tools do not replace "old school public diplomacy." He seized rare opportunities to appear on Russia's state-controlled television networks. Speaking in Russian with an American accent, he could tell jokes and win applause for naming Russian musicians. In interviews and op-ed columns in Russian print media he explained US policies. His "most pleasurable" tool for engaging Russians, as it had been for his predecessors, was Spaso House, the spectacular residence of the US ambassador, where he hosted concerts, academic lectures, and dinners with visiting American officials and celebrities.[24] He was a pioneer in the first generation of ambassadors to use social media.

Robert Ford. "Hi, I'm Robert," said the former Peace Corps volunteer, fluent Arab linguist, economic track Foreign Service officer, veteran of service in Iraq, former US ambassador to Algeria, and now ambassador to Syria Robert Ford. Tieless and with a book bag over his shoulder, he arrived at the US embassy in Damascus in 2011. Ford was intent on building connections with Syrian demonstrators and opposition groups. His strategy combined restraint, when his actions might provoke repression by the Assad government, and visits to Syria's provincial cities, including one notable visit to Hama. "I thought I needed to go there myself," he recalled. His presence did more than words to convey to the people of Hama they had a right to assemble and express themselves peacefully. "This was another example of an experienced diplomat taking risks to get out from behind embassy walls to do the job right," Secretary Clinton observed.[25]

Soon there were threats on his residence and "rent a crowd" demonstrations outside his meetings with opposition leaders. "I don't particularly care [if Syria's government is angry], because we have to show our solidarity with peaceful protestors," he declared. "I'd do it again tomorrow if I had to … I'm going to keep moving around the country."[26] As described by *Los Angeles Times* correspondent Paul Richter, Ford's social media accounts and the embassy's Facebook site "became a free-for-all—and a bracing departure from the usual bland State Department pronouncements." Arab TV stations followed his social media messages closely and reported when he made news. He posted US intelligence satellite photos on Facebook to rebut Syria's false claims about its military operations. In February 2012 he returned to Washington where he continued as US envoy to the Syrian opposition.[27]

In his Walter Roberts Endowment lecture at George Washington University in 2014, Ford emphasized the importance of social media, the value of being "seen," physically "being there," and reaching out to "regular people" as the most important lessons he had learned for successful public diplomacy. Ford also understood the value of exchanges, speeches, and other traditional tools. He recalled that as ambassador to Algeria he had requested a university speech be low key given widespread Arab opposition to the US occupation in Iraq. He was surprised by his large and enthusiastic welcome. English language programs and partnerships with US universities were popular. Students and teachers wanted more.[28]

Scholars use a variety of terms to describe the diplomacy typified by these ambassadors. Expeditionary diplomacy. Catalytic diplomacy. Entrepreneurial diplomacy. Guerrilla diplomacy. Even naked diplomacy. Doing things by the book and waiting for instructions is no longer sufficient. This is not a formula for going rogue. Foreign Service discipline is still required. Canadian diplomat Daryl Copeland summarized the traits of this new breed of diplomat: "autonomy, agility, acuity, and resilience; the ability to generate and use intelligence, personal and situational sensitivity; local knowledge, cultural awareness, and linguistic and communication skills; irregular representational capabilities and characteristics; an affinity for collaboration and teamwork; functionality in conflict situations … and a catalytic and transformational orientation."[29]

Expeditionary Diplomacy and Counterinsurgency

In Afghanistan and Iraq in 2005 small numbers of soldiers and diplomats turned to counterinsurgency—a political/military strategy neglected in the decades after the Vietnam War. The US needed to win the allegiance of local populations that provided support for extremists. Torture and rendition tactics undermined America's moral authority. Emphasis on military force and harsh rhetoric created the impression that the US was at war with Islam. Overcoming these pitfalls required a new approach to counterinsurgency.[30]

Military practitioners: David Kilcullen, John Nagl, David Petraeus. David Kilcullen, former Australian Army officer, scholar, and strategist skilled at challenging legacy mindsets, was the State Department's Coordinator for Counterterrorism in 2005–2006. He was General David Petraeus' counterinsurgency advisor in Iraq in 2007–2008. Al Qaeda's strategy, Kilcullen argued, was to provoke the US into actions that would destroy its credibility and heighten backlash against Western intervention. The best response was "hybrid warfare"—a population-centric strategy of political reform and development.[31]

Kilcullen's approach required "the study of social roles, groups, status, institutions, and relations within human population groups, in nonelite, nonstate-based frameworks." Many extremists were fighting because the US and its allies were in their space. They were "accidental guerrillas" fighting to be left alone. Rather than treating major combat operations as primary, his approach blended security, development, governance, and partnerships that gave host government officials the lead in building functioning institutions. Kilcullen deplored asymmetries within the military—capabilities overwhelmingly devoted to conventional war fighting and killing or capturing enemy personnel. Just as troubling was a Defense Department that dwarfed civilian capacity.[32] Changing this imbalance was critical, but reality proved intransigent. A Congressional Research Study in 2008 showed that approximately 94 percent of counterterrorism funding went to the Defense Department, with 6 percent for the State Department and foreign assistance.[33]

General David Petraeus, known for his Princeton PhD and command of the 101st Airborne Division's operations that restored local governance and basic services in the city of Mosul, transferred to Fort Leavenworth in 2006 to turn counterinsurgency ideas into doctrine. His team, which included Kilcullen and soldier/scholar John Nagl, produced the Army's popular *Counterinsurgency Field Manual*.[34] As Nagl summarized, it called for actionable intelligence, expeditionary diplomats, civilian specialists, public–private partnerships, law enforcement, strategic public engagement (public diplomacy and military information operations), and military security. Its goal: win the support of populations through long-term coordinated whole of government effort. Its methods: "Focus on protecting civilians over killing the enemy. Assume greater risk. Use minimum, not maximum force."[35] It was a radical shift for a US military focused on big battalions and quick decisive victories.

Civilian practitioners: Kael Weston, Kurt Amend, Carter Malkasian. Diplomats and other civilians served as advisors to combat forces and members of civil–military Provincial Reconstruction Teams (PRTs). The first PRTs, led by military officers with members from the State Department and other agencies, began operating in Afghanistan in 2002. Iraq's PRTs, launched in 2005, were led by Foreign Service officers and a military deputy. Their mission was to assist provincial governments in providing governance, basic services, rule of law, and economic development. Some PRT participants spoke positively about their work. "Working here at this time is fulfilling and historic, in spite of the dangers and the hardships and isolation," said Angela Williams. "I wanted to work where I could use my knowledge of Arabic, cross-cultural and interpersonal skills, and my knowledge of public diplomacy programming." Another public diplomacy officer, Kiki Munshi, stated, "What we do isn't traditional diplomacy. It is using diplomatic skills and techniques to do the things USIA used to do and USAID gives contracts to do, but all of it is hard to do in a war zone."[36]

The list of limitations and lessons learned is long. Some civilians pointed out they did not have the resources, personnel, authorities, or training to carry out "an expanded and better coordinated expeditionary advisory effort involving all agencies of the executive branch."[37] Diplomats reported feeling like "pins on a map," deployed so State could say they were there. Some lacked motivation. Some served for the danger pay. Others, unable to find good assignments elsewhere, saw it as a path to career advancement. In "Deadwood," a chapter in his book on Afghanistan, journalist Rajiv Chandrasekaran wrote vividly of the civilian surge. "We're past the B Team," he quoted Marc Chretien, a State officer in Helmand, "We're at Team C."[38]

Year-long assignments were a mismatch for a long-term effort. Just when PRT members gained experience and trust with local populations, they were transferred and new arrivals started the process all over. Security concerns limited travel and face-to-face meetings. Logistical deficiencies and cultural divides between civilians and soldiers added to the difficulties. As *Foreign Service Journal* editor Shawn Dorman concluded, "Unarmed diplomats flanked by armed personnel on military teams in active combat zones, outside of an embassy structure … may be the face of 'the expeditionary Foreign Service.'" But they should be sent with the skills and resources to do their jobs in places "where there is a chance that they can play an effective, meaningful role."[39]

Several civilian practitioners stand out in America's post 9/11 wars. Foreign Service officer Kael Weston served as a political advisor to US Marines for four years in Iraq. Embassy Baghdad's political counselor Robert Ford said Weston "had the toughest, most dangerous assignment of any State Department officer worldwide" and called him the bravest State officer he knew.[40] In Afghanistan, Weston worked with local Afghans as political advisor to Marine General Larry Nicholson. "Weston was a rare American diplomat in the war on terror who didn't live day and night behind blast walls and airlocked doors, chronically on email, sealed off from the country he was supposed to be trying to understand," wrote journalist George Packer. "He wore jeans instead of pressed khakis and spent his time in markets and combat outposts, talking with tribal elders and students, patrolling with American grunts and sharing their risks."[41] Weston left the Foreign Service and wrote a widely acclaimed book about his experiences.[42]

Two other State officers, Kurt Amend and Carter Malkasian, bridged the divide between theory and practice. Amend, after service in Afghanistan (2002–2003), addressed a central question. "How does a diplomat—outnumbered by the military in the field, lacking significant amounts of program funds, and dependent upon his colleagues in uniform for such basics as mobility and security—effectively pursue the political track, long seen as the decisive component of a counterinsurgency?" First, create a short, compelling narrative to explain the government's mission and interpret events at the tactical level. Second, develop a political strategy to win the support of local populations, and tailor it to security and governance situations on the ground. Third, learn as much as possible about the people, religious and ethnic groups, geography, local leadership, local economies, public services, and the enemy. Fourth, be prepared to assume roles unlike any discussed in Foreign Service training. Finally, be prepared to sit for long hours drinking tea and simply listening. What the US needs, he wrote, is "systematic development of a seasoned cadre of diplomat-counterinsurgents."[43]

Carter Malkasian, Oxford DPhil, teacher, and military analyst in Iraq, served with a PRT in Afghanistan's Kunar province in 2007 and as State's representative to the Garmser District in Helmand Province in 2009. He was known for his fluent Pashto, willingness to take physical and political risks, and warm reception by Afghans. In endless meetings and roadside conversations, he won their trust and the respect of US Marines who came and went during his years as a civilian advisor.[44]

Malkasian and Weston summarized what they had learned in an article in *Foreign Affairs*. State Department and USAID advisors should serve two-year tours and have adequate language training. They should run low-cost governance programs, not large infrastructure projects. They could not succeed bunkered in fortress embassies. "If posted far away from local government leaders and power brokers, civilian advisers will lose track of the intricacies of Afghan politics and will become too uninvolved in day-to-day events to react to problems." They need not live with Afghans; it would undermine their sovereignty. But they should see them daily, which means living in local districts.[45] They were voices in a growing call for a cadre of "expeditionary diplomats" trained to work in "fluid situations" (counterinsurgency, large-scale evacuations, earthquake relief) without a strong host government or US embassy infrastructure.

Cultural Diplomats

Cultural diplomacy practitioners after 9/11 emphasized first principles and greater investment in methods honed over six decades. The US should counteract anti-Americanism by providing more resources for cultural diplomacy even in countries hostile to the United States.[46] But they made their arguments to a Congress that wanted to secure borders, track students, and restrict entry to exchange visitors. There was a silver lining. Exchange organizations could use counterterrorism funds to expand their operations.

Immediately after the attacks, Senator Diane Feinstein (D-CA) called for a six-month moratorium on student visas. US educators responded that closing America's markets, minds, and doors would allow terrorists to succeed. Eventually they supported a compromise bill that gave special scrutiny to visa applications in countries on State's sponsors of terrorism list. After the World Trade Center bombing in 1993, Congress had authorized a Student and Exchange Visitors (SEVIS) tracking system in the Immigration and Naturalization Service. It was still not operational in 2001. But the US Patriot Act, passed six weeks after 9/11, made SEVIS a priority.[47] Computer tracking of students and scholars increased. Required face-to-face interviews meant long visa lines. Educators were soon lobbying lawmakers to reduce hassles that risked "irreparable damage to our competitive advantage in attracting international students, scholars, scientists, and engineers, and ultimately to our nation's global leadership."[48]

Most Americans were happy with immigration policies that strengthened homeland security by restricting access. At the same time, support increased for exchanges that could build understanding and friendly relations with the Islamic world. Side-by-side generalities were the usual rhetorical approach. "Security is always job one," Secretary Powell declared before quickly stating that "openness is a pillar of American influence and leadership."[49] The hard part was finding practical ways to achieve both.

Stricter border policies were a *fait accompli*, but cultural diplomats protested rules that restricted exchanges with Arab and Muslim countries. It was time to make exchanges "a national security imperative." In 2003 the Alliance that represented most US exchange organizations placed a full-page advertisement in *The New York Times* with the headline, "International Exchange Programs—An Investment in National Security." The US "must strike the right balance of protection by defending our country while preserving the openness that sustains legitimate exchange. Our security demands that we do both."[50] Resources for exchanges increased with new money for Partnerships for Learning Undergraduate Studies Program (PLUS), the Youth Exchange and Study Program (YES) that brought Muslim high school and college students to the United States, and other programs "critical in the war against terrorism." It was an investment, Secretary Rice told Congress, directly related to the 9/11 attack on America.[51]

Some cultural diplomats, however, voiced concerns about connections to war and foreign policy. "War invariably distorts cultural diplomacy and legitimizes propaganda," Richard T. Arndt maintained. "America's declared and undeclared wars have blurred the first purpose of cultural diplomacy—to build structures of peace over time." Others suggested campaigns to find common values might obscure legitimate differences in the interactions between individuals and communities in the US and Muslim worlds. A GAO report faulted State for operational deficiencies in language skills, staffing, evaluation, and learning from best practices.[52]

Broadcasters

US broadcasters wasted no time seizing the 9/11 moment. War and the media have a deep-rooted relationship. Audiences spike in a crisis. Journalists prioritize covering conflict. Lawmakers were quick to provide funds to reach Arab and Muslim audiences. By 2003 VOA and RFE/RL had ended broadcasts in Bulgarian, Czech, Estonian, Hungarian, Latvian, Lithuanian, Polish, Slovene, Slovak, Croatian, and Romanian—and expanded their broadcasts in Arabic, Farsi, Urdu, Dari, Pashto, and other languages in Muslim majority countries. They reorganized, developed new programs, and increased their use of FM radio, satellite TV, and digital technologies. Predictably, rivalries within and beyond broadcasting continued.

Voice of America. Seven months after 9/11, VOA's shortwave Arabic service, on air since 1950, was shut down. Research showed low audience ratings. Aging presenters and a one-size-fits-all seven-hour programming stream were not a good fit for countries with diverse audiences and a large youth demographic partial to short, fast-paced program blocks. The BBG and lawmakers wanted a fresh start with two new broadcasting services: Radio Sawa, an FM radio service, and Alhurra, a TV network.[53] VOA hands objected. "The disappearance of VOA Arabic at a time when it was needed most," Alan Heil declared, "ranks among the great tragedies in the history of U.S. international broadcasting."[54]

Radio Sawa. Norman J. Pattiz, CEO of Westwood One, America's largest radio network, and head of the BBG's Middle East Committee, appeared before Congress in June 2002. Radio Sawa (Arabic for "together") is "a prototype of the international broadcasting of the future," he stated. FM channels deliver a better signal. Research showed a menu of Arabic and Western popular music targeted at young listeners and drivers in their cars would have broad appeal. It was about "marrying the mission to the market."[55]

Radio Sawa had critics. What's the advantage of a pop music station, asked Tim Shamble, president of the union representing VOA's journalists. "You may gain a larger audience of teenagers. That's like feeding candy to kids."[56] Others asked, what about Arab intellectuals, reformers, and policymakers? When broadcasters lay claim to elites, Pattiz responded, "it is because they have failed to show a significant following among the general population."[57] Oversight bodies questioned Sawa's audience research and credibility.[58] An advisory panel led by Ambassador Djerejian complained that "Sawa needs a clearer objective than building a large audience." It must "move the needle" by changing Arab attitudes toward the United States.[59] A BBG press release bluntly countered that the panel failed to understand broadcasting's mission, ignored Sawa's news and current affairs content, and failed to "credit Radio Sawa as one of the most innovative public diplomacy initiatives in a generation."[60]

Radio Sawa quickly gained an audience as a first mover in the Middle East's FM radio environment with its attractive mix of Arab and Western music, but imitators soon diluted its market share. When it added call-in shows, public affairs content, programs on mobile devices, and an all-news website, RadioSawa.com, it was less attractive to young listeners. Audiences declined. Expensive transmitters gave way to online streaming services, and in 2018 Radio Sawa's broadcasts were terminated throughout the Middle East except in Iraq.[61]

Alhurra TV. The Middle East had television in abundance. Pan-Arab satellite television networks (Al Jazeera, Al Arabiya) and state-run stations dominated. Responding to criticism that US broadcasters had been slow to adopt satellite TV, the BBG in February 2004 launched Alhurra TV

(Arabic for "The Free One"). It would appeal to audiences seeking "fresh perspectives" through broadcasts of news and information about events in the region and programs on health, entertainment, sports, fashion, science, and technology. It also would bring audiences "the truth about the values and policies of the United States."[62]

Again, there were objections. Unlike Radio Sawa, Alhurra does not have a "superior product," wrote Middle East scholar Marc Lynch. Its much-touted state-of-the-art studios do not equate to good programming. He pointed to shortcomings in Alhurra's response to the Abu Ghraib prison scandal and failure to find space in Arab political conversations.[63] "Alhurra will not succeed ... [in] gaining a significant share of the news market in the region," Professor Shibley Telhami told Congress.[64] The GAO cited weakness in measuring impact and audience size.[65] Foreign Service officers argued the US needed more diplomats with TV-quality Arabic to appear on pan-Arab television networks.

Radio Free Europe/Radio Liberty. RFE/RL had turned to the Middle East and South Asia with Radio Free Iraq in 1998. It had emerged from the efforts of Iraq-born Ahmad Chalabi and his US-based Iraqi National Congress to overthrow Saddam Hussein. Conservative lawmakers looked to repurpose a clandestine station in Kuwait the CIA had used in the Persian Gulf War. "What we are talking about now is an open broadcast policy that supports the political opposition in Iraq," said Rep. Christopher Cox (R-CA).[66] Advocates targeted unused funds authorized in 1995 for a Farsi language service to be managed by VOA.

Critics again responded. Instead of beaming hostile propaganda, Rep. Lee Hamilton (D-IN) argued, "We should reprogram those funds for USIA exchanges." Every time Congress is unhappy with a policy, someone "suggests a 'Radio Free' something" an administration official stated on background. Officially, the Clinton administration supported increased Farsi broadcasting by VOA. Its purpose would not be to "beam anti-government propaganda into Iran," State's press spokesman Jamie Rubin stated, "rather this new service would provide more detailed factual reporting on political, social and foreign policy issues affecting Iran."[67] Broadcasters in VOA and RFE/RL lined up with their parent organizations.

On October 30, 1998, Radio Free Iraq and a Farsi service to Iran went on the air from RFE/RL's studios in Prague. "This is a double first," announced its president Thomas Dine. Although these languages are new for RFE/RL, "the mission of the Radios remains what it has always been—bringing accurate and objective news and responsible commentary to our listeners and thus promoting democratic values." RFE/RL, which had seen its staff and funding cut by more than half in the years since the Cold War, was now relevant to a new era.[68] Broadcasters, Secretary Albright, Kurdish leaders, Iraq's and Iran's pro-democracy groups in the US and Europe, and US conservatives, neoconservatives, and democracy promoters were all pleased.

In 2001 RFE/RL launched broadcasts in Dari and Pashto to Afghanistan, first as Radio Free Afghanistan and then as Radio Azadi. In 2002 VOA and RFE/RL aired broadcasts to Iran in a joint venture named Radio Farda, which in 2015 merged with Radio Sawa. In 2010 RFE/RL began broadcasts in local Pashto dialects to northwestern Pakistan and the border regions with Afghanistan. In 2014 RFE/RL's Ukrainian Service increased broadcasts to the Donbas region of eastern Ukraine and initiated "Current Time," a Russian language digital news network, in collaboration with VOA. Then, with populism growing in Europe, RFE/RL circled back to resume broadcasts in Romanian and Bulgarian in 2019 and Hungarian in 2020.[69]

VOA, Radio Sawa, Alhurra TV, and the "Radio Frees" coexisted uneasily in 9/11's long shadow. US broadcasters still faced hard questions. How much and what kind of broadcasting is needed compared to other instruments of public diplomacy? What language priorities are in the national interest? Why should taxpayers fund broadcasts when there is an overwhelming abundance of global news and information? What is the future of the mass audience?

Broadcasters were pouring old wine rationales into new technology bottles. Social media and streaming platforms joined radio and television. They shared content through YouTube, Facebook, and Twitter. They circulated audio and video podcasts on websites and ITunes. Bloggers extended their reach in Russian, Chinese, Farsi, English, and other languages. We are "platform agnostic" these government media practitioners maintained as they channeled national security concerns in making their case to officials and lawmakers. Former VOA director Geoffrey Cowan spoke of conversations at the highest levels of government and the private sector about using new technologies to confront the Islamic State. RFE/RL president Jamie Fly pointed to disinformation and slick lies by Russia, China, Iran, and other authoritarians.[70]

For the most part US broadcasting's rivals pursued separate paths. Surrogate broadcasters, hailing their distance from government as grantees, focused on providing unbiased news and information in regions where free media were beleaguered or nonexistent. VOA, a federal entity, remained committed to broadcasting US and global news, representing the role of a free press by example, and portraying America's values, institutions, and policies.

Democratizers

Four months after 9/11 the National Endowment for Democracy published a new strategy. Democracy building in the Muslim world was now "one of the most urgent challenges facing the NED." Previously it had been a low priority due to the small number of indigenous pro-democracy movements, fears that Islamic fundamentalists would manipulate elections to impose theocratic governance, and the views of some that democracy was a Western system incompatible with Islamic culture. Now democratization was "the surest way to sever the link between terror and tyranny."[71]

Support came not just from NED's labor, business, and political party advocates in American society. Voices across the political spectrum were calling for "a war of ideas" between liberal democracies and societies that sponsored terrorists. Neoconservatives viewed Saddam Hussein's removal as essential to a new era of democracy and economic modernization. Liberals talked about a war between incompatible ideologies. In his widely read *Terror and Liberalism*, Paul Berman, an outspoken voice on the left, argued it was a war to be fought "on the plane of theories, arguments, books, magazines, conferences, and lectures. It was going to be about the 'cultural influences' that penetrate the Islamic mind, about the deepest concepts of modern life, about philosophies and theologies, about ideas that draw on the most brilliant writers and the most moving of texts." It was to be fought with an activism akin to the anti-communism of intellectuals and civil society organizations during the Cold War. Michael Tomasky, George Packer, Christopher Hitchens, and other liberals followed Berman's lead.[72]

Few democracy practitioners still argued Islam and democracy could not coexist. They tried several strategies. An early option was cautious dialogue. But dialogue was difficult in states with monarchies and military governments—and where the strongest opposition groups were Islamists that supported imposition of Sharia, restrictions on women, and anti-Zionism.[73] State's Middle East Partnership supported pilot programs in education reform, campaign skills training for women candidates, and training for parliamentarians. NED emphasized civil society projects. The most important thing the US can do, Middle East expert Michele Dunne wrote, is "pay consistent attention" to democracy building through private dialogue with ruling officials and continued assistance to governments and NGOs. A Council on Foreign Relations Task Force led by former Secretary of State Albright and former Republican Congressman Vin Weber called on the US to oppose terrorist organizations, but otherwise support participation by any group or party committed to democratic rules and processes.[74]

Budgets for NED, USAID, and State Department democracy programs increased. For sixty years the US pursued stability at the expense of democracy in the Middle East while achieving neither, Secretary Condoleezza Rice stated in her Cairo speech in 2005.[75] Ten years after 9/11, NED President Carl Gershman would declare that "the Arab Spring has vindicated Bush's belief that Arab dictatorships were inherently unstable and democracy has more appeal to the people of the Middle East than jihadist violence and ideology."[76] But events in the next decade undermined this optimism.

Democratization came under assault from populist movements grounded in nativism, grievance politics, hostility to pluralism, and creeping authoritarianism. Critics argued US democracy assistance masked America's economic hegemony, projection of military power, and self-described "indispensable" leadership role.[77] When the US used the rationale of democratic nation-building in Iraq after failing to find weapons of mass destruction, Diamond declared, it "tarnished the idea of 'democracy promotion,' as well as perceptions of American democracy's effectiveness and ability to realize its will abroad."[78]

The West's democratization agenda also encountered revisionist attitudes in Europe. Ivan Krastev and Stephen Holmes, scholars who had embraced the "illusion that the end of the Cold War" signaled "an Age of Liberalism and Democracy," saw growing "resentment at liberal democracy's canonical status." Grievance over the way a no-alternative "imposed" Soviet communism was replaced by a no-alternative "invited" Western liberalism became an element in the revolt against the liberal world order. The West had promoted its model as "inescapable orthodoxy," they argued. Citizens in "replica democracies" harbored feelings of humiliation and resentment. "We don't want to be copies! We want to be ourselves!"[79]

The Clinton, Bush, and Obama administrations had remained committed to democratization. The Trump administration, however, downgraded democracy and human rights as a matter of policy. It made deep cuts in federally funded democracy programs, and failed to support democratic protests in Russia, Thailand, and Hong Kong. However, US support for pro-democracy elements in Venezuela and Iran, and the occasional pro-democracy rhetoric of Secretary of State Pompeo, conveyed a more mixed picture. Trump praised authoritarian regimes, touted his personal ties with autocrats, and criticized democratic leaders and multilateral organizations. "At the center of the current crisis of international democracy support," Thomas Carothers declared, "is the stunning abdication by the United States of its traditional role" in democracy assistance. Nevertheless, many US democracy programs continued with bipartisan Congressional support. For Carothers, democracy had "not so much retreated as plateaued."[80]

Malign efforts by Russia and China to undermine democracies bear little resemblance to public diplomacy or "the benign attraction of soft power," argued Christopher Walker, Jessica Ludwig, and others associated with NED. They coined the term "sharp power" and urged assertive responses that included unmasking Russian and Chinese disinformation activities and a stronger posture on behalf of democratic principles. They did more to define sharp power and imagine its potential, however, than develop strategies for democratizers. Joseph Nye responded that the deceptive use of information by Russia and China is not new; what's new is its speed and low cost. He called sharp power a form of hard power and warned democracies not to overreact or imitate disinformation methods.[81]

After the "War on Terror"

Public diplomacy's renaissance in America's "war on terror" continued for a decade after 9/11. But the dominant focus on terrorism reduced the bandwidth for other challenges. The financial crisis in 2007–2008 caused a global recession and contributed to increased populism and long-term global inequality. Leaders and diplomats continued to confront a buffet of entangled global trends, next-generation digitalization, unprecedented "wicked problems," and new geopolitical challenges.

Americans grew weary of long wars in Iraq and Afghanistan. Many came to view the Iraq war as a huge foreign policy mistake. US special forces killed Al Qaeda leader Osama bin Laden in Pakistan in 2011 bringing closure to the "war on terror" for many. US engagement in the region did not disappear. It backed Saudi Arabia in Yemen's civil war and led a coalition of Kurdish forces and Syrian Arabs against the Islamic State (ISIS). By the end of the Obama presidency in 2016, a new array of issues was shaping diplomacy's public dimension: a Joint Comprehensive Plan of Action (JCPOA) that put limits on Iran's nuclear weapons program; China's rising economy, cyber theft, and naval challenges in the South China Sea; tensions with a nuclear armed North Korea; and Russia's military operations in Georgia, Crimea, eastern Ukraine, and Syria.

Donald Trump's chaotic presidency, exit from the JCPOA, disdain for the NATO alliance and undermining of US diplomacy's institutions and career services raised tensions with allies and partners and eroded the US image. His relations with Vladimir Putin, Russia's disinformation campaigns, and its interference in US domestic politics dominated headlines. The US left the Paris Climate Accords and struggled to respond to the COVID-19 pandemic. Trump's attempt to coerce Ukraine's president Volodymyr Zelenskyy to provide damaging information about his

Democratic rival Joe Biden and son Hunter Biden led to his first impeachment. Career Foreign Service officers Marie Yovanovitch, William B. Taylor, George Kent, and David Holmes testified under subpoena in the House impeachment hearings.[82]

The election of Joe Biden and Kamala Harris in 2020 signaled a renewal of US diplomacy. The White House quickly issued an Interim National Security Strategic Guidance filled with U-turns and promises. Americans will again advance their interests and "universal values" by working with allies and renewing sources of strength at home. The US will "lead with diplomacy" as "our tool of first resort." Distinctions "between foreign and domestic are less meaningful than ever before." As with the George W. Bush and Obama administrations, "public diplomacy" was not mentioned but assumed to be integral to diplomacy.[83]

Actions accompanied words. The US returned to the Paris Climate Agreement, overturned Trump's intention to withdraw from the World Health Organization, launched a COVID-19 Global Action Plan, reversed Trump's decision to bar travelers from majority-Muslim countries, renewed cooperation with allies and partners, and agreed to talks with signatories to the Iran nuclear agreement. Areas of continuity with the Trump presidency included withdrawal from Afghanistan, denunciation of "forever wars," and a confrontational stance toward China. "America is back," Biden declared. Many around the world were pleased, but asked for how long.

Russia invaded Ukraine in February 2022 with devasting consequences. It was another geopolitical inflection point. Americans and Europeans supported harsh sanctions against Russia and provided weapons, financial assistance, and humanitarian support to Ukraine. Sweden and Finland applied to join NATO. Europeans increased defense spending and reduced their dependence on Russian oil and gas. Proponents of US leadership welcomed America's policies. Critics pointed to financial costs, questioned a return to interventions, and urged restraint.

The global trends profiled in this and the preceding chapter have uncertain consequences for diplomacy, governance, society, and the liberal world order. Predictions of future scenarios for US diplomacy's public dimension are risky, and practitioners will find it even harder to cope with accelerating change and the unexpected. The concluding chapter is an assessment of what practitioners can do to leverage their comparative advantages; transform their tools, structures, and modus operandi; and reckon with the American way of diplomacy.

Notes

1. "Text: Rumsfeld on NBC's 'Meet the Press,'" *Washington Post*, September 30, 2001.
2. *The Role of Public Diplomacy in Support of the Anti-terrorism Campaign, Hearing Before the Committee on International Relations*, 107th Cong. (2001).
3. Richard Holbrooke, "Get the Message Out," *Washington Post*, October 28, 2001.
4. Quoted in Robert G. Kaiser, "U.S. Message Lost Overseas: Officials See Immediate Need for 'Public Diplomacy,'" *Washington Post*, October 15, 2001.
5. "Hyde, Lantos Introduce Reform of U.S. Public Diplomacy: Will Improve America's Outreach to International Mass Audiences," International Relations Committee Press Release, Washington, DC, March 14, 2002, author's copy. It passed the House but not the Senate.
6. *The 9/11 Commission Report: Final Report of the National Commission on Terrorist Attacks Upon the United States* (W. W. Norton & Company, 2004), 369–379; *The 9/11 Commission Recommendations on Public Diplomacy: Defending Ideals and Defining the Message, Hearing Before the Subcommittee on National Security, Emerging Threats and International Relations*, 108th Cong. (2004) (statements of Thomas Kean, Chairman, and Jamie Gorelick, Commissioner).
7. Christopher Ross, "Public Diplomacy Comes of Age," *Washington Quarterly* 25, no. 2 (Spring 2002): 76; Peter Galbraith, email to National War College faculty, November 22, 1999, author's copy.
8. Matt Armstrong, "The Schrödinger's Cat of Public Diplomacy," *Arming for the War We're In* (blog), September 12, 2022, https://mountainrunner.substack.com/p/the-schrodingers-cat-of-public-diplomacy.
9. Anne Applebaum, "Think Again, Karen Hughes," *Washington Post*, July 27, 2005.

10. Richard Stengel, *The Information Wars: How We Lost the Global Battle Against Disinformation and What We Can Do About It* (Atlantic Monthly Press, 2019), 13, 58–59.

11. Daniel Benjamin and Steven Simon, *The Next Attack: The Failure of the War on Terror and the Strategy for Getting It Right* (Times Books, 2005), 218–219.

12. Department of Defense, *Report of the Defense Science Board Task Force on Strategic Communication* (2004). 39–47.

13. Department of State, "The 2010 Quadrennial Diplomacy and Development Review (QDDR): Leading Through Civilian Power," US Department of State, Archive Websites.

14. Dan Sreebny, "Public Diplomacy: The Field Perspective," in Kiehl, *America's Dialogue*, 101.

15. Mary Thompson-Jones, *To the Secretary: Leaked Embassy Cables and America's Foreign Policy Disconnect* (W. W. Norton, 2016), 62–67.

16. James Bullock, "The Role of the Embassy Public Affairs Officer After 9/11," in Rugh, *Arab & Islamic Worlds*, 44.

17. Public Diplomacy Front Line Working Group, "Public Diplomacy: A View from the Front Line," *Foreign Service* Journal 86, no. 10 (October 2009): 14–17.

18. Julie Gianelloni Connor, "PD: A View from the Promotion Panel," *Foreign Service Journal* 86, no. 10 (October 2009): 18–21.

19. Bruce Wharton, "Successful Public Diplomacy Officers in the Future," in Kiehl, *Last Three Feet*, 121–122.

20. Fulton, ed., *The Compleat Diplomat*, 18–19, 36–38, 56–57.

21. Clark, *Waging Modern War*, 60.

22. Hill, *Frontlines of American Diplomacy*, 74, 152, 188–191, 205–244.

23. Michael McFaul, *From Cold War to Hot Peace: An American Ambassador in Putin's Russia* (Houghton Mifflin Harcourt, 2018), 284, 299–315.

24. McFaul, *From Cold War*, 307–315.

25. Quoted in Paul Richter, *The Ambassadors: American Diplomacy on the Front Lines* (Simon & Schuster, 2019), 164, 169–171.

26. Quoted in Domani Spero, "JFK Profile in Courage Award Honors U.S. Ambassador to Syria, Robert S. Ford," *Diplopundit* (blog), May 7, 2012, https://diplopundit.net/tag/john-f-kennedy-profile-in-courage-award/.

27. Richter, *Ambassadors*, 177–179.

28. "5 Lessons From a Public Diplomacy Savvy Ambassador," *IPDGC Smart Power* (blog), November 19, 2014, https://blogs.gwu.edu/ipdgcsmartpower/2014/11/19/5-lessons-from-a-public-diplomacy-savvy-ambassador/.

29. Copeland, *Guerrilla Diplomacy*, 205–232; Brian Hocking, "Catalytic Diplomacy: Beyond 'Newness' and 'Decline'" in *Innovation in Diplomatic Practice*, ed. Jan Melissen (Palgrave Macmillan, 1999), 21–42; Kishan Rana, *The 21st Century Ambassador* (Oxford University Press, 2005), 192–196; Hocking, et al., *Futures for Diplomacy*, 69–73; Tom Fletcher, *Naked Diplomacy: Power and Statecraft in the Digital Age* (William Collins, 2016).

30. Kristin M. Lord, John A. Nagl, and Seth D. Rosen, *Beyond Bullets: A Pragmatic Strategy to Combat Violent Extremism* (Center for a New American Security, 2009).

31. David Kilcullen, *The Accidental Guerrilla: Fighting Small Wars in the Midst of a Big One* (Oxford University Press, 2009), 5–28, 265.

32. David J. Kilcullen, "New Paradigms for 21st Century Conflict," *Small Wars Journal*, June 23, 2007; Kilcullen, *Accidental Guerrilla*, 26, 28–38, 265–289.

33. *The Cost of Iraq, Afghanistan, and Other Global War on Terror Operations Since 9/11* (Congressional Research Service, 2014).

34. *U.S. Army/Marine Corps Counterinsurgency Field Manual* (University of Chicago Press, 2007).

35. Nathaniel C. Flick and John A. Nagl, "Counterinsurgency Field Manual: Afghanistan Edition," *Foreign Policy*, October 1, 2009.

36. Quoted in Shawn Dorman, "Iraq PRTs: Pins on a Map," *Foreign Service Journal* 84, no. 3 (March 2007): 22–23, 34.

37. John Nagl, "The Expeditionary Imperative," *Wilson Quarterly* 33, no.1 (Winter 2009): 56.

38. Rajiv Chandrasekaran, *Little America: The War Within the War for Afghanistan* (Alfred A. Knopf, 2012), 180.

39. Dorman, "Iraq PRTs," 21–39; John K. Naland, *Lessons from Embedded Provincial Reconstruction Teams in Iraq* (United States Institute of Peace, 2011); Chandrasekaran, *Little America*, 170–189; Judith Baroody Oral History, interviewed by Charles Stuart Kennedy, Foreign Affairs Oral History Collection, ADST, Arlington, VA; Carter Malkasian, *The American War in Afghanistan: A History* (Oxford University Press, 2021), 97–98, 227–228, 250–252.

40. Quoted in Rajiv Chandrasekaran, "The Renegade Diplomat: Kael Weston's Afghanistan Turnaround," *Newsweek*, November 5, 2012.
41. George Packer, *Our Man: Richard Holbrooke and the End of the American Century* (Alfred A. Knopf, 2019), 443.
42. J. Kael Weston, *The Mirror Test: America at War in Iraq and Afghanistan* (Vintage Books, 2016).
43. Kurt Amend, "Counterinsurgency Principles for the Diplomat," *Small Wars Journal*, July 19, 2008; Kurt Amend, "The Diplomat as Counterinsurgent," *Foreign Service Journal* 86, no. 9 (September 2009): 21–27.
44. Rajiv Chandrasekaran, "War Comes to the Garmser District, Praise for a U.S. Official's Tireless Work," *Washington Post*, August 13, 2011.
45. Carter Malkasian and J. Kael Weston, "War Downsized: How to Accomplish More with Less," *Foreign Affairs* 91, no. 2 (March/April 2012): 111–121; Carter Malkasian, *War Comes to Garmser: Thirty Years of Conflict on the Afghan Frontier* (Oxford University Press, 2013).
46. Barry Ballow, "Academic and Professional Exchanges with the Islamic World," in Rugh, *Arab & Islamic World*, 109–123.
47. Delma Campbell, "International Education and the Impact of the 'War on Terrorism,'" *Irish Studies in International Affairs* 16 (2005): 140–141.
48. Quoted in Christopher Connell, "Reactions Vary," *International Educator* (September–October, 2005): 34–39.
49. Colin Powell, "Secure Borders, Open Doors," *Wall Street Journal*, April 21, 2004.
50. Campbell, "International Education," 146–148.
51. Department of State, "The Budget in Brief: Fiscal Year 2006 Budget Request," https://2009-2017.state.gov/documents/organization/41676.pdf (accessed May 20, 2023); Campbell, "International Education," 153.
52. Richard T. Arndt, "Afterword: End of the Day or a New Dawn," [unpublished update to *First Resort of Kings*, 2008], author's copy; Cynthia Schneider, "Cultural Diplomacy: Hard to Define, But You'd Know It If You Saw It," *The Brown Journal of World Affairs* 13, no. 1 (Fall/Winter, 2006): 195–196; *U.S. Public Diplomacy: State Department Efforts to Engage Muslim Audiences Lack Certain Communication Elements and Face Significant Challenges* (US Government Accountability Office, 2006).
53. Norman J. Pattiz, "Radio Sawa and Alhurra TV: Opening Channels of Mass Communication in the Middle East," in Rugh, *Arab & Islamic World*, 69–89.

54. Alan L. Heil, Jr., "A History of VOA Arabic: A Half-Century of Service to the Nation and the Arab World," in Rugh, *Arab & Islamic World*, 49–68.
55. *S. Hrg. 107-692—America's Global Dialog: Sharing American Values and the Way Ahead for Public Diplomacy, Hearing Before the Committee on Foreign Relations*, 107th Cong. (2002) (statement of Norman J. Pattiz, Broadcasting Board of Governors).
56. Quoted in Michael Dobbs, "America's Arabic Voice," *Washington Post*, March 24, 2003.
57. Pattiz, "Radio Sawa and Alhurra," 76.
58. *US International Broadcasting: Management of Middle East Broadcasting Services Could Be Improved* (US Government Accountability Office, 2006); Marc Lynch, "America and the Arab Media Environment," in Rugh, *Arab & Islamic World*, 90–108.
59. *Changing Minds Winning Peace*, Advisory Group on Public Diplomacy in the Arab and Muslim World, 30.
60. "Broadcasting Board of Governors (BBG) Statement on 'Changing Minds, Winning Peace,'" October 9, 2003, USAGM website.
61. James Careless, "Radio Sawa to Scale Back Regional Broadcasts," *Radio World*, March 28, 2018.
62. Quoted in Paul Richter, "U.S. to Reach Out to Arabs Via TV," *Los Angeles Times*, February 5, 2004.
63. Lynch, "Arab Media Environment," 101–104.
64. *S.Hrg. 108-607—The Broadcasting Board of Governors: Finding the Right Media for the Message in the Middle East, Hearing before the Committee on Foreign Relations*, 108th Cong. (2004) (statement of Shibley Telhami, University of Maryland), 52.
65. *US International Broadcasting*, US General Accountability Office.
66. Walter Pincus, "Radio Free Iraq Proposal Gains Momentum, Support in Congress," *Washington Post*, March 1, 1998.
67. Lee H. Hamilton, "Reassessing U.S. Policy Toward Iran," remarks at Council on Foreign Relations, April 15, 1998, author's copy; US Department of State, Daily Press Briefing, April 15, 1998. https://irp.fas.org/news/1998/04/980415db-2.html.
68. RFE/RL, "RFE/RL Begins Broadcasts to Iran and Iraq," Press Release, October 30, 1998, author's copy; Frank Ahrens, "Radio Free Iraq's Strong Signal: U.S. News Service Heats Up for First Time Since Cold War," *Washington Post*, December 18, 1998.

69. Thomas Kent, "RFE/RL Today and Yesterday," remarks at Columbia University, March 27, 2017, https://ma.europe.columbia.edu/sites/default/files/content/documents/Thomas-Kent-RFE-3.24.17.pdf; RFE/RL, "History," Radio Free Europe/Radio Liberty Pressroom, https://pressroom.rferl.org/history.

70. Geoffrey Cowan, *Why the Voice of America Remains a Vital Force in the World* (Figueroa Press, March 2017); Jamie Fly, "How Biden Can Undo Damage to U.S. Outlets That Counter Authoritarian Propaganda," *Washington Post*, December 24, 2020.

71. National Endowment for Democracy, *Strategy Document*, January 2002.

72. Paul Berman, *Terror and Liberalism* (W. W. Norton, 2003), 184–191; George Packer, ed., *The Fight is for Democracy: Winning the War of Ideas in America and the World* (HarperCollins, 2003).

73. Daniel Benjamin and Steven Simon, *The Age of Sacred Terror: Radical Islam's War Against America* (Random House, 2003), 480–487.

74. Michele Dunne, "Time to Pursue Democracy in Egypt" (Carnegie Endowment, 2007); *In Support of Arab Democracy: Why and How* (Independent Task Force, Council on Foreign Relations, 2005).

75. Condoleezza Rice, "Remarks at the American University in Cairo," June 20, 2005, US Department of State, Archive Websites.

76. "Ten Years Later: A September 11th Symposium," *World Affairs* 174, no. 3 (September/October, 2011): 27–28.

77. William Galston, "The Populist Challenge to Liberal Democracy," *Journal of Democracy* 29, no. 2 (April 2018): 5–19; Diamond, *Ill Winds*, 59–107.

78. Larry Diamond, "Breaking Out of the Democratic Slump," *Journal of Democracy* 31, no. 1 (January 2020): 46–47.

79. Ivan Krastev and Stephen Holmes, *The Light That Failed: Why the West Is Losing the Fight for Democracy* (Pegasus Books, 2020).

80. Thomas Carothers, "Rejuvenating Democracy Promotion," *Journal of Democracy* 31, no. 1 (January 2020): 115, 117–119.

81. Christopher Walker and Jessica Ludwig, *Sharp Power: Rising Authoritarian Influence* (National Endowment for Democracy, 2017); Christopher Walker, "What is Sharp Power?" *Journal of Democracy* 29, no. 3 (July 2018): 9–21; Joseph S. Nye, Jr., "How Sharp Power Threatens Soft Power," *Foreign Affairs*, January 24, 2018.

82. Nicholas Fandos and Michael D. Shear, "Impeachment Hearings Open with Revelation on Trump's Ukraine Pressure," *New York Times*, November 13, 2019; Joe Davidson, "State Department Faces Its Biggest Crisis Since Joseph McCarthy's Hysteria," *Washington Post*, November 13, 2019.

83. White House, *Interim National Security Strategic Guidance*, 2021.

16

Looking Ahead

US diplomats entering the twenty-first century's third decade were gloomy about the state of American diplomacy and full of ideas about what needed to be done. William J. Burns and Linda Thomas-Greenfield, distinguished Foreign Service officers who had recently retired, wrote about a "badly broken US diplomacy" in the journal *Foreign Affairs*. "The wreckage at the State Department runs deep," they declared in a harsh critique of President Trump's "demolition" of the Department and threat to American democracy. His relentless tweets filled with lies and malicious content made life difficult for diplomats at home and abroad. They were just as clear that US diplomacy's problems also reflected "decades of neglect, political paralysis, and organizational drift." A bevy of reform reports echoed their concerns.[1]

In September 2021 President Biden announced a new era of "relentless diplomacy."[2] But American diplomacy's practitioners faced formidable challenges: the legacy of Trump's depredations, widening gaps between capabilities and global drivers of change, a deeply polarized country, the COVID pandemic, the chaotic exit from Afghanistan, tensions with Russia and China, and soon the Russia–Ukraine War.

Foreign Service. Diplomats were maligned and treated as disloyal in the Trump administration. Those who had worked on Obama era policies

© The Author(s), under exclusive license to Springer Nature Switzerland AG 2024
B. Gregory, *American Diplomacy's Public Dimension*, Palgrave Macmillan Series in Global Public Diplomacy, https://doi.org/10.1007/978-3-031-38917-7_16

were sidelined. Budget submissions for State and USAID were cut by 33 percent in 2017 and by similar amounts in the following years. A State planning document proposed cuts of 1410 Civil Service and 572 Foreign Service positions. Although Congress rejected most of these proposals, many diplomats left the Service. Senior positions in the first two years of the Trump presidency were only half filled. Promotions were cut by more than half. Applications dropped to the lowest levels in a decade.[3]

Many problems have deeper roots. Insufficient resources. Lack of adequate training. The near absence of professional education. Fortress embassies. The challenges of digitalization. Diversity reforms that consistently fall short. An inflexible bureaucracy, multiple clearance requirements, habits of waiting for guidance, and a "keep your head down" culture.[4]

Most diplomats had accepted USIA's 1999 merger with State, but it still cast a shadow. Trump's only Senate-confirmed Under Secretary of State for Public Diplomacy and Public Affairs, Irwin Steven Goldstein, arrived in December 2017 and lasted three months. The absence of a Senate-confirmed undersecretary continued until Biden's appointee Elizabeth Allen was confirmed in June 2023. "[W]hat you have now is a set of different PD institutions within State—public affairs, cultural affairs, policy, and planning—that don't work well together," observed the US Advisory Commission on Public Diplomacy's executive director Vivian Walker. "They're decentralized and stovepiped, and leadership is lacking."[5] Others pointed to a gap between the idea that "every officer is a PD officer" and insufficient training. "All Foreign Service officers must have the same understanding of public diplomacy as they have of writing cables," Wes Jeffers and Katherine Tarr observed.[6] "A lot of FSOs are analytical, risk averse, introverted, and maybe a little bit full of themselves," said Marcia Bosshardt. "For public diplomacy, you need a different kind of person."[7]

In 2019 the State Department combined its International Information Programs Bureau and domestically oriented Public Affairs Bureau into a single Bureau of Global Public Affairs (GPA). Its mission: "effectively communicating U.S. foreign policy priorities and the importance of diplomacy to American audiences, and engaging foreign publics to enhance their understanding of and support for the values and policies of the United States."[8] The merger addressed practical realities in digitalized diplomacy, and it drew little attention outside the Department. But decades of opposition to government propaganda at home kept open the possibility the GPA could be accused of partisan political agendas.

Cultural diplomats. The Trump administration targeted State's Bureau of Educational and Cultural Affairs (ECA) for a 47 percent cut in Fiscal Year 2018 and a massive 71 percent cut in 2019. Lobbying by Fulbright alumni, universities, and NGOs, with support from their allies in Congress, was largely successful in beating back these efforts. Many exchanges with China, however, were suspended or restricted. There was collateral damage from Trump's broader policies. Applicants seeking J-1 and F-1 visas for lawful stays in the US faced delays due to staffing shortfalls and regulatory issues. All diplomats encountered difficulties arising from Trump's narrow interpretation of "America First."

ECA's websites feature a glittering array of crosswalks, spreadsheets, and databases linking program goals and objectives to national security, public diplomacy, and Bureau strategies.[9] They are meant to project a strategically focused ECA, but it is hard to know how these indicators are used in program evaluation and cost/benefit trade-offs. Analysts called for closer integration of State's exchanges and foreign policy planning, consolidation and greater efficiencies in State's 90-plus exchange programs, expanded engagement with exchange alumni, and improved program evaluation.[10]

Government media. Congress transferred management authority for all federal and grantee media networks from the Broadcasting Board of Governors (BBG) to a presidentially-nominated, Senate-confirmed CEO in December 2016. Many welcomed the change as an improvement over management by an often dysfunctional, part-time nine-member board. Congress also established a new grantee, the Open Technology Fund, to support citizens seeking to counteract digital censorship in authoritarian countries. Obama appointee John F. Lansing, a respected media professional, served as CEO until 2019 when he left to chair National Public Radio. The BBG changed its name to US Agency for Global Media (USAGM) in 2018. Its annual reports highlight worldwide audience growth, engaging media content, award winning journalism, and trusted programs in a world of disinformation and extremist propaganda.

Oversight panels and outside observers called for elimination of duplication between USAGM's grantees and VOA, a clear implementation guide for VOA's policy editorials, audience data as percentages of population totals rather than absolute numbers, less reliance on self-reported audience data, and improved research methods to match industry standards.[11]

Trump's appointee to be USAGM's CEO Michael Pack, a documentary filmmaker and conservative activist, was confirmed by a Republican-led Senate in June 2020. He immediately fired every USAGM grantee president and board member. Five senior managers were placed on administrative leave pending dismissal; others were sidelined from regular duties or resigned in anticipation of being removed. Pack filled their positions with loyalists. His refusal to extend J-1 visas for foreign nationals working for USAGM raised prospects of uncertain fates on return to their countries of origin.

During his chaotic eight months, Pack insisted his actions were meant to restore impartiality in a "deep state" organization he claimed was filled with partisan bias, corruption, and foreign spies. VOA's journalists responded in an open letter that charged Pack with endangering their personal security, crippling the organization, and engaging in practices comparable to the McCarthy "Red Scare" of the 1950s. Widespread news coverage ensued. Lawsuits were filed. Oversight bodies weighed in.[12] Pack resigned a few hours after President Biden's inauguration. Biden named veteran VOA journalist Kelu Chao as Acting CEO until Amanda Bennett became CEO in December 2022. Senior officials returned to their positions.[13] A report released by the US Office of Special Counsel in 2023 documented abuse of authority, whistleblower retaliations, violations of regulations, and waste of public funds during Pack's tenure.[14]

Soldiers. Military commanders and public affairs officers kept their heads down at the beginning of the Trump administration, aware that Defense Secretary James Mattis was talking less to the press than his predecessors. But nine months into the Trump presidency, Mattis addressed the issue in a closed-door meeting with senior officers. His guidance, soon made public, stated that "communications is the job of the commander, not just the PAO." A "DoD Communication Playbook" encouraged more frequent on-camera press engagements. Military leaders were "to feel free, even obligated, to speak, in their lane, about their efforts."[15]

Simultaneously, Mattis designated information as a seventh joint function to be added to six other core military functions codified twenty years earlier. New information technologies, social media, and widely available wireless communications had "dramatically impacted operations and changed the character of modern warfare." It was past time to institutionalize information as an instrument of national power.[16] Pentagon doctrine writers, educators in military colleges, and analysts in military-funded research organizations went to work. In 2018 a revised publication on *Joint Operations* explained the significance of information in all military operations. It recognized that cognitive effects are as important as physical effects in warfare. The capacious term "information" embraces an array of knowledge categories and activities that enable commanders and staffs "to understand and leverage the pervasive nature of information, its military uses, and its application during all military operations."[17]

There were objections to this new capstone doctrine. We already do it. It's someone else's job. It will cut resources for combat capabilities.[18] The Army chose not to establish information as a seventh joint function, contending it was unnecessary since information is already integral to all warfighting functions. But some Army officers welcomed the new doctrine. Its designation as a joint function, wrote Gregory M. Tomlin, "would benefit the Army by elevating the importance of thinking more critically about and better resourcing the deliberate integration of strategic communications, public affairs, IO, electronic warfare (EW), and cyber operations." Deeper commitment to "information" can limit the need to deploy troops in combat and advance national security goals.[19]

Democratizers. In the third year of the Biden administration, the global decline in democracy continued. Rising authoritarianism in India, Turkey, Hungary, Poland, and other countries was accompanied by an increase in coups and coup attempts. American democracy was in a parlous state. Trump's refusal to concede the 2020 election, the January 6 insurrection at the US Capitol, and a mass movement based on Trump's election lies were leading indicators in America's "backsliding democracy."[20]

Democratizers faced a new challenge. The US had a history of advocating democracy while compromising its principles when circumstances required. But the idea that the nation's democratic institutions were in danger of systemic failure was new. The problem, William A. Galston and Elaine Kamarck wrote, was not that a majority of Americans wanted authoritarian government. Rather, democracy can fail if "an organized, purposeful minority seizes strategic positions within the system and subverts the substance of democracy while retaining its shell—while the majority isn't well organized, or doesn't care enough, to resist."[21]

President Biden's virtual Summit for Democracy in December 2021 signaled America was again supporting democratization. It got mixed reviews. Critics questioned its modest agenda and vague commitments to concrete actions. Supporters welcomed the event but reserved judgment on whether the US would address thorny issues in country-specific strategies.[22] Following a second Summit for Democracy in March 2023, democratizers again were underwhelmed.

Some analysts called for radical reassessment of democracy promotion's assumptions. Instead of *promoting* democracy where it does not exist, democratizers should focus on *protecting* democracies seriously at risk.[23] The US should attend to its own problems instead of promoting democracy abroad. Others argued this would be a mistake. "Now more than ever the world needs the United States to support democracy," Stanford University's Larry Diamond wrote, even as it strengthens democratic institutions at home. He called for more multilateral initiatives, rhetoric that emphasized universal values, not "US democratic values," and technologies to scale firewalls in repressive countries.[24] Journalist Anne Applebaum, a member of NED's board, complained modest spending on democracy projects and US government media fell well short of the billions spent by Russia and China on state media.[25] Former US ambassador to Russia Michael McFaul urged privatizing USAGM's networks in NED-like foundations and massive funding for educational exchanges.[26] He also called for "a new multilateral organization to support non-governmental democratic activists and liberal democratic ideas around the world."[27] It garnered little support.

Presidential aides. There were no serious attempts to create an NSC structure to manage interagency coordination of the government's international communication during the Obama and Trump years. The budget and staff of the Global Engagement Center (GEC), established in 2016 to support government-wide counterterrorism communication activities abroad, continued to grow. Its mission: "To direct, lead, synchronize, integrate, and coordinate efforts of the Federal Government to recognize, understand, expose, and counter foreign state and non-state propaganda and disinformation efforts aimed at undermining or influencing the policies, security, or stability of the United States, its allies, and partner nations."[28] But the GEC is not a comprehensive effort to coordinate America's practitioner communities on a broad range of issues. It is narrowly focused on countering foreign disinformation and propaganda.

Tomorrow's Possibilities

US diplomacy benefits from skilled practitioners, but in sharp contrast to the nation's military, it does not have enough diplomats, money, or support from the American people. The 2022 defense budget authorized at nearly $770 billion, $24 billion more than requested, far exceeded the $58.5 billion requested for State, USAGM, and USAID.[29] The June 2023 debt ceiling legislation set military spending at $886 billion, a 3.3 percent increase over current levels. Congressional leaders in both parties immediately anticipated supplemental defense spending bills. Military hardware is expensive, but there is more to the story. This preference for hard power is a central characteristic of the American way of diplomacy

What does this mean for US diplomacy's public dimension?

First, transformational changes, although not impossible, are unlikely. Consider this thought experiment. Since 1947 the US has tried unsuccessfully more than a dozen times to create a structure in the NSC or the State Department to "coordinate" global communication activities of US civilian and military entities. What if the answer lies not in repeated efforts to make one of these models work, but in creating a new model?

The Pentagon's Defense Science Board (DSB) conceptualized a new model in two task force studies by stakeholders in diplomacy, the military, and academe in the 2000s. They concluded traditional interagency coordination models were destined to fail without new legislation that would give the NSC three capabilities: (1) authority to assign tasks in public diplomacy, public affairs, and military information operations to departments and agencies, but not direct their execution; (2) the right to concur in the appointment of top executive branch communication officials; and (3) authority to transfer limited funds between agencies within appropriations cycles as unexpected circumstances might warrant. These authorities would enable the NSC to engage in *strategic direction* in addition to *strategic coordination*.[30]

The DSB's task force reports prompted a few lawmakers to draft implementing legislation.[31] Their efforts ended in 2010 when the NSC in a report to Congress stated the existing "interagency process for communication and engagement planning" already allowed "the interagency to develop strategies to address current and emergent areas of national security concern."[32] The US persists in willing the ends of interagency coordination using problematic NSC and State Department models. Advisory panels repeat familiar calls for reform.[33] The "NSC Coordinator for Strategic Communications" John Kirby "will coordinate interagency efforts to explain United States policy," President Biden announced on May 20, 2022.[34] Kirby was primarily the NSC's spokesperson. The DSB's proposal remains the most creative idea on the books. Its prospects are dim. Transformational change is rare absent an attack on the homeland. Threats such as climate change, pandemics, and cyber-attacks have not had similar effects.

Second, near-term changes are likely to be incremental. Buried in the 2165-page Defense Authorization Act in December 2021 was the first State Department authorization in twenty years. Buried in State's authorization was a small "public diplomacy modernization" section focused on research and evaluation.[35] In the Defense Authorization Act a year later, another small section on public diplomacy authorized appropriations for international fairs and exhibitions, mandated a report on the merger of information and public affairs bureaus to form the Bureau of Global Public Affairs, and included a Sense of Congress statement on the value of music diplomacy.[36] Aspirational taglines, "leading with diplomacy," and top-down frameworks, such as Secretary Blinken's five pillars for modernizing the State Department, are not roadmaps for making hard choices. For these reasons, bottom-up innovation in the tools and methods of diplomacy's practitioner communities holds greater promise than a new Foreign Service act or a radical remaking of America's foreign relations toolkit.[37]

An example of practitioner-led change is the State Department's "Public Diplomacy Staffing Initiative" (PDSI), a new organizational structure for field operations launched by the Office of Public Diplomacy and Public Affairs in 2017. Described as "one of the most important transformations" since the merger of USIA and State, it replaces the siloed PAO/Public Affairs/Cultural Programs model with a PAO and three "clusters" of collaborative work units. A Public Engagement cluster seeks to influence actions and views of opinion leaders, emerging voices, and the media. A Strategic Content Coordination cluster focuses on planning, audience analysis, research, digital production, and community management. A Resource Coordination cluster encompasses budget development and matching resources to policy priorities.[38]

Unsurprisingly, there were critics. Some in ECA objected that exchanges require special expertise and have long been strategic and "policy-focused."[39] For others, it was unclear how PAOs would leverage the public engagement of other mission elements, cities, and civil society groups. Nor was there clarity in the meanings of strategic planning, strategic plans, strategic goals, strategic content, strategic intent, strategic activities, strategic messaging, strategic engagement, strategic value, strategic results, and the State Department's PD strategic framework—terms sprinkled throughout explanations of the project. Case studies are needed to show how PDSI enables mission X to respond more effectively to complex problem Y in carrying out policy Z.

Thinking About Change

If incremental changes are more likely in the near term, how might we *think* about change, and then seek to *achieve* change, in the broad context of the practitioner communities discussed in this book? Consider first they have one big thing in common. They approached change, not with revolutionary blueprints, but with pragmatic ideas based on their experiences. They sought to blend new methods with the basics of their modus operandi. Four approaches to thinking about change have value for each of these communities: iterative micro-strategies, cross-category knowledge, leveraging diplomacy's comparative advantages, and a reckoning with American exceptionalism. Each is relevant to diplomacy's public dimension and diplomatic practice broadly conceived.

Iterative micro-strategies. Too often, strategies are checklists of objectives, tools, and methods wrapped in catch phrases—"winning hearts and minds," "support for freedom and democracy." Some are five-year "strategic plans" filled with overarching goals, baskets of objectives, and brief descriptions of projects and priorities presented with public relations intent.[40] These are not roadmaps to desired end states. They are not much help in making cost/benefit choices. Crosscutting strategies that embrace multiple practitioner communities are rare. Field operations, exchanges, government media, democratization, and military information operations expand and contract separately. Budgets are made by asking how much did we spend this year? Do we need more or less next year?

Diplomacy reforms with greatest promise in the 2020s are more likely to come through micro-strategies understood as agile and iterative ways of planning and acting on a broad range of issues. Practitioners can benefit from small cross-functional tiger teams and designed games to test concepts, tame bureaucracies, and assess alternative approaches to hard problems. They should not be parallel bureaucracies or reactive task forces, argues career diplomat Zed Tarar. They should be proactive, project-oriented, and deployed to address crises and unexpected contingencies.[41]

Lawrence Freedman in his magisterial *Strategy: A History* makes two relevant points. First, strategies are limited by unexpected contingencies and what others do. Strategies that are just a broad orientation to circumstances or fixed plans to achieve a predetermined goal are unlikely to work. In contested complex environments, diplomacy's natural domain, there are multiple actors and plenty of chances something will go wrong. Fixed plans give advantage to those with greater flexibility. "Plans are worthless," he quotes President Eisenhower as saying, "planning is everything." Second, micro-strategies and plans that are flexible and inventive are worthwhile. "Without some prior deliberation it might be even harder to cope with the unexpected, pick up the cues of a changing situation, challenge set assumptions, or consider the implications of uncharacteristic behavior."[42]

Cross-category knowledge. The US long ago decided diplomacy's center of gravity on financial, trade, commercial, agricultural, and development issues belonged not to State but to others in government. The US Trade Representative leads in trade negotiations; Health and Human Services leads in global health. As policy domains multiply, questions arise about what practitioners should know. They cannot possibly possess operational knowledge on all of today's complex issues. Nor can they be experts on contingencies sure to appear tomorrow, next year, or in five years.

Success in whole of government diplomacy lies in recruiting, training, and educating practitioners with *broad issue awareness.* They may be knowledgeable on one or two complex issues, but breadth means they must also have lateral skills and enough understanding of the "languages" of policy issues and knowledge domains to connect experts in ways that are diplomatically productive. They need sufficient knowledge to be able to find and leverage expertise elsewhere in government and society. This means going beyond what is familiar and beyond country or regional expertise. It also means experts must be willing to discuss the policy implications of their knowledge and provide insights that are operationally useful.

Critical thinking and a capacity to innovate are crucial. With change coming fast, journalist Thomas L. Friedman and scholar Michael Mandelbaum argue, every profession depends on practitioners who bring "something extra," an ability to adjust quickly when tasks change. "*Innovation that happens from the top down tends to be orderly but dumb,*" they maintain, quoting SRI International CEO Curtis Carlson. "*Innovation that happens from the bottom up tends to be chaotic but smart*" [emphasis in the original]. The job of leaders is "to find ways to inspire, enable, and unleash innovation" in their practitioner communities.[43]

It also matters where diplomats come from in society. In 2020 the top four Foreign Service ranks were Whiter than in 2000. In the Foreign Service overall only 7 percent were Black and 7 percent were Hispanic. Women in the Foreign Service were about 25 percent below female representation in the wider US labor force.[44] Efforts to rectify these imbalances matter not only in building a Foreign Service that looks like the

United States, they hold promise for diplomatic practice. Children of immigrants often have foreign language skills and cultural competence that can amplify what is learned in Foreign Service language and area studies. Indigenous Americans and people of color represent America not only by what they know but who they are.[45]

Leveraging comparative advantages. In 2013 US diplomat Roxanne Cabral kicked off a discussion with students at George Washington University by asking how a handful of American officers and local staff at the Consulate in Guangzhou, China, could manage public diplomacy programs in a province with a population nearly that of the Russian Federation. Her answer: make better use of the Consulate's power to leverage visits of mayors, corporate executives, government officials, and civil society experts to diplomatic advantage. Later, in a paper written on assignment at the Atlantic Council, she argued the traditional approach to engaging audiences "is no longer perfectly suited for a changing world." Diplomats must prioritize their power to convene and connect; use data to understand and engage local populations; focus more on cities; and in a "whole of society" mindset, collaborate with organizations to advance entrepreneurship, innovation, sustainability, civic involvement, empowerment in education, and programs of value to youth and women.[46]

Diplomats have always leveraged private visits of Americans, but as a lower priority in the context of government program alternatives, lack of sufficient notice, and previously planned mission activities. Today, taking advantage of the "accidental" visit of an MIT scientist, a Silicon Valley executive, or a Native American cultural scholar should be a field priority. Growth in the international activities of cities and states fits nicely with this logic. A younger generation of diplomats welcomes these developments. The State Department appointed its first Special Representative for City and State Diplomacy in 2022.[47]

Diplomats and foreign ministries often lament their loss of primacy in whole of government diplomacy, but they retain substantial advantages. Compared with most practitioners in military services and other government departments, diplomats have better foreign area and cross-cultural communications skills. Most have higher levels of global awareness.

Many are skilled at managing teams, engaging in multilateral forums, policy analysis, and advising political leaders. Ambassadors and embassies have standing and symbolic value in other societies, which makes them ideal hubs for addressing transnational issues. Successful diplomacy is contingent on knowing what happened last year or many years ago. Diplomats have well-established networks with stakeholders, and foreign ministries have institutional awareness of diplomacy's usable past.

American exceptionalism. The "death of American exceptionalism" was much remarked on in the wake of the January 6, 2021 insurrection. "What has happened should put an end to the notion of American exceptionalism, of an eternal shining city on a hill," opined Council on Foreign Relations President Richard Haass. "Whether American Exceptionalism in any form will survive the Apocalypse of 2020 ranks as an open question," the Quincy Institute's Andrew Bacevich declared. But after a run of four centuries, RIP American exceptionalism is likely premature. "On Twitter and television," journalist Suzy Hansen wrote, "we heard things like: 'This doesn't look like America,' 'This isn't the America I recognize,' 'Is this America?'" These remarks, she observed, were making the case for exceptionalism. For historian Ian Tyrrell, American exceptionalism is an entrenched "set of sedimentary deposits on American memory." It "is not about to die."[48]

Diplomats are more likely to succeed, John Dickson advises, if they remember and acknowledge those parts of America's past "that run counter to an exceptional nation spreading liberty." In assignment after assignment, he encountered the need for a broader "historical sensibility"—an experience widely shared by Foreign Service colleagues. A few weeks of foreign area studies does not solve the problem. It requires changes in American education and the Foreign Service. The point is not to dwell on America's mistakes. It's that greater awareness of ways in which self-image and history do not match up in the eyes of others is key to communicating America's current reckoning with the past, its values, and considerable achievements. Theologian Reinhold Niebuhr remains relevant. Americans must recognize they are fallible. In their democracy and diplomacy, they should reject the belief they can manage history.[49]

Achieving Change

As recent studies by scholars and practitioners suggest, there are sweet spots where a degree of transformational change and adaptation intersect. They require different mindsets. They come with resource costs. But they are achievable. Consider six possibilities with broad applicability to diplomacy's public dimension.

Create a Learning Culture. In the late 1920s, the State Department paid for two years of "tuition, textbooks, and living expenses" in Germany for George Kennan and other Foreign Service officers to study Russian language, literature, and history. They were to achieve an "education similar to that which an educated Russian of the prerevolutionary era would have received."[50] A similar investment a century later is hard to imagine.

The problem, Ambassador William Burns explains, is that my generation "had plenty of specialists in nuclear arms control and conventional energy issues; missile throw-weights and oil-pricing mechanisms were not alien concepts." But in recent years, "I spent too much time in meetings on the seventh floor of the State Department and the White House Situation Room with smart, dedicated colleagues, all of us collectively faking it on the intricacies of cyberwarfare or the geopolitics of data." Burns has a solution. State "can begin by taking a cue from the U.S. military's ... culture of professional education."[51] Others agree. Any attempt to rebuild American diplomacy without significant changes in education and training "will fall flat," argue veteran diplomats David Miller, Thomas R. Pickering, and Rand Beers. For smart diplomacy today, "professional education is not just useful but essential."[52]

Creating a learning culture was prominent in multiple diplomacy reform reports written for the incoming Biden administration, so far with marginal impact. Secretary Blinken's modernization plan is aspirational on training and silent on professional education. Understanding the reasons is key to building a roadmap to change. First, practitioners have long relied on mentors and adapting to circumstances on their own. "The Foreign Service has traditionally believed in an apprenticeship, 'on the job training,' or the 'you'll figure it out' model," declared Harvard's American Diplomacy Project. Diplomacy today cannot be learned by osmosis. Mentors can teach skills. Experiential learning has value. But the pace of today's diplomacy means diplomats lack time to reflect on their experiences and mentor the career development of subordinates. Mentors themselves need training and education.[53]

Second, training and professional education are not incentivized and treated as career enhancing. "I have never seen an institution work so hard to select people and do so little to train them once on board," Ambassador David Miller told a Senate committee in 2021. Promotion panels treat a year of professional education "as a lost year."[54] Solutions lie in a mix of rewards and requirements: more good quality courses that connect training to assignments and functions—and mandated career-spanning professional education. The American Diplomacy Project proposed six months of residential training at each of four career milestones combined with opportunities to study at American graduate schools and US military colleges. Managers should be rewarded and held responsible for authorizing training. Assignments should take into account relevant educational achievement.[55] One modest step would be to reconstitute State's only year-long interagency professional development course, the Senior Seminar, which was discontinued in 2004 after a run of forty-six years.

A third reason is that State lacks a 15 percent "training float"—the military's standard for the percent of the workforce engaged in training and education at any given time. Lack of resources is the usual explanation. Blinken promised to push for a training float "without sacrificing our readiness."[56] But small diplomacy budgets are a reason to emphasize, not forego, education, and funding for new positions is not the only solution. Reducing diplomacy's operational footprint (fortress embassies, diplomatic security) can provide offsets for training and education. Other suggestions include "greater attention to recruiting more officers with language skills," and "requiring multiple assignments in language-designated positions."[57]

Create a diplomacy reserve. Support is growing for a diplomacy reserve analogous to the US military's reserve services and National Guard. The State Department's inclination to stretch current staff to meet unanticipated requirements (new embassies in former Soviet republics, provincial reconstruction teams in Iraq and Afghanistan) has well documented shortcomings. Redundant staffing as a hedge against the unexpected is unrealistic. Predictions of future scenarios are often wrong. What the US needs, several reform reports contend, is a flexible, readily available "Diplomatic Reserve Corps with annual training requirements and activation commitments."[58]

A diplomacy reserve has many benefits. For the American Diplomacy Project, "reservists with specialized scientific or technical expertise in areas such as quantum computing, data science, cybersecurity, refugees and migration, and climate change could be called upon to bolster" existing personnel. Reserves would reduce dependency on expensive contractors. They would open doors to increased diversity and give former practitioners with much to contribute a way to maintain knowledge and skills. Importantly, "These part-time citizen diplomats would serve as 'Ambassadors' in their home communities, enhancing the understanding of America's role in the world and the importance of diplomacy."[59]

The idea of a diplomacy reserve is not new. Two presidents of the American Foreign Service Association have called for a Foreign Service Reserve Corps. Public diplomacy practitioners proposed a reserve corps in 1997 and 2002.[60] In addition to the military's reserves, USAID's "Disaster Assistance Response Teams (DART) and the Federal Emergency Management Agency's Community Emergency Response Teams are possible models. A reserve corps "would have landed in the 'too hard' pile when we were serving," Burns and Thomas-Greenfield wrote. But the need for a diplomatic surge capacity today is "inescapable."[61]

Create a diplomacy research and development center. The military has long benefited from government-funded research and development organizations such as RAND and from research in military service colleges. Since 1956 the Defense Science Board has harnessed the expertise of academic and other civil society experts. Since 1957 the Defense Advanced Research Projects Agency (DARPA) has worked with experts in and out of government to put US armed forces at the cutting edge of technological change. A Defense Innovation Board was established in 2016 to provide new ideas and critical thinking on strategies, operations, and technologies. The intelligence community has its IARPA, and a National Intelligence Council draws on expertise in academe and the private sector to broaden the knowledge of practitioners. There is no federally-funded independent, non-profit center to provide knowledge, skills, and services to diplomacy practitioners.

Proposals differ on ways to remedy this deficiency, but there is consensus that bridging gaps between diplomatic capacity and relevant knowledge is essential. Some would create an external government-funded entity to provide services and contract with academic, commercial, and non-government organizations. Its expertise and professional resources would serve all of diplomacy's practitioner communities. Others would strengthen existing research and analysis activities within government. A State Department analog to DARPA, an autonomous "skunk works" unhampered by bureaucracy to work on advanced technology projects relevant to diplomacy, is one approach.[62]

Eliminate Foreign Service Career Tracks. There is long-standing and now growing support for ending the career track system that separates Foreign Service officers into political, economic, public diplomacy, consular, and management "cones." In 1998 a report signed by more than 50 diplomacy practitioners called for an integrated Foreign Service with two categories of professionals: a merged category of political, economic, and public diplomacy officers whose assignments would focus on particular countries and regions, and a second category of management and consular officers deployed worldwide.[63]

Fast forward to the present. For the American Diplomacy Project, "an internal caste system [that] ranks some job categories as more important than others ... creates distrust both inside the Foreign Service and between the Foreign Service and the Civil Service." It perpetuates "the false notion that consular, economic, management, public diplomacy, and political officers do separate and unequally valued work." Or, as Burns and Thomas-Greenfield contend, "the State Department simply cannot afford to continue its bad habits of offering inflexible career tracks, imposing self-defeating hiring constraints, and encouraging tribal inbreeding among its cloistered ranks." Rigid specialization creates inflexibilities. It does not reflect the reality that cross-cone assignments are increasing, and it is incongruent with the "messy multilateralism" of diplomacy's environment.[64]

Supporters of the cone system contend different Foreign Service functions require specialized expertise, training, and personnel categories.

Not every diplomat can be adept at managing an exchange program, engaging journalists in a media briefing, or advising leaders and military commanders. True enough. However, this is the case not only *within* the public diplomacy cone but in the Foreign Service as a whole. The US is virtually the only diplomatic service that uses cones. Most countries deploy diplomats who see "external relationships as an integrated whole, where each specialized functional area serves also a larger, interconnected purpose."[65]

Acquiring skills and expertise. The challenges of modern diplomacy require knowledge, skills, and diversity in greater abundance. Pathways to critical expertise in advanced technologies, global health, cyber security, and other complex domains, however, are littered with obstacles. Security clearances take months or years. Government salaries are not competitive. Hiring rules are diverse and complex for Foreign and Civil Service recruitment, as well as special hiring authorities for individuals in "scientific, professional, and technical positions." State launched a fast-track hiring process for data scientists in 2022 with some success, but still lost applicants due to delays and salaries below private sector standards. Within the Department, some question the value of data-based diplomacy and zero-sum trade-offs with existing programs.[66]

To provide expertise and greater diversity in the ethnic, geographic, and cultural composition of diplomacy's practitioner communities, diplomats and policy analysts are calling for expanded mid-career lateral entry of persons with specialized skills. There is broad consensus on the merits and goals of lateral entry. Differences exist on the means. Should lateral entrants serve fixed or renewable terms? How should the selection process avoid partisan political manipulation and ensure compatibility with career systems? The American Diplomacy Project's detailed proposal recommends a pilot lateral entry program closely aligned with maintaining the hierarchy, discipline, and equities of the career Foreign Service. Anne-Marie Slaughter urges transforming the Foreign Service into a "Global Service" with very different rules. She would recruit talent "from the corporate, finance, NGO, social enterprise, educational, medical, scientific, religious, and other sectors that do globe-spanning work" for fixed "five-to ten-year rotations," renewable once or twice "at every level of seniority." Critics argue her proposal would lead to "rampant politicization" and unnecessary "de-professionalization."[67]

Together with other reforms—a learning culture, professional education, federally-funded nonprofit research and skills centers, a reserve corps for surge diplomacy—lateral entry is a proven way to meet pressing needs in diplomacy and build innovative, relevant career services. Reports recommending diplomacy reforms are filled with good ideas and end-state goals. Missing are roadmaps and detailed plans. One exception is a follow-up report by authors of the American Diplomacy Project. In 2023 they published draft language for regulations and legislation, written by experienced diplomats, to implement their reform recommendations.[68]

Diplomacy and technology, not technology diplomacy. This book has treated paradigm changes in technology as diplomacy turning points. Each paradigm shift brought changes that happened *to* diplomacy and were used *by* diplomacy. But they did not *become* diplomacy. Which is why phrases like digital diplomacy, data diplomacy, and quantum diplomacy mislead. They put the technology cart before the diplomacy horse.

Putting diplomacy first means it is important to distinguish between technology awareness and technology fluency. The former connotes recognition of value and possibility, the latter expertise and viability. Practitioners need to adopt communication technologies as they evolve. But their priority should be knowledge of how technologies can facilitate or complicate their diplomatic agendas. Most cannot possess expertise on successive waves of digitalization, artificial intelligence, and virtual realities. They must be technology literate, but they need specialists within and outside their communities to make technologies work to diplomatic advantage. Imaginative practitioners are key. In 2021 a team of current and former State practitioners concluded "New tools to analyze the social media landscape and other datasets offer immense sources of information on what conversations are taking place, what arguments are being mustered for or against certain policies, and how audiences are responding to our messages."[69]

The Department released a data strategy in September 2021 intended to empower its workforce with the "skills and tools to derive actionable mission insights from data," to secure and effectively manage data assets, and equip the Department to "lead America's foreign policy in the

twenty-first century." Its goals: cultivate a data culture, accelerate decisions through analytics, establish mission-driven data management, and
enhance data governance. Well-intended and described as a "paradigm
shift," it nevertheless failed to provide a blueprint with cost/benefit trade-
offs to achieve these goals. Critics pointed to its few operational details
and its treatment of data as a product rather than central to the policy
process.[70]

Science and technology not only shape diplomacy's tools, they serve as
historically contingent metaphors for understanding diplomacy and
world politics. Newton's mechanistic physics in the seventeenth century
gave meaning to government-to-government relations, balance of power,
correspondence to an intrinsic reality "out there," and cause and effect in
rational choice diplomacy. When science vocabularies become outdated,
theorists adopt new metaphors. Newton's physics gave way to quantum
physics. Notably it was a practitioner, former Secretary of State George
Shultz, who introduced the term "quantum diplomacy" in 1997 when he
compared diplomacy to this quantum theory axiom: "when you observe
and measure some part of a system, you inevitably disturb the whole
system." For Shultz, the process of observation and selectivity (such as a
TV camera) causes distortions in systems (such as diplomacy) in which
information and knowledge are raw materials.[71]

A quarter century later, quantum theory emerged full flower in diplomacy and international relations through the speculative insights of
James Der Derian, Alexander Wendt, and other scholars. Quantum
approaches are superior to classical physics, they argue, for their potential
to provide meaning in international relations and operational effect in
diplomacy, war, and addressing human needs. Quantum is ascending in
a world where observers and reality are seen to be interdependent, computers with new algorithms are blindingly fast, and "big data" processing
has potential to make "wicked problems" more solvable. Enthusiasts
expect quantum computing, communications, and artificial intelligence
(AI) to transform "the nature, production, and distribution of power and
knowledge." They debate "when, how and at what scale quantum behavior is actual, potential or 'merely' metaphorical."[72] Skeptics argue the
quantum turn constitutes an "imaginary" by which we know and interpret the world. There is no correspondence between quantum as theory

and a truthful reality "out there"—only the possibility of an interpretive consensus that is better for now than any imagined alternative.[73]

The "cash value" of theoretical debates for diplomacy practitioners turns on quantum's operational relevance. Corporations, governments, and foundations are investing billions in quantum's potential. Quantum theory, which enabled technologies from nuclear fission to mobile phones, former US diplomat Stephen Del Rosso observes, holds promise for new medicines, fertilizer production, carbon dioxide extraction, and improved power grids.[74] Fp21, a nonpartisan thinktank populated by scholars and practitioners, "aims to support a new generation of government officials eager to inject data and rigor into the policy process." Their recommendations seek to achieve evidence-based diplomacy, strengthen personnel and organizational structures, and foster a new culture of data literate practitioners.[75]

Conclusion

This book began with the diplomacy of European settlers and Native Americans in seventeenth-century North America. Theirs was a bridging of differences in a complex mix of state, sub-state, and non-state actors. Publics were both participants in their diplomacy and objects of their diplomacy. Government leaders, appointed "go-betweens," soldiers, and traders stepped in and out of diplomatic roles. Boundaries between governance and civil society were porous. Digitalization and the Internet were unimaginable, but wampum, Covenant Chains, and print technology had their own complexities in diplomacy between literate and oral societies. Then as now, diplomacy evolved with trends in the environment—epidemics, new technologies, population growth, and increasingly dense webs of global and local connections. In many ways, their diplomacy is more comparable to the twenty-first century's "societized diplomacy" than the state-centric diplomacy of the nineteenth and twentieth centuries.

Today's diplomacy is in the midst of one paradigm shift, societized diplomacy, and on the cusp of a second but related paradigm shift: the potential for powerful new artificial intelligence technologies to transform society. A tsunami of discourse is now emerging on how AI has evolved from a seemingly manageable tool to large creative models with existential risk and power to fundamentally change how people live, fight, and collaborate. AI's generative systems are black boxes known only by inputs and outputs, not by their internal processes. A technology that can "think" better and act "faster" than humans and their institutions is raising extraordinary concerns by experts.[76] How AI will change diplomacy is a conversation diplomacy scholars and practitioners are only beginning to have, and it is beyond the scope of this book.[77]

But the societization of diplomacy is an older conversation. It has generated a large literature and important questions. Diplomacy scholar Jan Melissen writes about a "new public diplomacy" as an activity "woven into the fabric of mainstream diplomatic activity." Today, governments and foreign ministries are turning more toward "dialogue with 'ordinary people'—the smallest units of society—in their domestic environments."[78] For Geoffrey Wiseman, diplomacy's boundaries are shifting in complex ways. Building on state-centric *bilateral* diplomacy (state-state relations) and *multilateral* diplomacy (relations between three or more states), his typology adds *polylateral* diplomacy (state-non-state relations) and *omnilateral* diplomacy (relations between non-state entities).[79]

"Sovereignty free" diplomacy actors are no longer viewed as unusual or an oxymoron. Scholars identify global firms, foundations, museums, churches, celebrities, sports associations, and social media influencers, examples from a very long list.[80] Some, however, have stretched diplomacy to include almost any individual or group seeking to negotiate interests and social meaning. Costas M. Constantinou's humanistic approach treats diplomacy as a "knowledge practice" and "mode of living." In his definition, "diplomacy is about *how we can live together in difference* [emphasis in the original]."[81] R.S. Zaharna's humanity-centered diplomacy argues assumptions of separateness are no longer sustainable. She breaks from a sovereignty-centric diplomacy that reinforces difference and neglects human needs to support a diplomacy that increasingly aligns with shared needs and goals of humanity.[82]

Shifting boundaries and thicker government/society connections raise a fundamental question. Is it still necessary to distinguish between diplomacy and other forms of social interaction? Yes. We need boundaries because not all political and social actors are diplomats and much that happens in governance and society is not diplomacy.

Three boundaries are essential. First, diplomatic actors are agents. They represent governance actors and the interests, values, and goals of groups—understood as both foreign policies of states and solutions to shared problems pursued in humanity-centered collaboration. Second, diplomacy is an instrument of governments and governance, meaning rules and norms that steer human collectives. This boundary distinguishes diplomacy from cross-cultural cosmopolitanism and other categories of connection such as global markets. A third boundary rests on a distinction between public and private interests. Diplomatic actors are accountable to the public interests of groups as a whole. Private interests motivate firms and most civil society actors in sectoral domains—markets, journalism, religion, education, issue-based activism. We need to keep these boundaries even as societization creates hugely complex conceptual and operational gray zones. As Vincent Pouliot argues persuasively, "if doing diplomacy becomes essentially the same as practicing human relationships ... then the notion risks becoming redundant and could lose its utility and specificity."[83]

America's diplomacy practitioners exist in a diplomacy that is whole of government and more whole of society. The institutionalization of US diplomacy's public dimension that began in World War I is now firmly embedded in multiple practitioner communities with well-established modus operandi. Changes required by today's complexities can be addressed most effectively by practitioners with broad lateral knowledge in a culture of learning, who are not risk averse, who put diplomacy first as they integrate new technologies, who are skilled at convening and connecting others in government and civil society to diplomatic advantage, and who are imaginative in coping with the constraints of the American way of diplomacy.

By the time these words are read, it is a safe bet that geopolitics, global issues, leaders, practitioners, and technologies will have materially changed. But it is likely the following characteristics of today's diplomacy will remain. Change's arrow points to the centrality of diplomacy's public dimension in the relations of states, associations of states, and some substate and non-state entities. Foreign ministries will remain important.

They have unique advantages that can strengthen the diplomacy of other government departments, military services, cities, and civil society organizations with standing in global governance. These diplomatic actors will bridge differences *between* groups and navigate politics *within* the groups they connect at home and abroad. As they have in the past, innovative practitioners in rival communities of practice will achieve change that blends adaptation and degrees of transformation. This book has identified ways this should happen in the American context. There are other contexts and other possibilities, and it is prudent to keep in mind that surprise confounds forecasts.

Notes

1. William J. Burns and Linda Thomas-Greenfield, "The Transformation of Diplomacy: How to Save the State Department," *Foreign Affairs* 100, no. 6 (November/December, 2020): 100–112; Anne-Marie Slaughter, "Reinventing the State Department," *Democracy: A Journal of Ideas*, September 15, 2020; Nicholas Burns, Marc Grossman, and Marcie Ries, *American Diplomacy Project: A U.S. Diplomatic Service for the 21st Century* (Harvard Kennedy School, 2020); Uzra S. Zeya and John Finer, *Revitalizing the State Department and American Diplomacy* (Council on Foreign Relations, 2020).
2. White House, "Remarks by President Biden Before the 76th Session of the United Nations General Assembly," September 21, 2021.
3. Harry W. Kopp and John K. Naland, *Career Diplomacy: Life and Work in the US Foreign Service* (Georgetown University Press, 2021), 30–34.
4. Burns and Thomas-Greenfield, "Transformation of Diplomacy."
5. Quoted in Kopp and Naland, *Career Diplomacy*, 67.
6. Wes Jeffers and Katherine Tarr, "Looking Back, Moving Forward: Public Diplomacy at 20," *American Ambassadors Review*, Fall 2019.
7. Quoted in Kopp and Naland, *Career Diplomacy*, 68.
8. US Department of State, Bureau of Global Public Affairs, https://www.state.gov.
9. US Department of State, Bureau of Educational and Cultural Affairs, "ECA Functional Bureau Strategy," "External Strategy Crosswalk," "Monitoring Data for ECA (MODE) Framework," https://eca.state.

gov/impact/eca-monitoring-evaluation-learning-and-innovation-meli-unit/mode-reporting (accessed May 22, 2023).

10. *2020 Comprehensive Annual Report on Public Diplomacy and International Broadcasting*, US Advisory Commission on Public Diplomacy Reports, 15–16, 33.

11. *US International Broadcasting: Background and Issues for Reform* (Congressional Research Service, 2016); *2018 Comprehensive Annual Report on Public Diplomacy and International Broadcasting*, US Advisory Commission on Public Diplomacy Reports, 41; *U.S. Agency for Global Media: Additional Action Needed to Improve Oversight of Broadcasting Networks* (US Government Accountability Office, 2021). For an overview of US government media in the 2020s, see Shawn Powers, "International Broadcasting," in Gilboa, *Research Agenda*, 231–248.

12. Department of State, *Targeted Inspection of the U.S. Agency for Global Media: Editorial Independence and Journalistic Standards and Principles*, Office of Inspector General, 2022.

13. Sarah Ellison and Paul Farhi, "New Voice of America Overseer Called Foreign Journalists a Security Risk. Now the Staff is Revolting," *Washington Post*, September 2, 2020; Paul Farhi, "Controversial Head of Voice of America Resigns Hours After President Biden Takes Office," *Washington Post*, January 20, 2021; Martha Bayles, "News They Can Use," *National Affairs* 46 (Winter 2021).

14. US Office of Special Counsel, *Review of Management Actions June 2020-February 2021* (2023).

15. Kevin Baron, "Mattis to Generals: Start Talking to the Press," *Defense One* (blog), October 9, 2017, https://www.defenseone.com/policy/2017/10/mattis-generals-start-talking-press/141639/.

16. James Mattis to the Department of Defense, memorandum, "Information as a Joint Function," September 15, 2017, https://www.rmda.army.mil/records-management/docs/SECDEF-Endorsement_Information_Joint%20Function_Clean.pdf (accessed May 20, 2023).

17. Joint Chiefs of Staff, *Joint Operations*, JP 3.0 (January 17, 2017, incorporating change 1, October 22, 2018), xiii, III-17–III-27, https://irp.fas.org/doddir/dod/jp3_0.pdf.

18. Scott K. Thomson and Christopher E. Paul, "Paradigm Change: Operational Art and the Information Joint Function," *Joint Force Quarterly* 89, 2nd Quarter (2018): 12–13.

19. Gregory M. Tomlin, "The Case for an Information Warfighting Function," *Military Review* (September–October, 2021): 90–99.

20. "Countering Coups: How to Help Rebuild Democratic Rule" (US Institute of Peace, 2022); Miriam Berger, "U.S. Listed as a 'Backsliding' Democracy for First Time in Report by European Think Tank," *Washington Post*, November 22, 2021.

21. William A. Galston and Elaine Kamarck, *Is Democracy Failing and Putting Our Economic System at Risk?* (Brookings, 2022).

22. Frances Z. Brown and Thomas Carothers, "Democracy Talk is Cheap," *Foreign Affairs*, January 10, 2022.

23. Yascha Mounk, "Democracy on the Defense: Turning Back the Authoritarian Tide," *Foreign Affairs* 100, no. 2 (March/April, 2021): 163–173.

24. Larry Diamond, "All Democracy is Global: Why America Can't Shrink from the Fight for Freedom," *Foreign Affairs* 101, no. 5 (September/October, 2022): 184–185.

25. Anne Applebaum, "The Autocrats are Winning," *The Atlantic* (December 2021), 53.

26. Michael McFaul, "ACPD Official Meeting Minutes: April 13, 2023," US Advisory Commission on Public Diplomacy, https://www.state.gov/acpd-official-meeting-minutes-april-13-2023/.

27. Michael McFaul, "It's Time to Up Our Democracy Promotion Game," *American Purpose*, November 12, 2021.

28. Department of State, Global Engagement Center, https://www.state.gov/bureaus-offices/under-secretary-for-public-diplomacy-and-public-affairs/global-engagement-center/.

29. Glenn Thrush, "Biden Signs $770 Billion Defense Bill," *New York Times*, December 27, 2021; Department of State, "State Department and U.S. Agency for International Development (USAID) FY 2022 Budget Request," May 28, 2021.

30. Department of Defense, *Defense Science Board Task Force on Strategic Communication* (2004), 62–65; Department of Defense, *Defense Science Board Task Force on Strategic Communication* (2007), 94–95.

31. Thom Shanker, "U.S. Fails to Explain Policies to Muslim World, Panel Says," *New York Times*, November 24, 2004. Senators Richard Lugar and Joseph Biden introduced a bill to enact the DSB's recommendations. Rep. Mac Thornberry did so in the House. The bills were not enacted.

32. White House, *National Framework for Strategic Communication*, n.d. [circa March 2010], https://man.fas.org/eprint/pubdip.pdf (accessed May 20, 2023).

33. *2019 Comprehensive Annual Report on Public Diplomacy & International Broadcasting*, US Advisory Commission on Public Diplomacy Reports, 22.

34. White House "President Biden Announces John Kirby as NSC Coordinator for Strategic Communications," May 20, 2022.

35. Senate Committee on Foreign Relations, "Chairman Menendez Celebrates Passage of State Department Authorization Bill," December 15, 2021.

36. Public Law No: 117-263, Sections 9601–9604, December 23, 2022.

37. Department of State, "Secretary Antony J. Blinken on the Modernization of American Diplomacy," October 27, 2021; Gordon Adams, *Responsible Statecraft Requires Remaking America's Foreign Relations Tool Kit* (Quincy Institute, 2021).

38. Department of State, *Review of the Public Diplomacy Staffing Initiative*, Office of Inspector General, April 2021; *Putting Policy & Audience First: A Public Diplomacy Paradigm Shift (2021)*, US Advisory Commission on Public Diplomacy Reports, 3, 7; *2022 Comprehensive Annual Report on Public Diplomacy and International Broadcasting*, US Advisory Commission on Public Diplomacy Reports, 17, 23. PDSI's change agents included Amelia Arsenault, Kelly Daniel, Roya Ellis, Jennifer Hall Godfrey, and Paul Kruchoski in the Office of the Under Secretary, and Vivian Walker and Shawn Baxter on the Commission's staff.

39. *Putting Policy & Audience First*, Advisory Commission, 24.

40. US Agency for Global Media. *Truth Over Disinformation: Supporting Freedom and Democracy, USAGM Strategic Plan 2022–2026*, March 2022.

41. Zed Tarar, "Analysis | When a Crisis Ensues, Embrace Dynamic Teams," *The Diplomatic Pouch* (blog), February 15, 2022, https://medium.com/the-diplomatic-pouch/analysis-when-a-crisis-ensues-embrace-dynamic-teams-6d2acf1a0d77; Robert Domainque, "Why the State Department Needs an Office of Diplomatic Gaming," *Foreign Service Journal* 99, no. 9 (November 2022): 21–23.

42. Lawrence Freedman, *Strategy: A History* (Oxford University Press, 2013), 607–615.

43. Thomas L. Friedman and Michael Mandelbaum, *That Used to Be Us: How America Fell Behind in the World It Invented and How We Can Come Back* (Farrar, Straus and Giroux, 2010), 81–98.
44. Burns and Thomas-Greenfield, "Transformation of Diplomacy," 106.
45. Slaughter, "Reinventing the State Department."
46. Roxanne Cabral, et al., *Diplomacy for a Diffuse World* (Atlantic Council, 2014).
47. Maryum Saifee, "Subnational Diplomacy: A National Security Imperative," *Foreign Service Journal* 99, no. 1 (January-February 2022): 22–24; FSJ Editorial Board, "On a New Approach to City and State Diplomacy," *Foreign Service Journal* 99, no. 1 (January-February 2022): 20–21.
48. Richard Haass, "Present at the Destruction," *Foreign Affairs*, January 11, 2021; Andrew Bacevich, *After the Apocalypse: America's Role in a World Transformed* (Metropolitan Books, 2021), 157; Suzy Hansen, "The End of the End of American Exceptionalism," *New York Magazine*, July 2, 2021; Ian Tyrrell, *American Exceptionalism: A New History of an Old Idea* (University of Chicago Press, 2021), 19, 207.
49. Dickson, *History Shock*, 205, 210–212; Niebuhr, *Irony of American History*, 174.
50. John Lewis Gaddis, *George Kennan: An American Life* (Penguin Press, 2011), 55.
51. William J. Burns, "The Lost Art of American Diplomacy: Can the State Department Be Saved?" *Foreign Affairs* 98, no. 3 (May/June, 2019): 98–107.
52. David C. Miller, Jr., Thomas R. Pickering, and Rand Beers, "Revitalizing State—Closing the Education Gap," *Foreign Service Journal* 98, no. 4 (May 2021): 20–21.
53. Burns, Grossman, and Ries, *American Diplomacy Project*, 30; Miller, Pickering, and Beers, "Revitalizing State," 21.
54. David Miller, statement before the Subcommittee on State Department and USAID Management, Senate Foreign Relations Committee, hearing on "Training the Department of State's Workforce for the 21st Century," November 2, 2021, https://www.foreign.senate.gov/imo/media/doc/110221_Miller_Testimony2.pdf.
55. Burns, Grossman, and Ries, *American Diplomacy Project*, 32–34.
56. Blinken, "Modernization of American Diplomacy."

57. Zeya and Finer, *Revitalizing the State Department*, 27; Joshua J. Marcuse, statement before the Subcommittee on State Department and USAID Management, Senate Foreign Relations Committee, hearing on "Training the Department of State's Workforce for the 21st Century," November 2, 2021, https://www.foreign.senate.gov/imo/media/doc/110221_Marcuse_Testimony.pdf.

58. Burns, Grossman, and Ries, *American Diplomacy Project*, 7; Burns and Thomas-Greenfield, "Transformation of Diplomacy," 104–105; Zeya and Finer, *Revitalizing the State Department*, 30.

59. Burns, Grossman, and Ries, *American Diplomacy Project*, 45.

60. Ted Wilkinson, "AFSA Views: Calling Up Our Own Reserves," *Foreign Service Journal* 67, no. 11 (November 1990): 2; Susan R. Johnson, "President's Views: Time for the Foreign Service Reserve Corps," *Foreign Service Journal* 88, no. 1 (January 2011): 5; Richard Burt, Olin Robison, and Barry Fulton, *Reinventing Diplomacy in the Information Age* (Center for Strategic and International Studies, 1998), 61–62; Public Diplomacy Council to the Department of State, "Proposal to Create a Public Diplomacy Reserve Corps," June 13, 2002, author's copy.

61. Burns and Thomas-Greenfield, "Transformation of Diplomacy," 104.

62. Lord, *Voices of America*, 17–30; Department of Defense, *Defense Science Board Task Force on Strategic Communication* (2007), 88–95; Council on Foreign Relations Task Force, *Finding America's Voice: A Strategy for Reinvigorating US Public Diplomacy* (Council on Foreign Relations, 2003).

63. Burt et al., *Reinventing Diplomacy*, 60.

64. Burns, Grossman, and Ries, *American Diplomacy Project*, 21, 39; Burns and Thomas-Greenfield, "Transformation of Diplomacy," 106; Zeya and Finer, *Revitalizing the State Department*, 24; Richard Haass, "The Case for Messy Multilateralism," *Financial Times*, January 5, 2010.

65. Rana, *21st Century Diplomacy*, 254.

66. Department of State, *Evaluation of the Department of State's Use of Schedule B Hiring Authority*, Office of Inspector General, 2019; David Nyczepir, "State Department Launching New Assessment Based Recruitment Process for Data Scientists," FEDSCOOP, March 25, 2022.

67. Burns, Grossman, and Ries, *American Diplomacy Project*, 41; Anne-Marie Slaughter, testimony before the Subcommittee on State Department and USAID Management, Senate Committee on Foreign Relations, July 20, 2021, https://www.foreign.senate.gov/imo/media/doc/072021_Slaughter_Testimony.pdf.

68. Mark Grossman and Marcie Ries, *Blueprints for a More Modern U.S. Diplomatic Service* (The American Diplomacy Project II, Arizona State University, 2022); Mark Grossman and Marcie Ries, "Toward a More Modern Foreign Service: Next Steps," *Foreign Service Journal* 100, no. 3 (March 2023): 23–26.

69. Marta Churella, et al., "Upgrading US Public Diplomacy: A New Approach for the Age of Memes and Disinformation" (Atlantic Council, September 15, 2021).

70. Department of State, *Enterprise Data Strategy: Empowering Data Informed Diplomacy*, 2021; Dan Spokojny, "State's New Data Strategy: A (potentially) historic step," *fp21* (blog), September 2021, https://www.fp21.org/publications/states-new-data-strategy-data-informed-diplomacy.

71. George P. Shultz, "Diplomacy in the Information Age" (US Institute of Peace, 1997), 15.

72. James Der Derian and Alexander Wendt, *Quantum International Relations: A Human Science for World Politics* (Oxford University Press, 2022); James Der Derian and Alexander Wendt, "'Quantizing International Relations': The Case for Quantum Approaches to International Theory and Security Practice," *Security Dialogue* 51, no. 5 (2020): 399–413.

73. Christopher McIntosh, review of *Quantum Social Theory for Critical International Relations Scholars, Quantizing Critique*, by Michael Murphy, H-Diplo Review Essay 385, November 3, 2021.

74. Stephen J. Del Rosso, "Making the Case for Quantum International Relations" (Carnegie Corporation of New York, June 2, 2022).

75. *Less Art, More Science: Transforming U.S. Foreign Policy Through Evidence, Integrity, and Innovation* (fp21, September 8, 2020).

76. "The Age of Pseudocognition," *The Economist*, April 22, 2023, 15–16.

77. Ilan Manor, "The AI Moves In: ChatGPT's Impact on Digital Diplomacy," *CPD* (blog), March 10, 2023, https://uscpublicdiplomacy.org/blog/ai-moves-chatgpt's-impact-digital-diplomacy.

78. Jan Melissen, *Beyond the New Public Diplomacy* (Netherlands Institute of International Relations 'Clingendael,' 2011); Jan Melissen and HwaJung Kim, "The Democratic Elite, The People at Home and Democratic Renewal," *CPD* (blog), November 4, 2022, https://uscpublicdiplomacy.org/blog/diplomatic-elite-people-home-and-democratic-renewal.

79. Wiseman, "Public Diplomacy and Hostile Nations," 151. Wiseman defines his fourth dimension as "*the conduct of relations between at least two non-state entities, with a modicum of international standing, in which there is a reasonable expectation of systematic relationships, involving some form of reporting, communication, negotiation and representation, but not involving mutual recognition as sovereign, equivalent entities* [emphasis in the original]."

80. Bernard Badie, "Transnationalizing Diplomacy in a Post-Westphalian World," in Kerr and Wiseman, *Diplomacy in a Globalizing World*, 90–109; Alisher Faizullaev, *Diplomacy for Professionals and Everyone* (Brill Nijhoff, 2022), 32–34.

81. Costas M. Constantinou, "Between Statecraft and Humanism: Diplomacy and its Forms of Knowledge," *International Studies Review* 15, no. 2 (2013): 141–142.

82. R. S. Zaharna, *Boundary Spanners of Humanity: Three Logics of Communication and Public Diplomacy for Global Collaboration* (Oxford University Press, 2022).

83. Vincent Pouliot, "Beyond the Profession, Into the Everyday? Grasping the Politics of Diplomatic Practices," in Constantinou, et al., "Thinking with Diplomacy: Within and Beyond Practice Theory," *International Political Sociology* 15, no. 4 (2021): 566.

Selected Bibliography

Books and Book Chapters

Adams, Gordon and Shoon Murray, eds. *Mission Creep: The Militarization of US Foreign Policy.* Georgetown University Press, 2014.

Allison, Graham and Philip Zelikow. *Essence of Decision: Explaining the Cuban Missile Crisis,* 2nd ed. Longman, 1999.

Arndt, Richard T. *The First Resort of Kings.* Potomac Books, 2005.

Arsenault, Amelia. "Public Diplomacy 2.0." In *Toward a New Public Diplomacy: Redirecting US Foreign Policy,* edited by Philip Seib, 135–153. Palgrave Macmillan, 2009.

Barnhisel, Greg. *Cold War Modernists: Art, Literature, and American Cultural Diplomacy.* Columbia University Press, 2015.

Barrett, Edward T. *Truth is Our Weapon.* Funk & Wagnalls, 1953.

Barry, John M. *Roger Williams and the Creation of the American Soul: Church, State, and the Birth of Liberty.* Penguin Books, 2012.

Bjola, Corneliu and Marcus Holmes, eds. *Digital Diplomacy: Theory and Practice.* Routledge, 2018.

Blackhawk, Ned. *The Rediscovery of America: Native Peoples and the Unmaking of U.S. History.* Yale University Press, 2023.

© The Author(s), under exclusive license to Springer Nature Switzerland AG 2024   **443**
B. Gregory, *American Diplomacy's Public Dimension*, Palgrave Macmillan Series in Global Public Diplomacy, https://doi.org/10.1007/978-3-031-38917-7

————. *Violence Over the Land: Indians and Empire in the Early American West.* Harvard University Press, 2006.

Brooks, Rosa. *How Everything Became War and the Military Became Everything.* Simon & Schuster, 2016.

Burnett, Stanton H. "U.S. Informational and Cultural Programs." In *Public Diplomacy: USA Versus USSR,* edited by Richard F. Staar, 69–81. Hoover Institution Press, 1986.

Calloway, Colin G. *Pen and Ink Witchcraft: Treaties and Treaty Making in American Indian History.* Oxford University Press, 2013.

Carothers, Thomas. *Aiding Democracy Abroad: The Learning Curve.* Carnegie Endowment, 1999.

————. *Critical Mission: Essays on Democracy Promotion.* Carnegie Endowment, 2004.

Castells, Manuel. *Communication Power.* Oxford University Press, 2009.

Caute, David. *The Dancer Defects: The Struggle for Cultural Supremacy During the Cold War.* Oxford University Press, 2003.

Cave, Alfred A. *The Pequot War.* University of Massachusetts Press, 1996.

Chandrasekaran, Rajiv. *Little America: The War Within the War for Afghanistan.* Alfred A. Knopf, 2012.

Clark, Wesley K. *Waging Modern War.* PublicAffairs, 2001.

Clarke, Torie. *Lipstick on a Pig: Winning in the No-Spin Era with Someone Who Knows the Game.* Free Press, 2006.

Cohen, Eliot A. *Conquered into Liberty: Two Centuries of Battles Along the Great Warpath That Made the American Way of War.* Free Press, 2011.

Cohen, Raymond. "Diplomacy Through the Ages." In *Diplomacy in a Globalizing World,* 2nd ed., edited by Pauline Kerr and Geoffrey Wiseman, 21–36. Oxford University Press, 2018.

Coombs, Philip H. *The Fourth Dimension of Foreign Policy: Educational and Cultural Affairs.* Harper & Row, 1964.

Copeland, Daryl. *Guerrilla Diplomacy: Rethinking International Relations.* Lynne Rienner, 2009.

Cull, Nicholas J. *The Cold War and the United States Information Agency.* Cambridge University Press, 2008.

————. *The Decline and Fall of the United States Information Agency: American Public Diplomacy, 1989–2001.* Palgrave Macmillan, 2012.

————. *Public Diplomacy: Lessons from the Past.* Figueroa Press, 2009.

Dewey, John. *The Public and Its Problems.* Swallow Press, 1954. First published 1927 by Henry Holt and Company.

Diamond, Larry. *Ill Winds: Saving Democracy from Russian Rage, Chinese Ambition, and American Complacency.* Penguin Press, 2019.

Dickson, John. *History Shock: When History Collides with Foreign Relations.* University Press of Kansas, 2021.

Dowd, Gregory Evans. *Groundless: Rumors, Legends, and Hoaxes on the Early American Frontier.* Johns Hopkins University Press, 2015.

Doyle, Don H. *The Cause of All Nations: An International History of the American Civil War.* Basic Books, 2015.

Dunn, Charles W., ed. *American Exceptionalism.* Rowman & Littlefield, 2013.

Eicher, Peter D. *Raising the Flag: America's First Envoys in Faraway Lands.* Potomac Books, 2018.

Fisher, Glen H. *Mindsets: The Role of Culture and Perception in International Relations*, 2nd ed. Intercultural Press, 1997.

———. *Public Diplomacy and the Behavioral Sciences.* Indiana University Press, 1972.

Fitzpatrick, Kathy R. *The Future of US Public Diplomacy: An Uncertain Fate.* Martinus Nijhoff, 2010.

———. "Public Relations." In *A Research Agenda for Public Diplomacy*, edited by Eytan Gilboa, 139–152. Edward Elgar, 2023.

Foreman, Amanda. *A World on Fire: Britain's Crucial Role in the American Civil War.* Random House, 2010.

Frankel, Charles. *The Neglected Aspect of Foreign Affairs: American Educational and Cultural Policy Abroad.* Brookings, 1965.

Fulton, Barry, ed. *Dr. Walter R. Roberts: The Compleat Public Diplomat.* CreateSpace, 2016.

Gaddis, John Lewis. *The Landscape of History: How Historians Map the Past.* Oxford University Press, 2002.

Gienow-Hecht, Jessica C. E. and Mark C. Donfried, eds. *Searching for a Cultural Diplomacy.* Berghahn Books, 2010.

Gilboa, Eytan, ed. *A Research Agenda for Public Diplomacy.* Edward Elgar, 2023.

Gotlieb, Allan. *'I'll be with you in a minute, Mr. Ambassador': The Education of a Canadian Diplomat in Washington.* University of Toronto Press, 1991.

Graham, Sarah Ellen. *Culture and Propaganda: The Progressive Origins of American Public Diplomacy.* Ashgate Publishing Company, 2015.

Grandin, Greg. *The End of the Myth: From the Frontier to the Border Wall in the Mind of America.* Metropolitan Books, 2019.

Greenberg, David. *Republic of Spin: An Inside History of the American Presidency.* W. W. Norton, 2016.

Hall, Edward T. *The Silent Language*. Doubleday, 1959.

Hamilton, John Maxwell. *Manipulating the Masses: Woodrow Wilson and the Birth of American Propaganda*. Louisiana State University Press, 2020.

Hamilton, Keith and Richard Langhorne. *The Practice of Diplomacy: Its Evolution, Theory, and Administration*, 2nd ed. Routledge, 2011.

Harris, Mark. *Five Came Back: A Story of Hollywood and the Second World War*. Penguin Press, 2014.

Hart, Justin. *Empire of Ideas: The Origins of Public Diplomacy and the Transformation of U.S. Foreign Policy*. Oxford University Press, 2013.

Heil, Alan L. Jr. *Voice of America: A History*. Columbia University Press, 2003.

Heine, Jorge. "From Club to Network Diplomacy." In *The Oxford Handbook of Modern Diplomacy*, edited by Andrew F. Cooper, Jorge Heine, and Ramesh Thakur, 54–69. Oxford University Press, 2013.

Hench, John B. *Books as Weapons: Propaganda, Publishing, and the Battle for Global Markets in the Era of World War II*. Cornell University Press, 2010.

Henderson, John W. *The United States Information Agency*. Frederick A. Praeger, 1969.

Hill, Christopher R. *Outpost: Life on the Frontlines of American Diplomacy*. Simon & Schuster, 2014.

Hixson, Walter L. *Parting the Curtain: Propaganda, Culture, and the Cold War*. St. Martin's Griffin, 1997.

Hocking, Brian. "The Ministry of Foreign Affairs and the National Diplomatic System." In *Diplomacy in a Globalizing World*, 2nd ed., edited by Pauline Kerr and Geoffrey Wiseman, 129–149. Oxford University Press, 2018.

Holbrooke, Richard. *To End a War*. Random House, 1998.

Huijgh, Ellen. *Public Diplomacy at Home: Domestic Dimensions*. Brill | Nijhoff, 2019.

Immerwahr, Daniel. *How to Hide an Empire: A History of the Greater United States*. Picador, 2020.

Iriye, Akira. *Cultural Internationalism and World Order*. Johns Hopkins University Press, 1997.

Isaacson, Walter. *Benjamin Franklin: An American Life*. Simon & Schuster, 2003.

Israel, Jonathan. *The Expanding Blaze: How the American Revolution Ignited the World, 1775–1848*. Princeton University Press, 2017.

Jansen, Sue Curry. *Walter Lippmann: A Critical Introduction to Media and Communication Theory*. Peter Lang, 2012.

Jennings, Frances, ed. *The History and Culture of Iroquois Diplomacy: An Interdisciplinary Guide to the Treaties of the Six Nations and Their League.* Syracuse University Press, 1985.

Johansen, Bruce Elliott. *The Native Peoples of North America: A History.* Rutgers University Press, 2006.

Johnson, A. Ross. *Radio Free Europe and Radio Liberty: The CIA Years and Beyond.* Stanford University Press, 2010.

Johnson, A. Ross and R. Eugene Parta, eds. *Cold War Broadcasting: Impact on the Soviet Union and Eastern Europe.* Central European University Press, 2010.

Jones, Jeffrey B. "The Third Wave and the Fourth Dimension." In *Special Operations Forces: Roles and Missions in the Aftermath of the Cold War,* edited by Richard H. Schultz, Robert L. Pfaltzgraff, and W. Bradley Stock, 225–239. Diane Publishing, 1996.

Jönsson, Christer and Martin Hall. *Essence of Diplomacy.* Palgrave Macmillan, 2005.

Kerr, Pauline and Geoffrey Wiseman, eds. *Diplomacy in a Globalizing World,* 2nd ed. Oxford University Press, 2018.

Kiehl, William P., ed. *America's Dialogue with the World.* Public Diplomacy Council, 2006.

———, ed. *The Last Three Feet: Case Studies in Public Diplomacy.* Public Diplomacy Council, 2012.

Kopp, Harry W. *The Voice of the Foreign Service: A History of the American Foreign Service Association.* Foreign Service Books, 2015.

Kopp, Harry W. and John K. Naland. *Career Diplomacy: Life and Work in the US Foreign Service.* Georgetown University Press, 2021.

Lepore, Jill. *The Name of War: King Philip's War and the Origins of American Identity.* Vintage Books, 1999.

———. *These Truths: A History of the United States.* W.W. Norton, 2018.

Lippmann, Walter. *Public Opinion.* 1922. Reprinted with a foreword by Ronald Steel. Free Press Paperbacks, 1997.

Lord, Carnes. *Losing Hearts and Minds: Public Diplomacy and Strategic Influence in the Age of Terror.* Praeger Security International, 2006.

Malkasian, Carter. *War Comes to Garmser: Thirty Years of Conflict on the Afghan Frontier.* Oxford University Press, 2013.

Malone, Gifford D. *Political Advocacy and Cultural Communication: Organizing the Nation's Public Diplomacy.* University Press of America, 1988.

Mandelbaum, Michael. *The Ideas That Conquered the World: Peace, Democracy, and Free Markets in the Twenty-first Century.* PublicAffairs, 2004.

Manor, Ilan. *The Digitalization of Public Diplomacy.* Palgrave Macmillan, 2019.

Mazower, Mark. *Governing the World: The History of an Idea.* Penguin Press, 2012.

McCullough, David. *John Adams.* Simon & Schuster, 2001.

McFaul, Michael. *From Cold War to Hot Peace: An American Ambassador in Putin's Russia.* Houghton Mifflin Harcourt, 2018.

McMurry, Ruth and Muna Lee. *The Cultural Approach: Another Way in International Relations.* University of North Carolina Press, 1947.

Meacham, Jon. *The Soul of America: The Battle for Our Better Angels.* Random House, 2018.

———. *Thomas Jefferson: The Art of Power.* Random House, 2013.

Mead, Walter Russell. *Special Providence: American Foreign Policy and How It Changed the World.* Routledge, 2002.

Melissen, Jan, ed. *The New Public Diplomacy: Soft Power in International Relations.* Palgrave Macmillan, 2005.

Menand, Louis. *The Free World: Art and Thought in the Cold War.* Farrar, Straus and Giroux, 2021.

Merrell, James H. *Into the American Woods: Negotiators on the Pennsylvania Frontier.* W. W. Norton, 1999.

Meyer, Cord. *Facing Reality: From World Federalism to the CIA.* Harper and Row, 1980.

Mock, James and Cedric Larson. *Words That Won the War: The Story of the Committee on Public Information, 1917–1919.* Princeton University Press, 1939.

Muravchik, Joshua. *Exporting Democracy: Fulfilling America's Destiny.* AEI Press, 1992.

Nelson, Michael. *War of the Black Heavens: The Battles of Western Broadcasting in the Cold War.* Syracuse University Press, 1997.

Neumann, Iver B. *At Home with the Diplomats: Inside a European Foreign Ministry.* Cornell University Press, 2012.

Nickles, David Paull. *Under the Wire: How the Telegraph Changed Diplomacy.* Harvard University Press, 2003.

Niebuhr, Reinhold. *The Irony of American History.* 1952. Reprinted with an introduction by Andrew J. Bacevich. University of Chicago Press, 2008.

Ninkovich, Frank. *The Diplomacy of Ideas: U.S. Foreign Policy and Cultural Relations, 1938–1950.* Cambridge University Press, 1981.

———. *The Global Republic: America's Inadvertent Rise to World Power.* University of Chicago Press, 2014.

Nye, Joseph S. Jr. *The Future of Power.* PublicAffairs, 2011.

————. *Soft power: The Means to Success in World Politics.* PublicAffairs, 2004.

Osgood, Kenneth. *Total Cold War: Eisenhower's Secret Propaganda Battle at Home and Abroad.* University Press of Kansas, 2006.

Paget, Karen M. *Patriotic Betrayal.* Yale University Press, 2015.

Pamment, James. *New Public Diplomacy in the 21st Century: A Comparative Study of Policy and Practice.* Routledge, 2013.

Paul, Christopher. *Strategic Communication: Origins, Concepts, and Current Debates.* Praeger, 2011.

Peraino, Kevin. *Lincoln in the World: The Making of a Statesman and the Dawn of American Power.* Crown Publishers, 2013.

Pomar, Mark G. *Cold War Radio: The Russian Broadcasts of the Voice of America and Radio Free Europe/Radio Liberty.* Potomac Books, 2022.

Pool, Ithiel de Sola, Frederick W. Frey, Wilbur Schramm, Nathan Maccoby, and Edwin B. Parker, eds. *Handbook of Communication.* Rand McNally, 1973.

Powers, Shawn. "International Broadcasting." In *Research Agenda for Public Diplomacy,* edited by Eytan Gilboa, 231–247. Edward Elgar, 2023.

Price, Monroe E. *Media and Sovereignty: The Global Information Revolution and Its Challenge to State Power.* MIT Press, 2002.

Rana, Kishan S. *21st Century Diplomacy: A Practitioner's Guide.* Continuum International, 2011.

Richmond, Yale. *Cultural Exchange and the Cold War: Raising the Iron Curtain.* Pennsylvania State University Press, 2003.

————. *Practicing Public Diplomacy: A Cold War Odyssey.* Berghahn Books, 2008.

Richter, Paul. *The Ambassadors: American Diplomacy on the Front Lines.* Simon & Schuster, 2019.

Rothkopf, David. *Running the World: The Inside Story of the National Security Council and the Architects of American Power.* PublicAffairs, 2005.

Rugh, William A., ed. *Engaging the Arab & Islamic Worlds Through Public Diplomacy.* Public Diplomacy Council, 2004.

————. *Front Line Diplomacy: How U.S. Embassies Communicate with Foreign Publics.* Palgrave Macmillan, 2014.

Saunders, Frances Stonor. *The Cultural Cold War: The CIA and the World of Arts and Letters.* New Press, 2000.

Schindler, Caitlin E. *The Origins of Public Diplomacy in US Statecraft.* Palgrave Macmillan, 2018.

Scott-Smith, Giles. "Cultural Diplomacy." In *Global Diplomacy: Theories, Types and Models,* edited by Alison R. Holmes and J. Simon Rofe, 176–190. Westview Press, 2016.

———. "International Exchanges." In *Research Agenda for Public Diplomacy*, edited by Eytan Gilboa, 249–264. Edward Elgar, 2023.

———. *The Politics of Apolitical Culture: The Congress for Cultural Freedom and the Political Economy of American Hegemony 1945–1955*. Routledge, 2002.

Seib, Philip, ed. *Toward a New Public Diplomacy: Reflecting U.S. Foreign Policy*. Palgrave Macmillan, 2009.

Shannon, Timothy. *Indians and Colonists at the Crossroads of Empire: The Albany Congress of 1754*. Cornell University Press. 2000.

———. *Iroquois Diplomacy on the Early American Frontier*. Penguin Books, 2008.

Sharp, Paul. *Diplomatic Theory of International Relations*. Cambridge University Press, 2009.

Shirky, Clay. *Here Comes Everybody*. Penguin Books, 2008.

Slaughter, Anne-Marie. *The Idea That Is America*. Basic Books, 2007.

———. *A New World Order*. Princeton University Press, 2004.

Smith, Paul A. Jr. *On Political War*. National Defense University Press, 1989.

Smith, Tony. *America's Mission: The United States and the Worldwide Struggle for Democracy*. Princeton University Press, 2012.

Snow, Nancy and Nicholas J. Cull, eds. *Routledge Handbook of Public Diplomacy*, 2nd ed. Routledge, 2020.

Snow, Nancy and Philip M. Taylor, eds. *Routledge Handbook of Public Diplomacy*. Routledge, 2009.

Sorenson, Thomas C. *The Word War: The Story of American Propaganda*. Harper & Row, 1968.

Stahr, Walter. *Seward: Lincoln's Indispensable Man*. Simon & Schuster, 2013.

Steel, Ronald. *Walter Lippmann and the American Century*. Transaction Publishers, 1999.

Taylor, Alan. *American Colonies: The Settling of North America*. Penguin Books, 2001.

———. *American Republics: A Continental History of the United States, 1783–1850*. W. W. Norton, 2021.

———. *American Revolutions: A Continental History, 1750–1804*. W. W. Norton, 2016.

Taylor, Philip M. *Global Communications, International Affairs and the Media Since 1945*. Routledge, 1997.

———. *Munitions of the Mind: A History of Propaganda from the Ancient World to the Present Day*, 3rd ed. Manchester University Press, 2003.

Thompson-Jones, Mary. *To the Secretary: Leaked Embassy Cables and America's Foreign Policy Disconnect*. W. W. Norton, 2016.

Thomson, Charles A. H. *Overseas Information Service of the United States Government.* Brookings, 1948.

Thomson, Charles A. H. and Walter H. C. Laves. *Cultural Relations and U.S. Foreign Policy: A New Dimension in Foreign Relations, Education, Science, Art, and Technical Skills.* University of Indiana Press, 1963.

Tomlin, Gregory M. *Murrow's Cold War: Public Diplomacy for the Kennedy Administration.* Potomac Books, 2016.

Tuch, Hans N. *Communicating with the World: U.S. Public Diplomacy Overseas.* St. Martin's Press, 1990.

Tyrrell, Ian. *American Exceptionalism: A New History of an Old Idea.* University of Chicago Press, 2021.

Wainwright, Nicholas B. *George Croghan, Wilderness Diplomat.* University of North Carolina Press, 1959.

Weston, J. Kael. *The Mirror Test: America at War in Iraq and Afghanistan.* Vintage Books, 2016.

Whitman, Daniel, ed. *Outsmarting Apartheid: An Oral History of South Africa's Cultural and Educational Exchange with the United States, 1960–1999.* State University of New York Press, 2014.

Wilford, Hugh. *The Mighty Wurlitzer: How the CIA Played America.* Harvard University Press, 2008.

Winkler, Alan. *The Politics of Propaganda: The Office of War Information 1942–1945.* Yale University Press, 1978.

Wiseman, Geoffrey. "Diplomacy." In *The Sage Handbook of Political Science,* edited by Dirk Berg-Schlosser, Bertrand Badie, and Leonardo Morlino, 1193–1213. Sage, 2020.

———. "Distinctive Characteristics of American Diplomacy." In *American Diplomacy,* edited by Paul Sharp and Geoffrey Wiseman, 1–25. Martinus Nijhoff Publishers, 2012.

———. "'Polylateralism' and New Modes of Global Dialogue." In *Diplomacy: Problems and Issues in Contemporary Diplomacy,* edited by Christer Jönsson and Richard Langhorne, 36–57. Sage, 2004.

Wolfe, Audra J. *Freedom's Laboratory: The Cold War Struggle for the Soul of Science.* Johns Hopkins University Press, 2018.

Zaharna, R. S. *Battles to Bridges: U.S. Strategic Communication and Public Diplomacy After 9/11.* Palgrave Macmillan, 2010.

———. *Boundary Spanners of Humanity: Three Logics of Communication and Public Diplomacy for Global Collaboration.* Oxford University Press, 2022.

Zaharna, R. S., Amelia Arsenault, and Ali Fisher, eds. *Relational, Networked and Collaborative Approaches to Public Diplomacy: The Connective Mindshift.* Routledge, 2013.

Zegart, Amy B. *Flawed By Design: The Evolution of the CIA, JCS, and NSC.* Stanford University Press, 1999.

Zimmerman, Warren. *First Great Triumph: How Five Americans Made Their Country a World Power.* Farrar, Straus and Giroux, 2002.

Zuckerman, Ethan. *Rewire: Digital Cosmopolitans in the Age of Connection.* W. W. Norton, 2013.

Journal Articles

Adler, Emanuel and Vincent Pouliot. "Fulfilling the Promises of Practice Theory in IR." *The Practice Turn in International Relations: An International Studies Quarterly Online Symposium.* July 23, 2017: 2–4.

Adler-Nissen, Rebecca and Kristin Anabel Eggeling. "Blended Diplomacy: The Entanglement and Contestation of Digital Technologies in Everyday Diplomatic Practice." *European Journal of International Relations* 28, no. 3 (2022): 640–666.

Amend, Kurt. "The Diplomat as Counterinsurgent." *Foreign Service Journal* 86, no. 9 (September 2009): 21–27.

Brown, John L. "But What Do You Do?" *Foreign Service Journal* 41, no. 6 (June 1964): 23–25.

Burns, William J. and Linda Thomas-Greenfield. "The Transformation of Diplomacy: How to Save the State Department." *Foreign Affairs* 99, no. 6 (November/December 2020): 100–112.

Castells, Manuel. "The New Public Sphere: Global Civil Society, Communication Networks, and Global Governance." *The Annals of the American Academy of Political and Social Science* 616, no. 1 (March 2008): 78–93.

Constantinou, Costas M., Jason Ditmer, Merje Kuus, Fiona McConnell, Sam Okoth Opondo, and Vincent Pouliot. "Thinking with Diplomacy: Within and Beyond Practice Theory." *International Political Sociology* 15, no. 4 (December 2021): 559–587.

Cowan, Geoffrey and Amelia Arsenault, "Moving from Monologue to Dialogue to Collaboration." *The Annals of the American Academy of Political and Social Science* 616, no. 1 (March 2008): 10–30.

Cull, Nicholas J. "Public Diplomacy: Taxonomies and Histories." *The Annals of the American Academy of Political and Social Science* 616, no. 1 (March 2008): 31–54.

Dewey, John. "Review of 'Public Opinion' by Walter Lippmann." *New Republic* 30, no. 387 (May 3, 1922): 286–288.

Gilboa, Eytan. "Searching for a Theory of Public Diplomacy." *The Annals of the American Academy of Political and Social Science* 616, no. 1 (March 2008): 55–77.

Gregory, Bruce. "American Public Diplomacy: Enduring Characteristics, Elusive Transformation." *The Hague Journal of Diplomacy* 6, no. 3–4 (March 2011): 351–372.

———. "Mapping Boundaries in Diplomacy's Public Dimension." *The Hague Journal of Diplomacy* 11, no. 1 (November 2016): 1–25.

———. "Public Diplomacy: Sunrise of an Academic Field." *The Annals of the American Academy of Political and Social Science* 616, no. 1 (March 2008): 274–290.

Grossman, Mark and Marcie Ries. "Toward a More Modern Foreign Service: Next Steps." *Foreign Service Journal* 100, no. 3 (March 2023): 23–26.

Huijgh, Ellen, ed. "The Domestic Dimension of Public Diplomacy." *The Hague Journal of Diplomacy* 7, no. 4 (2012).

Keith, Kenton. "Troubled Takeover: The Demise of USIA." *Foreign Service Journal* 76, no. 9 (September 1999): 18–23.

Kelley, John Robert. "The New Diplomacy: Evolution of a Revolution." *Diplomacy & Statecraft* 21, no. 2 (2010): 286–305.

La Porte, Teresa. "The Impact of 'Intermestic' Non-State Actors on the Conceptual Framework of Public Diplomacy." *The Hague Journal of Diplomacy* 7, no. 4 (2012): 441–458.

Lord, Carnes. "The Past and Future of Public Diplomacy." *Orbis* 42 (Winter 1998): 49–72.

Lucas, Scott. "Campaigns of Truth: The Psychological Strategy Board and American Ideology, 1951–1953." *The International History Review* 18, no. 2 (May 1996): 279–302.

Malkasian, Carter and J. Kael Weston. "War Downsized: How to Accomplish More with Less." *Foreign Affairs* 91, no. 2 (March/April 2012): 111–121.

Parry-Giles, Shawn J. "The Eisenhower Administration's Conceptualization of the USIA: The Development of Overt and Covert Propaganda Strategies." *Presidential Studies Quarterly* 24, no. 2 (Spring 1994): 263–276.

Pouliot, Vincent and Jeremy Cornblut. "Practice Theory and the Study of Diplomacy." *Cooperation and Conflict* 50, no. 3 (September 2015): 297–315.

Price, Monroe, Susan Haas, and Drew Margolin. "New Technologies and International Broadcasting: Reflections on Adaptations and Transformations." *The Annals of the American Academy of Political and Social Science* 616, no. 1 (March 2008): 150–172.

Roberts, Walter R. "The Evolution of Diplomacy." *Mediterranean Quarterly* 17, no. 3 (Summer 2006): 55–64.

Ross, Christopher. "Public Diplomacy Comes of Age." *The Washington Quarterly* 25, no. 2 (Spring 2002): 75–83.

Roth, Lois W. "Public Diplomacy: 1952–1977." *The Fletcher Forum* 8 (Summer 1984): 353–395.

Sablosky, Juliet Antunes. "Reinvention, Reorganization, Retreat: American Cultural Diplomacy at Century's End, 1978–1998." *The Journal of Arts Management, Law, and Society* 29 (March 31, 2010): 30–46.

Scott-Smith, Giles. "Mapping the Undefinable: Some Thoughts on the Relevance of Exchange Programs Within International Relations Theory." *The Annals of the American Academy of Political and Social Science* 616, no. 1 (March 2008): 173–195.

Slaughter, Anne-Marie. "Reinventing the State Department." *Democracy: A Journal of Ideas.* (September 15, 2020).

Wiseman, Geoffrey. "Diplomatic Practices at the United Nations." *Cooperation and Conflict* 50, no. 3 (September 2015): 316–333.

———. "Public Diplomacy and Hostile Nations." *The Hague Journal of Diplomacy* 14 (2019): 134–153.

Reports and Documents

Advisory Group on Public Diplomacy in the Arab and Muslim World. *Changing Minds Winning Peace: A New Strategic Direction for U.S. Public Diplomacy in the Arab & Muslim World.* 2003.

Burns, Nicholas, Marc Grossman, and Marcie Ries. *American Diplomacy Project: A U.S. Diplomatic Service for the 21st Century.* Harvard Kennedy School, November 2020.

Burt, Richard, Olin Robison, and Barry Fulton. *Reinventing Diplomacy in the Information Age.* Center for Strategic and International Studies, 1998.

Cabral, Roxanne, Peter Engelke, Katherine Brown, and Anne Terman Wedner. *Diplomacy for a Diffuse World*. Atlantic Council, September 2014.

Council on Foreign Relations Task Force. *Finding America's Voice: A Strategy for Reinvigorating US Public Diplomacy*. Council on Foreign Relations, 2003.

Department of Defense. *Report of the Defense Science Board Task Force on Managed Information Dissemination*. 2001.

Department of Defense. *Report of the Defense Science Board Task Force on Strategic Communication*. 2004.

Department of Defense. *Report of the Defense Science Board Task Force on Strategic Communication*. 2007.

Espinosa, J. Manuel. *Inter-American Beginnings of U.S. Cultural Diplomacy, 1938–1948*. Department of State, 1976.

Fairbank, Wilma. *America's Cultural Experiment in China, 1942–1949*. Department of State, 1976.

Gregory, Bruce. *The Broadcasting Service: An Administrative History* (1970). RG 306, Entry A1-1089: HISTORIES OF THE USIA, 1969–1999. Records of the United States Information Agency. National Archives and Records Administration, College Park, MD.

———. *The Paradox of US Public Diplomacy: Its Rise and "Demise."* Institute for Public Diplomacy and Global Communication. George Washington University, 2014.

Grossman, Marc and Marcie Ries. *Blueprints for a More Modern U.S. Diplomatic Service*. The American Diplomacy Project 2. Arizona State University, 2022.

Hocking, Brian and Jan Melissen. *Diplomacy in the Digital Age*. Clingendael. Netherlands Institute of International Relations, 2015.

Hocking, Brian, Jan Melissen, Shaun Riordan, and Paul Sharp. *Futures for Diplomacy: Integrative Diplomacy in the 21st Century*. Clingendael. Netherlands Institute of International Relations, 2012.

———. *Wither Foreign Ministries in a Post-Western World?* Clingendael Institute, 2013.

Johnson, A. Ross. *Setting the Record Straight: Role of Radio Free Europe in the Hungarian Revolution*. Woodrow Wilson Center, 2006.

Lawson, Murray and Bruce Gregory. *The United States Information Agency: A History, Origins, 1933–1945* (1970). RG 306, Entry A1-1089: HISTORIES OF THE USIA, 1969–1999. Records of the United States Information Agency. National Archives and Records Administration, College Park, MD.

Lawson, Murray G., Bruce N. Gregory, Hugh W. Olds, Jr., and Irving R. Wechsler. *The United States Information Agency During the Johnson*

Administration, 1963–1968 (1970). RG 306, Entry A1-1089: HISTORIES OF THE USIA, 1969–1999. Records of the United States Information Agency. National Archives and Records Administration, College Park, MD.

Lord, Kristin M. *Voices of America: U.S. Public Diplomacy for the 21st Century.* Brookings, 2008.

Lundberg, Kirsten. *The Accidental Statesman: General Petraeus and the City of Mosul, Iraq.* Kennedy School of Government Case Program. Harvard University, 2006.

Paul, Christopher. *Whither Strategic Communication? An Inventory of Current Proposals and Recommendations.* RAND, 2009.

Public Diplomacy and the Future: Hearings Before the Subcommittee on International Operations. 95th Cong. (1977).

US Advisory Commission on Public Diplomacy. *Data-Driven Public Diplomacy: Progress Toward Measuring the Impact of Public Diplomacy and International Broadcasting Activities.* 2014.

Walker, Christopher and Jessica Ludwig. *Sharp Power: Rising Authoritarian Influence.* National Endowment for Democracy, 2017.

Wallin, Matthew. *The Challenges of the Internet and Social Media in Public Diplomacy.* American Security Project, 2013.

White, Barbara. "U.S. Government Overseas Communication Programs: Needs and Opportunities in the Seventies" (1973). Walter R. Roberts Papers. Box 1. George Washington University Library.

Zeya, Uzra S. and Jon Finer. *Revitalizing the State Department and American Diplomacy.* Council on Foreign Relations, 2020.

Manuscript Collections

American Presidency Project. UC Santa Barbara. https://www.presidency.ucsb.edu

Congressional Research Service Reports. https://crsreports.congress.gov

Founders Online, National Archives. https://founders.archives.gov

Freedom of Information Act Electronic Reading Room. Central Intelligence Agency. https://www.cia.gov/readingroom/home

Historical Documents. Department of State. https://history.state.gov/historicaldocuments

Joint Publications Operations Series. Joint Chiefs of Staff, https://www.jcs.mil/Doctrine/Joint-Doctrine-Pubs/3-0-Operations-Series/

Leo P. Crespi Papers. Princeton University Library. https://findingaids.princeton.edu/catalog/MC235_c006

National Archives and Records Administration. Records of the United States Information Agency. RG 306. https://www.archives.gov/research/foreign-policy/related-records/rg-306

National Security Archive. George Washington University. https://nsarchive.gwu.edu

Presidential Directives and Executive Orders. Federation of American Scientists. https://irp.fas.org

Public Papers of the Presidents of the United States. University of Michigan Digital Library. https://babel.hathitrust.org/cgi/mb?a=listis;c=1429005971

US Advisory Commission on Public Diplomacy Reports. US Advisory Commission on Information. US Advisory Commission on Educational and Cultural Affairs. https://www.state.gov/reports-u-s-advisory-commission-on-public-diplomacy/

US Department of State. Archive Websites. https://www.state.gov/u-s-department-of-state-archive-websites/

US Government Accountability Office Reports. Name changed from US General Accounting Office in 2004. https://www.gao.gov/reports-testimonies

Walter R. Roberts Papers. George Washington University Library. https://searcharchives.library.gwu.edu/repositories/2/resources/838

Oral Interviews

Foreign Affairs Oral History Collection. Association for Diplomatic Studies and Training (ADST). Arlington, VA. https://adst.org/oral-history/oral-history-interviews/#gsc.tab=0

Anderson, Burnett. Interviewed by Jack O'Brien.

Bardos, Arthur A. Interviewed by Hans N. Tuch.

Baroody, Judith. Interviewed by Charles Stuart Kennedy.

Beecham, Charles Robert. Interviewed by Jack O'Brien.

Bishop, Donald Michael, Interviewed by Charles Stuart Kennedy.

Blackburn, Paul. Interviewed by Charles R. Beecham.

Chatten, Robert L. Interviewed by Fred A. Coffey, Jr.

Child, Julia. Interviewed by Jewell Fenzi.

Fulton, Barry. Interviewed by Charles Stuart Kennedy.

Galbraith, Peter. Interviewed by Charles Stuart Kennedy.

Gregory, Bruce. Interviewed by Charles Stuart Kennedy.

Keith, Kenton. Interviewed by Charles Stuart Kennedy.

Kinney, Stephanie Smith. Interviewed by Charles Stuart Kennedy.

Klieforth, Alexander A. L. Interviewed by Cliff Groce.

Lenderking, William. Interviewed by Charles Stuart Kennedy.

Loomis, Henry. Interviewed by "Cliff" Groce.

McBride, Tessa. Interviewed by Jewell Fenzi.

Oglesby, Donna. Interviewed by Charles Stuart Kennedy.

Oleksiw, Dan. Interviewed by Hans N. Tuch.

Rugh, William. Interviewed by Charles Stuart Kennedy.

Ryan, Hewson. Interviewed by Richard Nethercut.

Yates, Kenneth. Interviewed by Charles Stuart Kennedy.

Zorthian, Barry. Interviewed by Cliff Groce.

Harry S. Truman Library. Independence, MO. https://www.trumanlibrary.gov/library/oral-histories/oralhis

Barrett, Edward W. Interviewed by Richard D. McKinzie.

Gray, Gordon. Interviewed by Richard D. McKinzie.

Marshall, Charles Burton. Interviewed by Neil M. Johnson.

Index[1]

[1] Note: Page numbers followed by 'n' refer to notes.